Table of Contents

PART ONE

Career Counseling in the 21st Century: Evolving Contexts, Challenges, and Concepts

PART TWO
Client Goal or Problem Identification,
Clarification, and Specification

FOURTH EDITION

CAREER COUNSELING

Holism, Diversity, and Strengths

NORMAN C. GYSBERS

MARY J. HEPPNER

JOSEPH A. JOHNSTON

AMERICAN COUNSELING
ASSOCIATION

5999 Stevenson Avenue I Alexandria, VA 22304 I www.counseling.org

FOURTH EDITION

CAREER COUNSELING

Holism, Diversity, and Strengths

10   9   8   7   6   5   4   3

American Counseling Association
5999 Stevenson Avenue
Alexandria, VA 22304

Associate Publisher   Carolyn C. Baker

Production Manager   Bonny E. Gaston

Copy Editor   Susan B. Klender

Editorial Assistant   Catherine A. Brumley

Cover and text design by Bonny E. Gaston.

Library of Congress Cataloging-in-Publication Data

Gysbers, Norman C.
  Career counseling: holism, diversity, and strengths/Norman C. Gysbers,
Mary J. Heppner, Joseph A. Johnston.—Fourth Edition.
    pages cm
  Includes bibliographical references and index.
  ISBN 978-1-55620-333-6 (alk. paper)
  1. Vocational guidance—Study and teaching.   2. Personality and occupation.
I. Heppner, Mary J.   II. Johnston, Joseph A.   III. Title.
  HF5381.G95 2014
  158.7—dc23   2013037326

Dedication

To all our graduate students
and colleagues worldwide who have
supported and encouraged the
development and writing
of this book

PART THREE
Client Goal or Problem Resolution

Preface

The USA is bigger, older, more Hispanic and Asian and less wedded to marriage and traditional families than it was in 1990. It also is less enamored of kids, more embracing of several generations living under one roof, more inclusive of same-sex couples, more cognizant of multiracial identities, more suburban, less rural and leaning more to the South and West.

—Nasser & Overberg, 2011

Vast and far-reaching changes are taking place in the nature and structure of the social and economic systems in which people live and the industrial and occupational structures in which they work (U.S. Department of Labor, 2013). The values and beliefs individuals hold about themselves, about others, and about the world are changing too. More and more people are seeking meaning and coherence in their lives. Our society also is becoming multiracial, multilingual, and multicultural. Women are entering the labor force in record numbers, and men are questioning traditionally held beliefs about their roles.

Demographic trends in the 2000s showed the continuing separation of family and household because of factors such as childbearing among single parents, the dissolution of cohabiting unions, divorce, repartnering, and remarriage. The transnational families of many immigrants also displayed this separation, as families extended across borders. In addition, demographers demonstrated during the decade that trends such as marriage and divorce were diverging according to education. Moreover, demographic trends in the age structure of the population showed that a large increase in the elderly population will occur in the 2010s. Overall, demographic trends produced an increased complexity of family life and a more ambiguous and fluid set of categories than demographers are accustomed to measuring.

—Cherlin, 2010, p. 403

Far from being a standard or rote procedure, career counseling, in response to these social and economic changes, has become a dynamic, creative, and highly individualized process. The continually emerging and evolving ideas about the nature and structure of individuals' career development are providing practitioners with new ways to understand and work with clients of all ages and circumstances. To keep abreast of these changes you may wish to update your knowledge about the ever-changing contexts and conditions in which people will live and work in the 21st century. You may wish to revisit and revitalize how you conceptualize the career development of individuals and the structure of the career counseling you do with clients. You may be looking for specific interventions, including qualitative and quantitative assessments, to help you and your clients gather information about their goals and problems, to work together to understand and interpret this information, and to choose interventions that will assist them in reaching their goals or resolving their problems.

Purpose of the Book

The purpose of this book is to help you expand and extend your understanding of individuals' career development as well as your vision of career counseling and the skills and techniques in your career counseling repertoire. Specifically, this book is designed to help you update and add to the knowledge and skills you already have. It will help you better understand and interpret client information gathered and behavior observed during career counseling by using concepts from traditional and new and emerging postmodern conceptualizations of career development. It also will help you better understand and interpret client information and behavior in terms of *life career themes*, or the ideas, beliefs, attitudes, and values clients hold about themselves, others, and the world in which they live. Finally, it will help you assist clients of all ages and circumstances to more effectively understand and use such information and behavior in their quest to achieve their career goals or resolve their career concerns.

This book incorporates the strongest parts of the traditional understanding of the career counseling process with the ever-changing social and economic demands of the 21st century. In addition, it incorporates new and emerging postmodern career development concepts into career counseling practices, further strengthening your understanding of the career counseling process. This is important, because we believe that the process of career counseling has long been overlooked, as if this particular brand of counseling were devoid of process. We propose a process for career counseling, and we focus particular attention on how this process can be helpful in expanding options and empowering the authentic life choices of women; men; racial and ethnic minorities; gay, lesbian, bisexual, and transgender clients; and individuals with disabilities. Although we are keenly aware that these categories do not cover all forms of diversity in human life, we choose to highlight them and hope that much of what we express is transferable to the issues of other diverse groups as well.

To help you gain these specific skills, this book brings together selected concepts and techniques from the disciplines of counseling, psychology, sociology, and economics in general, and the discipline of career psychology specifically. It is a book for you if you are looking to enhance your theoretical knowledge and expand your practice skills through an in-depth examination of specifically selected career counseling interventions, including various qualitative and quantitative assessments. It is a book for you if you are looking to update and expand your ability to gain insights into client behavior, to develop hypotheses about such behavior, and to apply this knowledge in the selection of effective career counseling techniques and assessments.

Overview of the Contents

This book presents a theory-based, practice-focused approach to career counseling. It presents career counseling holistically using life career development as a way to view and understand overall human development in general and career development specifically. It is a strengths-based, theoretically sound conception of career counseling that is practitioner friendly and very usable with clients of all ages and circumstances. Specific attention is given to the critical life contexts in which career development unfolds and career counseling takes place, including gender, culture/race, sexual orientation, social class, spirituality, and disability. Specific attention is also given to the ever-changing work world, including the implications of globalization and the interactions of work and family.

Because the book is theory based and practice oriented, there is an emphasis on the nature and structure of the working alliance as central to the career counseling process. A strength of the book is the use of postmodern theories, including constructivism, social constructionism, and chaos theory. It focuses on narratives to identify life career themes used by clients to organize their thoughts, feelings, and ideas. To assist career counselors in gathering client information, understanding and hypothesizing client behavior, and helping clients develop and carry out action plans, the book includes very practical and highly usable presentations of a number of qualitative career assessments along with several quantitative instruments. A unique emphasis in the book focuses on dealing with resistant clients, why and how these clients may resist, and how to work with such resistance. Finally, the book describes how to use information in career counseling, how to help clients develop and use action plans, how to use social media, and how to bring closure to the career counseling process.

Part I, "Career Counseling in the 21st Century: Evolving Contexts, Challenges, and Concepts," provides you with foundation knowledge and perspectives concerning our changing world in the 21st century. Chapter 1 focuses on the career counseling process and the phases that are involved in working with clients. It describes the career counseling process from a life career development perspective and presents information about the Career Counseling Self-Efficacy Scale. Chapter 2 describes the evolution of career development theory building and presents selected traditional and postmodern theories and approaches to understanding career development, with an emphasis on the use of theoretical constructs in the practice of career counseling. Chapters 3, 4, and 5 highlight the implications of increasing diversity, focus on the impact of social class, describe women's and men's issues as they affect career counseling, and discuss sexual orientation issues and concerns. Finally, Chapter 6 focuses on empowering the life choices of people with disabilities, whereas Chapter 7 examines the changes that are occurring in the worlds of work and family and the impact these changes have on the lives of individuals.

Part II, "Client Goal or Problem Identification, Clarification, and Specification," provides in-depth discussions of issues and selected techniques and instruments, all tied to the first phases of the career counseling process detailed in Chapter 1. Chapter 8 examines the opening phase of career counseling, focusing on the working alliance and its importance in the career counseling process. Chapter 9 describes the concept of life career themes, shows how life career themes are identified and described by using example career themes, and details how these life career themes assist in understanding client goals, behavior, or concerns. Chapters 10, 11, and 12 feature postmodern qualitative techniques— a structured interview, the genogram, an occupational card sort—that provide structure and stimuli to help clients tell their stories and identify their life career themes during the information-gathering phase of career counseling. Then Chapter 13 presents an in-depth discussion of how selected standardized tests and inventories provide information about clients' interests and personalities. Chapter 14 presents assessments that focus on clients' styles and strengths. Finally, Chapter 15 deals with resistant clients, the kinds of resistance they may exhibit, and ways to respond to clients who resist.

Part III, "Client Goal or Problem Resolution," emphasizes career counseling strategies to use to assist clients in reaching their goals or resolving their concerns. Chapter 16 pays attention to the use of information in the career counseling process and presents the details of how clients can set goals and develop career plans based on the outcomes clients and counselors have arrived at through their work in career counseling. Chapter 17, a new chapter, focuses on the use of social media in career counseling. Finally, Chapter 18 examines closure in career counseling. The topic of how to bring closure to the career counseling process and the issues that are involved in closing the working alliance between client and counselor are featured.

Who Should Read This Book?

This book is designed for a variety of readers. First, practicing counselors in many different work settings who do career counseling will find this book to be an excellent in-depth update of traditional and contemporary postmodern career theories, issues, and techniques. But it is more than just an update for practitioners. With its three carefully crafted and connected parts, all organized around a holistic perspective of career development and the career counseling process, this book is a source of renewal for practitioners. Second, this book is also for counselors-in-training in counseling psychology, counselor education, and other helping relationship programs because it provides them with the prerequisite knowledge and skills to do career counseling. It features the career counseling process based on a life career development perspective, with particular attention to diversity, social class, disability, sexual orientation, and gender issues. The book takes counselors-in-training through the phases of the career counseling process, providing in-depth presentations of selected techniques and assessment procedures. It offers a framework for integrating postmodern qualitative and traditional quantitative assessment techniques and information into the career counseling process directly and naturally, something that many counselors-in-training have difficulty doing.

New to This Edition

Because interest in career counseling continues to increase, and because the literature on career counseling trends, issues, and practices has expanded substantially, it was clear that the third edition of *Career Counseling* was in need of revision. In this, the fourth edition, we thoroughly updated our chapters with current literature and research concerning the many contextual variables that influence our work as career counselors as well as the theory and practice of career counseling. Our goal was to enhance the theoretical foundations and contextual underpinnings of our field while maintaining our emphasis on the practical. Some of the most significant revisions and additions include the following:

- The title of the book was changed to emphasize holism, diversity, and strengths, major themes that are interwoven through the book.
- The chapter on ways to understand career behavior was expanded to provide a brief overview of the evolution of career theory building as well as coverage of postmodern theories of career development, including constructivism, social constructionism, and chaos theory.
- A new chapter has been added focusing on the role of social media in career counseling.

References

Cherlin, A. J. (2010). Demographic trends in the United States: A review of research in the 2000s. *Journal of Marriage and Family, 72*, 403–419.

Nasser, H. E., & Overberg, P. (2011). Census tracks 20 years of sweeping change. *USA Today*. Retrieved from http://www.usatoday.com

U.S. Department of Labor. (2013). *Occupational outlook handbook, 2013–2014 ed.* St. Paul, MN: Jist Publishing.

Acknowledgments

This book was written with the support, encouragement, and tangible contributions of many colleagues. We particularly acknowledge the contributions of Lisa Flores, Patrick Handley, Puncky Heppner, John Kosciulek, and Amanda Nell: Lisa for her substantial contributions to Chapter 3, "Empowering Life Choices: Career Counseling in the Contexts of Race and Class"; Patrick for his contribution to Chapter 14 concerning the INSIGHT Inventory; Puncky for his substantial contributions to Chapter 5, "Empowering Men's Life Choices: An Examination of Gender and Sexual Orientation"; John for writing Chapter 6, "Facilitating the Career Development of Individuals With Disabilities Through Empowering Career Counseling"; and Amanda for writing Chapter 17, "Using Social Media in Career Counseling." We also thank Kathleen Kerr for her help in researching portions of the book. Thank you, Lisa, Patrick, Puncky, John, Amanda, and Kathleen.

Finally, this book could not have been completed without the very effective and efficient work of our administrative associate, Linda Coats, who has now helped us through three editions of this book. Thank you, Linda.

About the Authors

Norman C. Gysbers, PhD, is a Curators' Distinguished Professor in the Department of Educational, School, and Counseling Psychology at the University of Missouri in Columbia, Missouri. He received his bachelor's degree from Hope College in Holland, Michigan, in 1954. He was a teacher in the Muskegon Heights Michigan School District (1954–1956) and served in the U.S. Army Artillery (1956–1958). He received his master's (1959) and doctorate (1963) from the University of Michigan. He joined the faculty of the College of Education at the University of Missouri–Columbia in 1963 as an assistant professor. In addition to his duties as an assistant professor, he also served as the licensed school counselor at the University Laboratory School until 1970.

He was awarded a Franqui Professorship from the Universite Libre de Bruxelles, Belgium, and lectured there in February 1984. He was a visiting scholar at the University of Hong Kong in May 2000, 2002, and 2004; a visiting scholar at the Chinese University of Hong Kong in January 2001; and a scholar in residence at the University of British Columbia in July/August 2000. He also was an International Visiting Scholar at National Taiwan Normal University in 2011.

His research and teaching interests are in career development, career counseling, and school guidance as well as in counseling program development, management, and evaluation. He is the author of 96 articles, 40 chapters in published books, 15 monographs, and 22 books, one of which has been translated into Italian, Korean, Japanese, and Chinese, and one into Chinese.

He has received many awards, most notably the National Career Development Association's Eminent Career Award in 1989; the Missouri Career Development Association's Lifetime Career Achievement Award in 2013; the American School Counselor Association's Mary Gehrke Lifetime Achievement Award in 2004; the William T. Kemper Award for Excellence in Teaching in 2002; the Governor's Award for Excellence in Teaching in 2004; the Faculty/Alumni Award from the University of Missouri–Columbia in 1997; and the Distinguished Faculty Award from the Mizzou Alumni Association, University of Missouri, in 2008.

Gysbers was editor of *The Career Development Quarterly* (1962–1970), president of the National Career Development Association (1972–1973), president of the American Counseling Association (1977–1978), and vice president of the Association of Career and Technical Education (1979–1982). He was also editor of the *Journal of Career Development* from 1978 until 2006.

Mary J. Heppner, PhD, is a full professor of counseling psychology at the University of Missouri. Dr. Heppner graduated from the University of Minnesota–Morris with her bachelor's, the University of Nebraska–Lincoln with her master's, and the University of Missouri–Columbia with her doctorate. She has written in the areas of women's career development and adult career transitions. She is coauthor of the texts *Career Counseling: Process, Issues, and Techniques* (1998, 2003), *Career Planning for the Twenty-First Century* (2000), and *A Guide to Successful Theses, Dissertations, and Publishing Research* (2004) and is coeditor of and contributor to the *Handbook of Career Counseling for Women* (2006). She is author of the Career Transitions Inventory and coauthor of the Career Counseling Self-Efficacy Scale. Her most recent research has been in the area of examining which aspects of the process of career counseling lead to effective outcomes. In addition, she has a programmatic line of research on the prevention of sexual assault in middle school, high school, and college populations.

She has been a Fulbright scholar in Taiwan. She is a Fellow in the Society of Counseling Psychology of the American Psychological Association. She has won the John Holland Award for Research in Career Development and the Early Scientist Practitioner Award, both from the Society of Counseling Psychology. She was also awarded the National Career Development Association Merit Award. On the University of Missouri campus she has won the William T. Kemper Award for Outstanding Teaching, the Robert S. Daniel Junior Faculty Teaching Award, the College of Education Outstanding Graduate Mentor Award, and the Graduate School's Outstanding Mentor Award. She was also awarded the Provost's Committee on the Status of Women's First Annual Tribute to Mizzou Women Award for contributions and commitment to the University and to the women who work and study at the University of Missouri.

Joseph A. Johnston, PhD, is a professor in the Department of Educational, School, and Counseling Psychology at the University of Missouri, where he is also director of the university career center. His bachelor's, master's, and doctoral degrees are all from the University of Michigan. He regularly teaches courses in career development. He is a founder of the Wakonse Foundation, an organization helping to elevate and improve college teaching. His memberships include the American Association for Counseling and Development, American College Personnel Association, and National Career Development Association.

He initiated the A Way With Words literacy program, the A Way With Numbers tutoring program, and the Jumpstart program at the University of Missouri in response to the America Reads Challenge. He has published in numerous professional journals, organized workshops, and presented at professional meetings nationally and internationally. He has served on the editorial boards of several professional journals. He has a strong commitment to career theory and practice, leadership, self-directed learning, faculty development, entrepreneurship, and positive psychology.

His awards and achievements include the following: Research Award in Career Development Scholarship named in his honor, February 2000; Excellence in Education Award, May 1996, Division of Student Affairs, University of Missouri; Certificate of Recognition of Service, April 2002, Kiwanis Club of Columbia, Missouri; Distinguished Membership, National Society of Collegiate Scholars, September 2002; Sam M. Walton Free Enterprise Fellow, 2005; Honorary Member of the National Residence Hall Honorary, 2005; Member, Board of Directors, Funding African Children's Education, Inc. (FACE); Member, Planning Committee for MU Colleague Circles, 2000–2007; Faculty Advisors, MU Student Entrepreneurs, 2005–2006. He was awarded the Missouri Career Development Association's Lifetime Career Achievement Award in 2013.

About the Contributors

Lisa Y. Flores, PhD, is an associate professor in the Department of Educational, School, and Counseling Psychology at the University of Missouri.

Patrick Handley, PhD, is a professional speaker and trainer, and developer of the INSIGHT Inventory.

P. Paul Heppner, PhD, is a Curator's Distinguished professor at the University of Missouri as well as the cofounder and codirector of the Center for Cultural Competence.

John F. Kosciulek, PhD, CRC, is a professor in the Department of Counseling, Educational Psychology, and Special Education at Michigan State University in East Lansing.

Amanda Nell, MA, is a Senior Student Services Coordinator in the Career Center at the University of Missouri.

PART ONE
Career Counseling in the 21st Century
Evolving Contexts, Challenges, and Concepts

Chapter 1

Career Counseling: A Life Career Development Perspective

> Careers are person-specific and created by the choices we make throughout our lives. Careers emerge from the constant interplay between the person and the environment. They include activities engaged in prior to entering the workforce and after formal activity as a worker has been completed. Careers encompass the total constellation of life roles that we play. Thus, managing our careers effectively also involves integrating the roles of life effectively. In a very real sense, careers are the manifestations of our attempts at making sense out of our life experiences. The career development process is, in essence, a spiritual journey reflecting our choices concerning how we will spend our time on Earth.
>
> —Niles & Harris-Bowlsbey, 2005, p. 30

The theory and research base of career development and the practice of career counseling has evolved and changed as the 21st century has continued to unfold. Modern normative, science-based theories such as Holland's theory of vocational personalities and work environments continue to be useful in guiding the practice of career counseling (R. W. Lent, 2013). At the same time, there has been "a proliferation of career counselling approaches underpinned by postmodern and constructivist philosophies" (McMahon, Watson, Chetty, & Hoelson, 2012, p. 127).

The combination of modern theories and postmodern theories is stimulating a reexamination of the nature and structure of career development and the career counseling practices used to facilitate it. This reexamination is also stimulating new ways of gathering client information as career counseling unfolds. Just as important, it is giving us new ways to think about and develop hypotheses concerning client information and behavior. It is opening up new ways to apply these hypotheses to the selection of interventions used to assist clients in resolving their problems and achieving their goals.

To set the stage for the rest of the book, the first part of Chapter 1 examines the nature and structure of career counseling in light of the changes occurring in career development theory building. This discussion is presented to provide a perspective and an organizer for the career counseling interventions that are described in the chapters that follow. Then, in the second part of Chapter 1, a holistic view of career development, called *life career development*, is described to provide a conceptual foundation and point of departure for career counseling with clients of all ages and circumstances. The chapter closes with a discussion of competencies for counselors who do career counseling. The Career Counseling Self-Efficacy Scale (O'Brien & Heppner, 1995) is presented and described.

Career Counseling

What is career counseling? Is it different from other forms of counseling? Is it the same? Is there overlap? These questions are being asked with increasing frequency today as attempts are being made to clarify this form of counseling (Amundson, Harris-Bowlsbey, & Niles, 2009; Capuzzi & Stauffer, 2012; Savickas, 2011). Central to the ongoing discussion about career counseling are two issues. First is the issue of the nature of career counseling. What are its intrinsic characteristics and qualities? Are psychological processes involved? Second is the issue of structure. Does career counseling have structure? If so, what is the configuration, sequence, and interrelationships of the phases and subphases involved?

The Nature of Career Counseling

"Historically, career and vocational counseling have served as the cornerstones upon which the counseling profession was built" (Dorn, 1992, p. 176). Unfortunately, along the path of history, career counseling became stereotyped. In many people's minds it became time limited, it was devoid of psychological processes, and it focused on outcomes and methods (Osipow, 1982). Swanson (1995), paraphrasing the work of Manuele-Adkins, underscored this point:

> Manuele-Adkins (1992) described elements of a stereotypic view of career counseling that discredit its psychological component and affect the quality and delivery of career counseling services. In this stereotypic view, career counseling is a rational process, with an emphasis on information-giving, testing, and computer-based systems; it is short-term, thus limiting the range of possible intervention strategies and obscuring psychological processes such as indecision; and it is different from personal counseling, thus lowering the perceived value of career counseling and increasing a false separation between work and nonwork. (p. 222)

Young and Domene (2012) added to this historical debate by stating there is still a disconnect "between career counseling and counseling for other areas of life, such as family, emotional difficulties and relationship issues" (p. 16). They pointed out that unfortunately practitioners in career counseling and counseling even have different professional identities, practices, and professional associations, which further adds to the separation. As a result, they noted, there is often failure to connect with each other and use each other's professional literature.

This separation has led some individuals to see counselors who do career counseling as active and directive because they use qualitative and quantitative assessments and information. Counselors who do personal–emotional counseling, in contrast, are seen by others as facilitative and exploratory because they focus on psychological processes, that is, on client–counselor interactions (Imbimbo, 1994). This dichotomy of views has led to the classic stereotype of career counseling as "three interviews and a cloud of dust" (Crites, 1981, pp. 49–52). It is not surprising, therefore, that career counseling does not fare well in the eyes of practitioners when compared to personal–emotional counseling, given the classic stereotype.

In addition, we believe this dichotomy has caused the public to form spurious beliefs and ideas about the nature of career counseling. Amundson et al. (2009) labeled these spurious beliefs and ideas as *career counseling myths*:

1. Career counselors have at their disposal standardized assessments that can be used to tell people which occupation they should choose.
2. Work role decisions can be made in isolation from other life roles.
3. Career counseling does not address "personal" issues.
4. Career counselors do not need extensive counseling expertise to do their work competently.
5. Career counseling does not address the client's context and culture.
6. Career counseling is required only when a career decision must be made.
7. Career counseling ends when a career decision is made. (p. 5)

Contrary to the classic stereotype, we believe that career counseling belongs in the general class of counseling because it has the same intrinsic characteristics and qualities that all forms of counseling possess. It differs from the rest of the class, however, because presenting problems often focus on work and career issues, and quantitative and qualitative assessment procedures and information are used more frequently. Swanson (1995) suggested this characterization of career counseling when she defined it as "an ongoing, face-to-face interaction between counselor and client, with the primary focus on work- or career-related issues; the interaction is psychological in nature, with the relationship between counselor and client serving an important function" (p. 245).

As those of you who are practicing counselors know, client presenting problems often are only a beginning point, and as counseling unfolds, other problems emerge. Career issues frequently become personal–emotional issues and family issues, and then career issues again (Andersen & Vandehey, 2012). Psychological distress is often present (Multon, Heppner, Gysbers, Zook, & Ellis-Kalton, 2001). Thoughts, emotions, and feelings are all involved. As Kidd (2004) pointed out, "We . . . need to know more about how the expression of emotion affects career development" (p. 443). Hartung (2011a) supported Kidd's point by stating,

> Emotion holds promise for providing answers to questions about the *why* of vocational behavior. It seems time to examine emotion's role in career theory and practice more broadly and specifically in fostering goal directedness, shaping purpose, constructing meaning, increasing narratability, and promoting intentionality in life-career design. (p. 302)

The stereotyped division of counseling into the separate classes of personal–emotional and career is artificial and cannot stand in practice because many clients are dealing with multiple personal–emotional and career problems simultaneously, many of them connected and intertwined (R. E. Lent & Brown, 2013). This is not a new idea. Years ago, Super (1957) said, "The distinction between vocational and personal counseling seems artificial, and the stressing of one at the expense of the other seems uncalled for" (p. 196). More recently, Flores (2007) stated, "Both the personal and career life spheres are understood to occur concurrently and to operate interdependently with one another" (pp. 3–4). As Amundson (1998) suggested, "Most people come to counseling with life problems that do not fall neatly into the categories of career or personal: life just does not define itself that neatly" (p. 16).

If career counseling belongs to the same class as other forms of counseling, then why do we use the term *career counseling* at all? We advocate the use of the term partly because of history. As stated earlier, the use of the word *vocational*, now *career*, is part of our heritage.

History alone, however, is not a sufficient reason to continue to use the term *career counseling*. There is another reason—the need to focus attention on client problems dealing with work and career issues that require theoretical conceptions and interventions originating from career development theory, research, and practice. These needed theoretical conceptions and interventions are not usually found in the literature that surrounds other forms of counseling. At the same time, theoretical conceptions and interventions that emerge from and undergird personal–emotional counseling perspectives are not usually found in the literature that surrounds career counseling. According to Collin (2006),

> Career represents the coexistence of the objective and the subjective, both the social reality and the individual's experience of it; even when the focus is on the former, the latter, though submerged, is still present. Career also represents other dualities: individual and collective, and rhetoric and praxis. Its two faces make career inherently ambivalent. It is not "either/or" but "both/and," making career a very powerful and fascinating construct that can continue to offer meaning for the twenty-first century. (p. 63)

In the worlds of today and tomorrow, theoretical conceptions and practical interventions from both the career and personal–emotional arenas are needed to work effectively with many clients (Fouad et al., 2007). Our starting point should be our clients, not predetermined distinctions of counseling. Zunker (2002) made this same point when he stated, "We are not just career counselors, we counsel individuals" (p. 7). The emphasis on client problems to guide and work with clients was suggested by Blustein and Spengler (1995) in their domain-sensitive approach:

> A domain-sensitive approach refers to a way of intervening with clients such that the full array of human experiences is encompassed. The goals of such an intervention are to improve adjustment and facilitate developmental progress in both the career and noncareer domains. The term *domain* pertains to the scope of the client's psychological experiences, encompassing both career and noncareer settings. By following *domain* with the term *sensitive*, we are attempting to capture counselors' inherent openness, empathy, and interest with respect to both the career and noncareer domains and their ability to shift between these content domains effectively. In effect, a domain-sensitive approach is characterized by the counselor's concerted interest in and awareness of all possible ramifications of a client's psychological experience and its behavioral expressions. In this approach, the counselor clearly values the client's experiences in both the career and noncareer domains. The counselor bases a decision about where to intervene on informed judgments about where the problem originated and where it is most accessible for intervention. (p. 317)

In the domain-sensitive approach, the career problems clients have are not automatically converted to personal–emotional problems because career (work) issues require full attention in the career counseling process (Blustein, 2006). Nor are personal–emotional problems automatically converted to career problems. "The underlying asset of a domain-sensitive approach is that interventions are not based on discrete or arbitrary distinctions between treatment modalities but are determined by the unique attributes of each client's history and presenting problem" (Blustein & Spengler, 1995, p. 318). The terms *career counseling* and *personal–emotional counseling* should remain as ways to organize theory and research but not as ways to restrict our view of clients and limit our work with them. Many years ago, Super (1955) stated it this way: "One counsels people rather than problems" (p. 4).

The Structure of Career Counseling

Based on our discussion of the nature of career counseling, the next task is to consider a way to organize the work of clients and counselors in career counseling. Can the work of clients and counselors in career counseling be organized into phases and subphases? If so, how are the phases and subphases arranged and sequenced? Are they interrelated?

Beginning with Parsons (1909), many writers have described possible ways to structure career counseling (Amundson et al., 2009; Crites, 1981; Kidd, 2004; McDaniels & Gysbers, 1992; Savickas, 2011). For the purposes of this book, the structure of career counseling that we suggest has two major phases (*Client Goal or Problem Identification, Clarification, and Specification* and *Client Goal or Problem Resolution*) and a number of subphases. An outline of these phases and subphases appears in Table 1-1.

In addition, because we agree with Swanson's (1995) statement that the relationship between counselor and client serves an important function in career counseling, Table 1-1 also pictures how we envision the counselor–client relationship or working alliance in the various phases and subphases of career counseling. We see the working alliance evolving during career counseling—moving from forming the working alliance, to strengthening

Table 1-1. The Structure of Career Counseling

Phases and Subphases	*Working Alliance*
Client Goal or Problem Identification, Clarification, and Specification Opening • Defining and clarifying client–counselor relationships and responsibilities and informed consent issues, including confidentiality • Identifying initial client presenting goals or problems • Listening for internal thoughts and feelings and underlying dynamics	*Forming the working alliance* • Identifying initial goals to be addressed • Specifying beginning tasks to be undertaken • Creating the bond between counselor and client
Gathering Client Information Using counselor leads, quantitative instruments, and qualitative procedures to clarify and specify presenting goals or problems for the purposes of • Exploring clients' views of themselves, others, and their worlds (worldviews) as well as how social, historical, and cultural contexts may affect them 　• Language clients use to represent their views 　• Racial/gender identity status • Exploring clients' ways of making sense out of their life roles, settings, and events: past, present, and future • Reviewing possible personal and environmental barriers or constraints • Identifying clients' decision styles	*Strengthening the working alliance* • Pursuing and/or modifying mutual goals and tasks, adding new goals and tasks, dropping goals and tasks no longer applicable • Enhancing the bond between counselor and client
Understanding and Hypothesizing Client Behavior Applying the language and constructs from career, counseling, and personality theories as well as multicultural and gender literature to understand and interpret client information and behavior in light of clients' presenting (and possible subsequent) goals or problems by • Forming hypotheses based on theory/literature concerning client goals or problems to guide intervention selection • Focusing on culture-/gender-specific variables that may influence client behavior • Listening for and responding to possible client resistance	
Client Goal or Problem Resolution *Taking action*—using theory–research-based interventions, including counseling techniques, quantitative and qualitative assessments, and information to assist clients to achieve their goals or respond to their problems in the context of the working alliance	*Fulfilling the working alliance* • Achieving clients' goals through tasks and completion; setting aside some goals as unfinished business • Completing the bond between counselor and client
Developing career goals and plans of action—developing with clients career goals and plans of action to achieve goals, resolve problems, and overcome environmental and bias barriers when and where present	
Evaluating results and closing the relationship—closing the relationship when clients' goals are achieved or problems are resolved	*Closing the working alliance*

it, to fulfilling it, to finally closing it upon completion of career counseling. How important is a good relationship? Amundson (2006) stated it this way: "All counselling interventions are dependent on the foundation of a good relationship" (p. 7). (A full discussion of the working alliance—including setting goals, establishing tasks to be completed, and creating the bond between counselor and client—appears in Chapter 8.)

Keep in mind that all of the phases and subphases of career counseling may take place during one session, but more likely they will unfold over a number of sessions. In some agencies and institutions, policies dictate the number of sessions possible. In this case, it is important that clients and counselors understand these time constraints and make decisions about what can be accomplished in the time available. In these situations, there may be agreed-upon unfinished business when the relationship is closed.

Also keep in mind that, although these suggested phases and subphases logically follow one another on paper, in actual practice they may not. There often is a back-and-forth flow to career counseling in that it may be necessary to backtrack to earlier phases or subphases before moving on again. Sometimes one reaches the taking action subphase only to realize that other interventions not anticipated may be needed, which necessitates a return to the gathering client information subphase. To picture this point, you can see that the phases and subphases of career counseling presented in linear outline form in Table 1-1 are placed in a circular format in Figure 1-1. Note how the working alliance evolves and interacts with the phases and subphases and how central it is to the structure of career counseling.

Finally, keep in mind that not everyone who seeks help wants or needs to go through the full process of career counseling. Some may want or need only limited assistance. Other clients, however, may need to be involved in the full process over time but may be resistant to this. Dealing with resistance may be a first priority in the opening subphase as the working alliance is beginning to be formed. Even if resistance is seemingly handled then, be aware that it may reoccur again and again, perhaps later in career counseling as some clients struggle with their problems. Remember, for these clients, dealing with reoccurring resistance is part of the psychological processes involved in career counseling. (See Chapter 15 for a detailed discussion of resistance in career counseling.)

Life Career Development: A Holistic Perspective

As we have seen, a major task in career counseling is gathering information concerning clients' presenting and subsequent goals and problems. Equally important

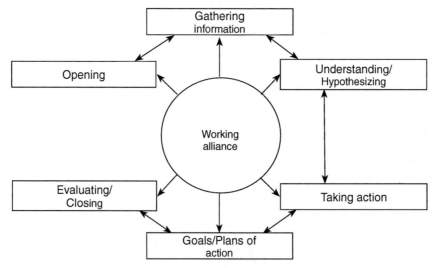

Figure 1-1. The Structure of Career Counseling

are the tasks of understanding clients' goals and problems, developing hypotheses about them, and selecting appropriate interventions to empower clients to reach their goals and resolve their problems. To aid you and your clients in working through these career counseling tasks, we advocate a broad, holistic perspective of career development called *life career development* to guide your work with individuals of all ages and circumstances. This broad, holistic perspective was also advocated by Amundson et al. (2009) when they stated that their definition "of career counseling emphasizes a life span and holistic approach" (p. 7). Westergaard (2012) supported the broad, holistic perspective of career development by suggesting a need for an "emphasis on a more holistic approach to 'life-designing,' where 'career' means more than simply 'work' " (p. 336).

What Is Life Career Development?

The Initial Definition

First proposed in 1973 by Gysbers and Moore and more fully described in the article "Beyond Career Development—Life Career Development" (Gysbers & Moore, 1975), *life career development* was defined as self-development over the life span through the interaction and integration of the roles, settings, and events of a person's life. The word *life* in the term *life career development* meant that the focus was on the whole person— the human career. The word *career* identified and related the roles in which individuals were involved (worker, participant in leisure, learner, family member, and citizen); the settings where they found themselves (home, school, community, and workplace); and the events, planned and unplanned, that occurred over their lifetimes (entry job, marriage, more advanced positions, divorce, and retirement). Finally, the expression *life career development* brought these separate meanings together, but at the same time a greater meaning emerged. Life career development described people holistically, with a diversity of lifestyles.

An Expanded Definition

Can the original concept of life career development, first described in 1973, be made more relevant for today and tomorrow? The answer is yes. Although the basic configuration of life roles, life settings, and life events interacting and unfolding over a lifetime is still of value, it is clear that other important factors are at work that influence the life career development of all individuals and that need to be added to the model. Mc-Daniels and Gysbers (1992) responded to this concern by adding the factors of gender, ethnic origin, religion, and race to the original conception of life career development. These were added to underscore the importance they have on shaping the life roles, life settings, and life events of individuals of all ages and circumstances. In addition, they were added to provide individuals with greater explanatory power to understand the dynamics of their life career development.

Figure 1-2 depicts this broader definition of career development in life career development terms. Note the headings *Life Settings*, *Life Roles*, and *Life Events*. The words circled underneath each heading are examples of various life settings (e.g., home, school, and work), life roles (e.g., parent, spouse), and life events (e.g., marriage, retirement, entry job, divorce). Near the bottom of the figure, the words *Gender*, *Ethnic Origin*, and *Race* remain from the first edition of this book. For the third edition, we changed the word *Religion* to *Spirituality* and the words *Socioeconomic Status* to *Social Class*. These changes were made to reflect the current thinking in our discipline. In addition, we added a new factor, *Sexual Orientation*. These changes and the new factor provided even greater explanatory power to the panoptic concept of life career development. We continue to emphasize the importance of all of these factors in this fourth edition.

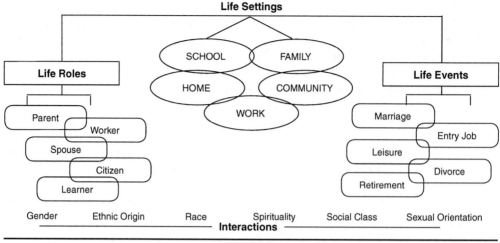

Figure 1-2. Life Career Development

Note. Adapted from *Counseling for Career Development,* by C. McDaniels and N. C. Gysbers, 1992, San Francisco: Jossey-Bass. This material is reproduced with permission of John Wiley & Sons, Inc.

Providing individuals with the ability to more fully explain and understand the what, why, and how of their overall life career development; the career goals they may have; or the career problems they may face is important, particularly in today's complex society. We live in a nation that is a part of a world economy (Friedman, 2007). This nation is increasingly diverse racially, spiritually, and ethnically, yet it has common themes that connect us all. This nation continues to change its views on what it means to be female or male educationally and occupationally. Social class and sexual orientation continue to play important roles in shaping individuals' socialization and their current and future status. Spirituality is also an important part of many individuals' lives. Paloutzian and Lowe (2012) underscored these points when they stated:

> we live in a multicultural, multiethnic, intergroup, many-valued world, with a seeming infinite array of religious, a-religious, and spiritual variations. This world's people are now so interconnected and interdependent, largely through work-related economic activities and institutions, that it would be an error to *not* equip people and their work cultures to see, understand, and accept each other, with their differences, with a binding commitment from all to fit within and collaborate with each other in mutually beneficial ways. (p. 194)

Thus, the influences of all of these factors on the life career development of individuals need to be understood more completely and reckoned with more directly if clients are to achieve their goals or resolve their problems.

A Goal of Life Career Development— Creating Career Consciousness in Individuals

What Is Career Consciousness?

A major goal of having individuals use life career development as a wide-angle lens to identify, describe, and understand the dynamics of their development past, present, and future is to create within themselves *career consciousness*. What is career consciousness? Gysbers and Moore (1975) defined career consciousness as the ability to visualize possible life career roles, analyze them, and relate them to present situations and conditions. We expanded and extended this original conceptualization and define career consciousness as individuals' inner sense of optimism and continuity of time (Ickes, 1981) that enables them to visualize, plan, and be planful about their current and future life careers so that they can engage "in an active life style to generate unexpected events, to remain alert to new opportunities, and to capitalize on the opportunities they find" (Krumboltz, 2009, p. 152).

The concept of career consciousness that we propose has a broad action-oriented meaning. "Included within the idea of consciousness is a person's background, education, politics, insight, values, emotions, and philosophy" (Reich, 1971, p. 15). But consciousness, according to Reich, is more than this. It is the whole person. It is that person's way of creating his or her own life. We incorporated Reich's definition of consciousness into our concept to highlight its broad action-oriented meaning, and we added the word *career* to focus attention on the human career. People have careers; the work world has occupations.

We believe the challenge for career counseling in the 21st century is to assist individuals of all ages and circumstances to become career conscious, enabling them to project themselves into and make sense of their current and future life roles, life settings, and life events. Involved in this challenge is the task of helping individuals to assess, reflect, and take purposeful action on the meanings they derive from what they see. Through meaning making, the career counseling process "helps people reduce their sense of discrepancy between appraised and global meanings and restore a sense of the world as coherent and their own life as meaningful" (Park, 2012, p. 25). We believe further that to meet this challenge the career counseling process must unfold in context, understanding the important ways that gender, ethnic origin, race, social class, sexual orientation, and disability can shape the reflection, meaning-making, and action processes.

Career Consciousness Is Multifaceted
Career consciousness is a multifaceted concept. It contains a number of elements such as possible selves, counterfactual thoughts, and calling, not as separate and distinct entities but as integrated parts of the whole person.

Possible Selves
Contained within the concept of career consciousness is the notion of possible selves, first described by Markus and Nurius (1986). What are possible selves? "Possible selves represent individuals' ideas of what they might become, what they would like to become, and what they are afraid of becoming, and thus provide a conceptual link between cognition and motivation" (Markus & Nurius, 1986, p. 954). We endorse Collin and Guichard's (2011) point that possible selves are "not given but constructed" (p. 93) and are "never complete" (p. 94).

Why are possible selves important? "Possible selves are important, first, because they function as incentives for future behavior (i.e., they are selves to be approached or avoided) and, second, because they provide an evaluative and interpretive context for the current view of self" (Markus & Nurius, 1986, p. 954). Oyserman and Fryberg (2006) described possible selves similarly.

> Possible selves are the selves we imagine ourselves becoming in the future, the selves we hope to become, the selves we are afraid we may become, and the selves we fully expect we will become. Possible selves can be distally imagined—'the self I will become as an adult,' or more short term—'the self I will become next year.' (p. 17)

Counterfactual Thoughts—Feeling of Regret
The concept of career consciousness can also contain counterfactual thoughts, such as thinking about how things might have been or what could have happened (Roese, 2005).

> Whenever we say "if only" or "almost," or use words like "could," "would," or "should," we may be expressing a counterfactual thought: *If only I were taller . . . I almost won that hand . . . I could have been a contender . . . I would have caught that ball, if not for the sun in my eyes.* (p. 1)

Counterfactual thoughts can result in feelings of regret in individuals, or feelings of sadness and disappointment that then current situations would have been better if only they had made different decisions in the past (Beike, Markman, & Karadogan, 2009; Berg, Grant, & Johnson, 2010). Obodaru (2012) underscored this point as follows:

> Even though we follow a certain path, we do not always forget the forgone options; instead, we wonder about them and generate ideas about what we might have encountered at the end of those alternative paths, and these ideas color our perception of the present as well as our vision of the future. (p. 51)

Calling

In addition to containing the concepts of possible selves and counterfactual thoughts such as regret, career consciousness can also contain the idea of *calling*. The concept of calling in career consciousness has deep roots in history and often had religious connotations. However, according to Dik and Duffy (2012), religious meanings have been largely lost: "Callings have largely lost the religious connotation and tend to be defined in the secular sense as consisting of enjoyable or pleasurable work that the individual believes is making the world a better place" (p. 10).

Dik and Duffy (2012) pointed out that constructing successful careers is not simply a matter of having talent, motivation, and opportunity. They stated,

> A successful career also requires the consistent belief that one can do what is required well, and that doing what is required actually leads to outcomes that matter. Not only that, but when facing obstacles, people have the capacity (to the extent that external constraints allow) to mold and shape their work into something that encourages, facilitates, and provides a means of living out their callings. (p. 19)

Using Life Career Development in Career Counseling

The concept of life career development serves as a wide-angle lens that can bring into focus a broad, holistic picture of individuals' life career development. It can provide them with potential realistic, graphic representations of their major life possibilities and responsibilities as well as language to describe themselves, enabling them to develop career consciousness. It is difficult to develop career consciousness, however, if the lens being used by them to view and give meaning to their past, present, and future is too narrow to capture the full scope of their life career development, and the screen on which it is being projected is not large enough to portray its many dimensions, dynamics, and relationships. Things not seen cannot be a part of individuals' career consciousness. "A spotlight only lights a spot. Everything outside it is obscured" (Heath & Heath, 2013, p. 2).

The life career development view of human development and behavior also provides ways to analyze and understand individuals' development and behavior in career terms, to expand their vision of career from a work-only focus to a broader view involving life roles, life settings, and life events that include work, all interacting over the life span. This allows them to focus on a specific life role while connecting that life role to other life roles (to appreciate the influence various life settings may have on life roles) and to anticipate the possible impact that planned and unplanned events or nonevents may have on career planning and decision making (Amundson et al., 2009; Anderson, Goodman, & Schlossberg, 2012; Hartung, 2011a). With the addition of the factors of gender, ethnic origin, spirituality, race, social class, sexual orientation, and disability, a broadened real-life frame is available on which individuals can display, organize, and understand the impact these factors may have on their current and possible selves—in essence, their life career development.

To appreciate the potential of this conceptualization, consider individuals who are struggling with work-related concerns. Sometimes these work-related concerns are not well understood. They often consist of a jumble of thoughts, feelings, and meanings. They may also involve other life roles, settings, and events. Hartung (2011b) emphasized this point when he stated:

> Counsellors . . . should first recognize and address the relative importance clients ascribe to various life roles rather than assuming that the work role constitutes the main focus of the client's problems and concerns. (p. 107)

The life career development view of human development and behavior can also address older clientele who are seeking new opportunities. Leider and Webber (2013) used the term *Life Reimagined* to describe this phenomenon. They suggested that Life Reimagined gives a way to think about aging; it gives us a way to talk with older clients about new opportunities, or what Leider and Webber called "encore careers" (p. 6). They pointed out that increasing longevity and better health offers individuals the potential of making transitions to new life roles, life settings, and life events, regardless of age.

Life career development provides individuals with a wide-angle lens through which they can view and understand work concerns as well as how other life role issues may impact these concerns. Add the factors of gender, ethnic origin, race, spirituality, social class, sexual orientation, and disability, and the wide-angle lens becomes even more powerful. Now individuals have a way of bringing their personal histories and the histories of their reference groups into focus. Now they can see how these factors have directly or indirectly influenced them and their views of themselves, others, and the world in which they live. Now they have these additional factors to use to understand and respond to various life roles, including work concerns. As a result they have new language. This new language is important because as Savickas (2011) pointed out, "As we talk, so we make. Words provide a resource for living that enables thinking and making meaning" (p. 16). Lago and Smith (2010) stressed the same point. "A common argument in discussions about the power of language is that language not only describes reality, it *determines* reality" (p. 7).

One way to assist individuals to practice the new language of life career development is to use the Adlerian *acting as if* technique. Ask them to imagine and describe being the person they would like to be. Then ask, How would that feel? What would that mean? and What would you do if you were that person? According to Watts (2013),

> The purpose of the procedure is to bypass potential resistance to change by neutralizing some of the perceived risk. Acting "as if" affords clients the opportunity to enact alternative or preferred outcomes and possibly *restory* oppressive aspects of their personal metanarrative (or "style of life" in Adlerian parlance). (pp. 49–50)

Implications for Career Counseling

The broadened understanding of career development in life terms makes it clear that we must respond to the developmental needs of people as well as to their crisis needs. Obviously, crises in individuals' lives must be dealt with, but crises are not the only emphasis in career counseling. Such thinking has a number of implications. Here are three.

Prediction and Development

The first implication revolves around the words *prediction* and *development*. Traditional career counseling practices emphasize the assessment of individuals' abilities, aptitudes, personality, values, and interests to aid them in selecting appropriate educational programs or making occupational choices. This emphasis, although important, is not sufficient. What is needed, in addition, is attention to individuals' life career development so that goal achievement and problem resolution can be based on the broadest and most well-informed perspective possible. We believe what Tennyson wrote in the 1970s was relevant then and is equally relevant today:

> By concentrating upon assessment of abilities presumed to be related to choice out-comes, counselors have neglected to concern themselves with the development of abilities and aptitudes. While it is generally recognized that what a person is able to do depends to a considerable extent upon what he has learned or practiced, guidance personnel have been inclined to capitalize upon aptitudes already developed rather than cultivating new talents. (Tennyson, 1970, p. 262)

Strengths and Deficits

The second implication focuses on the words *strengths* and *deficits*. A major focus of career counseling is on helping individuals deal effectively with problems. Personal crises; a lack of information about training opportunities and the job market; and inef-fective relationships with spouses, children, fellow employees, or supervisors are exam-ples of problems to which counselors frequently are asked to respond. This focus must continue, and better ways of helping individuals with their problems must be found.

At the same time, we believe that a preventive positive focus is needed to help indi-viduals develop and use their strengths to create a better world for themselves and for society (Snyder, Lopez, & Pedrotti, 2011). The preventive positive focus is not new. It has been a part of the counseling language and literature for more than 100 years. What is new, however, is a sense of urgency about the importance of helping people develop and focus on their strengths rather than on their deficits only. Although some individuals do not think of themselves as having strengths, everyone possesses a substantial number of strengths, and their identification and use is an important part of positive growth and development. Snyder et al. (2011) underscored this point by stating that individuals need to identify their strengths and move toward balance in their lives. "One characteristic of a happy and productive life is a sense of balance in one's views and actions" (p. 480).

Stability and Change

The third implication features the words *stability* and *change*. Sometimes these words are seen as opposites, not as two sides of the same coin. Pryor and Bright (2011) stated that individuals who stress either stability or change in career development sometimes acknowledge the opposite view but seldom incorporate it into their work. Pryor and Bright stressed the need to include both perspectives in our understanding of career development and in our work with clients.

> Complex dynamical systems incorporate both stability and change, structure and surprise, as linked, recursive and perpetual potential influences at the one time in the one system. Thus stability leads to change, and change may lead back again to stabil-ity. Indeed, some parts of such systems may be undergoing change at the same time that they are establishing stability in another part. (p. 29)

Ensuring Counselor Competence

The broadened understanding of career development in life terms requires that coun-selors who work from this holistic perspective have appropriate competencies to work with clients of all ages and circumstances (Hiebert, 2006). They must also have the self-confidence to use these competencies. What competencies are required? O'Brien and Heppner (1995) identified 25 competencies they thought career counselors should pos-sess. The 25 competencies form the items for an instrument they developed called the Career Counseling Self-Efficacy Scale (CCSES). It assesses the level of confidence that counselors have in their ability to perform the task involved in each competency. The CCSES with its 25 competencies appears in Table 1-2.

The CCSES evidenced moderate to high internal consistency and strong test–retest reliability over a 2-week period (O'Brien, Heppner, Flores, & Bikos, 1997). Convergent validity was supported by correlations with years of career counseling experience and several scales of an emotional–social counseling self-efficacy measure. Discriminant validity was evidenced through an absence of relations between the CCSES total score and years of an emotional–social counseling self-efficacy measure. Discriminant validity also was evidenced through an absence of relations between the CCSES total score and years of emotional–social counseling experience, emotional–social counseling self-efficacy, and research self-efficacy. In addition to the above, construct validity was evidenced by increases on the CCSES after a career course and varying levels of efficacy commensurate with status in the field (i.e., practicing psychologists held higher self-efficacy beliefs

Table 1-2. Career Counseling Self-Efficacy Scale

Below is a list of activities regarding counseling. Indicate YOUR CONFIDENCE IN YOUR CURRENT ABILITY TO PERFORM EACH ACTIVITY by circling the appropriate answer next to each question according to the scale defined below. Please answer each item based on how you feel now, not on your anticipated (or previous) ability.

0	1	2	3	4
Not Confident		*Moderately Confident*		*Highly Confident*

1. Select an instrument to clarify client's career abilities. 0 1 2 3 4
2. Provide support for a client's implementation of her/his career goals. 0 1 2 3 4
3. Assist a client in understanding how his/her non-work life (e.g., family, leisure, interests, etc.) affects career decisions. 0 1 2 3 4
4. Understand special issues related to gender *in career decision-making*. 0 1 2 3 4
5. Develop a therapeutic relationship with a career client. 0 1 2 3 4
6. Select an instrument to clarify aspects of a career client's personality which may influence career planning. 0 1 2 3 4
7. Explain assessment results to a career client. 0 1 2 3 4
8. Terminate counseling with a career client in an effective manner. 0 1 2 3 4
9. Understand special issues related to ethnicity in the workplace. 0 1 2 3 4
10. Understand special issues that lesbian, gay, and bisexual clients may have *in career decision-making*. 0 1 2 3 4
11. Provide knowledge of local and national job market information and trends. 0 1 2 3 4
12. Choose assessment inventories for a career client which are appropriate for the client's gender, age, education, and cultural background. 0 1 2 3 4
13. Assist the career client in modulating feelings about the career decision-making process. 0 1 2 3 4
14. Apply knowledge about current ethical and legal issues which may affect the career counseling process. 0 1 2 3 4
15. Understand special issues present for lesbian, gay, and bisexual clients *in the workplace*. 0 1 2 3 4
16. Communicate unconditional acceptance to a career client. 0 1 2 3 4
17. Select an instrument to assess a career client's interests. 0 1 2 3 4
18. Select an instrument to clarify a career client's values. 0 1 2 3 4
19. Understand special issues related to gender *in the workplace*. 0 1 2 3 4
20. Understand special issues related to ethnicity *in career decision-making*. 0 1 2 3 4
21. Listen carefully to concerns presented by a career client. 0 1 2 3 4
22. Synthesize information about self and career so that a career client's problems seem understandable. 0 1 2 3 4
23. Help a career client identify internal and external barriers that might interfere with reaching her/his career goals. 0 1 2 3 4
24. Use current research findings to intervene effectively with a career client. 0 1 2 3 4
25. Be empathic toward a career client when the client refuses to accept responsibility for making decisions about his/her career. 0 1 2 3 4

Note. Permission to use this scale for research purposes is granted by the authors. Copyright by Karen M. O'Brien and Mary J. Heppner. Additional requests for information regarding this scale should be directed to Karen M. O'Brien, Department of Psychology, University of Maryland, College Park, MD 20742.

than graduate students). Finally, four factors emerged that accounted for 73% of the variance. The above findings and the use of this instrument for training and evaluating counselors who provide career counseling are discussed in the O'Brien et al. article.

Both total and scale scores can be calculated for this instrument. The total score is calculated by summing all of the items. Scores on each of the four factors are obtained by summing the items composing each factor. Higher scores indicate considerable confidence in one's ability to perform career counseling.

The first factor is Therapeutic Process and Alliance Skills and is composed of 10 items with factor loadings ranging from .65 to .88. This factor assesses the counselor's confidence in developing a therapeutic relationship, providing support, synthesizing information, identifying barriers, and terminating the career counseling relationship in an effective manner. The following items load on this factor: 2, 3, 5, 8, 13, 16, 21, 22, 23, and 25.

The second factor, consisting of six items, is Vocational Assessment and Interpretation Skills and has factor loadings from .69 to .97. This factor assesses confidence in one's ability to select appropriate instruments to assess interests, values, and personality and to explain assessment results to career clients. Items 1, 6, 7, 12, 17, and 18 compose this factor.

The third factor is Multicultural Competency Skills and consists of six items with factor loadings from .56 to .92. This factor addresses the importance of multicultural counseling competencies in interventions with career clients. Specifically, this factor assesses confidence in understanding the special issues related to ethnicity, gender, and sexual orientation in both the workplace and career decision making. Included in this factor are Items 4, 9, 10, 15, 19, and 20.

The final factor is Current Trends in the World of Work, Ethics, and Career Research and consists of three items with factor loadings from .77 to .80. This factor assesses knowledge of current research findings, ethical and legal issues, and local and national job market trends. Items 11, 14, and 24 compose this factor.

What Do We Know About Career Development and Career Counseling?

Before we close Chapter 1, it is important to stop and review what we know about career development and career counseling. Work on these topics has been unfolding for almost 100 years, and a substantial body of descriptive and empirical literature is available. It is not possible to present a complete review of all of this literature here. However, it is possible to present a brief summary of some key points from recent literature.

Fouad (2007) reviewed the empirical work in career development and career counseling since 1995. She summarized her findings as follows:

1. Job satisfaction is more fully explained by variables other than congruence, but other aspects of Holland's theory were supported. Holland's theory appears to be most applicable for cultural groups similar to Caucasians.
2. Children's career dreams and aspirations do not very accurately predict their occupations in adulthood. Those eventual choices are influenced by parental socioeconomic status, schooling, and educational/environmental opportunities. However, aspirations can mediate the effects of an impoverished background.
3. Career exploration is best promoted by an individual's career adaptability, positive relationships, openness to experiences, and social and psychological capital.
4. An individual's beliefs in his/her ability to accomplish career-related tasks are critical predictors of career choice, particularly in nontraditional careers.
5. The context in which an individual lives is shaped by his/her gender, race/ethnicity, social class, and sexual orientation. All of these factors influence an individual's actual and perceived career opportunities and choices.

6. Career decision-making difficulties may be related to an individual's need to continue exploring various options and lack of readiness to make a decision. However, decision-making difficulties also may be related to other types of psychological concerns, such as general anxiety and indecisiveness.
7. Career counseling and interventions are effective. The most effective type of career counseling is individual counseling that contains homework, assessment interpretations, information on the world of work, social support, and exposure to role models.

Whiston and Blustein (2013) supported Finding 7 by stating "considerable evidence exists supporting the efficacy of career development interventions" (p. 4). They went on to state that career counseling is effective in helping individuals improve their career decision-making skills and handling career development tasks more effectively. They also indicated that career services are cost effective and useful in helping individuals make transitions to work.

As you are reading the chapters that follow, keep these findings in mind. You will find that they are discussed and emphasized in many of the chapters. When you finish reading the book, return to this list to remind yourself of these key findings concerning career development and career counseling. You will discover that we have substantial knowledge about the process of career development and the impact of career counseling on the lives of individuals of all ages and circumstances.

Closing Thoughts

Wolfe and Kolb (1980) summed up the dynamic life-centered view of career development that has evolved over the past decades when they described career development as involving one's entire life:

> Career development involves one's whole life, not just occupation. As such, it concerns the whole person, needs and wants, capacities and potentials, excitements and anxieties, insights and blind spots, warts and all. More than that, it concerns him/her in the ever-changing contexts of his/her life. The environmental pressures and constraints, the bonds that tie him/her to significant others, responsibilities to children and aging parents, the total structure of one's circumstances are also factors that must be understood and reckoned with. In these terms, career development and personal development converge. Self and circumstances—evolving, changing, unfolding in mutual interaction—constitute the focus and the drama of career development. (pp. 1–2)

Note that Wolfe and Kolb (1980) closed their definition of career development with the words *the drama of career development*. We label it *the drama of the ordinary*, because it is unfolding and evolving every day and thus is not often seen or appreciated by individuals. It is veiled in ordinariness. As a result, clients may fail to understand its dynamic nature and the substantial impact it has throughout their lives. They may fail to understand that what they "do in their daily lives is core to career" (Young, Marshall, & Valach, 2007, p. 8). By using the broader concept of life career development with clients as an orientation for understanding their human growth and development—the human career—we propose to make the drama of career development *the drama of the extraordinary*. It is the *drama of the extraordinary* because "each person is an individual traveller who navigates his or her career in a personal context" (Inkson & Elkin, 2008, p. 90).

References

Amundson, N. E. (1998). *Active engagement: Enhancing the career counseling process.* Richmond, British Columbia, Canada: Ergon Communications.

Amundson, N. (2006). Challenges for career interventions in changing contexts. *International Journal for Educational and Vocational Guidance, 6,* 3–14.

Amundson, N. E., Harris-Bowlsbey, J., & Niles, S. (2009). *Essential elements of career counseling: Processes and techniques* (2nd ed.). Upper Saddle River, NJ: Pearson Education.

Andersen, P., & Vandehey, M. (2012). *Career counseling and development in a global economy* (2nd ed.). Belmont, CA: Brooks/Cole, Cengage Learning.

Anderson, M. L., Goodman, J., & Schlossberg, N. K. (2012). *Counseling adults in transition: Linking Schlossberg's theory with practice in a diverse world* (4th ed.). New York, NY: Springer.

Beike, D. R., Markman, K. D., & Karadogan, F. (2009). What we regret most are lost opportunities: A theory of regret intensity. *Personality and Social Psychology Bulletin, 35,* 385–397.

Berg, J. M., Grant, A. M., & Johnson, V. (2010). When callings are calling: Crafting work and leisure in pursuit of unanswered occupational callings. *Organizational Science, 21,* 973–994.

Blustein, D. L. (2006). *The psychology of working: A new perspective for career development, counseling, and public policy.* Mahwah, NJ: Erlbaum.

Blustein, D. L., & Spengler, P. M. (1995). Personal adjustment: Career counseling and psychotherapy. In W. B. Walsh & S. H. Osipow (Eds.), *Handbook of vocational psychology: Theory, research, and practice* (pp. 295–329). Hillsdale, NJ: Erlbaum.

Capuzzi, D., & Stauffer, M. D. (2012). *Career counseling: Foundations, perspectives, and applications* (2nd ed.). New York, NY: Routledge.

Collin, A. (2006). Career. In J. H. Greenhaus & G. A. Callanan (Eds.), *Encyclopedia of career development* (Vol. 1, pp. 60–63). Thousand Oaks, CA: Sage.

Collin, A., & Guichard, J. (2011). Constructing self in career theory and counseling interventions. In P. J. Hartung & L. M. Subich (Eds.), *Developing self in work and career: Concepts, cases, and contexts* (pp. 89–106). Washington, DC: American Psychological Association.

Crites, J. O. (1981). *Career counseling: Models, methods, and materials.* New York, NY: McGraw-Hill.

Dik, B. J., & Duffy, R. D. (2012). *Make your job a calling.* West Conshokocken, PA: Templeton Press.

Dorn, F. J. (1992). Occupational wellness: The integration of career identity and personal identity. *Journal of Counseling & Development, 71,* 176–178.

Flores, L. Y. (2007). Introduction to a special issue. *Journal of Career Development, 34,* 3–4.

Fouad, N. A. (2007). Work and vocational psychology: Theory, research, and applications. *Annual Review of Psychology, 58,* 543–564.

Fouad, N. A., Chen, Y., Guillen, A., Henry, C., Kantamneni, N., Novakovic, A., . . . Terry, S. (2007). Role induction in career counseling. *The Career Development Quarterly, 56,* 19–33.

Friedman, T. L. (2007). *The world is flat.* New York, NY: Picador/Farrar, Straus & Giroux.

Gysbers, N. C., & Moore, E. J. (1975). Beyond career development—Life career development. *Personal and Guidance Journal, 53,* 647–652.

Hartung, P. J. (2011a). Barrier or benefit? Emotion in life–career design. *Journal of Career Assessment, 19*(3), 296–305.

Hartung, P. J. (2011b). Career construction: Principles and practice. In K. Maree (Ed.), *Shaping the story: A guide to facilitating narrative career counseling* (pp. 103–120). Rotterdam, The Netherlands: Sense.

Heath, C., & Heath, D. (2013). *Decisive: How to make better choices in life and work.* New York, NY: Crown Business.

Hiebert, B. (2006). Career counseling competences. In J. H. Greenhaus & G. A. Callanan (Eds.), *Encyclopedia of career development* (Vol. 1, pp. 92–93). Thousand Oaks, CA: Sage.

Ickes, J. L. (1981). *The psychology of career consciousness: The causal relationship between subjective future and career maturity* (Unpublished doctoral dissertation). Kent State University, Kent, OH.

Imbimbo, P. V. (1994). Integrating personal and career counseling: A challenge for counselors. *Journal of Employment Counseling, 31*, 50–59.

Inkson, K., & Elkin, G. (2008). Landscape with travellers: The context of careers in developed nations. In J. A. Athanasou & R. Van Esbroeck (Eds.), *International handbook of career guidance* (pp. 69–94). New York, NY: Springer.

Kidd, J. M. (2004). Emotion in career contexts: Challenges for theory and research. *Journal of Vocational Behavior, 64*, 441–454.

Krumboltz, J. D. (2009). The happenstance learning theory. *Journal of Career Assessment, 17*, 135–154.

Lago, C., & Smith, B. (2010). Ethical practice and best practice. In C. Lago & B. Smith (Eds.), *Anti-discriminatory practice in counseling and psychotherapy* (2nd ed., pp. 1–12). London, England: Sage.

Leider, R. J., & Webber, A. M. (2013). Life reimagined: The new story of aging. *Career Developments, 29*(3), 5–9.

Lent, R. E., & Brown, S. D. (2013). Understanding and facilitating career development in the 21st century. In S. D. Brown & R. W. Lent (Eds.), *Career development and counseling* (pp. 1–26). Hoboken, NJ: Wiley.

Lent, R. W. (2013). Career–life preparedness: Revisiting career planning and adjustment in the new workplace. *The Career Development Quarterly, 61*, 2–14.

Markus, H., & Nurius, P. (1986). Possible selves. *American Psychologist, 41*, 954–969.

McDaniels, C., & Gysbers, N. C. (1992). *Counseling for career development: Theories, resources, and practice.* San Francisco, CA: Jossey-Bass.

McMahon, M., Watson, M., Chetty, C., & Hoelson, C. N. (2012). Examining process constructs of narrative career counselling: An exploratory case study. *British Journal of Guidance & Counselling, 40*(2), 127–141.

Multon, K. D., Heppner, M. J., Gysbers, N. C., Zook, C., & Ellis-Kalton, C. A. (2001). Client psychological distress: An important factor in career counseling. *The Career Development Quarterly, 49*, 324–335.

Niles, S. G., & Harris-Bowlsbey, J. (2005). *Career development interventions in the 21st century* (2nd ed.). Upper Saddle River, NJ: Pearson Education.

Obodaru, O. (2012). The self not taken: How alternative selves develop and how they influence our professional lives. *Academy of Management Review, 37*, 34–57.

O'Brien, K. M., & Heppner, M. J. (1995). *The Career Counseling Self-Efficacy Scale.* (Available from K. M. O'Brien, Psychology Department, University of Maryland, College Park, MD 20742)

O'Brien, K. M., Heppner, M. J., Flores, L. Y., & Bikos, L. H. (1997). The Career Counseling Self-Efficacy Scale: Instrument of development and training applications. *Journal of Counseling Psychology, 44*, 20–31.

Osipow, S. H. (1982). Research in career counseling: An analysis of issues and problems. *The Counseling Psychologist, 10*(4), 27–34.

Oyserman, D., & Fryberg, S. (2006). The possible selves of diverse adolescents: Content and function across gender, race, and national origin. In C. Dunkel & J. Kerpelman (Eds.), *Possible selves: Theory, research and applications* (pp. 17–39). New York, NY: Nova Science.

Paloutzian, R. F., & Lowe, D. A. (2012). Spiritual transformation and engagement in workplace culture. In P. C. Hill & B. J. Dik (Eds.), *Psychology of religion and workplace spirituality* (pp. 179–199). Charlotte, NC: Information Age.

Park, C. L. (2012). Religious and spiritual aspects of meaning in the context of work life. In P. C. Hill & B. J. Dik (Eds.), *Psychology of religion and workplace spirituality* (pp. 25–42). Charlotte, NC: Information Age.

Parsons, F. (1909). *Choosing a vocation.* Boston, MA: Houghton Mifflin.

Pryor, R., & Bright, J. (2011). *The chaos theory of careers.* New York, NY: Routledge.

Reich, C. A. (1971). *The greening of America*. New York, NY: Bantam Books.

Roese, N. (2005). *If only: How to turn regret into opportunity*. New York, NY: Broadway Books.

Savickas, M. L. (2011). *Career counseling*. Washington, DC: American Psychological Association.

Snyder, C. R., Lopez, S. J., & Pedrotti, J. T. (2011). *Positive psychology: The scientific and practical explorations of human strengths* (2nd ed.). Thousand Oaks, CA: Sage.

Super, D. E. (1955). Transition: From vocational guidance to counseling psychology. *Journal of Counseling Psychology, 2,* 3–9.

Super, D. E. (1957). *The psychology of careers*. New York, NY: Harper & Brothers.

Swanson, J. L. (1995). The process and outcome of career counseling. In W. B. Walsh & S. H. Osipow (Eds.), *Handbook of vocational psychology: Theory, research, and practice* (pp. 217–259). Hillsdale, NJ: Erlbaum.

Tennyson, W. (1970). Comment. *Vocational Guidance Quarterly, 18,* 261–263.

Watts, R. E. (2013). Reflecting 'as if.' *Counseling Today, 55,* 48–53.

Westergaard, J. (2012). Career guidance and therapeutic counseling: Sharing 'what works' in practice with young people. *British Journal of Guidance & Counselling, 40,* 327–339.

Whiston, S. C., & Blustein, D. L. (2013). *The impact of career interventions: Preparing our citizens for the 21st century jobs* (Policy brief). Retrieved from the National Career Development Association (www.ncda.org) and the Society for Vocational Psychology (www.div17.org/vocpsych/).

Wolfe, D. M., & Kolb, D. A. (1980). Career development, personal growth, and experimental learning. In J. W. Springer (Ed.), *Issues in career and human resource development* (pp. 1–56). Madison, WI: American Society for Training and Development.

Young, R. A., & Domene, J. F. (2012). Creating a research agenda in career counselling: The place of action theory. *British Journal of Guidance and Counselling, 40*(1), 15–30.

Young, R. A., Marshall, S. K., & Valach, L. (2007). Making career theories more culturally sensitive: Implications for counseling. *The Career Development Quarterly, 56,* 4–18.

Zunker, V. G. (2002). *Career counseling: Applied concepts of life planning*. Pacific Grove, CA: Brooks/Cole.

Chapter 2

Ways of Understanding
Career Behavior and Development:
Selected Theories

"Why study theory?" "What does theory have to do with practice?" "Most of the courses I took in my training to become a counselor were too theoretical!" "Theory gets in
my way when I am trying to listen to and respond to my clients!" These and similar
questions and comments are heard frequently when counselors get together and discuss
their current work and previous training. Why do they express these attitudes? Partly
because there is, in fact, a gap between theory and practice. Many books and articles describe theory. Fewer books and articles explain how theoretical concepts and language
can be used in counseling.

Theory provides us with a way to see and understand human behavior. Anderson,
Goodman, and Schlossberg (2012) stated, "A theory is a set of abstract principles that
can be used to predict facts and to organize them within a particular body of knowledge" (p. 4). Krumboltz (2005) suggested, "A theory is just one way of oversimplifying
a complex situation so that it is easier for you to see the big picture" (p. 34). For us,
a theory summarizes and generalizes a body of information. It facilitates our understanding of and provides an explanation for the phenomena described by that body of
information. It acts as a predictor of future developments, and it also stimulates further
research (Young, Marshall, & Valach, 2007).

Thus, theories provide foundation knowledge from which you can draw useful concepts and language to explain client behavior. Theories offer a framework within which
client behavior can be examined and hypotheses formed about the possible meanings
of that behavior. In turn, this knowledge helps you identify, understand, and respond to
clients' goals or problems.

How do clients, the counseling process, and theory interact? Clients often become
involved in career counseling because they are in transition, either by their own choice
or because of conditions over which they have only limited control or no control at
all. Internal thoughts and feelings concerning these transitions abound, often without
shape or form. They may appear jumbled and confused, at least on the surface. What
should I do? In which direction should I go? How should I respond to and resolve my
problem or achieve my goal? These are the kinds of questions clients may be struggling

with. Sometimes the questions, let alone any possible answers, are not clearly formed in clients' minds.

So how does theory inform practice to help you and your clients deal with these issues? Theory helps us identify and interpret client behavior and information. It provides us with ways to give meaning to the internal thoughts and feelings of our clients. That meaning can then be connected to practical strategies for assisting clients in pursuing career goals or resolving problems.

In addition to helping us understand and respond to clients' problems and goals, career theories provide us with insights into the possible outcomes of counseling for career development. Super (1990) made this point a number of years ago, and we feel it is still valid today.

> Career development theory makes clear what is to be fostered—occupational self-concept clarification and implementation and handling of the developmental tasks. It is growth in autonomy, time perspective, and self-esteem; exploration in breadth and then in depth for the crystallization, specification, and implementation of occupational self-concepts, interests, and a vocational preference; establishment with trial, stabilization, consolidation, and perhaps advancement; maintenance with adaptability, which means at least holding but better still keeping up, innovating, and in some cases transferring; and decline, or disengagement, and the shift of role emphases. (p. 254)

This chapter opens with an overview of how our understanding of career behavior and development has evolved over the years from the late 1800s to today. Then brief descriptions of selected theories that attempt to explain the nature, structure, and processes of career behavior and development are presented. We do not provide overviews of all career theories because a number of excellent books available today do that. Instead, our intent is to describe several theories from different time periods to illustrate how the constructs from these theories can facilitate our understanding of client behavior as well as facilitate clients' understanding of their own behavior.

The Evolution of Our Understanding of Career Behavior and Development

Many years ago, Crites (1969) identified three broad overlapping eras to describe the evolution of career behavior and development theory building. His first era, *Observational*, covered a period of time from the late 1800s to the mid-1920s. His second era, *Empirical*, focused on the time from World War I to the end of World War II, roughly 1914 to 1945. His third era, *Theoretical*, began in the late 1940s and continues today.

Observational Era

From the mid-1800s into the early years of the 1900s, the United States was deeply involved in the Industrial Revolution. It was a period of rapid industrial growth, social protest, social reform, and utopian idealism. Social protest and social reform were being carried out under the banner of the Progressive Movement, a movement that sought to change negative conditions associated with the Industrial Revolution. *Vocational guidance*, the term used in the early years, was born during the height of the Progressive Movement as "but one manifestation of the broader movement of progressive reform which occurred in this country in the late 19th and early 20th centuries" (Stephens, 1970, p. 5).

During the early part of this period, efforts to provide vocational guidance to individuals were sponsored by the Young Men's Christian Association (YMCA) and by individuals such as Lysander Richards, who in 1881 published his book *Vocophy: The New Profession*. According to Savickas and Baker (2005), practitioners during these years used phrenology, physiognomy, and palmistry in their vocational guidance work. "This pseudoscience recognized individual differences but assessed their meaning . . . by measuring crania, facial features, and body shapes" (p. 20). Although these pseudoscience techniques were still being talked about in the early 1900s, they were largely discredited as more scientific approaches to vocational guidance were being developed and used.

The foundation for vocational guidance as we know it today was laid by a number of individuals and social institutions in the early 1900s. Frank Parsons has been identified as "the dominant visionary and architect of vocational guidance" (Herr, Cramer, & Niles, 2004, p. 19) during this time period. He opened the Vocational Bureau in a settlement home called the Civic Service House in January 1908, where he used the term *vocational guidance* for the first time. In his book *Choosing a Vocation*, published in 1909, he described his three-step approach, giving vocational guidance "its status as a science" (Savickas & Baker, 2005, p. 24):

> In the wise choice of a vocation there are three broad factors: (1) a clear understanding of yourself, your aptitudes, interests, ambitions, resources, limitations, and their causes; (2) a knowledge of the requirements and conditions of success, advantages and disadvantages, compensation, opportunities, and prospects in different lines of work; (3) true reasoning on the relations of these two groups of facts. (Parsons, 1909, p. 5)

To carry out his three-step approach, Parsons depended "on self-analysis by the candidate himself, shrewd intuition on the part of the counselor, and even physiognomatic observations" (Hale, 1980, p. 122). His methods involved seven steps: Personal Data, Self-Analysis, The Person's Own Choice and Decision, Counselor's Analysis, Outlook on the Vocational Field, Induction and Advice, and General Helpfulness in Fitting in the Chosen Work (Parsons, 1909). He also began relying on the new field of testing to measure mental capacities. He called on Hugo Munsterberg, director of the Harvard Psychology Laboratory, to test Vocational Bureau clients using mental tests (Hale, 1980).

The use of mental tests (i.e., tests of intelligence) spread rapidly in the 1910s. Individuals such as James Cottell, Hugo Munsterberg, and H. L. Hollinworth were among the advocates who urged the use of these tests. The first large-scale administration of paper-and-pencil tests of intelligence—the Army Alpha and Beta tests—occurred when the United States entered World War I (Crites, 1969). Following the war, these tests were increasingly used in schools and industry (Savickas & Baker, 2005).

Empirical Era

According to Savickas and Baker (2005), the Observational Era came to an end in the mid-1920s. They described the close of the Observational Era and the beginning of the Empirical Era:

> In its observational era, vocational psychology had concentrated on vocational orientation activities and intelligence testing. In its empirical era, vocational psychology would crystallize its identity as a psychological science by merging the streams of Parsons' vocational guidance and Binet's intelligence testing into a current of aptitude and interest testing. (p. 37)

During the 1920s, 1930s, and 1940s, many tests that focused on aptitude, abilities, and interests were developed and used. For example, in 1927 E. K. Strong published the first edition of what is today the Strong Interest Inventory. Later, in the early 1930s, the Minnesota Mechanical Ability Tests were published. During this same period, the Minnesota Employment Stabilization Research Institute at the University of Minnesota was established, partly in response to the depression that gripped the economy. According to Savickas and Baker (2005), this organization conducted numerous research projects and developed many tests.

In 1933, the Wagner–Peyser Act was passed by Congress. It created the U.S. Employment Service:

> When it was founded, the Employment Service surveyed 25,000 employers and 100,000 employees to gather occupational information, develop measures of proficiency and potentiality, study the transferability of skills, and write job descriptions. (Savickas & Baker, 2005, p. 39)

World War II saw many psychologists using tests for personnel classification. The major test used for this purpose was the Army General Classification Test. Some 9 million men were tested. According to Crites (1969), the problems encountered in selecting and classifying soldiers caused the field to grow quickly and revise its view of individuals' relationships to work. "What had been called the Matching Men to Jobs approach in the 1930s gave way to what became known as Trait and Factor theory in the 1940s" (p. 8).

Theoretical Era

The Theoretical Era can be subdivided conceptually into two categories labeled *modern* and *postmodern*. Modern theories began appearing in the 1950s. Postmodern theories began to emerge in the late 1980s and early 1990s.

Modern Theories

Up until the 1950s, the trait and factor approach to career counseling dominated. In keeping with Parsons (1909), the word *trait* focused on characteristics of the individual, whereas the word *factor* looked at the requirements of the workplace. The Empirical Era provided the instruments and information needed to operationalize this approach.

Then in 1951, Ginzberg, Ginsburg, Axelrad, and Herma startled the profession by stating that vocational counselors counseled without theory to guide them. Vocational guidance was a process without a base in theory:

> Vocational counselors are busy practitioners anxious to improve their counseling techniques. They are constantly on the lookout for helpful tools, and the research-minded among them devote what time they can to devising better techniques. They are not theoreticians working on the problem of how individuals make their occupational choices, for, though they have no bias against theory, they have had little time to invest in developing one. (p. 7)

Ginzberg et al. (1951) responded to the lack of theory by proposing a theory of occupational choice that they suggested extended over a period of 10 years. Later, Super (1953) presented a life-long view of career development in 10 propositions that summarized a comprehensive theory. Then Roe (1956) published her book *The Psychology of Occupations*. Holland followed in 1959, presenting a theory of vocational choice "in terms of the occupational environments, the person and his development, and the interactions of the person and the vocational environment" (p. 35).

In the years and decades that followed, many theories were developed to explain and understand career behavior and development. They typically are grouped under such titles as trait and factor theories, developmental theories, learning theories, and socioeconomic theories (Brown, 2007). It is important to remember that modern theories are still in use today, as noted by Savickas and Baker (2005). "Many of these theories are not 'history'; they or their direct descendants are still being used today" (p. 42).

Postmodern Theories

According to McMahon (2010), modern theories are "informed largely by a logical positivist philosophy" (p. 1) that is based on the assumption that there is a reality that can be objectively observed and measured through scientific inquiry. Postmodern theories depart from the logical positivist philosophy by stressing that individuals construct their own ideas about their world as they try to make sense out of their real-life experiences. "Postmodernism embraces multicultural perspectives and emphasizes the belief that there is no one fixed truth but, rather, we construct our own realities and truths" (Niles & Harris-Bowlsbey, 2005, p. 104). Postmodern theories also tend to stress that career counseling should be "less expert and assessment driven, more culturally and contextually sensitive and more inclusive of qualitative and subjective processes" (McMahon & Watson, 2013, p. 284).

Postmodern theories such as constructivist and social constructionist theories began to emerge in the 1980s and 1990s. It is important to note, however, that some of the fundamental concepts used in these theories go back in history to the work of theorists such as Adler, as noted by Watts (2003).

> There is a growing body of literature demonstrating that Adlerian therapy resonates with both cognitive constructivist and social constructionist theories and approaches to therapy. (p. 139)

Selected Theories From the Modern and Postmodern Eras

It is our intent to describe several theories from the modern and postmodern eras to illustrate how the constructs from these theories can facilitate our understanding of client behavior as well as facilitate clients' understanding of their own behavior. The modern theories we have chosen to describe are (a) Super's life-span, life-space theory of career development; (b) Holland's theory of vocational personalities and work environments; (c) Schlossberg's adult career development transition model; (d) Lent, Brown, and Hackett's social cognitive career theory; (e) Krumboltz's happenstance learning theory; and (f) Cook, Heppner, and O'Brien's ecological theory. The postmodern theories we have chosen to describe are (a) constructivism/social constructionism and (b) the chaos theory of careers.

The presentation of each theory begins with a brief description of its basic tenets. Then we identify their implications for clients, counselors, and the counseling process. Emphasis is placed on how the constructs of these theories help us understand client behavior and information more fully and select practical interventions to assist clients in achieving their goals and resolving their problems.

Modern Theories of Career Development

Super's Life-Span, Life-Space Theory of Career Development

Super (1990) described his theory as "a segmental theory . . . a loosely unified set of theories dealing with specific aspects of career development, taken from developmental, differential, social, personality, and phenomenological psychology and held together by self-concept and learning theory" (p. 199). His initial ideas for his theory began forming in the late 1930s. According to Super, Savickas, and Super (1996), these ideas originated in his interest in work and occupations, the developmental studies of Buehler (1933), and the studies of occupational mobility by Davidson and Anderson (1937). These beginning ideas were brought together in Super's (1942) book *The Dynamics of Vocational Adjustment*, in which he presented a developmental view of career choice. The point that career choice was a process, not an event, was "Super's single most important idea" (Super et al., 1996, p. 122).

In the early 1950s, Super (1953) introduced the first outline of his theory in his presidential address to the Division of Counseling and Guidance (now the Division of Counseling Psychology) of the American Psychological Association, in part in response to a challenge by Ginzberg et al. (1951) that vocational counselors lacked a theory to guide their work. In his address, he identified the elements that he thought made up an adequate theory of vocational development. These elements included individual differences; multipotentiality; occupational ability patterns; identification and the role of models; continuity of adjustment; life stages; career patterns; the idea that development can be guided; the idea that development is the result of interaction; the dynamics of career patterns; job satisfaction, individual differences, status, and role; and work as a way of life. He then presented a series of 10 propositions that organized these elements into what he called "a summary statement of a comprehensive theory" (Super, 1953, p. 189). Later, another two propositions were included, and still later two more were added, making a total of 14 (Super, 1990).

In developing his final 14 propositions, Super (1990) drew upon four diverse domains, namely differential psychology, developmental psychology, occupational sociology, and personality theory. Differential psychology provided a knowledge base about the various traits individuals possess and the variety of occupational requirements. Developmental psychology contributed insights into how individuals develop abilities and interests and the concepts of life stages and developmental tasks. Occupational sociology offered new ideas about occupational mobility and the impact of environmental influences. Finally, personality theory contributed the concepts of self-concept and person–environment theory.

The first three propositions emphasize that people have different abilities, interests, and values, and because of this, they may be qualified for various occupations. No person fits only one occupation; a variety of occupations are available for an individual, and occupations accommodate a wide variety of individuals. The next six propositions focus on self-concept and its implementation in career choices, on life stages with their mini- and maxicycles, and on the concepts of career patterns and career maturity. The next four propositions deal with the synthesis and compromise between individual and social factors and work and life satisfactions. Finally, the last proposition looks at work and occupation as the focus for personality organization as well as the interplay of such life roles as worker, student, leisurite, homemaker, and citizen.

In 1951, a major research program called the Career Pattern Study was undertaken in Middletown, New York, to test some of the hypotheses of Super and his colleagues. The Career Pattern Study began following 138 eighth-grade boys and 142 ninth-grade boys. Super and his colleagues theorized that the movement of individuals through life stages was a typical process that could be loosely tracked according to an age-referenced timeline. The participants were followed up briefly at age 21, more intensively at age 25, and then again at about age 36. The findings from the Career Pattern Study have been made available periodically in a series of monographs (Jordaan & Heyde, 1979; Super & Overstreet, 1960), in an article by Super (1985), and in a dissertation by Fisher (1989).

Super's (Super et al., 1996) life-span, life-space approach to career development organizes the concepts of life roles and life stages into an interactive system. This system is represented by a Life–Career Rainbow model. Five life stages shown in relationship to age ranges appear on the upper outside rim. These life stages are labeled growth, exploration, establishment, maintenance, and decline. Super called them *maxicycles*, and, although they are linear, not everyone goes through these stages in the same way or at the same age. Transitions from one stage to the next often involve *minicycles*, or going back through various stages before moving on. Within each of the stages, developmental tasks are to be mastered before movement to the next stage occurs. "Success in adapting to each developmental task results in effective functioning as a student, worker, or retiree [for example] and lays the groundwork for mastering the next task along the developmental continuum" (Super et al., 1996, p. 131).

In addition to life stages, the Life–Career Rainbow features life roles located in the space and time of life stages (life space). Super identified six life roles in which individuals participate over the life span: homemaker, worker, citizen, leisurite, student, and child. Individuals often participate in multiple roles at the same time; the amount of time and effort varies by life stage and age. Individuals' participation in these life roles flucuates depending on age and other circumstances across the life span. Some roles are more important during certain ages than others. "By combining the life space with the life-span or developmental perspective, the Rainbow model shows how the role constellation changes with life stages. As Super noted, life roles wax and wane over time" (Sverko, 2006, p. 791).

An important concept in Super's formulation of career development is that of *career maturity*. Although there are differences of opinion about the definition of career maturity, there is general agreement that this term denotes a readiness to engage in the developmental tasks appropriate to the age and level at which one finds oneself. Maturity, however, is not something that is ever reached, but instead is the goal relative to where one is at any given time. This formulation of the concept helps to promote a life span notion rather than a static, irreversible pattern of career development. Later, Super refined his notion of career maturity. He suggested that the term for adults should be *career adaptability*. Included in his formulation of career maturity (adaptability) are the constructs of planfulness (including autonomy, self-esteem, and reliance on a time perspective), exploration, information, decision making, and reality orientation.

Although Super's work on theory building was substantial and continuous over a long period of time, he also saw the need to concentrate on the use of his theory in practice. He was particularly interested in applying his theoretical concepts to career counseling. To that end, he, along with a number of colleagues, developed the career development assessment and counseling (C-DAC) model (Niles & Harris-Bowlsbey, 2005; Super, Osborne, Walsh, Brown, & Niles, 1992).

According to Super et al. (1996), the C-DAC begins with a session that focuses on the client's concerns and a review of data about the client. Then four phases of assessment are undertaken, with the first phase being the assessment of the importance of the work role in relationship to other life roles. Then in the next phase, attention is given to determining the career stage and career concerns of the client, followed by identifying resources for making and implementing choices as well as assessing resources for adapting to the work world. Next, interests, abilities, and values are assessed by following the trait and factor methodology. The last phase focuses on the assessment of the client's self-concept and life themes by using qualitative assessment procedures:

> The final step in the C-DAC is the integration of assessment and interview data into a meaningful whole. A final step integrates the interview material and the assessment data into a narrative that realistically and sensitively portrays the client's vocational identity, occupational self-concept, and coping resources and then locates the individual in the context of multiple roles with their developmental tasks. Comparing this narrative to the client's career concerns begins the process of formulating, in collaboration with the client, a counseling plan designed to foster the client's career development. (Super et al., 1996, p. 151)

Super (1990) summarized the status of his theory as follows:

> During the past decade, this career development model has been refined and ex-
> tended. Differential psychology has made technical, but not substantive, advances.
> Operational definitions of career maturity have been modified, and the model has
> been modified with them. Our understanding of recycling through stages in a mini-
> cycle has been refined, but the basic construct is essentially the same as when it was
> first formulated, years ago. Ideas about how to assess self-concepts have evolved as
> research has thrown light on their measurement, and knowledge of how applicable
> self-concept theory is to various subpopulations has been extended, but this segment
> of the model has not greatly changed. Life-stage theory has been refined but mostly
> confirmed by several major studies during the past decade. The role of learning the-
> ory has been highlighted by the work on social learning, but to the neglect of other
> kinds of interactive learning. The career model is perhaps now in the maintenance
> stage, but health maintenance does not mean stasis but rather updating and innovat-
> ing as midcareer changes are better recognized and studied.
>   The concept of life stages has been modified in recent years, from envisioning
> mainly a maxicycle to involving minicycles of growth, exploration, establishment,
> maintenance, and decline, linked in a series within the maxicycle. Reexploration and
> reestablishment have thus attracted a great deal of attention, and the term *transition*
> has come to denote these processes. . . . Important, too, is the greater emphasis on the
> fact that the typical impetus for any specific transition is not necessarily age itself, for
> the timing of transitions (stage) is a function of the individual's personality and abili-
> ties, as well as of his or her situation. (pp. 236–237)

Implications of Super's Life-Span, Life-Space Theory for the Practice of Career Counseling

1. Because individuals' life career development involves more than the choice of occupation and the adaptation to it (work role), career counseling should focus attention
   on how work roles interact with other life roles (Niles & Harris-Bowlsbey, 2005).
2. Because occupational decisions are related to other life decisions and often continue to be made throughout the life span, career counseling needs to be provided
   to individuals of all ages and circumstances.
3. Because career development can be described as a stage process with developmental tasks at each stage, and because the nature of these stages is not linear but
   cyclical, counselors need to help clients understand that they are not venturing
   outside of normalcy if they cycle back to earlier developmental stages.
4. Because people who are at different stages of development may need to be counseled in different ways, and because people at similar stages but with different
   levels of career maturity (adaptability) also need to be counseled in different
   ways, it is important to learn how to use life stages and tasks to make diagnoses
   and select appropriate intervention strategies.

Holland's Theory of Vocational Personalities and Work Environments

Holland has a gift for making us think about theory in practical terms. He opened his
text (Holland, 1997) by stating that his theory is designed to provide some explanations
for three common and fundamental questions:

1. What personal and environmental characteristics lead to satisfying career decisions, involvement, and achievement, and what characteristics lead to indecision,
   dissatisfying decisions, or lack of accomplishment?
2. What personal and environmental characteristics lead to stability or change in the
   kind and level of work a person performs over a lifetime?
3. What are the most effective methods for providing assistance to people with career problems? (p. 1)

From the beginning to the end of his book, Holland emphasized the practical application of the theory. In fact, he summarized the theory in a few pages, leaving the rest of the book for an elaboration of practical ways to apply the theory. We follow his lead here. The theory in its simplest terms suggests that at first people can be characterized in terms of their resemblance to each of six personality types: Realistic, Investigative, Artistic, Social, Enterprising, and Conventional (hence the reference to it being the RIASEC model). The more closely people resemble a type, the more they exhibit the traits and behaviors of that type. Also, environments can be characterized in terms of their resemblance to and support of the types. Holland went on to state, "The pairing of persons and environments leads to outcomes that we can predict and understand from our knowledge of the personality types and the environmental models" (1997, p. 2).

It should then be obvious that it is important to know all we can about how to describe the personality types and the corresponding environments. Research supports Holland's contention that there are six distinct personality types and that these types differ in terms of their interests, vocational and avocational preferences, goals, beliefs, values, and skills. Table 2-1 outlines what we know about the types, and you can read elsewhere in this book about the various instruments that can be used to assess a person's resemblance to the types.

To apply the theory, you need to know the distinguishing features of the personality types and understand a few key principles. Table 2-1 provides a comprehensive description and an overview of the salient characteristics of the types. The table comes directly from *Making Vocational Choices: A Theory of Vocational Personalities and Work Environments* (Holland, 1997), an assessment instrument commonly used to determine a person's resemblance to the types. You would do well to read this guide thoroughly if you use the instrument. You can go to the technical manual (Holland et al., 1994) for an even more complete description of the characteristics associated with the types.

Beyond understanding the six types and the corresponding environments, one can use a number of other key principles to make appropriate use of the theory. These include knowing the relationship of one type to another (calculus) or understanding the hexagon in Figure 2-1 (Holland, 1997, p. 6), and appreciating the consistency of the types as well as the environments, congruence of types with environments, differentiation of types, and vocational identity.

Calculus—Visualizing the Relationship Within and Between Types and Environments

First, and probably most important, is to understand the calculus, or relationship, of one type to another. One can best see this visually by placing each type at a particular point and in a particular order on a hexagon (see Figure 2-1). Start with Realistic, next is Investigative, Artistic, Social, Enterprising, and finally Conventional. With the types placed in this order (RIASEC), you can visualize the resemblance of one to another. The closer one type is to another type on the hexagon, the more it resembles the other. R and I are next to each other, for example, and these two types are close in terms of how they are described and how they can work together, whereas R is farthest away from S, which is the type most unlike R. A person's resemblance to the various types, ones that may be close to or far away from one another, predicts the ease or difficulty of finding environments that will support that person's particular pattern of traits.

Consistency—Defining the Relatedness Between Types and Environments

Once you understand this principle, you begin to see how the theory predicts the ease or difficulty of people making a career choice. If people identify with types that are close to one another on the hexagon, Holland defined that as being consistent. Their career exploration proceeds much easier than would be the case for those with inconsistent identifications (i.e.,

Table 2-1. Personality Types and Salient Characteristics

	Realistic	Investigative	Artistic	Social	Enterprising	Conventional
Traits	Hardheaded Unassuming Practical Dogmatic Natural Uninsightful	Intellectual Curious Scholarly Open Broad interests	Open Nonconforming Imaginative Intuitive Sensitive Creative	Agreeable Friendly Understanding Sociable Persuasive Extroverted	Extroverted Dominant Adventurous Enthusiastic Power-seeking Energetic	Conservative Unimaginative Inhibited Practical-minded Methodical
Life goals	Inventing apparatus or equipment Becoming outstanding athlete	Inventing valuable product Theoretical contribution to science	Becoming famous in performing arts Publishing stories Original painting Musical composition	Helping others Making sacrifices for others Competent teacher or therapist	Being community leader expert in finance and commerce Being well liked and well dressed	Expert in finance and commerce Producing a lot of work
Values	Freedom Intellectual Ambitious Self-controlled Docility	Intellectual Logical Ambitious Wisdom	Equality Imaginative Courageous World of beauty	Equality Self-respect Helpful Forgiving	Freedom Ambitious (−) Forgiving (−) Helpful	(−) Imaginative (−) Forgiving
Identifications	Thomas Edison Admiral Byrd	Madame Curie Charles Darwin	T. S. Eliot Pablo Picasso	Jane Addams Albert Schweitzer	Henry Ford Andrew Carnegie	Bernard Baruch John D. Rockefeller
Aptitudes and competencies	Technical	Scientific	Arts	Social and educational Leadership and sales Interpersonal	Leadership and sales Social and educational Business and clerical Interpersonal	Business and clerical
Self-ratings	Mechanical ability	Math ability Research ability	Artistic ability	—	—	Clerical ability
Most competent in	Mechanics	Science	Arts	Human relations	Leadership	Business

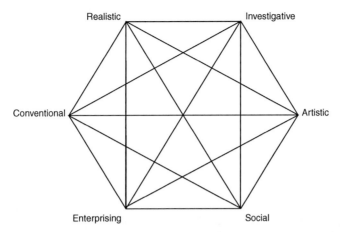

Figure 2-1. A Hexagonal Model for Defining the Psychological Resemblances Among Personality Types and Environments and Their Interactions

Note. Reproduced by special permission of the publisher, Psychological Assessment Resources, Inc., 16204 North Florida Avenue, Lutz, FL 33549 from *Making Vocational Choices: A Theory of Vocational Personalities and Work Environments,* third edition, by J. L. Holland. Copyright 1973, 1985, 1992, 1997 by Psychological Assessment Resources, Inc. All rights reserved.

preferences for working in environments that are across from one another on the hexagon). This concept is used to describe both the personality types and the work environments.

Congruence—Defining the Fit Between Types and Environments
It would be a logical expectation that the theory would provide additional help in predicting how one will find satisfaction or dissatisfaction with a choice. For that, Holland introduced the principle of congruence, that is, thinking about the agreement between a person's personality type and the environment (i.e., the more agreement or congruence, the more satisfaction with the choice). When an R type finds an R environment or an I type finds an I work environment, then we are dealing with congruence; when an R type is in an S work environment or an I type is in an E environment, then we describe this as incongruent. Predictions about the ease or difficulty of making a career choice or finding satisfaction with that choice flow in a fairly logical way from this and some other concepts still to be discussed.

Of course, this would appear to be an oversimplification of matching personalities with work environments. But when you realize all people have some identification with all six personality types, more so with some than with others, you realize that describing this theory as a matching process hardly does it justice. The same applies to the concept of work environments. All environments may be described as being mainly composed of people with particular personality patterns; we never find pure environments. Nor are people represented equally in any environment. So the matching becomes more complex in terms of both our description of it and its practical application. Holland introduced a principle of differentiation to further refine the process.

Differentiation—Defining How Well a Person or Environment Can Be Described
Differentiation helps one refine or modify predictions of vocational behaviors. Although we all relate in some way to each of the personality types and the six environments as well, some of us bear much stronger resemblance to one type than to another. A highly differentiated type, for example, might strongly identify with one type and bear little or no identification with another type. A less differentiated type might bear strong resem-

blance to all types or no types. But employing the principle of differentiation is another way to help us make practical use of the theory.

Identity—Describing the Clarity or Stability of One's Goals, Interests, and Talents
The personality types; the work environments; and the principles of consistency, congruence, and differentiation all help us think creatively when applying the theory. Still another idea emerged from Holland's efforts at refining the theory. That concept is vocational identity. It is establishing how clear a picture one has of one's current career plans or simply who or where one is in a vocational sense. Holland developed the instrument My Vocational Situation (Holland, Daiger, & Power, 1980; Holland et al., 1994) to measure the state of one's identity (see Chapter 13 for a description). One can be assessed as having a clear or an unclear picture of career goals and of the tasks needed to make the goal clear. The vocational identity concept, and the instrument to measure it, has proven to be another way of making practical what is offered by the theory. The theory makes clear that career decisions are easy for some and difficult for others. Offering help with decision making, career explorations, and the like can be easier if one has a sense of the vocational identity of those requesting help. The concept can also be used to describe work environments; they too can be defined as clear or unclear in terms of goals, tasks, and rewards provided.

Vocational identity, then, is one more way we can add to our ability to answer the three basic questions posed by Holland (1997). Along with the other principles discussed, we have some basis for talking about how and why people make the career decisions they do, why some are satisfied and others are not, why some persist with their career choices and others do not, and, finally, why some interventions are better than others at providing career assistance.

*Implications of Holland's Theory of Vocational Personalities and
Work Environments for the Practice of Career Counseling*

1. We can help clients assess their personalities and work environments and then help them see the relationships between the two. Either the Vocational Preference Inventory or the Self-Directed Search can help with the process. Given limited time, the Party Exercise (Bolles, 2001, p. 289) popularized in *What Color Is Your Parachute?* may prove effective. For a visual representation of the theory, go online to the University of Missouri Career Center to take the Career Interests Game (http://career.missouri.edu/students/explore/thecareerinterestsgame.php).
2. Consider using an occupational card sort with clients that classifies all occupational titles according to the Holland codes. Use the Occupational Dreams Inventory to stimulate discussion of client aspirations and then assign Holland codes to the dreams (this and the Self-Directed Search are described in Chapter 13).
3. Work with clients to help them see how their traits, life goals, values, aptitudes and competencies, and involvements and achievements can be associated with the match of personality with work environment.
4. Use the My Vocational Situation to quickly establish client needs for help.
5. Consider using the Career Attitudes and Strategies Inventory developed by Holland and Gottfredson (1994) to help employed people assess their current work environments.
6. Organize and reference your career and occupational information according to the Holland codes. Use the Gottfredson and Holland (1996) *Dictionary of Holland Occupational Titles*, which classifies all occupations according to the codes, as a guide.
7. Learn to listen carefully for clients' personal career theories (PCTs) or their career narratives. It will always be a good way to start, and it may be all that is needed.

Defining the Career Intervention and Change Approach

Holland (1997) offered three basic assumptions for this approach: (a) Everyone has a theory about careers (i.e., everyone has a PCT; p. 205). (b) When that theory does not seem to work, a person seeks help of some sort, sometimes from professionals like us. (c) When asked, we can provide interventions that will help the person implement, revise, or refine that theory. It follows that a first step for us in working with a client is to do what we can to understand that client's PCT. Holland offered that we apply a diagnostic scheme as we listen. We can listen for evidence of how we should best describe the theory. He suggested that we think of the PCT in terms of three dimensions: its validity, its complexity, and its comprehensiveness. When a client comes for help, we define interventions based on what we have come to know as most effective given these particulars of the theory. We cannot stress how important it becomes, then, both to listen for all the clues as to how to describe the theory and to come to know what works best to help one implement, refine, or revise the theory.

As for a framework for using this approach, we suggest starting with the three continua suggested by Holland (1997, pp. 205–206) and listening for what the client provides until you can judge where it belongs along each of these three dimensions (Gottfredson & Cook, 1984; Prochaska, Norcross, & DiClemente, 1994):

> Assessing One's PCT
> 1. invalid .... valid
> 2. primitive .... complex
> 3. incomplete .... comprehensive

You can then let your experience guide you with what works best if you need to help with implementation of an only somewhat valid theory, refinement of a primitive theory, or maybe revision of an incomplete theory. Clearly we will begin to see particular interventions as more effective with one versus another kind of PCT.

Holland (1997), always at the forefront with suggestions for implementing ideas, offered, for example, a "four-level diagnostic and treatment plan":

Level 1 for people with valid [complex and comprehensive] personal theories . . .

Level 2 for people whose theories have an occupational knowledge section that requires extension, revision, or adaptation to an unusual work or unemployment situation;

Level 3 for people whose theories have a weak translation unit or lack a reliable formula for relating personal characteristics to occupations, special occupational roles, or specialization, or for managing job changes;

Level 4 for people whose personal theory has pervasive weaknesses. (pp. 207–208)

Level 1 describes people who need little help, as they have a well-developed PCT, whereas Level 2 describes people who need some help with at least some part of their theory—a minor extension, revision, or adaptation may suffice. Level 3 describes people who have difficulties seeing themselves in particular occupations or making changes in their jobs. They need substantial help, probably one-on-one career counseling focused on resolving a particular weakness in their thinking. Level 4, however, describes people who need extensive help, as there are major flaws or weaknesses in their PCTs.

Although not the last word or not as fully developed a diagnostic system as will be forthcoming in time, this four-level model does help us begin to think of clients as truly unique in terms of what they bring to us. It suggests that our experience is important in helping us develop and provide appropriate career services for each and every one. Although we may have something for everyone, it should not be the same for everyone.

Implications of the Career Intervention and Change Approach for the Practice of Career Counseling

1. As counselors, we need to recognize that every person has a PCT that informs his or her life decisions. Our role is to help that person articulate and refine that theory.
2. We can encourage clients to describe how they understand their PCT, and, while they are talking, we can be thinking about its validity, complexity, and comprehensiveness.
3. If a client has developed a PCT that seems valid, complex, and comprehensive, perhaps what is needed most is career information and reassurance that he or she seems on the right track.
4. If parts of the PCT seem to lack validity (e.g., conclusions built on faulty reasoning, irrational beliefs) or are overly simplified understandings or incomplete in important ways, the counselor can then help flesh out the theory to help clients better describe their life circumstances.
5. All of the other theories and models presented in this chapter can be used to help individuals flesh out a PCT. For example, one might help them understand where they are in their developmental progression (Super); how their choices reflect person–environment fit (Holland); how their self-efficacy and outcome expectations may be influencing their interests, choices, or goal attainment (Lent, Brown, & Hackett); how being in a transition is influencing their life course (Schlossberg); how macro-, exo-, meso-, and microforces are shaping and reshaping their choices (Cook, Heppner, & O'Brien); and how chance events have shaped and will continue to shape their life course (Krumboltz).

Thus, in some ways the theory of career intervention and change can be seen as recognizing individual differences and how various aspects of career theory can be applied to help clients describe their own unique career paths. Ultimately, our theories must ring true to the people they are designed to help. They must be seen as useful in actually explaining career behavior. By encouraging our clients to design their own PCTs, we capitalize on their own wealth of self-understanding, which may ultimately lead to the most valid, complex, and comprehensive theories for them to use in guiding their own life pattern.

Schlossberg's Adult Career Development Transition Model

> The transition model provides a systematic framework for counselors, psychologists, social workers, and others as they listen to the many stories—each one unique—of colleagues, friends, and clients. The transitions differ, the individuals differ, but the structure for understanding individuals in transition is stable. (Anderson et al., 2012, p. 38)

The adult career development transition model has three major parts, according to Anderson et al. (2012). The first part focuses on approaching the transition, including transition identification and process. The second part deals with identifying coping resources, and the third part emphasizes strategies that can be used to take charge of the transition.

Approaching Transitions

To understand transitions, it is important to identify their type. Anderson et al. (2012) identified three types. The first type is the *anticipated transition*. This transition is caused by expected events that occur as a part of one's life cycle. The second type is the *unanticipated transition* caused by life events that are not predictable. It is not planned for. The last type is called the *nonevent transition*. This type of transition is caused by events that were anticipated and planned for but that did not happen.

In understanding transitions, it also is important to appreciate that what is anticipated by one individual may not be by another. The context of the events that shape transitions is another important consideration. Does the event occur to the individual or to another person? Is it personal or interpersonal? Finally, the impact of the transition on the individual is important to consider. Sometimes, too, transitions come in bunches; while an individual is experiencing one transition, other transitions occur.

The Transition Process

"Although the onset of a transition may be linked to one identifiable event or non-event, transitions are really a process over time" (Anderson et al., 2012, p. 48). While in transitions, clients pass through a series of identifiable phases. At first transitions are pervasive. There is often total preoccupation with the transitions and the complete disruption in clients' lives. There is disbelief ("This can't be happening"), then a sense of betrayal ("I worked for this organization for 30 years"), confusion ("What do I do now?"), anger ("I'll sue somebody!"), and, finally, after a period of time, resolution ("I have many skills and I can get another job!").

It is tempting to oversimplify these phases and what is involved in them. Anderson et al. (2012) stressed that transitions often contain many complex dynamics and that their satisfactory resolution depends on the characteristics of the clients and the nature of the contexts in which the transitions take place. Sometimes, for some clients, transitions end in deterioration. There is no satisfactory resolution.

How do counselors assess where clients are in the transition process? Schlossberg (1984) advised starting with clients' perceptions, because some clients view where they are in transitions differently from other clients who are involved in the same transitions. Another means of appraisal is to assess how preoccupied clients are with their transitions. Schlossberg (1984, p. 56) suggested that the continuum counselors assess begins with "pervasiveness" (transitions completely permeate clients' attitudes and behaviors) and ends with "boundedness" (transitions are contained and integrated into clients' self-concepts). Finally, measures of life satisfaction can be used to assess where clients are in their transitions, with the assumption being that clients will express more satisfaction with their lives as they move toward transition resolution.

Factors That Influence Transitions

Anderson et al. (2012) pointed out that four major factors influence how individuals handle transitions. They are the situation, the self, support, and strategies.

The Situation. What are the variables characterizing the transition that counselors need to understand? Some of these variables are the trigger (what triggered the transition?), timing (does the transition relate to the social clock?), the source (where does control lie?), role change (does the transition involve role change?), duration (permanent or temporary?), previous experience with similar transitions, and concurrent stress.

The Self. To understand the coping resources available to clients, it is necessary to identify clients' personal situation and psychological resources. Personal and demographic variables that need to be considered include socioeconomic status, culture/race/ethnicity, gender role, age and stage of life, and state of health. Psychological resources encompass variables related to ego development, personality, outlook, and commitment and values.

According to Anderson et al. (2012), the following questions can be used to assess clients' selves:

- Are they able to deal with the world in an autonomous way? Can they tolerate ambiguity?
- Are they optimists? Do they see the glass as half full or half empty?

- Do they blame themselves for what happens?
- Do they feel in control of their response to the transition?
- Do they believe that their efforts will affect the outcomes of a particular course of action?
- Do they have a sense of meaning and purpose?
- Do they have characteristics that contribute to resiliency? (p. 83)

Support. The last category of variables to consider is those that focus on clients' environments. As counselors work with clients in transitions, it is important to consider the social support clients have (intimate relationships, family, friendship networks, and institutions), functions of the support available to them (affect, affirmation, aid, and feedback), and their options (actual, perceived, used, and created).

The following questions can be used to assess support:

- Is this client getting what he or she needs for the transition in terms of affect? Affirmation? Aid?
- Does the client have the range of support—spouse or partner, other close family or friends, co-workers? Colleagues? Neighbors, organizations, strangers, and institutions?
- Has the client's support system or "convoy of social support" been interrupted by this transition?
- Does the client feel the support system for this transition is a low or high resource? (Anderson et al., 2012, p. 87)

Strategies. Coping responses to transitions can include trying to control the situation, its meaning, and the stress associated with the transition. Anderson et al. (2012) suggested that "an individual's ability to cope with transitions depends on the changing interaction and balance of his or her assets and liabilities" (p. 91). They recommended that the following questions could be used to understand one's balance:

- What are the variables characterizing the particular situation in terms of timing, assessment, and duration?
- What are the personal and demographic characteristics of the individual at the time of the transition—the Self?
- Is the client sick or well?
- What is the client's level of ego development, personality, and outlook?
- What coping strategies does he or she use?
- What types of support does the client have?
- What are his or her actual and perceived options? (p. 92)

Implications of Schlossberg's Adult Career Development Transition Model for the Practice of Career Counseling

1. Because more individuals are changing occupations at later stages of their career development, counselors should be open to clients who want to change and should understand and empathize with the frustration, pain, and joy involved in the transition process.
2. Because clients who are going through transitions are often experiencing anxiety and emotional upheaval, it is essential to provide a safe environment—a counseling relationship that focuses on the use of listening and responding skills, and attending and focusing skills.

3. Because clients involved in transitions often have difficulty reframing and re-focusing their situations, counselors need to provide new perspectives to them through interpretation, theme identification, and the presentation of internal and external information.
4. Because clients involved in transitions usually need assistance moving on, it is important to help them develop problem-solving, decision-making, and coping skills.
5. Because social support is key to successfully coping with transitions, counselors should provide clients with skills that aid them in developing social support systems and networks.

Lent, Brown, and Hackett's Social Cognitive Career Theory

Social cognitive career theory (Lent, 2013; Lent, Brown, & Hackett, 1994) is a relatively new theory in comparison to the foundational theories of Super and Holland. It is unique from the other theories in its "focus on the personal constructions that people place on events related to career decision making" (Swanson & Fouad, 1999, p. 340). It has also been noted for its utility in explaining the vocational behaviors of racial and ethnic groups and for its greater attention to contextual factors that influence career development. Indeed, since this theory was proposed, it has spawned several research studies with racially diverse samples (e.g., Flores & O'Brien, 2002; Fouad & Smith, 1996; Gainor & Lent, 1998; Lent, 2013; Morrow, Gore, & Campbell, 1996; Tang, Fouad, & Smith, 1999).

Lent and his colleagues (1994) developed this comprehensive theory to explain three intricately linked aspects of career development: (a) the development of interests, (b) the choice of educational and career options, and (c) performance and persistence in educational and vocational realms. Lent et al. extended Bandura's (1986) social cognitive theory and Hackett and Betz's (1981) career self-efficacy theory to develop this theory of career development that hypothesizes the influence of individual and contextual factors on the sociocognitive mechanisms of self-efficacy, outcome expectations, and goals and their influence on interests, actions, and performance. We briefly describe the portions of the theory relevant to our interests but refer the reader to the original monograph that describes each component in a great deal more depth (Lent et al., 1994). In addition, in a recent chapter Lent (2013) more thoroughly described the theory and its relation to career development and counseling.

Figure 2-2 depicts the theorized sociocognitive determinants of interest. Thus, the theory hypothesizes that self-efficacy beliefs and outcome expectancies both predict academic and career interests. *Self-efficacy beliefs* are defined as "people's judgments of their capabilities to organize and execute courses of action required to attain designated types of performance" (Bandura, 1986, p. 391). *Outcome expectancies* are defined as "personal beliefs about probable response outcomes" (Lent et al., 1994, p. 83). Thus, people's beliefs about their abilities in particular areas and their beliefs about probable outcomes both lead to the development of interests. These interests (together with self-efficacy beliefs and outcome expectancies) predict goals that in turn lead to the selection of activities and the practice of activities. This in turn leads to experiencing performance attainment (e.g., goal fulfillment and attainment), trying out various activities, and feeling successful at them. Thus, our perceptions of self-efficacy and outcome likelihood are hypothesized to figure prominently in the development of our career interests.

Implications of Lent, Brown, and Hackett's Social Cognitive Career Theory for the Practice of Career Counseling

1. Counselors should help clients examine the importance of the learning process and the specific learning experiences they have had that have helped to shape their current career path.

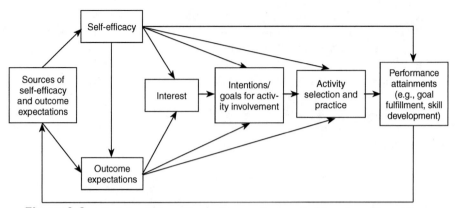

Figure 2-2. Model of How Basic Career Interests Develop Over Time

Note. The model highlights cognitive and behavioral influences during childhood and adolescence. From "Toward a Unifying Social Cognitive Theory of Career and Academic Interest, Choice, and Performance," by R. W. Lent, S. D. Brown, and G. Hackett, 1994, *Journal of Vocational Behavior, 45*, p. 116. Copyright 1994 by Elsevier. Reprinted with permission.

2. Specifically, the theory suggests an investigation of both how previous learning has helped to shape clients' confidence or self-efficacy about their career plans and how these experiences may have shaped clients' outcome expectations and eventual career interests.

3. It may be very useful to examine how career-related self-efficacy beliefs developed and what barriers the clients experienced in the development of their confidence around various career-related experiences.

4. The theory emphasizes the need to carefully examine person inputs such as gender, race, sexual orientation, level of ability or disability, and social class in the formation of self-efficacy beliefs.

5. It may also be helpful to examine past performance attainment and the clients' perceptions of future performance goals. Specifically, it would be useful to examine both clients' self-efficacy beliefs and their outcome expectancies with regard to their future performance level.

6. According to this theory, an important role for counselors is in helping clients examine positive and realistic expectations for themselves and helping them develop specific goals to meet these expectations.

The Happenstance Learning Theory

The happenstance learning theory (HLT) is Krumboltz's (2009) latest thinking concerning career development. He stated that it "is an attempt to explain how and why individuals follow different paths through life and to describe how counselors can facilitate that process" (p. 135). He based his current thinking on the work of many others, including Bandura (1982), Betsworth and Hansen (1996), and Cabral and Salomone (1990).

Krumboltz (2009) summarized the essence of the HLT by stating:

> The HLT posits that human behavior is the product of countless numbers of learning experiences made available by both planned and unplanned situations in which individuals find themselves. The learning outcomes include skills, interests, knowledge, beliefs, preferences, sensitivities, emotions, and future actions. (p. 135)

In explaining his theory, Krumboltz began by describing nine factors that influence individuals' behavior. First, he believes that *genetics* play a part in that "many important psychological variables are associated with genetic variation" (p. 137). Second, the *learn-*

ing experiences individuals have can play an important role. Third, *instrumental learning experiences* through which individuals observe their own behavior and its consequences can influence their behavior. Fourth, *associate learning experiences*, whereby individuals observe the behavior of others, can be influential. Fifth, *environmental conditions and events* can play a substantial role in influencing individuals' behavior. Sixth, the impact of *parents and caretakers* can have significant impact on behavior as well. Seventh, *peer groups* have been found to play a role in shaping individuals' behavior. Eighth, the kind of *structured educational settings* individuals experience while growing up can have substantial impact on their behavior, good or bad. And finally, ninth, Krumboltz stated that the *imperfect world* in which we live provides opportunities for some and not for others.

Fundamental Propositions

Krumboltz (2009) stated that "career counselors should teach their clients the importance of engaging in a variety of interesting and beneficial activities, ascertaining their reactions, remaining alert to alternative opportunities, and learning skills for succeeding in each new activity" (p. 135). To accomplish this he identified four fundamental propositions that undergird the HLT.

> *Proposition 1:* The goal of career counseling is to help clients learn to take actions to achieve more satisfying career and personal lives—not to make a single career decision (p. 141).
> *Proposition 2:* Career assessments are used to stimulate learning, not to match personal characteristics with occupational characteristics (p. 143).
> *Proposition 3:* Clients learn to engage in exploratory actions as a way of generating beneficial unplanned events (p. 144).
> *Proposition 4:* The success of counseling is assessed by what the client accomplishes in the real world outside the counseling session (p. 145).

Applying HLT

When you use HLT with clients, Krumboltz (2009) recommended that you consider taking the following five actions. First, it is necessary to orient client expectations and help them understand that any possible anxiety they may have is normal, that a goal of career counseling is to help them create satisfying lives (which may involve considering many factors), that individuals' lives are influenced by many unplanned events, and that identifying an occupation becomes a starting point for more exploration. Second, it is necessary to identify the clients' concerns as a starting point. Remember, start where clients are, not where you are. Third, use clients' successful past experiences with unplanned events as a basis of current actions and ask them to describe how unplanned events may have influenced their behavior. Fourth, sensitize clients to recognize potential opportunities and help them reframe unplanned events into positive opportunities. Finally, help clients overcome blocks to action by using such leads as "What is stopping you from taking action?" and "What can you do now to take action to reach your goal?"

In addition to taking the five actions, Krumboltz (2009) stressed the need to evaluate the outcomes of counseling. He pointed out that evaluation should not take place during counseling; rather it should take place based on what happens after counseling. He stated that "to evaluate the effects of counseling, counselors need to find out the extent to which clients' thoughts, feelings, and behaviors in the real world have changed" (p. 148).

Reexamining Our Role as Career Counselors

Incorporating happenstance may mean we need to encourage clients to be open minded. When a client comes to us for help in career planning, we often assume our role is to resolve ambiguity, reduce anxiety, find quick solutions, administer interests tests, or deliver a barrage of career information. But an alternative might be to help clients become comfortable with their present situation so they can remain open to opportunities that constantly present themselves—opportunities that will not be recognized while they are under such stress. Uncertainty too often narrows our perspective and thinking, and happenstance is then not seen for what it could be.

Gelatt and Gelatt (2003) proposed that being uncertain about career goals might be what will lead one to discover new ideas or opportunities. Once decided, we tend to focus only on affirming our choice. We may not be as open to seeing chance events as new opportunities. Helping clients tolerate the ambiguity of not knowing may emerge as an appropriate task for career counselors.

Implications of the HLT for the Practice of Career Counseling

1. We need to change our thinking so as not to minimize the importance of happenstance but rather to recognize and find ways to increase its importance in the career counseling process.
2. We need to understand that "indecision" should not be stigmatized as undesirable but rather viewed as a desirable stance.
3. We need to advocate for open-mindedness as a stance that may most help clients find direction.
4. We need to help clients view unplanned events as opportunities and to take advantage of them.

Race/Gender Ecological Model of Career Development

"Human life is fundamentally connected with the world around us" (Cook, 2012, p. 6). A career development model that was designed to examine contextual factors in the vocational development of individuals was developed by Cook, Heppner, and O'Brien (2002). They used an ecological model to develop what they called a *race/gender ecological approach to career development*. The ecological model states that human behavior results from the ongoing, dynamic interaction between the person and the environment. Behavior is the result of a multiplicity of factors at the individual, interpersonal, and broader sociocultural levels (Cook, 2012). Vocational behavior can then be understood as an "act-in-context" (Landrine, 1995, p. 5), where the context is essential to the naming and meaningfulness of the individual's behavior. This model has been used to understand and intervene in the vocational behavior of diverse women (see Cook, Heppner, & O'Brien, 2004, 2005). For example, Ancis and Davidson (2012) used ecological theory to understand women's and girls' issues related to education and the workplace, sexual violence, and legal issues. Bieschke and Toepfer-Hendey (2006) applied this model to career interventions with lesbian women, and Heppner and O'Brien (2006) used it with women in poverty. Ecological thinking has also been applied extensively to understanding the levels of change necessary to promote social justice (Pitt-Catsouphes & Swanberg, 2006).

Bronfenbrenner (1977) developed the most widely cited ecological model and the one Cook and her colleagues used as their guiding theoretical framework. Bronfenbrenner identified four major subsystems that influence human behavior: (a) the microsystem, which includes the interpersonal interactions within a given environment, such as home, school, or work setting; (b) the mesosystem, which constitutes interaction between two or more microsystems, such as the relation between an individual's school and his or her work environment; (c) the exosystem, which consists of linkages between subsystems that indirectly influence the individual, such as one's neighborhood or the media; and (d) the macrosystem, which is the ideological components of a given society, including norms and values.

The race/gender ecological model of career development recognizes that by their very nature, humans live interactionally in a social environment. The model recognizes that every person has both a gender and a race and that these factors decisively shape the individual's career throughout life as he or she encounters opportunities or obstacles because of race or gender. It reminds us that career behavior does not occur in a vacuum but rather emerges from a life-long dynamic interaction between the person and his or her environment. For example, as Ancis and Davidson (2012) described, ecologically based career counseling could assist women "struggling with sexual harassment in the workplace ... to view such oppressive behavior as one of power, rooted in societal/cultural beliefs (macrosystems), rather than operating solely at the individual level" (p. 69).

In addition, career behavior is thought to be determined by the interrelationships between the subsystems in a larger ecosystem (Bronfenbrenner, 1977). Implicit in the model is the knowledge that interrelationships occur simultaneously on multiple levels, so a focus on any one level of interaction is by definition a limited picture of the dynamics shaping career behavior at any one time. The model also recognizes that although individuals of the same biological sex or race may encounter similar circumstances because of their demographics, each career path is unique because of individual circumstances and the unique interactions of the subsystems. Clients bring their ecosystems into counseling primarily by conveying how they understand and react to their circumstances (e.g., perceptions of opportunities or the lack of opportunities, positive or negative comparisons of self to desired models, optimistic or pessimistic conceptions of the future, or internalization of stereotypes as personally salient or irrelevant). Individuals are also thought to shape the environment around them in complex ways as they overtly reward or punish the career behaviors of others.

In applying the race/gender ecological model, an example might be helpful. The larger culture, operating as a macrosystem, perpetuates career myths and stereotypes that are related to race and gender and, in fact, institutionalizes forms of race/gender discrimination. This macrosystem embodies values such as White male privilege, Eurocentric worldviews, race-/gender-appropriate ideologies, or race/gender typing of occupational choices. Macrosystem values may be internalized by the individual (e.g., internalized oppression) and may, on the microsystem level, influence how others treat a person because of his or her gender or race.

Implications of the Race/Gender Ecological Model for the Practice of Career Counseling

1. The model reminds us as career counselors that we can change the person–environment interaction in numerous ways for any given client. Examples include changing the environment through counselor or client initiatives, helping the client identify and practice skills to cope more effectively with the environment, and addressing the cognitive processes that shape the client's interactions with the environment.
2. In addition to engaging in more traditional career counseling interventions that help the individual alter perceptions about desirable and appropriate career alternatives, this model calls on counselors to serve as client advocates working toward environmental and societal changes that may facilitate the development of present and future clients.
3. Careful assessment of the client's ecosystem determines how and where career counseling interventions can be most effectively implemented for an individual.
4. The counselor serves as a liaison, working as a partner with the client to effect more successful and satisfying interactions with the world of work.
5. The counselor uses diverse methodologies and emphasizes that clients are best served when a diverse range of conceptualizations and interventions are considered.
6. The model requires a range of skills not typically required in intrapsychically oriented interventions but respects the complexity of influences shaping an individual's life over time.

Postmodern Theories of Career Development

Constructivism/Social Constructionism

Beginning in the late 1980s, but particularly in the 1990s and the first 2 decades of the 21st century, a number of theorists began to shift their attention away from modern theories based on a logical positionist philosophy to theories they labeled as postmodern.

Terms such as *constructivism, constructivist, constructionism, social constructionism, contextualist,* and *narrative* are being used by various authors as work continues to identify and clarify what constitutes a postmodern approach to career development (McIlveen & Schultheiss, 2012; McMahon & Watson, 2012; Meier, 2012; Sharf, 2010). While discussion continues concerning how to define and describe postmodern theories (McIlveen & Schultheiss, 2012), consensus seems to be forming around the use of two overarching terms, constructivism and social constructionism (Young & Collin, 2004). Following Young and Collin's (2004) lead, we focus our attention on these two terms to describe two separate yet closely interrelated postmodern theories.

Constructivism is defined as a type of learning theory that describes how individuals construct their own ideas about themselves, others, and their worlds as they try to make sense out of their real-life experiences. "Constructivist epistemology holds that knowledge is constructed by people, that is, it does not reflect an actual reality that exists independent of those who have constructed it as such" (Young & Popadink, 2012, p. 10).

Social constructionism, in contrast, "covers a range of views from acknowledging how social factors shape interpretations to how the social world is constructed by social processes and relational practices" (Young & Collin, 2004, p. 377). Hence, the emphasis is on how social or external processes shape the career development of individuals rather than on how individuals shape their career development based on how they view themselves, others, and their worlds (internal processes). According to social constructionism, careers are "constructed in a social, historical context" (Young & Collin, 2004, p. 381).

Constructivism and social constructionism are two postmodern approaches concerning individuals' career development. Each view offers researchers and theorists fruitful areas of inquiry concerning the processes that form and shape individuals' career development. The literature continues to provide discussion of these views, helping us understand more completely the nature and structure of internal cognitions (constructivism) and external processes (social constructionism) and the impact they have on individuals' career development. (For example, see the special issue of the *Journal of Vocational Behavior,* Volume 64, Issue 3, June 2004, on Constructivism, Social Constructionism, and Career as well as the special issue of the *International Journal for Educational and Vocational Guidance,* Volume 7, Issue 3, November 2007, on New Methods and Emerging Paradigms in Vocational Psychology.)

Although theorists and researchers separate these postmodern perspectives for research and theory-building purposes, we believe that individuals, as they live their lives, do not. We believe that individuals construct and live their lives using both internal (self) and external (social) processes. They can describe how they see themselves, others, and their worlds as well as grasp the impact that culture, history, and social structures have on their career development. We agree with Young and Collin (2004) that "career represents a unique interaction of self and social experience" (p. 381). We believe that individuals are "active agents striving to make sense of their experiences" and that "individuals need to be studied in the context of their environments" (McMahon & Watson, 2007, p. 171).

The idea that individuals construct and live their lives using both internal (self) and external (social) processes is not new. For example, Hughes (1937) stated, "A career is the moving perspective in which the person sees his life as a whole and interprets the meaning of his various attributes, actions, and things which happen to him" (pp. 409–410). Twenty years later, Super (1957) made the same point:

> The individual is born with certain neural and endocrine tendencies or potentialities. These may be thought of as his personal resources. He finds himself in an environment which contains tendencies or potentialities which are independent of the indi-

vidual, but with which the developing individual interacts. These may be considered cultural resources. As the individual makes use of the resources in his environment, and brings his own tendencies and potentialities to bear on them in the performance of the developmental tasks which constitute social expectation, interaction takes place. (p. 283)

Career counseling that uses both constructivism and social constructionism approaches "requires the counselor to enter into the psychosocial sphere of a person's career system" (McIlveen, Ford, & Dun, 2005, p. 31). This means using the narrative approach within the career counseling process to help clients tell their story starting where they are in their own language. This means helping clients describe their life career development past, present, and future in terms of life career themes and patterns.

Cochran (2011) noted the importance of using the narrative approach within the career counseling process when he stated:

> Perhaps the best description of a client entering career counselling is that he or she is clouded. It is not just that a life plot is a tacit pattern of meaning, but that the plot is clouded by distortions, negative assessments, recent influences, dubious connections and the like. Largely, the work of narrative career counselling involves an uncovering of thematic strands of meaning and the way that they form into a coherent whole. For the client, important connections might not have been seen before. The significance of particular desires, events, abilities and so on might not have been fully appreciated. In this sense, the function of a narrative career counsellor is to help clients see more clearly the meaningful patterns from their own life histories. (p. 13)

Table 1-1 in Chapter 1 describes the gathering client information phase of career counseling. As noted in Table 1-1, information can be gathered through quantitative and qualitative procedures. Qualitative procedures such as the Life Career Assessment (Chapter 10), career genograms (Chapter 11), and card sorts (Chapter 12) are particularly useful because they provide frameworks and stimuli that aid clients in telling their stories. The emphasis in this phase is on clients sharing how they view themselves, others, and their worlds; how they make sense out of their life roles, settings, and events past, present, and future; and how they talk about possible personal and environmental barriers and social constraints they may be facing.

> As individuals are reflecting on their real-life experiences through the medium of narratives, they are crafting their narrative identities. They are engaged in meaning making. To understand the identity formation process is to understand how individuals craft narratives from experiences, tell these stories internally and to others, and ultimately apply these stories to knowledge of self, others, and the world in general. (Singer, 2004, p. 437)

As noted in Chapter 1, the key to effective career counseling is the working alliance that is established between clients and counselors. The qualitative interventions used in the postmodern approaches of constructivism and social constructionism are particularly useful in establishing working alliances. When counselors help clients tell their stories from their own perspectives, using their own language, it conveys to clients that what they have to say is important; it conveys to them that counselors care and that clients are being listened to and understood. Bujold (2004), referencing Rugira, underscored this point by stating that "the transforming power of narrative rests on the existence of a relationship in which a person feels that he or she is acknowledged and accepted" (p. 473). Sinisalo and Komulainen (2008), paraphrasing Arthur, Inkson, and Pringle, suggested, "A career story is a personal moving perspective on what a person is and what he or she is able to do" (p. 47).

*Implications of the Postmodern Theories of Constructivism and
Social Constructionism for the Practice of Career Counseling*

1. Postmodern approaches to career development emphasize multicultural perspectives and focus on the belief that there is no fixed truth. Instead, individuals construct their own truths, their own realities (Niles & Harris-Bowlsbey, 2005).
2. Qualitative assessments provide frames and stimuli that assist clients in telling their stories about who they are, where they see themselves going, and the issues and circumstances they believe are impacting their career development.
3. "Constructivism has directed career practitioners towards the holistic experience of a person's career within their environmental context" (McIlveen et al., 2005, p. 31).
4. "Narrative therapists help clients see that their worlds are constructed through language and cultural practice and that clients can subsequently deconstruct and reconstruct their assumptions and perceptions" (Meier, 2012, p. 2).
5. "Client stories are face valid, that is, they have intrinsic value, and narrative therapists assume that client stories reflect some meaningful aspect of that person" (Meier, 2012, p. 4).

The Chaos Theory of Career Development

Chaos theory is a new way of looking at human behavior that has emerged from the disciplines of economics, mathematics, biology, and physics. It offers us a different way of understanding the complexity and uncertainty of human development in general and career development specifically. According to Briggs and Peat (1989), it moves us away from a reductionist view of human behavior to a view that emphasizes wholeness and change.

> Nature controlled by human thought is the essence of the reductionist dream. . . .
> Against this trend (toward isolation of parts and systems) rises the young science of
> chaos, wholeness, and change—a new insistence on the interrelationships of things,
> an awareness of the essential unpredictableness of nature and of the uncertainties in
> our scientific descriptions. (p. 201)

The chaos theory of career development views individuals as being complex dynamic systems. As individuals grow and develop they are subject to many different and continually changing life challenges. As their career development unfolds, they find themselves often dealing with such challenges as unplanned events, nonlinear change, unpredictability, and continual change.

The Concept of Attraction

Pryor and Bright (2011) defined attraction as a process used by individuals to organize a coherent self and then maintain and sustain it when change occurs. This process can be subdivided into four types of attraction called attractors. They are labeled *point attractor*, *pendulum attractor*, *torus attractor*, and *strange attractor*. They describe different patterns of behavior used to respond to changing life challenges (Pryor & Bright, 2011).

Point Attractor

Individuals who use the point attractor pattern of behavior often focus on choosing the best occupation based on a match between their personalities, abilities, and interests. At the extreme they may be seen as having "tunnel vision, exclusive preoccupation, over confidence in decision making, fixation on a choice option, ideological or goal-dominated thinking and/or obsessional or fearful behavior" (Pryor & Bright, 2011, p. 42). They may also discount the role of chance and uncertainty in their lives.

Pendulum Attractor

As indicated in the title, this attractor describes swings in behavior. According to Pryor and Bright (2011), individuals who use this pattern of behavior are likely to engage in dichotomous either–or thinking. They may hold rigid beliefs. Sometimes,

> Clients in the grip of pendulum thinking will rarely be able to generate win-win scenarios and, furthermore, solutions that present "balance" as the desirable outcome may be aggravating the situation by attempting to stop the pendulum at the lowest point: that is, at the point of compromise in which neither conflicting need is appropriately met, thereby aggravating both. (p. 43)

Torus Attractor

This pattern of behavior is described as "routine, habitual, and predictable thinking and behavior" (Pryor & Bright, 2011, p. 44). Individuals who use this pattern try to control their lives by organizing and classifying people and things. They like consistency and routine. At the extreme,

> Fear, insecurity, self-consciousness, uncertainty, worry about failure, desire to "play it safe" are sources of motivation that frequently constrain those in the torus attractor. When the illusion of their control is shattered by a major negative unplanned event, they typically try to regress to an earlier mode of coping, refuse to consider the consequences of change, deny or hope that it does not affect them, or simply lose all confidence in their ability to respond to the new set of circumstances confronting them. (pp. 44–45)

Strange Attractor

On the one hand, point, pendulum, and torus attractors are closed systems thinking, meaning that individuals who use these patterns of behavior tend to have a strong sense of control. Furthermore, they like order and stability. On the other hand, open systems thinking (strange attractor) recognizes "the possibility of change being non-linear in the sense that a small difference may result in every major reconfiguration of the system" (Pryor & Bright, 2011, p. 48). According to Pryor and Bright, strange attractor thinking promotes the ability for individuals to adopt and grow. Chance is not seen as the opposite of order but as part of one's existence.

Chaos Theory and Spirituality

Pryor and Bright (2011) pointed out that chaos theory emphasizes the importance of integrating spirituality into our conceptualizations of career development. Summarizing the work of Bloch (2006), Pryor and Bright described five dimensions of spirituality and career development that need to be considered in our work as career counselors. The first dimension is *connection*, which focuses on how we are interconnected with the human community, the world, and the universe. Second is *purpose* with its focus on "humans' sense of meaning, purpose and significance" (Pryor & Bright, 2011, p. 148). Third is *transcendence* with its emphasis on the idea that there is a greater power beyond our understanding. The fourth dimension is *harmony* with its attention to "how everything fits together into an intelligible whole" (Pryor & Bright, 2011, pp. 148–149). Finally, and fifth, is *calling*, or the idea that individuals often perceive that what they are doing with their lives is the result of being called.

Chaos Theory and Shiftwork

"Chaos theorists have observed that change can occur in systems either gradually or very quickly. However, the effect of change is to reconfigure the system" (Bright & Pryor, 2008, p. 64). When change occurs, it is called a phase shift because the system will have changed from its original configuration. Pryor and Bright (2011) used the term *shiftwork* to describe the work of career counselors helping clients deal with these phase shifts or changes in their lives, however and whenever change occurs. They described 11 phase shifts career counselors need to pay attention to:

Shift 1: From Prediction to Prediction and Pattern Making
Shift 2: From Plans to Plans and Planning
Shift 3: From Narrowing Down to Being Focused on Openness
Shift 4: From Control to Controlled Flexibility
Shift 5: From Risk as Failure to Risk as Endeavor
Shift 6: From Probabilities to Probably Possibilities
Shift 7: From Goals, Roles and Routines to Meaning, Mattering and Black Swans
Shift 8: From Informing to Informing and Transforming
Shift 9: From Normative Thinking to Normative and Scalable Thinking
Shift 10: From Knowing in Advance to Living with Emergence
Shift 11: From Trust as Control to Trust as Faith (p. 49)

Implications of the Chaos Theory of Career Development for the Practice of Career Counseling

How are these 11 phase shifts to be dealt with in career counseling? Bright and Pryor (2008) suggested that career counselors use the following four-step process:

1. To identify, where operative, clients' closed system thinking strategies.
2. To help clients to realize that such efforts at control, certainty, knowledge, and predictability are crucially limited.
3. To assist clients to recognize and utilize the stabilities and surprises of living in the strange attractor.
4. To enable people to be able to both perceive the dimensions of complexity and acknowledge and effectively negotiate uncertainty, change, and chance in constructive ways to fulfill their deepest aspirations. (p. 49)

Closing Thoughts

Career theories should ultimately help our clients understand the stories of their lives and the role that work and other important life roles have in those stories. The theories and approaches in this chapter are meant to provide a starting point for counselors as they work with clients to understand these unique life stories. Although some counselors work from a "unitheoretical" stance (Savickas, 1996, p. 193) in which they see all client behavior through one theoretical lens, most effective counselors find "theoretical eclecticism" (p. 193) a more useful stance. They seek to help clients understand their career behavior by flexibly using a repertoire of different theories and approaches, depending on the circumstances and life context of the individual client.

From our own experience, we have found theory to be an invaluable guide in our work with clients. The more knowledgeable we are about various theories the more flexibly we can use them, and the more helpful we ultimately are in working with clients. This flexibility does not come quickly or easily but rather through study, reflection, and practice. It comes from reading these theories in their original form rather than relying solely on the brief summaries provided in texts like ours. It comes from thinking deeply about the strengths and shortcomings of each theory for various populations, and it comes from working with individual clients, seeing firsthand what works best for which clients under which circumstances.

The ultimate test of any theory is in its ability to provide clarity and insight to clients about their life journeys. We believe that the theories briefly described here will help you in working with your clients as they explore, expand, and understand their own fascinating life stories.

References

Ancis, J. R., & Davidson, M. M. (2012). Gender and mental health in ecological/sociological context. In C. Z. Enns & E. N. Williams (Eds.), *The Oxford handbook of feminist multicultural counseling psychology* (pp. 67–86). Oxford, England: University Press.

Anderson, M. L., Goodman, J., & Schlossberg, N. K. (2012). *Counseling adults in transition* (4th ed.). New York, NY: Springer.

Bandura, A. (1982). The psychology of chance encounters and life paths. *American Psychologist, 37,* 747–755.

Bandura, A. (1986). *Social foundations of thought and action: A social cognitive theory.* Englewood Cliffs, NJ: Prentice Hall.

Betsworth, D. G., & Hansen, J.-I. C. (1996). The categorization of serendipitous career development events. *Journal of Career Assessment, 4,* 91–98.

Bieschke, K. J., & Toepfer-Hendey, E. (2006). Career counseling with lesbian women. In W. B. Walsh & M. J. Heppner (Eds.), *Handbook of career counseling for women* (pp. 351–386). Hillsdale, NJ: Erlbaum.

Bloch, D. P. (2006). Spirituality and careers. In J. H. Greenhaus & G. A. Callanan (Eds.), *Encyclopedia of career development* (Vol. 2, pp. 762–764). Thousand Oaks, CA: Sage.

Bolles, R. N. (2001). *What color is your parachute?* Berkeley, CA: Ten Speed Press.

Briggs, J., & Peat, F. D. (1989). *Turbulent mirror: An illustrated guide to chaos theory and the science of wholeness.* New York, NY: Harper & Row.

Bright, J., & Pryor, R. (2008). Shiftwork: A chaos theory of careers agenda for change in career counseling. *Australian Journal of Career Development, 17,* 63–72.

Bronfenbrenner, U. (1977). Toward an experimental ecology of human development. *American Psychologist, 32,* 513–531.

Brown, D. (2007). *Career information, career counseling, and career development* (9th ed.). Boston, MA: Pearson Education.

Buehler, C. (1933). *Der menschliche Lebenslauf als psychologisches Problem* [The course of human life as a psychological problem]. Leipzig, Germany: Herzel.

Bujold, C. (2004). Constructing career through narrative. *Journal of Vocational Behavior, 64,* 470–484.

Cabral, A. C., & Salomone, P. R. (1990). Chance and careers: Normative versus contextual development. *The Career Development Quarterly, 39,* 5–17.

Cochran, L. (2011). The promise of narrative career counseling. In K. Maree (Ed.), *Shaping the story: A guide to facilitating narrative career counseling* (pp. 7–19). Rotterdam, The Netherlands: Sense.

Cook, E. P. (2012). *Understanding people in context: The ecological perspective in counseling.* Alexandria, VA: American Counseling Association.

Cook, E. P., Heppner, M. J., & O'Brien, K. M. (2002). Career development of women of color and White women: Assumptions, conceptualizations, and interventions from an ecological perspective. *The Career Development Quarterly, 50,* 291–305.

Cook, E. P., Heppner, M. J., & O'Brien, K. M. (2004). An ecological model of career development. In R. K. Conyne & E. P. Cook (Eds.), *Ecological counseling: An innovative approach to conceptualizing person–environment interaction* (pp. 219–242). Alexandria, VA: American Counseling Association.

Cook, E. P., Heppner, M. J., & O'Brien, K. M. (2005). An ecological model of women's career development. *Journal of Multicultural Counseling and Development, 33,* 165–179.

Crites, J. O. (1969). *Vocational psychology: The study of vocational behavior and development.* New York, NY: McGraw-Hill.

48 Career Counseling in the 21st Century

Davidson, P. E., & Anderson, H. D. (1937). *Occupational mobility in an American community.* Stanford, CA: Stanford University Press.

Fisher, I. (1989). *Midlife change.* Unpublished doctoral dissertation, Teachers College, Columbia University, New York, NY.

Flores, L. Y., & O'Brien, K. M. (2002). The career development of Mexican American adolescent women: A test of social cognitive career theory. *Journal of Counseling Psychology, 49,* 14–27.

Fouad, N., & Smith, P. L. (1996). A test of a social cognitive model for middle school students: Math and science. *Journal of Counseling Psychology, 43,* 338–346.

Gainor, K. A., & Lent, R. W. (1998). Social cognitive expectations and racial identity attitudes in predicting the math choice intentions of Black college students. *Journal of Counseling Psychology, 45,* 403–413.

Gelatt, H. B., & Gelatt, C. (2003). *Creative decision making: Using positive uncertainty.* Boston, MA: Crisp.

Ginzberg, E., Ginsburg, J. W., Axelrad, S., & Herma, J. L. (1951). *Occupational choice: An approach to a general theory.* New York, NY: Columbia University Press.

Gottfredson, G. D., & Cook, M. S. (1984). *The psychology of everyday life: A theory of persons and environments with implications for social control.* Unpublished manuscript.

Gottfredson, G. D., & Holland, J. L. (1996). *Dictionary of Holland occupational titles.* Odessa, FL: Psychological Assessment Resources.

Hackett, G., & Betz, N. E. (1981). A self-efficacy approach to the career development of women. *Journal of Vocational Behavior, 18,* 326–339.

Hale, M., Jr. (1980). *Human science and social order.* Philadelphia, PA: Temple University Press.

Heppner, M. J., & O'Brien, K. (2006). Women and poverty: The need for a holistic approach to career interventions. In B. Walsh & M. J. Heppner (Eds.), *Handbook of career counseling for women* (pp. 75–102). Hillsdale, NJ: Erlbaum.

Herr, E. L., Cramer, S. H., & Niles, S. G. (2004). *Career guidance and counseling through the lifespan* (6th ed.). Boston, MA: Pearson Education.

Holland, J. L. (1959). A theory of vocational choice. *Journal of Counseling Psychology, 6,* 35–45.

Holland, J. L. (1997). *Making vocational choices: A theory of vocational personalities and work environments* (3rd ed.). Odessa, FL: Psychological Assessment Resources.

Holland, J. L., Daiger, D. C., & Power, P. G. (1980). Some diagnostic scales for research in decision-making and personality: Identity, information, and barriers. *Journal of Personality and Social Psychology, 39,* 1191–1200.

Holland, J. L., & Gottfredson, G. D. (1994). *Career Attitudes and Strategies Inventory.* Odessa, FL: Psychological Assessment Resources.

Holland, J. L., Powell, A. B., & Fritzsche, B. A. (1994). *The Self-Directed Search (SDS) professional user's guide.* Odessa, FL: Psychological Assessment Resources.

Hughes, E. C. (1937). Institutional office and the person. *American Journal of Sociology, 43,* 404–413.

Jordaan, J. P., & Heyde, M. B. (1979). *Vocational maturity during the high-school years.* New York, NY: Teachers College Press.

Krumboltz, J. D. (2005). Don't let theories boggle your mind. In S. G. Niles & J. Harris-Bowlsbey (Eds.), *Career development interventions in the 21st century* (p. 34). Upper Saddle River, NJ: Pearson Education.

Krumboltz, J. D. (2009). The happenstance learning theory. *Journal of Career Assessment, 17,* 135–154.

Landrine, H. (1995). *Bringing cultural diversity to feminist psychology: Theory, research, and practice.* Washington, DC: American Psychological Association.

Lent, R. W. (2013). Social cognitive career theory. In S. D. Brown & R. W. Lent (Eds.), *Career development and counseling: Putting theory and research to work* (pp. 115–146). Hoboken, NJ: Wiley.

Lent, R. W., Brown, S. D., & Hackett, G. (1994). Toward a unifying social cognitive theory of career and academic interest, choice, and performance. *Journal of Vocational Behavior, 45,* 79–122.

McIlveen, P., Ford, T., & Dun, K. (2005). A narrative sentence completion process for system career assessment. *Australian Journal of Career Development, 14*(3), 30–39.

McIlveen, P., & Schultheiss, D. E. (Eds.). (2012). *Social constructionism in vocational psychology and career development.* Rotterdam, The Netherlands: Sense.

McMahon, M. (2010). Career counseling and storytelling: Constructing a 21st century narrative for practice. In H. Ohlsson & H. Borg (Eds.), *Career development* (pp. 1–23). Hauppauge, NY: Nova Science.

McMahon, M., & Watson, M. (2007). An analytical framework for career research in the post-modern era. *International Journal for Educational and Vocational Guidance, 7,* 169–179.

McMahon, M., & Watson, M. (2012). Story drafting: Strategies for facilitating narrative career counseling. *International Journal for Educational and Vocational Guidance, 12,* 211–224.

McMahon, M., & Watson, M. (2013). Story telling: Crafting identities. *British Journal of Guidance & Counseling, 41,* 277–286.

Meier, S. T. (2012). *Language and narratives in counseling and psychotherapy.* New York, NY: Springer.

Morrow, S. L., Gore, P. A., & Campbell, B. W. (1996). The application of a sociocognitive framework to the career development of lesbian women and gay men. *Journal of Vocational Behavior, 48,* 136–148.

Niles, S. G., & Harris-Bowlsbey, J. (2005). *Career development interventions in the 21st century* (2nd ed.). Upper Saddle River, NJ: Pearson Education.

Parsons, F. (1909). *Choosing a vocation.* Boston, MA: Houghton Mifflin.

Pitt-Catsouphes, M., & Swanberg, J. E. (2006). Connecting social work perspectives to work–family research and practice. In M. Pitt-Carsouphes, E. F. Kossek, & S. Sweet (Eds.), *The work and family handbook: Multi-disciplinary perspectives and approaches* (pp. 327–366). Mahwah, NJ: Erlbaum.

Prochaska, J. O., Norcross, J. C., & DiClemente, C. C. (1994). *Changing for good.* New York, NY: Morrow.

Pryor, R., & Bright, J. (2011). *The chaos theory of careers.* New York, NY: Routledge.

Richards, L. S. (1881). *Vocophy: The new profession.* Marlboro, MA: Bratt Brothers.

Roe, A. (1956). *The psychology of occupations.* New York, NY: Wiley.

Savickas, M. L. (1996). A framework for linking career theory and practices. In M. L. Savickas & W. B. Walsh (Eds.), *Handbook of career counseling theory and practice* (pp. 191–212). Palo Alto, CA: Davies-Black.

Savickas, M. L., & Baker, D. B. (2005). The history of vocational psychology: Antecedents, origin, and early development. In W. B. Walsh & M. L. Savickas (Eds.), *Handbook of vocational psychology* (3rd ed., pp. 15–50). Mahwah, NJ: Erlbaum.

Schlossberg, N. K. (1984). *Counseling adults in transition: Linking practice with theory.* New York, NY: Springer.

Sharf, R. S. (2010). *Applying career development theory to counseling* (5th ed.). Belmont, CA: Thomson Wadsworth.

Singer, J. A. (2004). Narrative identity and meaning-making across the adult lifespan: An introduction. *Journal of Personality, 72,* 437–460.

Sinisalo, P., & Komulainen, K. (2008). The creation of coherence in the transitional career: A narrative case study of the woman entrepreneur. *International Journal for Educational and Vocational Guidance, 8,* 35–48.

Stephens, W. R. (1970). *Social reform and the origins of vocational guidance.* Washington, DC: National Vocational Guidance Association.

Super, D. E. (1942). *The dynamics of vocational adjustment.* New York, NY: HarperCollins.

Super, D. E. (1953). A theory of vocational development. *American Psychologist, 8,* 185–190.

Super, D. E. (1957). *The psychology of careers.* New York, NY: Harper & Brothers.

Super, D. E. (1985). Coming of age in Middletown: Careers in the making. *American Psychologist, 40,* 405–414.

Super, D. E. (1990). A life-span, life-space approach to career development. In D. Brown, L. Brooks, & Associates (Eds.), *Career choice and development: Applying contemporary theories in practice* (2nd ed., pp. 197–261). San Francisco, CA: Jossey-Bass.

Super, D. E., Osborne, W. L., Walsh, D. J., Brown, S. D., & Niles, S. G. (1992). Development career assessment and counseling. *Journal of Counseling & Development, 71,* 74–80.

Super, D. E., & Overstreet, P. L. (1960). *The vocational maturity of ninth-grade boys.* New York, NY: Teachers College Press.

Super, D. E., Savickas, M. L., & Super, C. M. (1996). The life-span, life-space approach to careers. In D. Brown, L. Brooks, & Associates (Eds.), *Career choice and development* (3rd ed., pp. 121–178). San Francisco, CA: Jossey-Bass.

Sverko, B. (2006). Super's career development theory. In J. H. Greenhaus & G. A. Callanan (Eds.), *Encyclopedia of career development* (Vol. 2, pp. 789–792). Thousand Oaks, CA: Sage.

Swanson, J. L., & Fouad, N. A. (1999). Applying theories of person–environment fit to the transition from school to work. *The Career Development Quarterly, 47,* 337–347.

Tang, M., Fouad, N. A., & Smith, P. L. (1999). Asian Americans' career choices: A path model to examine factors influencing their career choices. *Journal of Vocational Behavior, 54,* 142–157.

Watts, R. E. (2003). Adlerian therapy as a relational constructivist approach. *The Family Journal: Counseling and Therapy for Couples and Families, 11,* 139–147.

Young, R. A., & Collin, A. (2004). Introduction: Constructivism and social constructionism in the career field. *Journal of Vocational Behavior, 64,* 373–388.

Young, R. A., Marshall, S. K., & Valach, L. (2007). Making career theories more culturally sensitive: Implications for counseling. *The Career Development Quarterly, 56,* 4–18.

Young, R. A., & Popadink, N. E. (2012). Social constructionist theories in vocational psychology. In P. McIlveen & D. E. Schultheiss (Eds.), *Social constructionism in vocational psychology and career development* (pp. 9–28). Rotterdam, The Netherlands: Sense.

Chapter 3

Empowering Life Choices: Career Counseling in the Contexts of Race and Class

Lisa Y. Flores

If we seek to incorporate the full richness of Parsons' contributions, we need to ground our study of vocations in a broader understanding of social issues, with a focus on how interventions can help empower clients and change inequitable systems.
—Blustein, 2001, p. 174

There are four major goals of this chapter. First, I examine the historical and social factors that provided the impetus for the birth of the field of career development and resulted in six tenets based on Western European cultural values that have dramatically influenced our theory, research, and practice. Second, I briefly discuss the demographic and ethical imperatives for expanding the field of career development. Third, I examine critical individual differences constructs that are believed to impact the career development of culturally diverse individuals: worldview, acculturation, racial identity, and ethnic identity. And fourth, I outline the role of cultural context in all aspects of the career counseling process from recognition of the need for assistance through postcounseling follow-up. A number of excellent books are available that can provide information about the career development of individuals from diverse racial and ethnic groups or that focus on the implications of social class on the career development process. For example, Blustein's (2006) *The Psychology of Working: A New Perspective for Career Development, Counseling, and Public Policy* and (2013) *The Oxford Handbook of the Psychology of Working*; Liu's (2012) *Social Class and Classism in the Helping Professions: Research, Theory, and Practice*; Peterson and Gonzalez's (2005) *The Role of Work in People's Lives: Applied Career Counseling and Vocational Psychology* (2nd edition); and Walsh, Bingham, Brown, and Ward's (2001) *Career Counseling for African Americans* are among the growing body of resources that provide helpful information in this area.

Definition of Terms

Although there appears to be considerable interchangeability in the literature related to word usage, in this chapter I use the terms *ethnicity*, *race*, *culture*, and *social class* as described below. *Ethnicity*, or *ethnic origin*, refers to a shared unique sociogeographical and cultural heritage. The sociogeographical customs (e.g., language, religion, food, dance, values, ceremonies) commonly associated with specific ethnic groups are passed down from one generation to the next. Examples of ethnic groups include Italian Americans, Sioux, Mexican Americans, Korean Americans, and African Americans.

In contrast, *race* has generally been defined in the social science literature in two ways: natural/biological race and social race. *Natural race* refers to a shared genotype or physiology that often is outwardly manifested in a group's phenotype or physical characteristics, such as hair texture, body type, facial features, and skin pigmentation. Biologists and social scientists have long challenged the concept of natural race and have all but abandoned this usage. One reason for this desertion is the difficulty in defining a "pure" race; for example, the presence of offspring from "racially" different parents questions the validity of race as purely natural or biological. Moreover, social scientists have argued that one's physiology is not related to social behaviors or personality styles.

Currently, most social scientists view race as a social construct; that is, race is socially defined within a particular society or nation. It is important to emphasize that the social construction of race is very much related to the society in which one lives. It is not uncommon for residents who have immigrated to the United States from other countries to indicate that they never identified with a racial group familiar to the United States. For example, an immigrant might say, "I never thought of myself as Latino until I moved here. We do not think of ourselves in that way in my home country." *Social race* encompasses the shared sociohistorical experiences of a group of people (e.g., slavery and Black liberation movements for Blacks throughout the diaspora); shared experiences and social relationships between races significantly affect one's beliefs, behaviors, and sociopolitical and economic conditions. In the United States, five major "racial" groups have been constructed: Native American, Asian/Asian American, Black/African American, Latina/o American, and White American. Within each of these social races are numerous ethnic groups, such as Cherokee, Chinese Americans, African Americans, Puerto Ricans, and German Americans, respectively. White individuals have been identified as the majority race because they are the numerical majority in the United States, and, moreover, they have political and economic power.

Culture is an important concept that is related, but not equivalent, to race and ethnicity. In general, *culture* refers to the attitudes, values, norms, and behaviors of a social group. Members of cultural groups often acquire or learn the values and behaviors of their social group through a process of *enculturation*, or socialization within one's group. However, even though someone can be categorized into a particular racial or ethnic group, he or she may not necessarily be culturally affiliated with the attitudes, values, or norms commonly associated with that group. For example, a person who is ethnically Mexican American may not identify with cultural customs commonly practiced within the Mexican American community.

In the United States, social class is a construct that is intricately linked to race and ethnicity. That is, the economic inequalities that exist in the United States are racialized; a disproportionate number of African Americans, Latinas/os, and Native Americans are poor, whereas a disproportionate number of Whites are among the financially elite (Lui et al., 2006). To date, *social class* has been almost exclusively defined around socioeconomic status and has included educational, occupational, and financial status. However, economic factors do not tell the whole story of social class. Recently there has been a call to go beyond defining social class as only socioeconomic status and to include issues such as lifestyle, power, and prestige (Diemer & Ali, 2009; Liu et al., 2004). These researchers argue that only when we examine the combination of economic and social status variables can we understand the effects of social class on a person's career aspirations, choice, and development.

Social class has been demonstrated to affect a host of career-related variables, including perceptions of work (Chaves et al., 2004), career development progress (Blustein et al., 2002; Diemer & Blustein, 2006), and vocational expectations (Diemer & Hsieh, 2008; Lapour & Heppner, 2009). Until recently, social class has received little attention in the psychological literature (Fouad & Brown, 2000), particularly regarding the needs of poor clients (L. Smith, 2005); however, social class is a critical aspect in understanding the career development process of all clients regardless of their racial or ethnic group affiliation. Moreover, it is important to understand how social class influences everyone's career options, both those who are financially privileged as well as those from working and lower class backgrounds (Heppner & Scott, 2004; Lapour & Heppner, 2009), and that we as career counselors explore how social class bias may influence our work with clients (Liu & Ali, 2005).

The Birth of the Field

In the quote that begins this chapter, Blustein (2001, p. 174) refers to calls from several scholars today that career counseling research and practice "return to its roots." To better understand the reasons for this redirection, I provide a brief reminder about the historical roots of career counseling and the assumptions and practices that later developed out of those early roots.

The vocational guidance movement was born during a period of major transition in the country, and the movement developed largely in response to the social concerns of the time, which included tremendous population growth, migration to urban areas, high rates of immigration, and the introduction of child labor laws. This was a time when both economic turmoil and demographic change were coupled with the changes brought on by the Industrial Revolution and the need to train and place individuals into the labor force. Career services, originally operationalized by Frank Parsons in 1909, were designed to help European immigrants find their place in this new and vast country and its developing economic system. Thus, our roots were embedded in helping poor and marginalized groups. However, scholars have argued that later theoretical developments and subsequent research studies in the field have resulted in a practice that is largely geared toward a small, privileged segment of society: middle-class, educated, white-collar workers (Blustein, 2006; Fitzgerald & Betz, 1994; Richardson, 1993). Moreover, middle-class cultural values and beliefs have been reflected in the theoretical and intervention advances since the early 1900s. Next I highlight the ways in which these values have permeated the field.

Six Key Tenets

The European immigrants who were settling in the United States in the early 1900s sought to assimilate into American society, a society that encouraged exchanging one's ethnic identity for another ethnic identity, that of the White American. These immigrants were striving to learn English and to become part of the American "melting pot," in which Western European cultures blended together to create a new "White" culture. Against this backdrop, many of the antecedents of our current tenets about career development were formed. The six key tenets that were born out of this historical setting were based on the Western European experience and worldview, and they dramatically influenced the development of career theories, research, and practices in the United States. These six tenets are (a) universality; (b) individualism and autonomy; (c) affluence; (d) the structure of opportunity open to all who strive and the myth of meritocracy; (e) the centrality of work in people's lives; and (f) the linearity, progressiveness, and rationality of the career development process.

The Tenet of Universality

An important assumption within the career development area is that theories and practices can be applied universally and that they adequately explain the career decisions of a wide range of individuals regardless of their race, ethnicity, class, gender, or nationality. Moreover, the constructs and terms that we use to understand the career development process are assumed to be defined similarly across groups. This universal bias can be problematic because it favors Western perspectives, and it fails to consider individual, cultural, contextual, and generational differences that may explain one's career decisions.

Wrenn (1962) warned against cultural encapsulation that emphasizes a universal concept of what is healthy and normal behavior. In the United States, what has traditionally been considered healthy is centered on the Eurocentric tenets outlined in this section. This Eurocentric stance disregards cultural variation and assumes rigid uniformity (Sue & Sue, 2013). Some have questioned the validity of career theories, concepts, and instruments across cultural groups (e.g., Leong & Brown, 1995) and have called for more research with culturally diverse groups to determine culture-specific variables that may explain vocational behavior. At the same time, others have suggested that the theories are not the problem, but rather it is the manner in which career researchers and practitioners apply or test these theories (Hardin, 2007; Hardin, Robitschek, Flores, Navarro, & Ashton, 2013). Specifically, these researchers warned that career counselors and researchers may be narrowly operationalizing these theories and their related constructs to fit within a Western worldview, and if a broader and more culturally sensitive lens is used, the theories may be useful after all in understanding the career development of marginalized cultural groups in our society. Clearly, additional work is needed to determine which aspects of our theories and concepts are universal to all people, and more discussion is needed regarding how we can use these tools in a culturally sensitive manner with the diverse clients with whom we work.

The Tenet of Individualism and Autonomy

Another central tenet of career theory, research, and practice is the importance of the individual. The individual is the core unit and makes choices that ultimately shape his or her destiny. Western psychological theories emphasize separation and individuation from the family as a key developmental task. Virtually all traditional career theories focus on aspects of the self to determine career outcomes: How can we find a match between an individual's interests and the work world? How can we help the individual strive for self-actualization? How can we help the client develop individual-based career and life goals? How can we help the individual develop self-efficacy beliefs that will inform his or her career decisions? How does one's career define the self?

In career counseling we encourage the "healthy" developmental step of the adolescent separating from family and beginning to trust his or her own decision-making ability. Here, *healthy* is defined as part of the individuation process; that is, to be perceived as healthy one needs to separate from family and make individual decisions about one's life. This tenet is consistently reflected in career theories, interventions, and assessments. For example, most career theories use concepts such as individual interests, goals, personality, skills, self-efficacy beliefs, or self-concepts to explain career decisions, and career interventions often consist of one-on-one sessions with an individual and a career counselor. Career counselors typically use assessment instruments that evaluate person factors and do not consider environmental variables that may have an effect on the individual. It should be as important to conduct an environmental assessment regarding the role of institutional barriers, family, teachers, and culture in the career decision making of culturally diverse clients.

Individualism and autonomy may not be relevant or meaningful for individuals from collectivist cultures. For members of groups with collectivist values, membership in the family or community is of primary importance, and members place great value on their collective group membership. Vocational decision making and life planning may occur in consultation with others in the community and with one's community in mind, or the decision may be made by elders in the community. Thus, it may be a serious mistake to view this reliance on family support and collective decision making as being immature or overly dependent. This reliance is valued and respected in many Asian cultures, and studies have shown that family expectations, support, and obligations to the family are important in Asian Americans' career development (Fouad et al., 2008). Career choices are thus weighed in terms of the potential contribution they would make or benefits they would have to the family or community as opposed to the individual. Empirical data support the observation that individualism and autonomy may not be as culturally relevant in career planning as collectivism or community for some Asian Americans (Hardin, Leong, & Osipow, 2001) and that some individuals from diverse racial and ethnic groups may make career decisions based on factors other than personal interests (Tang, Fouad, & Smith, 1999) or self-efficacy beliefs (Flores & O'Brien, 2002).

The Tenet of Affluence

Another central tenet assumes a certain level of affluence on the part of the career client. Career development theory has at its core the assumption that individuals have the economic means to pursue their career interests and goals. This middle-class bias within the field (Liu & Ali, 2005; Richardson, 1993) has been pervasive in our career theories and approaches and is relevant to only a minority of people in the country. This tenet assumes that because of financial privileges, people are able to exercise a certain level of volition when making career choices (Blustein, 2006). Moreover, it assumes that prestigious occupations are ideal and that everyone in our society aspires to hold these jobs (Liu & Ali, 2005). Thus, the role of the career counselor is to assess interests, skills, and values and to help match individuals with appropriate, or high-status, career options. Those career options all have price tags, such as the cost of vocational–technical training, college, or relocating to where there are jobs in a chosen career field.

This tenet of affluence is not true for the majority of the world's population, nor is it true for many individuals in the United States. It is particularly not true for the poor and working-class Whites and racial and ethnic minorities living in our country. For many individuals from lower social classes, career decisions are made based on the need to provide the basic necessities for the family. Thus, finding a job—*any job*—that pays for shelter, food, and clothing is what is important. Indeed, one study reported that poor and working-class adolescents from an urban high school in the northeast were more likely to perceive work as a means of making money versus an opportunity for personal development or implementing one's identity (Chaves et al., 2004). Still, others might make career decisions based on factors other than salary, such as the quality of life it provides and the ability to spend time with family and/or children. The messages that one receives about work and working are largely shaped by family, and these messages can play an important role in how one approaches work as an adult (Fouad et al., 2008). The luxury of choosing a career to fulfill one's personal identity or to express one's interests is usually reserved for the college educated or financial elite. Very little is known about the interface between economic exploitation and racism experienced by racial and ethnic minorities and by Whites on career interests and development. Much more research is needed that elucidates the interaction between race and class as well as disentangles race from class to more fully understand the applicability of this tenet to both racial and ethnic minorities and White individuals.

The Tenet of the Structure of Opportunity Open to All Who Strive and the Myth of Meritocracy

This tenet emphasizes the construct of individual control in selecting, attaining, and ultimately being satisfied in a career field, and it contributes to the belief that we live in a *meritocracy*, or a society in which one advances because of individual merit. Those who operate under this assumption believe that the prestigious jobs in our society, along with wealth and resources, are distributed according to merit and effort. In essence, wealthy people accumulate their assets through hard work, whereas poor people get their just rewards because they are lazy. Thus, the assumption is made that the individual is in control of his or her efforts and that those who work hard enough can achieve the "American Dream," a belief that is held by many people in the United States (F. Miller & Clark, 1997). This tenet is reflected in the ideology that you can "pull yourself up by your bootstraps" and can make any occupational dream a reality.

In her book *Nickel and Dimed: On (Not) Getting By in America*, Ehrenreich (2001) described her undercover work at minimum-wage jobs in different cities around the United States. She reported that these jobs were strenuous and physically taxing and that her coworkers were among the most hard-working people she knew. Yet in spite of their hard work, many members of the working class have a difficult time making ends meet or moving up the social class ladder. McNamee and Miller (2004) challenged the belief that we live in a meritocratic society and suggested that a number of non-merit-based factors help to determine the jobs and other financial resources that one may accumulate. These non-merit factors include, but are not limited to, discrimination, social capital, inheritance, privilege, and unequal opportunities for quality public education. Career theorists have written about the role that non-merit variables, namely luck or happenstance, play in the career development process (Krumboltz, 1998; Krumboltz & Levin, 2004; Mitchell, Levin, & Krumboltz, 1999).

Color-blind racial ideology is a useful construct for underscoring the cultural relativity of this tenet. Specifically, individuals, groups of people, and systems that consciously or unconsciously operate from this ideological framework deny, distort, or minimize the role of racism (or classism) in people's lives and assume that to achieve equity, all people should be treated the same. People who ascribe to racial ideology use this to advocate for the dissolution of affirmative action programs, which are under threat in several states today. Research has found that racial ideology is linked to beliefs about affirmative action (Bobo, 1998; W. A. Smith, 2006). Color-blind racial ideology helps to legitimize blaming the individual for his or her circumstances instead of blaming the institutional structures and policies that prevent a person from fulfilling his or her career aspirations (Neville, Lilly, Duran, Lee, & Browne, 2000; Neville, Worthington, & Spanierman, 2001). In an ideal world, everyone would have the same opportunity to choose a career that would be personally meaningful, rewarding, and lucrative. Unfortunately, we do not live in an ideal world. We live in a society in which racism and class exploitation continue to exist, and these interlocking systems, in turn, structure an individual's career choice.

This tenet ignores the toll that discrimination has taken in the creation of social, psychological, institutional, political, and economic barriers that seriously erode the control that many people in our society have over various facets of their career development. Instead, it puts the responsibility on the individual to succeed, and it blames the individual for not working hard enough if he or she does not succeed. Indeed, in our society stereotypes are rampant about poor people (Lott, 2002) and racial and ethnic minorities (Niemann, 1999). They obviously can have harmful effects on the recruitment, hiring, and retention practices within an organization when members of the system rely on these stereotypes when making decisions about or interacting with diverse employees. Stereotypes also can serve as major career barriers when members of these groups internalize these messages. Evidence of the effects of institutional racism is apparent when one reviews labor market reports. Specifically, according to the U.S. Bureau of Labor Statistics (2013a, 2013b), Whites are more likely than African Americans, Latinas/os, and Asians to hold managerial and professional positions. Furthermore, African Americans and Latinas/os earn less than their White and Asian American counterparts (U.S. Bureau of Labor Statistics, 2013c). It is important to be aware of the many ways in which institutional racism (e.g., income disparities, lack of representation of one's racial or ethnic group among the employees or leaders in an organization) and individual racism (e.g., beliefs in stereotypes) may limit racial and ethnic minorities and persons from various social classes from examining or leaving an occupation or career field.

Sue and Sue (2013) proposed a four-quadrant model of locus of control (i.e., internal vs. external explanations for creating one's fate) and locus of responsibility (i.e., person vs. system attribution for one's life condition) that is helpful in career counseling with all clients regardless of race or social class. Most traditional career counseling approaches and interventions follow the internal control–personal responsibility philosophy, which is synonymous with the belief in one's ability to pull oneself up by the bootstraps. Given the existence of prejudice and discrimination, many racial and ethnic minority group members and working-class individuals may legitimately perceive institutional barriers that may impede their career development. However, little empirical research has examined the effect of both personality variables and perceived institutional racism on the career choices and satisfaction of members of these groups. Thus, little is known about the interface between perceived locus of control and responsibility on career development based on one's racial, ethnic, or social class background.

The Tenet of the Centrality of Work in People's Lives

This tenet assumes that work plays a central and pivotal role in a person's life and that it is thus critical to find a career that fulfills many of the person's needs. Work is thought to make up the core of a person's identity. Work provides the self-actualization that humans need to feel whole. Although the role of work is important in many people's lives, it may not have the center stage position many career theorists and researchers may give it (Blustein, 2006; Richardson, 1993). This lack of centrality may be the case because of forms of oppression (racism, classism, sexism) or cultural values. For example, racial and ethnic minority group members may experience institutional racism in the workplace and thus view it as a hostile or nonaffirming environment for them as individuals. On a related note, poor and working-class individuals may feel their labor is being exploited, which further adds to feelings of alienation from work. Cultural values might also create a greater tendency for other life roles, such as family, church, or leisure activities, to take on a more central role. Little research has examined the role of culture in creating and emphasizing the salience of environments other than the work setting to provide centrality and identity affirmation in people's lives. A greater understanding is needed regarding the intersecting effect of poverty and racial discrimination on the importance of work and in determining identity.

The Tenet of the Linearity, Progressiveness, and Rationality of the Career Development Process

Career counseling and one's career development process are often described in orderly, rational, and linear terms, and this is clearly evident in Parsons's (1909) formulation of the components of the three-part model for making a career choice: (a) an understanding of the self, (b) an understanding of the world of work, and (c) true reasoning of their relations. This linear progression has had a profound impact through the century and continues to provide a format for our current practice. Gelatt (1962, 1989) originally described the decision-making process as rational but later revised his thinking to incorporate flexibility, intuition, and irrationality. Thus, the efficacy of a linear, progressive, and rational approach for all clients, particularly racial and ethnic minority clients and clients who are poor and working class, is an important consideration for career counselors. Indeed, research has indicated that some individuals from diverse cultural groups do not experience their careers as either linear or rational (e.g., Gomez et al., 2001). Similarly, clients may approach counseling as a circular, rather than linear, process.

In today's global economy, the assumed linear nature of the world of work is becoming less true for all workers. Unlike in the past, career changes are not uncommon, and workers can expect to hold a number of jobs in their lifetime and are expected to possess transferable skills that can be applied to a range of careers. As I discuss in more detail later in the chapter, many of these assumptions born in the early part of the last century may no longer be true for the majority of workers of this century. If career counseling is to be truly empowering for the increasingly diverse workforce, we must examine the present-day accuracy of our basic operating tenets.

Demographic and Ethical Imperatives

The demographic landscape in the United States has changed dramatically since the conception of the field. In the early 1900s, when the U.S. Census Bureau first started tracking population data, the United States had 75 to 90 million residents, the majority of whom were European immigrants. The most recent census count in 2010 indicated that the U.S. population includes 308.7 million people (Mackun & Wilson, 2011), and the population reflects a highly diverse group of people in terms of their cultural backgrounds (Humes, Jones, & Ramirez, 2011). These population demographics are replicated in our social institutions, specifically the workplace and educational systems. As the demographic makeup of our society continues to shift, career counseling specialists can expect to work with a diverse group of clients. It is important that career counselors understand the implications of these demographic changes in their work and that they are knowledgeable of the professional and ethical obligations to provide effective career services to diverse individuals. The following statistics are provided to illuminate the changing demographics in the United States and the need to more fully attend to the career needs and development of culturally diverse clients:

- In 2011, 15.9% of the population lived in poverty (U.S. Census Bureau, 2011).
- The latest census data indicate that 16.3% of the population is Latina/o or Hispanic, making this the second largest racial or ethnic group behind Whites. Between 2000 and 2010, more than half of the U.S. population growth was attributed to the increase in the Latina/o population (Humes et al., 2011). The size of this group is expected to continue to rise dramatically in comparison to that of other groups, with the U.S. Census Bureau (2012b) projecting that Latinas/os and Hispanics will compose almost one-third of the population in 2060. The poverty rate among Latinas/os and Hispanics in 2011 was 25.8%, and their median income was $39,589 (U.S. Census Bureau, 2011).
- African Americans represent 12.6% of the population (Humes et al., 2011). In 2011, African American households had the lowest median income ($33,223) among all racial groups, which was about 62% of the average income in non-Hispanic White households (U.S. Census Bureau, 2011). Their poverty rate in 2011 was 28.1% (U.S. Census Bureau, 2011).

- Although Asian Americans compose only 4.8% of the total population, they are one of the two fastest growing racial or ethnic groups in the United States. The government projects that Asian Americans will double in size between 2012 and 2060, when they are expected to compose 8.2% of the population (U.S. Census Bureau, 2012b). Asian American households have the highest median income among all racial groups in the United States ($67,885) and had a poverty rate of 12.8% in 2011 (U.S. Census Bureau, 2011).
- Native Americans constitute 0.9% of the U.S. population (Humes et al., 2011). The poverty rate among Native Americans was 29.5% in 2011, the highest among all racial groups (U.S. Census Bureau, 2011). In 2010, fewer than 1% of 4-year college degrees were awarded to Native Americans (U.S. Department of Education, 2012).
- Although non-Hispanic Whites have the lowest poverty rate of any U.S. racial group at 11%, they represent 45% of people living in poverty (U.S. Census Bureau, 2011).
- The labor force is projected to become more racially and ethnically diverse. Labor force participation is expected to increase faster for Latinas/os and Hispanics, Asian Americans, and African Americans than for Whites; by 2020, Latinas/os, African Americans, and Asian Americans are expected to make up 40% of the labor force (Toossi, 2012).

If these projections are accurate and these demographic trends continue, in a few decades our society will be truly multiracial and multicultural, and no single racial or ethnic group will be a numerical majority. Today, almost 40% of our society is people of color (Latinas/os, African Americans, Asian Americans, and Native Americans), and it is projected that, collectively, they will compose the majority of the population in the United States by the middle of the century.

At the same time that we are seeing these demographic shifts, statistics indicate that significant disparities exist across these groups with regard to educational attainment, employment status, and earnings. According to the U.S. Census Bureau (2012a), a higher proportion of White adults (90%) reported at least a high school education, and Latinas/os had the lowest percentages with at least a high school diploma (61%). Moreover, Whites earn more money than Latinas/os and African Americans, and these disparities exist across all occupational fields and when education level is controlled (U.S. Bureau of Labor Statistics, 2011). It should be apparent that education, profession, and salary are interconnected, and each plays a critical role in a person's social and economic standing in the United States. For example, lifetime earnings increase and employment options expand with each progressive level of education.

What emerges from these data is a dramatic and profound need for career assistance for racial and ethnic minorities and persons from lower social classes as they more fully move and integrate into the schools and workplaces that have so long discriminated against and marginalized them. As mentioned by Blustein (2001) in the opening quote to this chapter, career counselors can play an important role in helping to rectify these social inequalities by providing culturally effective career services and by providing their diverse clients with information about and access to a broad range of educational training and career options. To affect our clients' career development, it is important to understand how race and social class intersect for them. It is especially critical that career counselors understand that although racial and ethnic minorities are overrepresented among the poor, a wide range of diversity exists within all racially and ethnically diverse communities.

Unfortunately, our existing knowledge base about the career development of racial and ethnic minorities is limited (Byars & McCubbin, 2001; Flores, Berkel, et al., 2006; Richardson, 1993). One of the early critics of the state of our research was Richardson, who noted that because the predominant orientation of theories and research was to White, middle-class individuals, the field had effectively marginalized the career development needs of racial and ethnic minorities and persons from lower social classes. According to an analysis of career development studies published in the leading U.S. vocational journals over a 36-year time span (1969–2004), only 6.7% of all studies (or a total of 281 articles) were related to the career development of diverse racial and ethnic groups in the United States (Flores, Berkel, et al., 2006). In addition, the career development literature has paid little attention to how social class affects the career decision process (Blustein, 2006; Diemer & Ali, 2009; Heppner & Scott, 2004; Liu & Ali, 2005; Richardson, 1993). To date, most of our knowledge about career development, career counseling, and career assessment has been based on studies conducted on White, middle-class individuals, and it is not proportionate to population demographics or labor force composition. We know much less about the considerably sizable groups as well as the fastest growing segments of our population, most notably individuals from diverse racial and ethnic backgrounds and persons representing the broad range of social classes. More research is needed with culturally diverse samples in terms of race, ethnicity, and social class to assist in the development of culturally relevant theories and models and culturally effective career interventions for a broad range of individuals.

What is not explicitly articulated in the statistics just outlined is the ethical obligation to provide quality, culturally sensitive, and relevant career counseling to all clients. Several years ago, psychologists argued that the provision of services to persons of culturally diverse backgrounds by professionals not knowledgeable about providing services to such groups was unethical (Korman, 1974). In spite of this recognition, scholars have argued that mental health services have not been sensitive to culturally diverse clients, and they have suggested that a number of factors may contribute to service underutilization in culturally diverse communities, such as stigma on seeking help, lack of culturally competent professionals, and culture- and class-bound professional practices (Sue & Sue, 2013).

Several areas should be considered to facilitate placing career counseling in cultural context(s) and to provide culturally sensitive career services. Specifically, the field of career counseling has been criticized for using culturally biased assessment tests that were originally developed on White Americans and that may or may not be valid for racial and ethnic minorities (Flores, Spanierman, & Obasi, 2003; Fouad, 1993). When assessing an instrument's cultural validity, one should consider the following criteria: (a) the extent to which the items are culturally relevant for the population, (b) the extent to which the semantic meaning of the items is similar for each culture, and (c) the extent to which the interpretation of the instrument is similar across populations (Paniagua, 1994). Models of career development also have been criticized for not including critical cultural variables, such as immigration disruption, racial discrimination, or poverty (Fouad & Bingham, 1995; Leong & Brown, 1995). Furthermore, some major career theories were built on the basis of primarily White middle-class men (e.g., Super's 1953 Middletown study), and the practices and assessments that are tied to these theories are based on the Eurocentric worldview and underlying tenets that characterized the field at its inception. The validity of many of these models for persons of color and persons across the social class spectrum is largely untested. Thus, it is critical that career counselors align their practices in accordance with professional ethical standards (e.g., National Career Development Association, American Psychological Association) and that career counselors possess the requisite knowledge, awareness, and skills (Hargrove, Creagh, & Kelly, 2003; Sue, Arredondo, & McDavis, 1992) to become proficient at providing services within cultural contexts. A recent study found that while professional career counselors self-reported above-average multicultural counseling competencies, assessments of their responses to specific career counseling practices were evaluated as being low on multicultural knowledge and skills (Vespia, Fitzpatrick, Fouad, Kantamneni, & Chen, 2010). While valuing, affirming, and being aware of diversity and differences is an important foundation for working with diverse career clients, it is important that career counselors receive ongoing training and feedback regarding their application of multicultural knowledge and skills in career counseling practice.

Individual Difference Variables: Worldview, Acculturation, and Racial and Ethnic Identity Development

When career counselors view their clients broadly as members of a specific cultural group, they risk relying on group stereotypes and may overlook the variables that make each client unique. Given the tremendous amount of within-group variability across all cultural groups, it is vital to consider individual difference variables when providing career counseling. Multicultural career research studies have been criticized because they are often designed to test between-group differences (in this case, middle-class Whites serve as the normative group against which others are compared) or because they ignore within-group factors and assume uniformity within groups (Leong & Flores, 2013; Worthington, Flores, & Navarro, 2004). In addition to the differences that exist across cultural groups based on gender, age, social class, sexual orientation, and ability status, career counselors should take note of the culture-specific variables that are gaining considerable theoretical and empirical support, such as worldview, acculturation, racial and ethnic identity, cultural values, and generation status. Understanding clients in terms of these culture-specific variables can lead to more culturally informed and sensitive career counseling interventions. These individual difference variables may affect each stage in the career counseling process, from the initial acknowledgment of the need for career assistance to the close of career counseling. Each of these constructs can be applied to clients from any cultural or socioeconomic background; however, research on these constructs has typically been conducted with specific cultural groups (Cokley, 2007). In this section, I review the cultural constructs of worldview, acculturation, and racial and ethnic identity and briefly highlight findings from career development research in these areas.

Worldview

Probably the broadest of these three individual difference variables is the construct of worldview. *Worldview* is defined as the frame of reference that a person uses to interpret and define events and make decisions and comprises a person's attitudes and values (Sue & Sue, 2013). Worldview is typically acquired via the enculturation process. That is, a person learns how to perceive his or her relation to self, community, and the world through cultural socialization into a racial, ethnic, or social class community. Although worldview consists of several components, such as group identity (cultural consciousness), individual identity (individual vs. collective self-concept), beliefs (assumptions), and language (communication patterns; Dana, 1993), critical elements of worldview consistently discussed in the literature concentrate on value dimensions. A value orientation reflects cultural components of the decision-making process, such as the relationship between people and nature (mastery over vs. harmony with), time orientation (future, present, past), interpersonal relations (individualistic, collateral), mode of activity (doing, being, being-in-becoming), and human nature (good, bad, neutral; Kluckhohn & Strodtbeck, 1961). Our value orientation in each of these areas is highly influenced by our cultural background and life experiences.

An assessment of these components of worldview with a career client can assist us in delivering services and the client in conceptualizing his or her career concerns. Worldviews may influence many aspects of one's career development as well as the career counseling process. Thus, it is critically important that we as career counselors examine our own worldview, because it may influence the questions that we ask, the interventions that we select, and our goals for counseling. Moreover, a career counselor's worldview orientation can also affect the pace and timing of career choice and the actual occupational content of job choices. The six basic tenets described in the beginning of this chapter reflect the worldview embraced in many Western European cultures; as I have noted, these tenets have shaped current career research theory and practice. To understand how worldviews may shape the career counseling process, consider a Native American woman seeking career counseling who has a present time orientation, values collateral relationships, and prefers a being-in-becoming activity dimension. Career counseling practice is future oriented (career goals, future career selection), relies heavily on individualistic values (individual choice, interests, goals), and expects that an individual will take control of his or her career development process and make a decision that is best for him or her. These differences between the Native American woman and career counseling practice are likely to manifest in counseling and may lead to premature termination or dissatisfaction with counseling if the career counselor does not modify the process to better fit the client's worldview orientation. Given the value of family and community and their role in the career decision-making process of U.S. racial and ethnic minorities (e.g., Flores, Robitschek, Celebi, Andersen, & Hoang, 2010; Fouad et al., 2008; Pearson & Bieschke, 2001), a culturally sensitive career counselor might consider using constructivist approaches, such as career narratives and family genograms, instead of the conventional career practices of setting individual career goals and completing traditional career assessments (interests, self-efficacy measures).

Acculturation

Acculturation is often used to understand individual differences within a specific ethnic group. *Acculturation* has been largely defined as a multidimensional psychosocial process that occurs when members of two or more cultures come into contact with one another. However, there is some debate as to whether all groups in a multicultural society undergo the acculturation process or if the process is unique to members of the nondominant culture (Berry, 2002). According to acculturation theory, as a result of coming into contact with other cultural groups, individuals from each group learn the cultural values and practices of a new culture while maintaining some degree of cultural affiliation to their traditional culture (Berry, 2002). The adaptation that occurs during acculturation can be either psychological (personal feelings about one's group membership) or sociocultural (relationships that are formed within or outside one's cultural group; Berry, 2002), and aspects of culture that are affected by acculturation include language, friendship patterns and social affiliations, customs, music, and food preferences. Acculturation models and assessments have generally been developed to describe and measure the adaptation process of individuals with ancestry from Mexico (Cuellar, Arnold, & Maldonado, 1995), Asia (Kim, Atkinson, & Yang, 1999; Suinn, Rickard-Figueroa, Lew, & Vigil, 1987), Africa (Landrine & Klonoff, 1996), and Latin America (Marin & Gamba, 1996; Norris, Ford, & Bova, 1996). Pan-ethnic acculturation measures are also available (Stephenson, 2000).

Acculturation models in the psychology literature have evolved over the past 20 years (Kim & Abreu, 2001), and today, bidimensional or multidimensional models of acculturation are widely recommended (M. J. Miller & Kerlow-Myers, 2009). In a multidimensional model, a person can be oriented to varying degrees to more than one culture (own culture, host culture, other cultures) at the same time. In essence, individuals can selectively maintain or discard certain traits from their traditional or new cultures depending on the adaptive utility of the trait. According to Berry's (1980) model, two broad queries can help career practitioners to determine a client's level of acculturation: (a) To what extent does the person wish to maintain his or her cultural heritage in regard to language, self-identity, and way of life? and (b) To what extent does the individual have contact with the dominant culture and want to participate in the dominant culture's practices?

Responses to these questions can help career counselors place individuals in one of four acculturation strategies. The first strategy, *integration* or *bicultural*, is characterized by wanting to maintain one's own culture while having daily interactions with other groups. An adult client who moved to the United States from Taiwan as a teenager may have learned to speak English fluently yet still speaks Mandarin with her family and practices traditional customs at home. In terms of her career, a career counselor may want to help her seek a job that builds on her strengths as a bicultural and bilingual person. Research has shown that integration strategies lead to more mentoring experiences (Nguyen, Huynh, & Lonergan-Garwick, 2007) as well as higher income levels (Valdivia et al., 2008) than other strategies. Another strategy is *assimilation*, which includes wishing to give up one's own cultural identity to become more a part of the dominant group. For example, a young man may ask to be called John instead of his given name, Juan, to distance himself from his Mexican heritage and may try hard to get rid of his Spanish accent. He believes that he will be accepted at school and work if he is oriented toward the dominant culture. Research has suggested that high orientation toward the dominant culture is related to career self-efficacy (Byars-Winston, Estrada, Howard, Davis, & Zalapa, 2010; Flores, Navarro, Smith, & Ploszaj, 2006; Flores et al., 2010; Patel, Salahuddin, & O'Brien, 2008; Rivera, Chen, Flores, Blumberg, & Ponterotto, 2007), career choices (Flores & O'Brien, 2002; Tang et al., 1999), and educational goals (Flores, Navarro, & Dewitz, 2008; Flores, Ojeda, Huang, Gee, & Lee, 2006). The third strategy, *separation*, describes wanting to retain one's own cultural identity and not interact with the majority group. A Latino or African American high school student may choose to attend a Hispanic-serving institution or a historically Black institution, respectively, to be immersed in a learning environment that reflects his or her cultural values and to be educated with other students and faculty from his or her cultural group. Empirical findings have found that orientation toward one's culture of origin is related to career self-efficacy (Flores et al., 2010) but unrelated to setting educational aspirations (Flores et al., 2008; Flores, Ojeda, et al., 2006). Finally, *marginalization* distinguishes persons by the fact that they are interested neither in maintaining their own ethnic identity nor in interacting with the dominant group. Individuals characterized by this acculturation strategy might include gang members or individuals belonging to religious sects who adopt an entirely new identity based on their membership in this group.

Understanding more about an individual's level of acculturation may help describe and explain critical aspects of vocational behavior. Research studies have found that acculturation influences the work experiences and career development of racial and ethnic minorities (e.g., Mexican Americans, Asian Americans, and Vietnamese Americans). Specifically, acculturation is related to a host of variables, such as career decision making self-efficacy (Patel et al., 2008), career self-efficacy (Rivera et al., 2007), career maturity (Hardin et al., 2001), family conflict about education and careers (Chung, 2001), job satisfaction (Leong, 2001), and employment skepticism (Valentine, 2006). In addition, one study found that work supervisors provided higher performance evaluations to acculturated employees (Leong, 2001). Because each of these career variables can play a strong role in work-related decisions, adjustment, and satisfaction, acculturation becomes a critically important area to assess when working with a culturally diverse client.

Acculturation level may also explain aspects of the career counseling process, including help-seeking behavior, counselor preference, levels of disclosure, and expectations of the career counselor and the counseling process in general. Traditional career interventions may be most appropriate for clients who are highly acculturated, whereas situating career interventions in a cultural context would be essential for clients who more closely adhere to their traditional cultural practices. For example, it seems appropriate to apply "traditional" career interventions with a fourth-generation Chinese American woman who was raised in a small, predominantly White, Midwestern community. However, this application does not preclude consideration of other class or culture-related concepts, such as social class worldview and racial identity, in devising an intervention plan.

Racial and Ethnic Identity Development

A number of theorists and researchers throughout the past 3 decades have proposed and investigated models of racial and ethnic identity development (e.g., Cross, 1971; Cross & Vandiver, 2001; Helms, 1984, 1990, 1995; Phinney, 1992). In the multicultural career literature (Byars & McCubbin, 2001; Flores, Berkel, et al., 2006), the examination of racial identity or ethnic identity is a widely used and culturally specific approach for examining within-group differences.

Racial identity and ethnic identity are two distinct constructs. *Racial identity* entails understanding oneself in a racially oppressive environment and describes how a person is socialized to think about his or her own racial group as well as other racial groups. Racial identity models assume that by virtue of living in an oppressive society, people develop attitudes and identities about racial groups (Helms, 1990). Racial identity development models have received increasing attention over the past 20 years, and models exist to describe a nonlinear process by which Whites and persons of color cycle through different stages or statuses that are distinguished by the specific attitudes people hold about their own racial group membership and those of other groups. *Ethnic identity*, in contrast, refers to how one self-identifies in terms of an ethnic group. Ethnic identity has been assessed via self-report measures pertaining to one's ethnic identity search and belonging and commitment to activities within a group (Phinney, 1992).

The Civil Rights Movement served as an impetus in the emergence of racial identity development theories. Cross's (1971) nigrescence theory was the first framework to describe the development of racial consciousness among Blacks. This theory has served as a foundation for a host of racial identity development models, all of which describe a developmental process whereby individuals increasingly become aware of racial oppression and of themselves as racial beings (Cross, 1971; Helms, 1990, 1995). Racial identity is a dynamic interplay between an individual's affective, cognitive, and behavioral attitudes and his or her environment.

The number of stages or statuses associated for each model, the description of each status, and the desired outcomes vary across models. For example, Cross's (1971) theory includes five stages (pre-encounter, encounter, immersion–emersion, internalization, and internalization–commitment), Helms's (1990, 1994) model for people of color includes five statuses (contact, dissonance, immersion/emersion, internalization, and integrative awareness), and Helms's (1995) White racial identity model has six statuses (contact, disintegration, reintegration, pseudo-independence, immersion/emersion, and autonomy). The outcomes associated with White identity development models generally describe the process of increasing racial awareness, the acknowledgement of racial oppression, and the ways in which one has benefited from this oppression. Conversely, the process for persons of color in the United States evolves from being in a state of obliviousness about racial issues to shedding the internalized negative messages about their racial group to making a commitment to all oppressed groups (Helms, 1995). It is important to note that these statuses are not mutually exclusive and that an individual may hold attitudes that are consistent with all of the statuses; however, the strength of these attitudes will differ across statuses and environments.

Scholars have hypothesized that racial identity attitudes may be linked to the career development of racial and ethnic minorities because of the racial climate in our society as well as the educational and work settings (Byars & Hackett, 1998; Cokley, Dreher, & Stockdale, 2004; Helms & Piper, 1994). It is important to note that these statuses may play an important role at different stages of the career development process and that they may be connected to a number of factors that inform one's career decisions. For example, clients who have strong attitudes that are consistent with the pre-encounter status may be largely oblivious to racial elements of the work world and may internalize negative evaluations from a supervisor that are contradictory to prior feedback without recognizing that the negative feedback may be rooted in the supervisor's biases and stereotypes. Individuals with attitudes that are characteristic of the immersion/emersion status may be distrustful of non-Black coworkers, and, consequently, this may affect perceived job satisfaction. Finally, persons who exhibit attitudes that are consistent with higher statuses may recognize that the additional work-related stressors that they experience may be related to pressure to prove themselves in a predominantly White work environment and may work to promote a multicultural workplace environment.

A few empirical studies have tested the relations of racial identity and associated constructs to career-related variables. Studies with African American samples have suggested that more developed racial identity attitudes are related to vocational identity (Jackson & Neville, 1996), life role salience (Carter & Constantine, 2000), and social cognitive variables (Byars-Winston, 2006; Gainor & Lent, 1998) but are unrelated to career decidedness (McCowan & Alston, 1998), number of occupations considered by a sample of high school students (Lease, 2006), and grades or standardized test scores (Awad, 2007). In addition, racial identity attitudes predict, over and above demographic variables such as age and gender, career development among African American students (Jackson & Neville, 1996). Racial identity has also been empirically linked to career maturity among Asian Americans (Carter & Constantine, 2000) and to work-related values among Whites (Carter, Gushue, & Weitzman, 1994).

An important area of research has focused on the relationship between racial attitudes and counseling skills. Preliminary studies have suggested that higher statuses of racial identity are associated with higher levels of self-reported multicultural counseling competencies (Middleton et al., 2005; Ottavi, Pope-Davis, & Dings, 1994). It is important that White career counselors be trained to be aware of their racial identity attitudes and how they might be related to the career counseling process, as these attitudes may have implications for the delivery of culturally sensitive career counseling to culturally diverse clients.

Ethnic identity may also play an important role in the career development of culturally diverse clients; however, the empirical literature in this area is thin. Findings with racially/ethnically diverse samples have indicated that ethnic identity was positively related to career decidedness, indecisiveness, comfort and career choice importance (Duffy & Klingaman, 2009), and career decision making self-efficacy (Gushue, 2006; Gushue & Whitson, 2006b; Rollins & Valdez, 2006), and it had an indirect effect on career planning outcome expectations via self-efficacy (Gushue, 2006). However, ethnic identity was not related to career-related self-efficacy in samples of African American students (Gushue & Whitson, 2006a) or racially diverse students (Byars-Winston et al., 2010). Although more research is needed to understand the connection between ethnic identity and career decisions, career practitioners are encouraged to assess a client's ethnic identity to understand how career decisions may have formed in relation to group affiliations and pride.

The Career Counseling Process Through the Lens of Culture

Culture is a critical factor in career counseling and career development and should be used both as a filter to understand the client and as a factor that may affect each phase of the process. What follows is a description of some of the culturally salient aspects of each phase in the career planning process outlined in Chapter 1. It is vital that career counselors engage in an ongoing exploration of their own cultural values and how these values may influence their work with clients who are racially, ethnically, socioeconomically, and culturally similar to or different from themselves. To assist with this exploration process, readers should examine their worldviews, racial and ethnic identities, and social class attitudes throughout their professional development, as these attitudes are likely to change through life experiences.

Phase 1: Client Goal or Problem Identification, Clarification, and Specification

Identification—Opening and Forming the Working Alliance
It is critical from the outset that counselors have an awareness of the myriad ways in which culture may influence a person's career development. Given the vast array of different cultural contexts a client may bring to the career counseling session, Leong's (1993) construct of creative uncertainty serves as a good place to begin. Even if we are uncertain about each client's cultural background and values and how these may have influenced the career counseling process, Leong reminds us to remain creative in our approach to helping the client. The more our knowledge and awareness of culturally relevant factors can inform our practice, the more creative we can be.

Along with the need for creativity comes the need to develop a strong working alliance with the client at the onset of counseling to prevent early termination (Bingham & Ward, 1994; Fouad & Bingham, 1995). Meara and Patton (1994) suggested that one reason for premature termination among career clients in general may be a lack of attention to the working alliance. Thus, regardless of the cultural background of the counselor and the client, there is a need to establish rapport with the client in a way that helps the client feel bonded with the counselor. This early connection can set the stage for the collaboration and mutuality necessary for effective career counseling to take place. The working alliance may also be facilitated by the counselor communicating an understanding and validation of the client's life experiences and by the counselor communicating a willingness and excitement about the client's life and future options.

At this opening phase in career counseling it may be helpful to try to assess the client's level of "racial salience," or the extent to which the individual perceives race to be influential in the career planning process, including in perceived work options, level of occupational stereotyping, and career decision making (Helms & Piper, 1994). It is also important to examine the client's level of class salience and how his or her current or previous social class identity may impact career development. All of this information can help to shape the discourse of career counseling.

Clarification—Gathering Client Information
Gathering information about the client should include assessing the culture-specific variables and individual differences discussed earlier. This assessment should extend beyond the traditional use of tests and inventories to incorporate qualitative assessments and interviews to understand various aspects of the client (Lonberg & Hackett, 2006; Ponterotto, Rivera, & Sueyoshi, 2000; Subich, 1996). The use of genograms (Gibson,

2005; Sueyoshi, Rivera, & Ponterotto, 2001), life and career narratives (Clark, Severy, & Sawyer, 2004; Galindo, Aragon, & Underhill, 1996), multicultural checklists (Ward & Bingham, 1993), vocational card sorts, and career/life timelines can be particularly useful approaches for gaining a better understanding of a client. Filtering this information through a cultural context and understanding how one's career development has been shaped by this cultural context (Blustein, Coutinho, Murphy, Backus, & Catraio, 2011; Heppner & Fu, 2010; Leong, Hardin, & Gupta, 2010) is an important skill for career counselors. In addition, the race/gender ecological model of career development discussed in Chapter 2 provides a template for helping the client examine the macro- and microsystems affecting his or her career development. For example, an assessment of the client's racial identity status as a microsystem influence is very important to understanding many of the dynamics of the career counseling process. This assessment of racial identity status can be accomplished with one of the racial identity scales or through a less formal verbal assessment based on the counselor's thorough understanding of the various racial identity statuses. Counselors would benefit from reading recent chapters on social class worldview, acculturation, and racial and ethnic identity and special journal issues that have been devoted to multicultural career counseling and assessment (e.g., *Journal of Career Assessment*, Volume 2, Number 3; *Journal of Vocational Behavior*, Volume 44, Number 2; *The Career Development Quarterly*, Volume 50, Number 4; *Journal of Multicultural Counseling and Development*, Volume 33, Number 3; *Journal of Career Development*, Volume 34, Number 3; *Journal of Career Development*, Volume 37, Number 1). As Helms (1994) indicated, to understand a client's racial identity status, the counselor may be able to assess how the client integrates racial information into his or her career self-conception, which may be a critical factor in effectively providing career planning assistance. It is especially important to examine how a client's racial identity might affect such constructs as racial salience in job selection, strategies for dealing with racism in the work environment, work adjustment, and work satisfaction.

In addition to gathering client information, this is also a phase of providing information that may be useful to the client. Particularly if the client is at a less developed racial identity status, he or she may be unaware of structural barriers in the career development process. Thus, it is important that the counselor help the client become aware of these barriers and discuss ways to circumvent these obstacles should they occur. The counselor may also point out the roles of the sociopolitical environment, culture, and social class in shaping individuals' self-concepts. This information will lay the groundwork for future discussion about how environmental and cultural factors may influence important aspects of the client's career development process.

Specification—Understanding and Hypothesizing About Client Information and Behavior

In attempting to gain greater specificity with the client, the counselor might explore, when appropriate, the roles that poverty, sexism, racism, or discrimination may have on both the client's self-efficacy concerning his or her probability of succeeding in the traditional labor market and the outcomes he or she perceives to be possible. The counselor may also explore the gendered, racialized, and classist nature of vocational self-concept and how it may influence job options. The counselor may further explore how perceptions of the vocational self may influence an individual to compromise his or her career choices in ways that may be detrimental. For example, if a client indicates low educational aspirations, the counselor should seek to understand the source of these low aspirations and attempt to widen the educational and occupational options the client is considering. Given the overrepresentation of African Americans and women in social occupations, the counselor may explore whether these are authentic interests or if the person is following socialized expectations for traditional careers. In addition, this phase of counseling may include the counselor testing hypotheses about culture-specific variables that may explain the client's vocational behavior. In particular, it may be helpful to examine how culture-specific variables can enhance the counselor's and client's understanding of the career development process. Culture-specific variables can be examined as unique strengths that the client brings to the career planning process and eventually to the workplace setting.

Phase 2: Client Goal or Problem Resolution

Taking Action

Some writers in the field of multicultural counseling (Sue & Sue, 2013) have indicated that some racially and ethnically diverse clients prefer directive- and action-oriented approaches to counseling rather than insight- or reflective-oriented approaches (Fusick & Bordeau, 2004; Okonji, Osokie, & Pulos, 1996), although these preferences may differ based on race, ethnicity, gender, acculturation, and social class. Almost no studies have been conducted on the effectiveness of career interventions with culturally diverse clients (M. T. Brown, Yamini-Diouf, & Ruiz de Esparza, 2005; S. D. Brown & Ryan Krane, 2000; Heppner & Heppner, 2003); however, many recommendations can be drawn from the extant multicultural counseling and career literatures. For example, research has found evidence that racial and ethnic group differences exist in perceived career opportunities and perceived career barriers, with racial and ethnic minorities reporting fewer career options and more perceived barriers than their White counterparts (Fouad & Byars-Winston, 2005). Given the tremendous impact environmental barriers have on racially and ethnically diverse and poor individuals' career development, it may be very important in this phase to help clients identify those aspects of the process that are within and beyond their personal control. This may be especially helpful for those clients who are living in poverty. It may also be very helpful to talk directly with clients about ways of overcoming certain barriers in the career planning and job search processes.

In addition, it may be particularly helpful to provide opportunities for culturally diverse clients to take part in group interventions, as some writers have indicated that this reinforces the collectivist worldview and allows individuals to connect with others from similar backgrounds who are experiencing similar career challenges (Bowman, 1993; Clark et al., 2004; Shea, Ma, & Yeh, 2007). In the action phase, this may take the form of a career exploration group or a job club, whereby individuals come together and provide support, leads, and resources as well as normalize the fears and feelings that may accompany these important life transitions. This may also be an appropriate time to introduce the client to culturally similar role models in a variety of career fields to expand awareness of possible career fields and to increase self-efficacy beliefs.

It may also be beneficial to include the family in the action phase, either by directly involving them in parts of the process or by inquiring about how the family would view particular options the individual is considering. Clients might be encouraged to use their immediate family, extended family, or community as resources in their career planning process. Delivery systems might include holding career planning workshops in community centers and collaborating with community leaders in the design and implementation of career planning services. This may be particularly advantageous for people living in lower socioeconomic neighborhoods with little access to transportation.

Some writers have indicated the importance of the counselor emphasizing clients' abilities to generate knowledge about themselves and to act on their own behalf in locating appropriate role models and developing networks. Although advocacy on the client's behalf is definitely warranted when the client is having difficulty negotiating predominantly White work environments, the more counselors emphasize client-generated rather than counselor-generated knowledge, the more self-efficacy and strength the client is likely to feel (Hawks & Muha, 1991).

Developing Career Goals and Plans of Action
The career counseling process continues with the development of an individual career plan. This specific plan can serve as a road map for a client as he or she navigates the action phase of the process. Here the counselor can help the client examine at a more micro level how to take action steps and how to overcome potential obstacles. For some of the action steps, the counselor may need to play the role of advocate for the client in the larger employment and educational system. The counselor can also help the client to creatively devise a repertoire of possible responses to situations of racism, classism, and discrimination that the client may face. At this stage, the lack of linearity in the process may become evident as the client sees the need to reevaluate and revisit previous steps. It is especially important at this time that the career counselor reinforces the client's decision-making style and unique strengths.

Evaluating Results and Closing the Relationship
This is the phase in which the counseling session is evaluated from both a content (what we did) and a process (how we did it) perspective. During this phase the counselor can emphasize the client's strengths and proficiency at various aspects of the career planning process. This is also a time to welcome clients to return if they need further help or assistance. This is especially important for culturally diverse clients for a couple of reasons. For one, Fouad and Bingham (1995) argued that many times individuals from diverse cultural backgrounds may ascribe expert or even familial status to the counselor. Returning to counseling after termination may be perceived as a failure or loss of face, especially for Asian American clients, and thus may be very difficult for the client. Thus, it is important that the counselor normalize coming back to counseling and help the client see it as simply a part of what often occurs in counseling relationships. Another reason for emphasizing the possibility of the client's return is the likelihood that the client will be met with race-related obstacles (racism, discrimination) and will need further assistance. If a strong relationship has been built between counselor and client, this is a natural place for the client to return and get help instead of having to develop an entirely new relationship with another counselor.

Closing Thoughts

In sum, it is imperative that each phase of the career planning process be examined through the filter of culture. Although much of what is included in each phase may be similar, cultural contexts can bring different needs to these phases that, when attended to, can lead to more effective and empowering career counseling. However, when the cultural context is ignored or unattended, counselors can do a great disservice to their culturally diverse clients. The more awareness and knowledge counselors have about culture-specific variables, the more equipped they will be to provide the best quality service and help empower the life choices of all people.

References

Awad, G. H. (2007). The role of racial identity, academic self-concept, and self-esteem in the prediction of academic outcomes for African American students. *Journal of Black Psychology, 33,* 188–207.

Berry, J. W. (1980). Acculturation as varieties of adaptation. In A. M. Padilla (Ed.), *Accul-turation: Theory, models and some new findings* (pp. 9–25). Boulder, CO: Westview Press.

Berry, J. W. (2002). Conceptual approaches to acculturation. In K. M. Chun, P. B. Or-ganista, & G. Marin (Eds.), *Acculturation: Advances in theory, measurement, and applied research* (pp. 17–37). Washington, DC: American Psychological Association.

Bingham, R. P., & Ward, C. M. (1994). Career counseling with ethnic minority women. In W. B. Walsh & S. Osipow (Eds.), *Career counseling with women* (pp. 165–195). Hillsdale, NJ: Erlbaum.

Blustein, D. L. (2001). Extending the reach of vocational psychology: Toward an inclusive and integrative psychology of working. *Journal of Vocational Behavior, 59,* 171–182.

Blustein, D. L. (2006). *The psychology of working: A new perspective for career development, counseling, and public policy.* Mahwah, NJ: Erlbaum.

Blustein, D. L. (2013). *The Oxford handbook of the psychology of working.* Oxford, England: Oxford University Press.

Blustein, D. L., Chaves, A. P., Diemer, M. A., Gallagher, L. A., Marshall, K. G., Sirin, S., & Bhati, K. S. (2002). Voices of the forgotten half: The role of social class in the school-to-work transition. *Journal of Counseling Psychology, 49,* 311–323.

Blustein, D. L., Coutinho, M. T. N., Murphy, K. A., Backus, F., & Catraio, C. (2011). Self and social class in career theory and practice. In P. J. Hartung & L. M. Subich (Eds.), *Developing self in work and career: Concepts, cases, and contexts* (pp. 213–229). Washington, DC: American Psychological Association.

Bobo, L. (1998). Race, interests, and beliefs about affirmative action: Unanswered questions and new directions. *American Behavioral Scientist, 41,* 985–1003.

Bowman, S. L. (1993). Career intervention strategies for ethnic minorities. *The Career Development Quarterly, 42,* 14–25.

Brown, M. T., Yamini-Diouf, Y., & Ruiz de Esparza, C. (2005). Career interventions for racial or ethnic minority persons: A research agenda. In W. B. Walsh & M. L. Savickas (Eds.), *Handbook of vocational psychology: Theory, research, and practice* (3rd ed., pp. 227–242). Mahwah, NJ: Erlbaum.

Brown, S. D., & Ryan Krane, N. E. (2000). Four (or five) sessions and a cloud of dust: Old assumptions and new observations about career counseling. In S. D. Brown & R. W. Lent (Eds.), *Handbook of counseling psychology* (3rd ed., pp. 740–766). New York, NY: Wiley.

Byars, A. M., & Hackett, G. (1998). Applications of social cognitive theory to the career development of women of color. *Applied & Preventive Psychology, 7,* 255–267.

Byars, A. M., & McCubbin, L. D. (2001). Trends in career development research with racial/ethnic minorities: Prospects and challenges. In J. G. Ponterotto, J. M. Casas, L. Suzuki, & C. Alexander (Eds.), *Handbook of multicultural counseling* (2nd ed., pp. 633–654). Thousand Oaks, CA: Sage.

Byars-Winston, A. M. (2006). Racial ideology in predicting social cognitive career variables for Black undergraduates. *Journal of Vocational Behavior, 69,* 134–148.

Byars-Winston, A. M., Estrada, Y., Howard, C., Davis, D., & Zalapa, J. (2010). Influence of social cognitive and ethnic variables on academic goals of underrepresented students in science and engineering: A multiple-groups analysis. *Journal of Counseling Psychology, 57,* 205–218.

Carter, R. T., & Constantine, M. G. (2000). Career maturity, life role salience, and racial/ethnic identity among Black and Asian American college students. *Journal of Career Assessment, 8,* 173–187.

Carter, R. T., Gushue, G. V., & Weitzman, L. M. (1994). White racial identity development and work values. *Journal of Vocational Behavior, 44,* 185–197.

Chaves, A. P., Diemer, M. A., Blustein, D. L., Gallagher, L. A., DeVoy, J. E., Casares, M. T., & Perry, J. C. (2004). Conceptions of work: The view from urban youth. *Journal of Counseling Psychology, 51,* 275–286.

Chung, R. H. G. (2001). Gender, ethnicity, and acculturation in intergenerational conflict of Asian American college students. *Cultural Diversity and Ethnic Minority Psychology, 7*, 376–386.

Clark, M. A., Severy, L., & Sawyer, S. A. (2004). Creating connections: Using a narrative approach in career group counseling with college students from diverse cultural backgrounds. *Journal of College Counseling, 7*, 24–31.

Cokley, K. O. (2007). Critical issues in the measurement of ethnic and racial identity: A referendum on the state of the field. *Journal of Counseling Psychology, 54*, 224–234.

Cokley, K., Dreher, G. F., & Stockdale, M. S. (2004). Toward the inclusiveness and career success of African Americans. In M. S. Stockdale & F. J. Crosby (Eds.), *The psychology and management of workplace diversity* (pp. 168–190). Malden, MA: Blackwell.

Cross, W. E., Jr. (1971). The negro-to-Black conversion experience: Toward a psychology of Black liberation. *Black World, 20*, 13–27.

Cross, W. E., Jr., & Vandiver, B. J. (2001). Nigrescence theory and measurement: Introducing the Cross Racial Identity Scale. In J. G. Ponterotto, J. M. Casas, L. Suzuki, & C. Alexander (Eds.), *Handbook of multicultural counseling* (2nd ed., pp. 371–393). Thousand Oaks, CA: Sage.

Cuellar, I., Arnold, B., & Maldonado, R. (1995). Acculturation Rating Scale for Mexican Americans–II: A revision of the original ARSMA scale. *Hispanic Journal of Behavioral Sciences, 17*, 275–304.

Dana, R. H. (1993). *Multicultural assessment perspectives for professional psychology.* Boston. MA: Allyn & Bacon.

Diemer, M. A., & Ali, S. R. (2009). Integrating social class into vocational psychology: Theory and practice implications. *Journal of Career Assessment, 17*, 247–265.

Diemer, M. A., & Blustein, D. L. (2006). Critical consciousness and career development among urban youth. *Journal of Vocational Behavior, 68*, 220–232.

Diemer, M. A., & Hsieh, C. (2008). Vocational expectations among lower socioeconomic status adolescents of color. *The Career Development Quarterly, 56*, 257–267.

Duffy, R. D., & Klingaman, E. A. (2009). Ethnic identity and career development among first-year college students. *Journal of Career Assessment, 17*, 286–297.

Ehrenreich, B. (2001). *Nickel and dimed: On (not) getting by in America.* New York, NY: Metropolitan Books.

Fitzgerald, L. F., & Betz, N. E. (1994). Career development in cultural context: The role of gender, race, class, and sexual orientation. In M. L. Savickas & R. W. Lent (Eds.), *Convergence in career development theories* (pp. 103–118). Palo Alto, CA: Consulting Psychologists Press.

Flores, L. Y., Berkel, L. A., Nilsson, J. E., Ojeda, L., Jordan, S. E., Lynn, G. L., & Leal, V. M. (2006). Racial/ethnic minority vocational research: A content and trend analysis across 36 years. *The Career Development Quarterly, 55*, 2–21.

Flores, L. Y., Navarro, R. L., & Dewitz, J. (2008). Mexican American high school students' post-secondary educational goals: Applying social cognitive career theory. *Journal of Career Assessment, 16*, 489–501.

Flores, L. Y., Navarro, R. L., Smith, J., & Ploszaj, A. (2006). Testing a model of career choice nontraditionality with Mexican American adolescent men. *Journal of Career Assessment, 14*, 214–234.

Flores, L. Y., & O'Brien, K. M. (2002). The career development of Mexican American adolescent women: A test of social cognitive career theory. *Journal of Counseling Psychology, 49*, 14–27.

Flores, L. Y., Ojeda, L., Huang, Y., Gee, D., & Lee, S. (2006). The relation of acculturation, problem solving appraisal, and career decision-making self-efficacy to Mexican American high school students' educational goals. *Journal of Counseling Psychology, 53*, 260–266.

Flores, L. Y., Robitschek, C., Celebi, E., Andersen, C., & Hoang, U. (2010). Social cognitive influences on Mexican Americans' career choices across Holland's themes. *Journal of Vocational Psychology, 76*, 198–210.

Flores, L. Y., Spanierman, L. B., & Obasi, E. M. (2003). Professional and ethical issues in career assessment with diverse racial and ethnic groups. *Journal of Career Assessment, 11*, 76–95.

Fouad, N. A. (1993). Cross-cultural vocational assessment. *The Career Development Quarterly, 42*, 4–13.

Fouad, N. A., & Bingham, R. P. (1995). Career counseling with racial and ethnic minorities. In W. B. Walsh & S. H. Osipow (Eds.), *Handbook of vocational psychology: Theory, research, and practice* (2nd ed., pp. 331–365). Mahwah, NJ: Erlbaum.

Fouad, N. A., & Brown, M. T. (2000). Role of race and social class in development: Implications for counseling psychology. In S. D. Brown & R. D. Lent (Eds.), *Handbook of counseling psychology* (pp. 379–408). New York, NY: Wiley.

Fouad, N. A., & Byars-Winston, A. M. (2005). Cultural context of career choice: Meta-analysis of race/ethnicity differences. *The Career Development Quarterly, 53*, 223–233.

Fouad, N. A., Kantamneni, N., Smothers, M. K., Chen, Y. L., Fitzpatrick, M., & Terry, S. (2008). Asian American career development: A qualitative analysis. *Journal of Vocational Behavior, 72*, 43–59.

Fusick, L., & Bordeau, W. C. (2004). Counseling at-risk Afro-American youth: An examination of contemporary issues and effective school-based strategies. *Professional School Counseling, 8*, 102–115.

Gainor, K. A., & Lent, R. W. (1998). Social cognitive expectations and racial identity attitudes in predicting the math choice intentions of Black college students. *Journal of Counseling Psychology, 45*, 403–413.

Galindo, R., Aragon, M., & Underhill, R. (1996). The competence to act: Chicana teacher role identity in life and career narratives. *Urban Review, 28*, 279–308.

Gelatt, H. B. (1962). Decision-making: A conceptual frame of reference for counseling. *Journal of Counseling Psychology, 9*, 240–245.

Gelatt, H. B. (1989). Positive uncertainty: A new decision making framework for counseling. *Journal of Counseling Psychology, 36*, 252–256.

Gibson, D. M. (2005). The use of genograms in career counseling with elementary, middle, and high school students. *The Career Development Quarterly, 53*, 353–362.

Gomez, M. J., Fassinger, R. E., Prosser, J., Cooke, K., Mejia, B., & Luna, J. (2001). *Voces abriendo caminos* (voices forging paths): A qualitative study of the career development of notable Latinas. *Journal of Counseling Psychology, 48*, 286–300.

Gushue, G. V. (2006). The relationship of ethnic identity, career decision-making self-efficacy and outcome expectations among Latino/a high school students. *Journal of Vocational Behavior, 68*, 85–95.

Gushue, G. V., & Whitson, M. L. (2006a). The relationship among support, ethnic identity, career decision self-efficacy, and outcome expectations in African American high school students: Applying social cognitive career theory. *Journal of Career Development, 33*, 112–124.

Gushue, G. V., & Whitson, M. L. (2006b). The relationship of ethnic identity and gender role attitudes to the development of career choice goals among Black and Latina girls. *Journal of Counseling Psychology, 53*, 379–385.

Hardin, E. E. (2007, August). *Cultural validity of career theories: A new perspective.* Symposium conducted at the 115th Annual Convention of the American Psychological Association, San Francisco, CA.

Hardin, E. E., Leong, F. T., & Osipow, S. H. (2001). Cultural relativity in the conceptualization of career maturity. *Journal of Vocational Behavior, 58*, 36–52.

Hardin, E. E., Robitschek, C., Flores, L. Y., Navarro, R., & Ashton, M. W. (2013). *The cultural lens approach to evaluating cultural validity of psychological theory.* Manuscript submitted for publication.

Hargrove, B. K., Creagh, M. G., & Kelly, D. B. (2003). Multicultural competencies in career counseling. In D. B. Pope-Davis, H. L. K. Coleman, W. M. Liu, & R. L. Toporek (Eds.), *Handbook of multicultural competencies in counseling and psychology* (pp. 392–405). Thousand Oaks, CA: Sage.

Hawks, B. K., & Muha, D. (1991). Facilitating the career development of minorities: Doing it differently this time. *The Career Development Quarterly, 39,* 251–260.

Helms, J. E. (1984). Toward a theoretical explanation of the effects of race on counseling: A black and white model. *The Counseling Psychologist, 12*(4), 153–165.

Helms, J. E. (Ed.). (1990). *Black and White racial identity: Theory, research and practice.* New York, NY: Greenwood Press.

Helms, J. E. (1994). Racial identity and career assessment. *Journal of Career Assessment, 3,* 199–209.

Helms, J. E. (1995). An update of Helm's White and people of color racial identity models. In J. G. Ponterotto, J. M. Casas, L. A. Suzuki, & C. M. Alexander (Eds.), *Handbook of multicultural counseling* (pp. 181–198). Thousand Oaks, CA: Sage.

Helms, J. E., & Piper, R. E. (1994). Implications of racial identity theory for vocational psychology. *Journal of Vocational Behavior, 44,* 124–136.

Heppner, M. J., & Fu, C. C. (2010). The gendered context of vocational self-construction. In P. J. Hartung & L. M. Subich (Eds.), *Developing self in work and careers: Concepts, cases, and contexts* (pp. 177–192). Washington, DC: American Psychological Association.

Heppner, M. J., & Heppner, P. P. (2003). Identifying process variables in career counseling: A research agenda. *Journal of Vocational Behavior, 62,* 429–452.

Heppner, M. J., & Scott, A. B. (2004). From whence we came: The role of social class in our families of origin. *The Counseling Psychologist, 32,* 596–602.

Humes, K. R., Jones, N. A., & Ramirez, R. R. (2011). *Overview of race and Hispanic origin: 2010.* Retrieved from http://www.census.gov/prod/cen2010/briefs/c2010br-02.pdf

Jackson, C. C., & Neville, H. A. (1996). Influence of racial identity attitudes on African American college students' vocational identity and hope. *Journal of Vocational Behavior, 53,* 97–113.

Kim, B. S., & Abreu, J. (2001). Acculturation measurement: Theory, current instruments, and future directions. In J. G. Ponterotto, J. M. Casas, L. Suzuki, & C. Alexander (Eds.), *Handbook of multicultural counseling* (2nd ed., pp. 394–424). Thousand Oaks, CA: Sage.

Kim, B. S. K., Atkinson, D. R., & Yang, P. H. (1999). The Asian Values Scale: Development, factor analysis, validation, and reliability. *Journal of Counseling Psychology, 46,* 342–352.

Kluckhohn, F. R., & Strodtbeck, F. L. (1961). *Variations in value orientations.* Evanston, IL: Row, Petersen.

Korman, M. (1974). National conference on levels and patterns of professional training in psychology. *American Psychologist, 29,* 441–449.

Krumboltz, J. D. (1998). Serendipity is not serendipitous. *Journal of Counseling Psychology, 45,* 390–392.

Krumboltz, J. D., & Levin, A. S. (2004). *Luck is no accident: Making the most of happenstance in your life and career.* Atascadero, CA: Impact.

Landrine, H., & Klonoff, E. A. (1996). *African American acculturation: Deconstructing race and reviving culture.* Thousand Oaks, CA: Sage.

Lapour, A. S., & Heppner, M. J. (2009). Social class privilege and adolescent women's perceived career options. *Journal of Counseling Psychology, 56,* 477–494.

Lease, S. H. (2006). Factors predictive of the range of occupations considered by African American juniors and seniors in high school. *Journal of Career Development, 32,* 333–350.

Leong, F. T. L. (1993). The career counseling process with racial-ethnic minorities: The case of Asian Americans. *The Career Development Quarterly, 42,* 26–40.

Leong, F. T. L. (2001). The role of acculturation in the career adjustment of Asian American workers: A test of Leong and Chou's (1994) formulations. *Cultural Diversity and Ethnic Minority Psychology, 7*, 262–273.

Leong, F. T. L., & Brown, M. T. (1995). Theoretical issues in cross-cultural career development: Cultural validity and cultural specificity. In W. B. Walsh & S. H. Osipow (Eds.), *Handbook of vocational psychology: Theory, research, and practice* (2nd ed., pp. 143–180). Mahwah, NJ: Erlbaum.

Leong, F. T. L., & Flores, L. Y. (2013). Multicultural perspectives in vocational psychology. In W. B. Walsh, M. L. Savickas, & P. J. Hartung (Eds.), *Handbook of vocational psychology: Theory, research, and practice* (4th ed., pp. 53–80). New York, NY: Routledge.

Leong, F. T. L., Hardin, E. E., & Gupta, A. (2010). Self in vocational psychology: A cultural formulations approach. In P. J. Hartung & L. M. Subich (Eds.), *Developing self in work and careers: Concepts, cases, and contexts* (pp. 193–211). Washington, DC: American Psychological Association.

Liu, W. M. (2012). *Social class and classism in the helping professions: Research, theory, and practice.* Thousand Oaks, CA: Sage.

Liu, W. M., & Ali, S. R. (2005). Addressing social class and classism in vocational theory and practice: Extending the emancipatory communitarian approach. *The Counseling Psychologist, 33*, 189–196.

Liu, W. M., Ali, S. R., Soleck, G., Hopps, J., Dunston, K., & Pickett, T., Jr. (2004). Using social class in counseling psychology research. *Journal of Counseling Psychology, 51*, 3–18.

Lonberg, S. D., & Hackett, G. (2006). Career assessment and counseling for women. In W. B. Walsh & M. J. Heppner (Eds.), *Handbook of career counseling for women* (2nd ed., pp. 103–166). Mahwah, NJ: Erlbaum.

Lott, B. (2002). Cognitive and behavioral distancing from the poor. *American Psychologist, 57*, 100–110.

Lui, M., Robles, B., Leondar-Wright, B., Brewer, R., & Adamson, R., with United for a Fair Economy. (2006). *The color of wealth: The story behind the U.S. racial wealth divide.* New York, NY: New Press.

Mackun, P., & Wilson, S. (2011). *Population distribution and change: 2000 to 2010.* Retrieved from http://www.census.gov/prod/cen2010/briefs/c2010br-01.pdf

Marin, G., & Gamba, R. J. (1996). A new measurement of acculturation for Hispanics: The Bidimensional Acculturation Scale for Hispanics (BAS). *Hispanic Journal of Behavioral Sciences, 18*, 297–316.

McCowan, C. J., & Alston, R. J. (1998). Racial identity, African self-consciousness, and career decision making in African American college women. *Journal of Multicultural Counseling and Development, 26*, 28–38.

McNamee, S. J., & Miller, R. K., Jr. (2004). *The meritocracy myth.* Lanham, MD: Rowman & Littlefield.

Meara, N. M., & Patton, M. J. (1994). Contributions of the working alliance in the practice of career counseling. *The Career Development Quarterly, 43*, 161–177.

Middleton, R. A., Stadler, H. A., Simpson, C., Guo, Y. J., Brown, M. J., Crow, G., . . . Lazarte, A. A. (2005). Mental health practitioners: The relationship between White racial identity attitudes and self-reported multicultural counseling competencies. *Journal of Counseling & Development, 83*, 444–456.

Miller, F., & Clark, M. A. (1997). Looking toward the future: Young people's attitudes about affirmative action and the American dream. *American Behavioral Scientist, 41*, 262–271.

Miller, M. J., & Kerlow-Myers, A. E. (2009). A content analysis of acculturation research in the career development literature. *Journal of Career Development, 35*, 352–384.

Mitchell, K. E., Levin, A. S., & Krumboltz, J. D. (1999). Planned happenstance: Construct-ing unexpected career opportunities. *Journal of Counseling & Development, 77,* 115–124.

Neville, H. A., Lilly, R. L., Duran, G., Lee, R. M., & Browne, L. (2000). Construction and initial validation of the Color-Blind Racial Attitudes Scale (CoBRAS). *Journal of Counseling Psychology, 47,* 59–70.

Neville, H. A., Worthington, R. L., & Spanierman, L. B. (2001). Race, power, and multi-cultural counseling psychology: Understanding White privilege and color-blind racial attitudes. In J. G. Ponterotto, J. M. Casas, L. Suzuki, & C. J. Alexander (Eds.), *Handbook of multicultural counseling* (2nd ed., pp. 257–288). Thousand Oaks, CA: Sage.

Nguyen, A. D., Huynh, Q., & Lonergan-Garwick, J. (2007). The role of acculturation in the mentoring-career satisfaction model for Asian/Pacific Islander American univer-sity faculty. *Cultural Diversity and Ethnic Minority Psychology, 13,* 295–303.

Niemann, Y. F. (1999). Stereotypes about Chicanas and Chicanos: Implications for coun-seling. *The Counseling Psychologist, 29,* 55–90.

Norris, A. E., Ford, K., & Bova, C. A. (1996). Psychometrics of a brief acculturation scale for Hispanics in a probability sample of urban Hispanic adolescents and young adults. *Hispanic Journal of Behavioral Sciences, 18,* 29–38.

Okonji, J. M. A., Osokie, J. N., & Pulos, S. (1996). Preferred style and ethnicity of counsel-ors by African American males. *Journal of Black Psychology, 22,* 329–339.

Ottavi, T. M., Pope-Davis, D. B., & Dings, J. G. (1994). Relationship between White racial identity attitudes and self-reported multicultural counseling competencies. *Journal of Counseling Psychology, 41,* 149–154.

Paniagua, F. A. (1994). *Assessing and treating culturally diverse clients.* Thousand Oaks, CA: Sage.

Parsons, F. (1909). *Choosing a vocation.* Garrett Park, MD: Garrett Park Press.

Patel, S. G., Salahuddin, N. M., & O'Brien, K. M. (2008). Career decision-making self-efficacy of Vietnamese adolescents: The role of acculturation, social support, socio-economic status, and racism. *Journal of Career Development, 34,* 218–240.

Pearson, S. M., & Bieschke, K. J. (2001). Succeeding against the odds: An examination of familial influences on the career development of professional African American women. *Journal of Counseling Psychology, 48,* 301–309.

Peterson, N., & Gonzalez, R. C. (2005). *The role of work in people's lives: Applied career coun-seling and vocational psychology* (2nd ed.). Belmont, CA: Thomson, Brooks/Cole.

Phinney, J. S. (1992). The Multigroup Ethnic Identity Measure: A new scale for use with diverse groups. *Journal of Adolescent Research, 7,* 156–176.

Ponterotto, J. G., Rivera, L., & Sueyoshi, L. A. (2000). The career in-culture interview: A semi-structured protocol for the cross-cultural intake interview. *The Career Develop-ment Quarterly, 49,* 85–96.

Richardson, M. S. (1993). Work in people's lives: A location for counseling psychologists. *Journal of Counseling Psychology, 40,* 425–433.

Rivera, L. M., Chen, E. C., Flores, L. Y., Blumberg, F., & Ponterotto, J. G. (2007). The effects of perceived barriers, role models, and acculturation on the career self-efficacy and career consideration of Hispanic women. *The Career Development Quarterly, 56,* 47–61.

Rollins, V. B., & Valdez, J. N. (2006). Perceived racism and career self-efficacy in African American adolescents. *Journal of Black Psychology, 32,* 176–198.

Shea, M., Ma, P. W. W., & Yeh, C. J. (2007). Development of a culturally specific career exploration group for urban Chinese immigrant youth. *The Career Development Quar-terly, 56,* 62–73.

Smith, L. (2005). Psychotherapy, classism, and the poor. *The American Psychologist, 60,* 687–696.

Smith, W. A. (2006). Racial ideology and affirmative action support in a diverse college student population. *Journal of Negro Education, 75,* 589–605.

Stephenson, M. (2000). Development and validation of the Stephenson Multigroup Acculturation Scale (SMAS). *Psychological Assessment, 12,* 77–88.

Subich, L. M. (1996). Addressing diversity in the process of career assessment. In M. L. Savickas & W. B. Walsh (Eds.), *Handbook of career counseling theory and practice* (pp. 277–290). Palo Alto, CA: Davies-Black.

Sue, D. W., Arredondo, P., & McDavis, R. J. (1992). Multicultural counseling competencies and standards: A call to the profession. *Journal of Multicultural Counseling and Development, 70,* 477–486.

Sue, D. W., & Sue, D. (2013). *Counseling the culturally diverse: Theory and practice* (6th ed.). New York, NY: Wiley.

Sueyoshi, L. A., Rivera, L., & Ponterotto, J. G. (2001). The family genogram as a tool in multicultural career counseling. In J. G. Ponterotto, J. M. Casas, L. A. Suzuki, & C. M. Alexander (Eds.), *Handbook of multicultural counseling* (2nd ed., pp. 655–671). Thousand Oaks, CA: Sage.

Suinn, R. M., Rickard-Figueroa, K., Lew, S., & Vigil, P. (1987). The Suinn-Lew Asian Self-Identity Acculturation Scale: An initial report. *Educational and Psychological Measurement, 47,* 401–407.

Super, D. E. (1953). A theory of vocational development. *American Psychologist, 8,* 185–190.

Tang, M., Fouad, D. A., & Smith, P. L. (1999). Asian Americans' career choices: A path model to examine factors influencing their career choices. *Journal of Vocational Behavior, 54,* 142–157.

Toossi, M. (2012, January). Labor force projections to 2020: A more slowly growing workforce. *Monthly Labor Review.* Retrieved from http://www.bls.gov/opub/mlr/2012/01/art3full.pdf

U.S. Bureau of Labor Statistics. (2011). *Labor force characteristics by race and ethnicity, 2010.* Retrieved from http://www.bls.gov/cps/cpsrace2010.pdf

U.S. Bureau of Labor Statistics. (2013a). *Employed persons by occupation, race, Hispanic or Latino ethnicity, and sex.* Retrieved from http://www.bls.gov/cps/cpsaat11.pdf

U.S. Bureau of Labor Statistics. (2013b). *Employed persons by sex, occupation, class of worker, full- or part-time status, and race.* Retrieved from http://www.bls.gov/cps/cpsaat12.pdf

U.S. Bureau of Labor Statistics. (2013c). *Median weekly earnings of full-time wage and salary workers by selected characteristics.* Retrieved from http://www.bls.gov/cps/cpsaat37.pdf

U.S. Census Bureau. (2011). *2011 American Community Survey.* Retrieved from http://www.census.gov/acs/www/about_the_survey/2011_acs_improvements/

U.S. Census Bureau. (2012a). *Educational attainment in the United States: 2009: Current population reports.* Retrieved from http://www.census.gov/prod/2012pubs/p20-566.pdf

U.S. Census Bureau. (2012b). *U.S. Census Bureau projections show a slower growing, older, more diverse nation in a half century from now.* Retrieved from http://www.census.gov/newsroom/releases/archives/population/cb12-243.html

U.S. Department of Education, National Center for Education Statistics. (2012). *The condition of education 2012* (NCES 2012-045). Retrieved from http://nces.ed.gov/fastfacts/display.asp?id=72

Valdivia, C., Dozi, P., Jeanetta, S., Flores, L. Y., Martinez, D., & Dannerbeck, A. (2008). The impact of networks and the context of reception on asset accumulation strategies of Latino newcomers in new settlement communities of the Midwest. *American Journal of Agricultural Economics, 90,* 1319–1325.

Valentine, S. (2006). Hispanics' self-esteem, acculturation, and skepticism of women's work. *Journal of Applied Social Psychology, 36,* 206–221.

Vespia, K. M., Fitzpatrick, M. E., Fouad, N. A., Kantamneni, N., & Chen, Y.-L. (2010). Multicultural career counseling: A national survey of competencies and practices. *The Career Development Quarterly, 59,* 54–71.

Walsh, W. B., Bingham, R. P., Brown, M. T., & Ward, C. M. (2001). *Career counseling for African Americans.* Mahwah, NJ: Erlbaum.

Ward, C. M., & Bingham, R. P. (1993). Career assessment of ethnic minority women. *Journal of Career Assessment, 1,* 246–257.

Worthington, R. L., Flores, L. Y., & Navarro, R. L. (2004). Career development in context: Research with people of color. In S. D. Brown & R. W. Lent (Eds.), *Career development and counseling: Putting theory and research to work* (pp. 225–252). Hoboken, NJ: Wiley.

Wrenn, C. G. (1962). The culturally encapsulated counselor. *Harvard Educational Review, 32,* 444–449.

Chapter 4

Empowering Women's Life Choices: An Examination of Gender and Sexual Orientation

> Worldwide, throughout history, one of the most salient predictors of virtually all aspects of one's work and career development is one's gender. In essence, being born male or female is a powerful predictor of a host of life factors including: whether one works inside or outside the home (or both), the type of jobs one perceives as appropriate, the type of jobs one will be hired to perform, how far one is likely to climb, the level and type of harassment one experiences, the amount of money one will receive, the amount of conflict or enrichment one gets from work and family life, the amount of job satisfaction one reports, and ultimately the quality of one's life.
>
> —Heppner, 2013, p. 187

Empowering girls and women to make authentic life choices in ways that provide both economic security and personal meaning is a critical role for career counselors. As we examine intersecting social identities and their impact on career development, gender remains a highly salient aspect influencing women's career choice and adjustment around the world (Hackett & Kohlhart, 2012; Watt & Eccles, 2008).

Although the second wave of feminism brought about important changes in social policy and legislation, there remain a host of gender-related issues influencing the life paths of girls and women (Heppner, 2013; Heppner & Jung, 2013; Ormerod, Joseph, Weitzman, & Winterrowd, 2012; Walsh & Heppner, 2006). For example, a recent United Nations report concluded that (a) women have not achieved equity with men in *any* country; (b) of the world's 1.3 billion poor, nearly 70% are women; (c) between 75% and 80% of the world's 27 million refugees are women and children; (d) out of the world's 1 billion illiterate adults, two thirds are women; (e) the majority of women earn an average of three fourths of the pay of men doing the same work in both developing and developed countries; and (f) women are chronically underrepresented in STEM (science, technology, engineering, and math) careers in developed countries around the world (Hausmann, Tyson, & Zahidi, 2010).

Thus, understanding the gendered context is important to being an effective career counselor. In addition, a woman's sexual orientation can have profound impact on her career development; thus, we also discuss the impact of this important aspect of women's lives on their career development.

To practice in a gender-blind (or sexual orientation–blind) manner as a career counselor can continue to perpetuate stereotypes and further reinforce the status quo. In our view, the profession of career counseling is meant to be quite the opposite. Career counselors should be dream restorers and social activists, they should empower people to resist the status quo if that brings with it discrimination and oppression, and they should be powerful social justice advocates. As a field, counselors have stressed their vision of social justice (Arredondo & Perez, 2003; Ratts, Toporek, & Lewis, 2010), and there is no clearer way for women to achieve social justice than through finding meaningful employment that allows them to have "full and equal participation in a society that is mutually shaped to meet their needs. Social justice includes a vision of society in which the distribution of resources is equitable and all members are physically and psychologically safe and secure" (Bell, 1997, p. 3).

We start this chapter by highlighting key aspects of the gendered context and their gender-specific outcomes. Whole texts (e.g., Walsh & Heppner, 2006) have been written on the topic of women's career development and should be consulted for a more in-depth analysis of these issues. Key issues are discussed here in order to highlight aspects of the gendered context and those specific to lesbian, bisexual, and transgender individuals that may impact our clients most directly. The second part of this chapter suggests specific assessments, techniques, and information to share with clients to make career counseling more empowering for lesbian, bisexual, transgender, and heterosexual women. This part also discusses the impact of gender and sexual orientation on the different phases of career counseling outlined in Chapter 1.

As we begin this chapter, it is important to note that although we have attempted to integrate career research on lesbian, gay, bisexual, and transgender (LGBT) individuals wherever possible, this body of literature, although growing in the last decade, remains quite small and incomplete. Whereas the literature on lesbian women and gay men is small, but growing, the literature on the career development of bisexual and transgender individuals is virtually nonexistent. Thus, we caution the reader that our ability to discuss and offer assistance in working with LGBT clients is limited because of the limited research base. We do, however, believe that it is important for LGBT issues to be addressed in the mainstream career literature, and thus we have tried to include references to this scholarship whenever possible. Two editions of the landmark book *Handbook of Counseling and Psychotherapy With Lesbian, Gay, Bisexual, and Transgender Clients* are now available, offering much valuable information about LGBT issues, including career and vocational issues (Bieschke, Perez, & DeBord, 2006; Perez, DeBord, & Bieschke, 1999; Prince, 2013; Szymanski & Hilton, 2012).

In the next sections we briefly review the literature on critical gender and sexual orientation influences, presenting them in a thematic and developmental progression. They are not, however, exclusive categories, nor are they linear. Men and women, for example, continue to experience the impact of sex role socialization from birth to death. The thematic schema is meant to provide an organizing framework for typical developmental influences and includes sections on the gendered overlay of sex role socialization in childhood, the gendered context of adolescence, and the gendered workplace context.

The Gendered Overlay: Sex Role Socialization in Childhood

The overlay for all of the critical aspects of the gendered context that follow is the pervasive sex role socialization of boys and girls. How we interact with and are reinforced by others from a very young age dramatically alters how we view ourselves and our options. Our acquisition of gender-typed personality traits, interests, and behaviors starts early in life (Matlin, 2012) and is reinforced by parents, teachers, peers, the media, and the church, among others. Occupational stereotyping starts early. Matlin (2012) reported that children between kindergarten and fourth grade become increasingly rigid about which occupations they perceive that men and women can hold. These findings support Gottfredson's (1981, 2005) theory of circumscription and compromise, in which she theorized that children's perceptions of appropriate occupations become circumscribed into a narrow range of acceptable sex-typed career options. This range is generally set by the time the child is 6 to 8 years old and is difficult to modify once set. As Mac Naughton (2007) indicated, "Many studies have highlighted how preschool children can talk in detail about gender marking what clothes you wear. The colors you like, your hairstyle, your voice, your play choices, your likes, your dislikes and your relationships with each other" (p. 263). However, it is important to also remember that gender identity develops alongside other social identities and is made even more complex by its intersection with race, class, and sexual orientation (Mac Naughton, 2007).

The role of sexual orientation identity in the vocational development of lesbian and bisexual women has been the focus of some research. Croteau, Anderson, Distefano, and Kampa-Kokesch (1999) discussed two areas of research that have prompted the most scientific inquiry: (a) Gender role socialization influences the development of vocational interest in gay and lesbian individuals in a distinct manner from this development in heterosexual individuals, and (b) gay and lesbian individuals internalize societal vocational stereotypes and use them to define their structures of opportunity.

Croteau et al. (1999) indicated that gay and lesbian individuals tend to be more gender nontraditional in their career interests than do their heterosexual counterparts. This nontraditionality has two potential outcomes. If gay and lesbian children are discouraged from pursuing nontraditional paths, this may lead to increased indecision, restricted choices, and less career satisfaction. There is some evidence, however, to suggest that lesbian women may be more likely to pursue nontraditional careers and that there may be more support for nontraditional career choice within the lesbian community (Fassinger, 1995, 1996).

In addition, writers have indicated that LGBT individuals may internalize stereotypes about appropriate career fields and limit their choices to ones they believe are appropriate. For example, several studies have provided evidence that LGBT individuals restrict their opportunities for working with children (Croteau et al., 1999). Thus, it appears that for heterosexual, lesbian, or bisexual women, early societal messages about what is gender appropriate may have powerful influences on their eventual career choices. This emphasizes the need for school counselors to play an active role in helping to change these messages before they become firmly implanted in the ways that boys and girls view the world of work.

The Gendered Context of Adolescence

As children enter into adolescence, that critical transition period between childhood and adulthood, a number of important influences shape their views of themselves in relation to the occupational world. This time period is especially critical in the development of a sense of self-identity. Several researchers have looked to the school environment as a major socializing and self-concept-forming influence.

A number of important studies have examined the differential treatment of boys and girls at all levels of the educational experience. In studies that examined gender bias in the classroom, researchers observed bias from the grade school level (Sadker & Sadker, 1994) through the college level (Fischer & Good, 1994; Ossana, Helms, & Leonard, 1992). Although some of the gender bias is blatant, such as professors telling sexist jokes, much of it is more subtle, such as the systematic ignoring of girls' and women's comments by professors, which leads the girls and women to feel devalued or invisible in the academic community. Freeman (1979) labeled this phenomenon the *null environment*. A null environment is one that neither actively discourages nor encourages, but rather ignores, the individual. In Freeman's study of college students, she found that both women and men felt ignored by educational institutions, but men felt more supported by friends and family. This process of ignoring women, which is so characteristic of the null environment, has been referred to as a form of passive discrimination (Betz, 1989). Although there has been growing awareness in this area, recent research has still indicated that in the United States, male and female teachers continue to provide greater attention to their male students' academic work (Good & Brophy, 2003). "Teachers select boys more for special learning opportunities, leadership roles, and academic awards, especially in mathematics and science" (Grant & Kimberly, 2007, p. 573).

Although much early research indicated that there appeared to be some gender bias on the part of school counselors who were poorly informed about women's employment and who reinforced stereotypical options (Betz, 2006), few studies have been conducted since that time to examine current attitudes and practices. Although most counselors are probably now aware of the need not to sex role stereotype occupational choices, it is unclear how more subtle messages are conveyed in the counseling context. Without behavioral research analogous to that conducted in classrooms by Sadker and Sadker (1994), it is difficult to determine what is actually being reinforced by school counselors. The few studies conducted that have examined the role of gender bias in career and lifestyle planning have unfortunately found gender-biased attitudes and practices (Robertson & Fitzgerald, 1990).

Homophobia refers to "systematic discrimination against gays and lesbians. . . . The term points to a sense of panic, suggesting an association with psychic or unconscious motives" (Ghaill, Haywood, & Popoviciu, 2007, p. 549). Research has also indicated that homophobic beliefs and attitudes are prevalent in all aspects of society (e.g., the media, curricula, peer group interactions; Ghaill et al., 2007; Mandel & Vitelli, 2007), and, thus, it is very likely that mental health professionals have acquired many of these attitudes at a conscious or unconscious level. Career counselors must be aware of their own homophobia and not encourage or discourage lesbian clients into certain careers based on stereotypical beliefs.

Although adolescence is for some a time of identity development around tentative career choices, if the adolescent is also involved in the process of sexual identity development, his or her vocational identity can be delayed. In one study, lesbian women reported feeling behind their heterosexual counterparts because of the time and emotional energy they had devoted to their sexual identity development and the coming-out process. For more information about LGBT adolescents, see Hershberger and D'Augelli (1999).

Kerr and her colleagues' (Kerr, Vuyk, & Rea, 2012) extensive research on academically gifted girls and women emphasized that even for this highly talented portion of the population, a lack of guidance and support can have drastic consequences. The authors indicated that what happens to these young women can hardly be called career development; rather, they described it as "a gently downward spiral as gifted young women adjust their interests, aspirations, and achievements to fit their own perceived limitations" (Kerr & Maresh, 1994, p. 207). Moreover, Kerr and her colleagues' research also indicates that although gifted girls and boys are more alike than different in their intelligence, creative abilities, and psychological adjustment, gendered practices in schools and other venues result in the eventual differences we see between males and females in their interests, achievements, and well-being (Kerr et al., 2012).

Thus, the gendered context of childhood and adolescence has a critical influence on the career aspirations of young men and women. As social cognitive learning theory and research makes clear, the earlier these messages are encoded in the schema of the individual, the more difficult they are to alter. Research indicates that when the individual leaves the educational institution and pursues employment, gender and sexual orientation biases continue to be reinforced. For lesbian and bisexual women and transgender individuals, these biases are compounded, as the intersection of multiple minority statuses increases the likelihood that these women will face discrimination based not only on gender but also on sexual orientation, in the forms of homophobia and heterosexism (Prince, 2013).

The Gendered Workplace Context

These gender-based roles for women may form the basis for the continued discrimination in hiring (Betz, 2006), in salaries (Watt & Eccles, 2008), and in sexual harassment on the job (Ormerod et al., 2012; Paludi, 2007) so consistent in the literature. Even if women do exceedingly well, there appears to be what some have referred to as a glass ceiling (Russell, 2006), such that women can rise only so far on the corporate ladder but not reach top-level executive positions. It appears that although there is increased awareness in organizations about the existence of sexual harassment, hostile environments that devalue women still exist, and informal networks that exclude women from top positions still predominate.

There is also convincing evidence that lesbian women experience significantly more employment discrimination than heterosexual women (Bieschke & Toepfer-Hendey, 2006; Ormerod et al., 2012). This is because, in addition to the bias they may receive due to their sex, they also must face the harassment and discrimination that come from our heterosexist, homophobic society. Although it might have become somewhat less socially acceptable to be blatantly discriminatory against some minority groups, research indicates it is still acceptable to express hostility toward lesbians and gay men. Lesbians continue to report fear of losing their jobs should they decide to be open about their sexual orientation. Studies indicate that these fears are not unfounded and that lesbians do face considerable levels of employment discrimination based on their sexual orientation.

Croteau et al. (1999) reported that employment discrimination against LGBT individuals is widespread, with between 25% and 66% of individuals studied reporting discrimination. This is often formal and involves discrimination in hiring, promotion, raises, and limited benefits for partners, but it may also be informal and include a hostile work environment and verbal harassment (Croteau, 1996).

Workplace sexual identity management has been identified in several reviews as being a "core issue in understanding the unique vocational experiences of LGB people" (Lidderdale, Croteau, Anderson, Tovar-Murray, & Davis, 2006, p. 245). The level of concealment of one's sexual orientation has been shown to relate to level of discrimination (Croteau & Lark, 1995). Griffin (1992) identified four categories of vocational identity management: (a) "passing," whereby the individual leads others to believe that he or she is heterosexual; (b) "covering," in which the individual tries to hide his or her orientation at work while not pretending to be heterosexual; (c) "implicitly out," whereby one is honest about one's life but does not actually describe oneself as lesbian or bisexual; and (d) "explicitly out," which involves openly labeling oneself as lesbian or bisexual at work. Griffin hypothesized that the choice of strategy involves a tension between fear of discovery and need for self-integrity (Croteau et al., 1999). Scholars indicate that the strength of this model is its ability to describe the range of strategies for concealment or openness that exist to individuals. However, the model has been criticized for being limited in that "key theoretical questions about how the strategies are learned and how they change over time remain unanswered. The influence of individual and contextual variables is not explained" (Lidderdale et al., 2006, p. 249). Lidderdale and colleagues (2006) developed a workplace sexual identity management model by using the theoretical framework of the social cognitive career choice model (Lent, Brown, & Hackett, 1994). The model presents four segments that nicely depict the multidimensional and conceptual nature of this construct. The four segments are (a) developing learning experiences about sexual identity management, (b) developing personally acceptable identity management strategies, (c) choosing and implementing sexual identity management strategies, and (d) learning from outcomes. Career counselors can use this model with clients to help them understand both contextual variables and the myriad of influences involved in sexual identity management, as well as develop sexual identity management self-efficacy beliefs (Lidderdale et al., 2006).

Gender-Specific Outcomes

The previous sections were an overview of some of the career-related aspects of the gendered environment that appear during early development, during adolescence, and in the workplace. Learning more about aspects of this environment is an important step in improving career counseling for lesbian, bisexual, and heterosexual women. Only when we as counselors have adequate information about the extent of the gendered context and issues relevant to sexual orientation can we be effective in our interventions with clients. This section discusses some of the most prevalent gender-specific outcomes that may result from these environments and that may dramatically influence career counseling. Specifically, these outcomes are limited participation in mathematics-related fields, lower expectations for success, lower self-efficacy beliefs about nontraditional careers, relational focus, and role conflict.

Limited Participation in Math Fields

On the topic of mathematics and girls, there is both good and bad news to report. First the good news: Math performance for girls and women has steadily increased over the past 2 decades, leading Boaler and Irving (2007) to assert, "As we survey the landscape of gender and mathematics relationships in various countries around the world . . . in many countries differences in boys' and girls' mathematics achievement that used to prevail have been eradicated" (p. 287). Various reasons have been posited for this good news—most often that mathematics classrooms have found ways to make math more girl-friendly. The bad news, however, is that in some countries, including the United States, greater math achievement has not led to greater participation in math-related occupations. Occupations that have a strong math or science base are referred to as STEM (science, technology, engineering, and mathematics) occupations. STEM fields are expanding rapidly in the U.S. economy, with a 2002 National Science Foundation study indicating they will grow at a rate 3 times as fast as that of occupations in general. Yet even though the number of women obtaining doctorates in STEM-related fields has increased fivefold in the past quarter century, women represent less than one fourth of the STEM labor market (Fassinger & Asay, 2006).

Given the high number of present and future occupations requiring mathematics skills, math has been labeled the "critical filter" for women's career development (Betz, 1994; 2006, p. 51). For women to have the option to participate in the full range of occupations, it is critical that interventions help women make the step into STEM-related fields. As Fassinger and Asay (2006) pointed out,

> Much of this work will require systemic changes that include: developing educational and workplace policies that affirm and support all workers (e.g., equitably distributed benefits, antidiscrimination statements); instituting educational and workplace practices that help to counter discriminatory attitudes (e.g., training in diversity,

transparent performance review and reward systems); implementing social policies and laws that support families in all diverse forms (e.g., accessible child care, medical and legal benefits available to all families); and, finally, transforming gender socialization practices so that all individuals have the freedom and support to actualize their best selves. (pp. 450–451)

It is important for career counselors to understand the underlying mechanisms and beliefs that help to keep this gender disparity in place. Correll (2010) investigated how boys and girls differ on their beliefs related to their math ability and found that boys assessed their math ability as being stronger even when test scores between boys and girls were exactly the same. Since belief in one's competence is an important predictor of persistence toward a mathematics career, these beliefs are highly salient. Correll concluded, "Boys do not pursue mathematical activities at a higher rate than girls do because they are better in mathematics. They do so, at least partially, because they *think* they are better" (p. 1724). Helping young women believe in their competence would seem like an important step in altering these STEM disparities (Heppner, 2013).

Lower Expectations for Success

Another pervasive outcome of the gendered context seems to be a consistent underestimation of abilities on the part of girls and women. Beginning at a very young age, girls perceive and report their career options to be much narrower than do boys. In a study reported by Unger and Crawford (1992), first- and second-grade children were asked the traditional question "What do you want to be when you grow up?" A total of 33 boys and 33 girls responded. The boys came up with 18 different occupational options, the girls only 8. Girls are significantly more likely to report that they are not smart enough or good enough to attain their desired careers (O'Brien, Friedman, Tipton, & Linn, 2000).

Studies report that college women also consistently indicate lower expectancies for success on exams and other measures of achievement in college (Matlin, 2012). This phenomenon seems to continue throughout a woman's development, with adult women also reporting lower expectations for what they can achieve in their lives. These underestimations were present even when the women's objective performance was found to be better than men's (Matlin, 2012).

Betz (2006) reported that lower expectations for success occur primarily for masculine-stereotyped tasks. Specifically, lower expectations are found for tasks that have as components social comparison, competition, and social evaluation and that lack clear performance feedback. As Betz argued, these are the very characteristics generally necessary for career success. Consequently, if women consistently underestimate their ability to perform in these situations, it is probably harmful to their overall career development.

A longitudinal study by O'Brien and her colleagues (2000) found that over the 5 years of the study, women chose less prestigious careers and more traditional careers than those to which they had aspired as high school seniors. In addition, these women chose careers that underutilized their abilities (O'Brien et al., 2000). Lesbian and bisexual woman may also express more limited expectations for success because of the perception that they will be entering more prejudicial and discriminatory work environments. This perception may limit the range of careers they pursue (Croteau et al., 1999).

Research has also indicated that women's underestimation of their ability is present in ability and interest inventories (Swanson & Lease, 1990). Swanson and Lease's (1990) research supported an earlier finding of Bailey and Bailey (1971), who reported that male college students rated themselves above a "typical male student" and women rated themselves below a "typical female student." Swanson and Lease urged career counselors to supplement self-ratings and to explore the authenticity of ratings whenever possible.

Lower Self-Efficacy Beliefs About Nontraditional Careers

Gender differences continue to persist in occupational pursuits, with women being less represented in sex-nontraditional fields (National Center for Education Statistics, 2012). Research has also indicated that, in addition to not choosing these fields initially, women tend to drop out of nontraditional fields at a higher rate than do men (Jacobs, Chhin, & Bleeker, 2006; Watt, 2006).

One potential reason for this lack of involvement in generally high-paying, high-prestige nontraditional careers is lower self-efficacy beliefs. *Self-efficacy* refers to one's confidence in one's ability to do the tasks necessary in a particular field. If a woman does not feel confident in her ability in a nontraditional field, she is less likely to pursue the field, and, once in the field, is less likely to stay if met with obstacles or barriers. Self-efficacy or confidence in nontraditional occupations is also related to the amount of intrinsic value placed on the occupation (Betz & Hackett, 1983; Larose, Ratelle, Guay, Senecal, & Harvey, 2006).

Family–Work Conflict or Mutual Enhancement

As more and more heterosexual women have left the home to enter the paid labor force, one would expect changes in role expectations to have occurred in the home. Data indicate, however, that heterosexual women who work full time outside the home continue to be responsible for 80% to 90% of the work within the home as well. This appears to be true across ethnic and cultural groups also. Research indicates that working two full-time jobs is placing great strain on female workers. In an examination of the role conflict of home and work responsibilities, lesbian couples were much more committed to an equitable division of home-related tasks than were their heterosexual counterparts. Addressing these unique role conflicts may include dealing with partner differences in sexual orientation, identity management at work, and the issues of benefits being denied to partners (Croteau et al., 1999).

Among heterosexual couples, however, the pattern is quite clear. Betz and Fitzgerald (1987) conducted an extensive review of the literature on the relationship of marital status to career involvement. In Betz's (1994) synopsis of this aspect of their review, she concluded that there is a "strong inverse relationship between being married and number of children and every measurable criterion of career involvement and achievement" (p. 21). Betz and Fitzgerald indicated that based on their review, they believe that role conflict is "the most salient factor in women's career development" (p. 203). Although these studies were done some time ago, recent studies support the same conclusions. Frome, Alfeld, Eccles, and Barber (2008) conducted a longitudinal study of low- to middle-income women and found that their desire for flexibility indeed was a factor in their career choice. The fact that young women still see themselves as needing to take more flexible or family-friendly jobs in order to be able to both work and manage home and family responsibilities appears to remain strong.

Assessments and Techniques for Empowering Women's Choices

The previous section examined several key aspects of the gendered context and their resultant gender-specific outcomes. Now we turn to examining various assessments and techniques for promoting women's awareness and understanding of how gender and sexual orientation have influenced their career development. We first describe assessment techniques for both counselor and client that will help the counselor understand the impact of gender and sexual orientation on the change process in counseling. Then we discuss the importance of helping clients acquire information with which to make more authentic life choices.

Assessing Your Own Counseling Philosophy

As we ask you to assess your philosophy of counseling, it is important for us to clarify our own. Much of what we suggest in actual career counseling strategies flows from this underlying philosophy. A wide diversity of philosophies guides career counseling, and counselors who hold these philosophies can be placed on a continuum. At one end of the continuum are career counselors who view their role as one of matching individuals and occupational roles. These counselors would see their role as largely a technical one: assessing the skills, interests, and abilities of the client and matching that individual to an occupation that would best use those personal characteristics. These counselors would find assessment skills and knowledge of labor market information of most value to them. At the other end of the continuum, and more congruent with our philosophy, are career counselors who view their role as being personal and societal change agents. These counselors use knowledge of assessment and occupational information, along with psychological knowledge and constructs, to understand how the environmental context may be limiting the range of options their clients are currently considering. Thus, the counselors examine and challenge underlying assumptions clients have about themselves and the world of work.

As this philosophy applies directly to the gender context of career planning, we believe it is important to focus on gender and sexual orientation as categories of analysis within the career counseling context. We view the role of the career counselor as one of helping clients to understand and work through the numerous societal obstacles that systematically keep women and men from envisioning and achieving economic security and balancing meaningful achievement and relational connectedness in their lives. We recognize that gender socialization brings with it a host of problems for women (e.g., lower expectations for success, low math participation, occupational stratification and segregation, and family and career conflict) that severely restrict women's aspirations and options. Similarly, as we explore in greater depth in Chapter 5, men's socialization brings with it performance anxiety, restricted emotional expression, limited interpersonal relationships, and shortened life expectancy. Therefore, we view the role of the career counselor as one that challenges gender-based homophobic and heterosexist assumptions and helps clients recapture dreams and restore options that have been discarded along the way.

This philosophy also incorporates affirmative counseling practices. It recognizes homophobia and heterosexism as critical barriers in the lives of lesbians and bisexual women and seeks ways to affirm and enhance the lives of LGBT individuals through career counseling.

This philosophy challenges the counselor to go far beyond the maintenance of the status quo typified by the matching of people and jobs. It calls on each of us to ensure that our clients have the information to make authentic life decisions. In doing so, some of our suggestions will run counter to the popular notion in career counseling that we must respect the client's own decision-making and career choices. Given the weight of gender socialization and the power of homophobia and heterosexism, we believe that many times women and men have not experienced the kind of environmental support and information necessary to lead them to authentic career decisions. This philosophy also emphasizes our role as change agents working for more humane and person-enhancing school and work environments. It views both our individual work with clients and our work in promoting change in the environment as being equally valid.

We urge you to clarify your own philosophy toward career counseling and to consider especially the role of multiple identities and how they impact a person's career path. We highlight here one approach, the critical feminist approach to career counseling with women, as it incorporates many of the important issues that we address in this and other chapters. We also present the construct of LGBT affirmativeness. We hope that both of these models will serve as a starting point for your own thinking about critical elements of your philosophy in working with women in career counseling.

A Critical Feminist Approach to Career Counseling With Women
(Chronister, McWhirter, & Forrest, 2006; McWhirter, 1994)

This model or approach to career counseling with diverse women is based on McWhirter's (1994) empowerment model. More recently, Chronister and her colleagues (2006) described the model in depth and applied it to cases. Readers interested in a more in-depth description of this approach are encouraged to investigate this source. We want to highlight this specific model of career counseling with women as we feel it complements and enhances many of the aspects of this book and our own model of the career counseling process. This model seems particularly important, as it embraces the concept of empowerment and, hence, has particular utility in working with diverse women—especially women of color, immigrant women, lesbian women, women living in poverty, and disabled women. Thus, it is in keeping with the social justice goals that we believe are so critical to the work we do as career counselors.

First of all, it is important to understand what is meant by *empowerment* in this particular model:

> The process by which people, organizations or groups who are powerless or marginalized (a) become aware of the power dynamics at work in their life contexts, (b) develop the skills and capacity for gaining some reasonable control over their lives, (c) which they exercise, (d) without infringing on the rights of others, and (e) which coincides with actively supporting the empowerment of others in their community. (Chronister et al., 2006, p. 170; see also McWhirter, 1994)

This approach has five constructs, the five Cs, to depict its central tenets. We believe these five are of critical importance to the career counseling process and complement and enhance many aspects of the career counseling process model we present in this text. Thus, we describe these components and highlight parallels within our own model and thinking.

Collaboration. This C speaks to the active roles necessary for both client and counselor in the career counseling process. This construct fits so well with our placement of the working alliance at the center of our model. Collaboration emphasizes that counselor and client work together to establish the goals of counseling, the tasks that will help to achieve those goals, and the importance of the relationship or bond between the counselor and client. In so doing, collaboration forms the very core of the process in our model.

Competence. This C speaks to the importance of recognizing and using the client's skills and helping him or her to develop new skills as well. It fits so well with our notions of building on strengths and specifically with using instruments such as the Clifton StrengthsFinder (see Chapter 14) to help clients identify and use their strengths. The tenet of competence seems rooted in the idea that every client comes with strengths and that we should start from there rather than looking for pathology and weakness—we assess and reinforce strengths.

Context. The third critical C is context. We believe context to be crucial in understanding an individual woman's career development. The ecological model (Cook, Heppner, & O'Brien, 2005) presented in Chapter 2 emphasizes most strongly the systems and subsystems that make up an individual's ecology. We believe any vocational behavior to be an act in context and, as such, intertwined with one's macro-, exo-, meso-, and microsystems. As the scope of whom we serve in career counseling becomes increasingly broad (immigrant women, women in poverty, etc.), it is critical that the context of each woman's life be central to understanding and assisting with her own personal empowerment.

Critical Consciousness. McWhirter (1994) drew on the integrated work of both Paulo Freire (1970) and Ignacio Martin-Baro (1994) in discussing the construct of *critical consciousness*, which she defined as involving the dual processes of power analysis (or identifying how power is manifested and expressed in a woman's life context) and critical self-reflection that generates awareness of how women can transform those dynamics. To be able to help clients do this kind of thinking, McWhirter emphasized the importance of counselors developing their own critical consciousness. She suggested that this be done through studying multicultural literature, having cross-cultural experiences, talking with people from different communities, and engaging in intense self-reflection.

This is the type of thinking and learning we urge counselors to do throughout this book. It is probably the most basic piece of advice we can give—that counselors must know themselves, their own prejudices and biases, the way they hold and use power, and the way they are controlled by others. They must know the ways in which racism, sexism, heterosexism, and all the other "-isms" affect them as counselors. All of this deep and many times hard learning and reflection is critical to really being able to empower others to look at the impact of these forces in their own lives.

Community. The final C is community, which entails both helping women find community to support them on their life journey and helping women find places where they can empower themselves by empowering others in their community. Early work with rape survivors and battered women illustrates the power that helping others can have in empowering oneself.

We believe McWhirter's (1994) critical feminist approach to career counseling with women is useful in operationalizing the essential elements of empowerment and thus making it more usable and achievable with the women we seek to help.

LGBT Affirmativeness (Worthington, Savoy, & Vernaglia, 2001)

LGBT affirmativeness among heterosexuals is conceptualized as "the range of attitudes beliefs, emotions and behaviors that express and assert the positive valuing of the sexual identity of, and an understanding of the realities faced by LGBT individuals within an oppressive society" (Worthington et al., 2001, p. 2). Affirmative individuals are not only knowledgeable about LGBT issues but also understanding of and comfortable with their own sexual identity and diverse sexual orientations. Having contact and involvement with LGBT individuals is an important component of the process of becoming an LGBT-affirmative career counselor. This contact is presumed to occur not only in one's professional role but also in other contexts, including personal, social, and familial networks. The model describes five states: Passive Conformity, Revelation and Exploration, Tentative Commitment, Synthesis and Integration, and Active Commitment. Becoming LGBT affirmative is a developmental process of movement from an unexamined, unconscious heterosexist or homophobic construction of the world; through a phase of intellectualized understanding of what it means to be LGBT affirmative; and finally to a more fully integrated level of awareness and expression, in which knowledge achieved at earlier phases is incorporated into one's personal, professional, and political spheres. LGBT-affirmative counselors use their self-awareness, knowledge, skills, and involvement with LGBT individuals to inform their practice with all clients, including lesbian, gay, bisexual, and heterosexual clients.

Helping Clients Acquire Information for Making Authentic Life Choices

In addition to continually working on your own philosophy of career counseling with women, it is also important to build a repertoire of useful tools and techniques, processes, and discussion points that you can draw on when working with women. This section contains two informal assessments: (a) the Environmental Assessment of the Gendered Context Growing Up and (b) the Environmental Assessment of the Gendered Context of Work. These assessments are followed by a discussion of ways to increase the authenticity of career decision making through knowledge that includes (a) informing clients about the rewards and costs of gender role traditionality; (b) teaching clients how to alter gender- and homophobia-based self-efficacy beliefs; (c) informing clients about the importance of continuing in math and science careers and considering nontraditional career fields; (d) reinforcing the importance of valuing the unique characteristics that women traditionally possess; (e) using specific awareness and skills to work with the unique issues of lesbian and bisexual women; and (f) educating yourself on the specific needs of groups of women, such as women living in poverty, disabled women, and others.

Environmental Assessment of the Gendered Context Growing Up
Although research indicates that sex role socialization is pervasive, there are numerous individual differences in both extent of exposure and impact. We recommend that an assessment be done to examine the level to which each client has been influenced by traditional sex role socialization. This assessment should include an examination of the various sources of active support and discouragement, as well as neutral treatment, that has influenced the client's life journey and perceived choices. Although these assessments will vary depending on life circumstances, the following questions provide a starting point:

- Think back to your childhood. What messages did you receive about the career options you might pursue?
- Who most actively supported the development of your interests and skills? What form did that active support take?
- Can you think of any discouragement you received regarding a potential interest area? What form did the discouragement take?
- In grade school (high school, college), did you feel support, discouragement, or a neutral atmosphere for the development of your interests?
- Were you more actively encouraged to pursue sex role–appropriate interests than nontraditional interests?
- If you were to graph your own sense of personal self-efficacy throughout your life, how would that graph look?
- Can you think of occupational areas you once dreamed of that you discarded at some point in your life? What were they, and what do you remember about the reasons why you discarded them?

This assessment can be done as part of the career counseling session or provided as a homework assignment for the client to ponder and write about independently. You may also want to use some variation of these questions while conducting a career genogram (see Chapter 11). The client can then process these reflections in the following sessions.

Environmental Assessment of the Gendered Context of Work
Much of the literature on career development focuses on adjustment or adaptation to the work environment. Fitting into the work culture and sharing similar interests and

skills as those currently employed in the field have both been seen as valued career skills. Although not questioning their overall importance, researchers have begun to point out the toxic quality of some work environments that promote neither the physical nor the psychological health of their workers (Carayon, 1993). In this chapter, we point to research on sexual harassment, the glass ceiling, lack of mentoring and support, and stereotypical definitions of working women as sex objects or iron maidens. Thus, fitting into these environments cannot be seen as an appropriate goal. Research indicates that these unhealthy environments may be especially detrimental to individuals who have previously been underrepresented and marginalized in particular work fields. Women and men who work in nontraditional fields may find themselves being asked to adapt to environments that may not value their uniqueness and in which they might suffer bias, discrimination, and harassment. Thus, it may be vitally important that career counselors help clients analyze the work environment. Is it an environment in which the goal of adaptation is a healthy choice? Or does the environment support a culture that is basically unhealthy for the individual worker? Again, although these assessments will vary greatly depending on the individual circumstances of the work environment, the following questions might be a starting point:

- In general, how does your work environment feel to you? Warm and friendly? Cold and hostile? What words would you use to describe your work atmosphere?
- What messages have you received in your work environment about what options you might pursue within the organization? Do these options seem limited due to your sex or your sexual orientation?
- What are the signs that your environment at work is healthy for the individuals who work there?
- Are your skills and interests being actively promoted and developed within the organization?
- Are the unique aspects that characterize you (which may not be characteristic of the environmental culture) valued in your work environment?
- Can you think of subtle or blatant experiences of harassment or discouragement experienced in your work environment that have diminished your sense of personhood?
- Have there been times when you felt singled out or ignored because of your sex or your sexual orientation?

Once an environmental assessment of this kind has been conducted, the counselor's role involves helping the client determine whether fitting in, becoming a change agent, or getting out of the system is the most healthy and functional life choice. Thus, these assessments are ways of helping you gain information about the influences of the gendered context on the individual. Although they should be adapted to fit the individual circumstances of the situation, they are provided here to stimulate your thinking about ways of addressing gender and sexual orientation issues in career counseling sessions.

Inform Women About the Rewards and Costs of Occupational Gender Role Traditionality

Research on the importance of achievement through paid employment in the lives of men and women is important knowledge to share with clients. Data are compelling that show that women who do not have outlets for achievement outside the homemaker role are more likely to suffer from psychological distress (Betz, 2006) and lower self-esteem than their employed counterparts. Although respecting our clients' ultimate choices is important, it is critical to examine the authenticity of those choices. Authentic choices can only be made through knowledge of both the costs and the rewards of those choices.

In addition to the psychological benefits of meaningful paid employment, women need to know about the likelihood that they will be economically independent during their lifetimes. More than two thirds of women in the United States are divorced, widowed, separated, single, or married to men whose income is below the poverty level (U.S. Department of Labor, 2007). Although most young women optimistically approach relationships with a vision of an economically stable future, they should be aware of the reality of many women's lives.

Thus, women need more information about adherence to traditional gender role prescriptions and the occurrence of psychological distress as well as financial need. The career counselor is in a unique role to explore how much the client already knows about these costs and rewards and to furnish additional information as needed.

Teach Clients How to Alter Gender- and Homophobia-Based Self-Efficacy Beliefs
Self-efficacy has been defined as "people's judgments in their capabilities to organize and execute courses of action required to attain designated types of performance" (Bandura, 1986, p. 391). Self-efficacy has been shown to predict choice of behavioral activities, effort expended on these activities, persistence despite obstacles, and actual performance (Bandura, 1977). The development of self-efficacy beliefs has been demonstrated to be facilitated by the following conditions: (a) performance attainment, or trying a behavior and having success with it; (b) verbal persuasion, or being told by others that you can do it; (c) vicarious reinforcement, or seeing others similar to oneself successfully perform a behavior; and (d) physiological input, or bodily sensations that give you information about how you are doing (Bandura, 1977, 1982).

Although gender-based self-efficacy beliefs may be embedded in how clients view themselves, it is important that career counselors provide information about the changeable nature of these beliefs. If men and women know that these beliefs can be altered, and if they know the procedures needed for change, they are in a better position to decide whether to alter these beliefs. Hackett and Betz (1981) hypothesized that Bandura's (1977, 1982) theoretical framework would have particular relevance to the area of women's career development, sparking a plenitude of important research on the impact of self-efficacy beliefs on career-related behavior. In the first empirical test of the application of Bandura's theory to women's career development, Hackett and Betz demonstrated considerable support for its application. Additional research has demonstrated that self-efficacy is related to performance in a myriad of other domains, such as academics (Bores-Rangel, Church, Szendre, & Reeves, 1990; Multon, Brown, & Lent, 1991), math (Pajares & Miller, 1995), and work-related behavior (Sadri & Robertson, 1993). Lent et al. (1994) also expanded Bandura's work by advancing a social cognitive theory of career and academic interest, choice, and performance. Using meta-analytic data, they suggested a direct relationship between self-efficacy and performance in academic and vocational areas. Social cognitive theory has also been applied to LGBT individuals (Morrow, Gore, & Campbell, 1996).

Career counselors can promote women's self-efficacy through a variety of theoretically based strategies. Performance attainment as a source of self-efficacy can be facilitated through women being encouraged to try out a variety of experiences and roles similar to one they might be considering. Internships, part-time jobs, and volunteer experiences provide valuable ways for women to realize that they are capable of more than they had thought was in their realm of possibilities. Verbal persuasion may come from any significant person in a woman's life, including her counselor. Letting the client know that you believe in her ability to accomplish her goals can be a powerful message. Vicarious reinforcement, another important source of self-efficacy beliefs, involves the client seeing other women who are similar to herself succeed in roles she is considering. Career counselors can help locate such role models and make arrangements for formal or informal contact. Thus, it is important that career counselors let women know that it is possible to alter their gender-based interest and behavior patterns. Giving clients specific information about how they can alter their beliefs in their abilities is an important step toward empowering them.

Inform Clients About the Importance of Pursuing Math and Science
Although the evidence reported earlier in this chapter about the occupational importance of continuing in math and science courses has been in the professional literature for a number of years, there is little evidence that parents and children are aware of these data. Career counselors can take an active role in helping girls and women understand the role of mathematics and science in their career development. The following are three specific techniques career counselors might use:

1. Girls should be presented with specific data, perhaps in graphic form, that depict the continually narrowing range of options available to those who lack math and science backgrounds.
2. Because girls and women are now taking more math courses than previously, it is important to reinforce with them the wide range of attractive occupations that use these skills.
3. The perception of how sociable people in the math and science fields are has also been the subject of investigation. For example, Lips (1992) found that study participants who believed that scientists are sociable were more likely to enjoy math and science courses and stated more interest in pursuing math- and science-related careers. These data highlight the importance of counselors exposing clients to role models who can help break preexisting stereotypes about mathematical and scientific occupations.

Valuing What Is Female: Integrating the Self-in-Relation Theory Into Career Counseling

One of the gender-related outcomes presented earlier in this chapter is that self-concept may be formed differently by men and women, with the relational component more critical to women's identity formation than to men's. This difference has a host of implications for both the process and the content of work with female clients:

1. Perhaps one of the most critical roles for the career counselor is helping female clients to value their uniqueness as women. From the earliest years, and across cultures, there is a valuing of masculine traits over feminine ones and of boys over girls (Basow, 1992). This phenomenon continues throughout life in varied environmental situations, often resulting in a devaluing of the self. Therefore, it is important that the counselor value the strong preferences women may have for connectedness and relationship and reinforce these characteristics as unique strengths rather than signs of immature dependency, as traditionally has been the case.
2. The counselor might help the client explore whether dissatisfaction in a work setting is a result of a lack of perceived connection with others. It may be especially important to help the client determine the advantages and disadvantages of various courses of action: Does she try to find a different work environment that better meets her relational needs, or does she try to change her need for connection from 9 to 5 and fit into the work environment? Does she try to change her work environment to make it a place that better fits her needs? Each of these courses of action requires additional assistance. For example, if the woman decides to change her work environment, the counselor can help her identify work environments that may promote a greater sense of relationship.

3. Although it seems critically important to overtly demonstrate that you value your client's need for connection and her relational competence, especially given how devalued these characteristics are in society, it is still important that the client examine the benefits as well as the costs of both the separate and connected perspectives when making career decisions (Hotelling & Forrest, 1985). The predominance of women in social occupations (e.g., nursing or teaching) may enable women to meet needs for connection and relationship, but because of the devalued status of these occupations, they may not provide the income needed to sustain a household. The counselor can also help the client identify when her emphasis on connection may lead to role overload and conflict because of too many relational demands. Especially during the stressful time of a career transition, the counselor may also need to emphasize to the client the importance of caring for her own wants and needs.

4. During the career counseling process, a client's relational perspective may mean that she would benefit from a greater connection with you as the counselor (Nelson, 1996), and she may wish for more self-disclosure from you about your own career and life planning decisions. This may be one way of building a strong working alliance with the client. Moreover, she may react negatively to, and find little benefit in, vocational exploration tools that she perceives as lacking human connection (e.g., computerized career information systems, batteries of vocational assessment instruments). One client recently characterized her career counseling experience as follows: "They just took my data, referred me to some boxes, and shuffled me out the door—no human connection. This is my life I want help with."

5. Although "the mainstream of vocational theory includes the implicit assumption that a career is a vehicle or opportunity leading to realization of self" (Forrest & Mikolaitis, 1986, p. 86), a client may benefit from a close examination of how her career choices also affect others in her relational community. It may, therefore, be beneficial for you to examine the importance the client perceives her career planning decisions will have for others in her environment (partner, children, employer, etc.). This self versus relational focus forms the theoretical basis for one of the factors on the Career Transitions Inventory, which is discussed in depth in Chapter 13. One factor, called *decision independence*, includes such items as "Career choices affect others and I must take the needs of others into account when making a career transition." The Career Transitions Inventory may be helpful in assessing a client's relational focus as it relates to her career decision making.

These ways of altering our view of healthy identity development to include the relational component may influence career counseling from both a content and a process perspective. The relational component emphasizes the importance of the life career perspective (McDaniels & Gysbers, 1992) in career counseling, in which one's vocation is only a part of the total life career.

In addition, this knowledge may be useful to clients to help them make the most well-informed decisions possible. Other information may be valuable given the client's specific demographics or situation. The Walsh and Heppner (2006) text provides in-depth research on a variety of topics, such as counseling women in management, women in science and engineering, dual-career relationships, immigrant women, women in poverty, and so on. This type of current information is indispensable when one is helping clients sort through gender-related life issues.

In Chapter 1 we outline a process of career counseling that consists of two major phases and a number of subphases. In the next section of the current chapter we discuss ways of integrating the issues relevant to the gendered context into this broad career planning process. Although more generic issues related to this model are presented in Chapters 8 through 17, the next section highlights those aspects of each phase that may have gender-related implications for girls and women.

Competence in Working With Lesbian and Bisexual Women

Although most of the recommendations made for working with girls and women in general are salient for lesbian and bisexual women, a host of unique skills and areas of awareness also need our attention. The following five skills are critical for becoming an effective career counselor for LGBT clients:

1. Being familiar with the Association for Lesbian, Gay, Bisexual, and Transgender Issues in Counseling's *Competencies for Counseling LGBQQIA Individuals* and *Competencies for Counseling With Transgender Clients* and the American Psychological Association's *Guidelines for Psychological Practice With Lesbian, Gay, and Bisexual Clients*. These guidelines provide a wealth of helpful suggestions for all human service providers, including career counselors. They are available online at www.algbtic.org/resources/competencies.html and www.apa.org/pi/lgbc/publications/guidelines.aspx, respectively.
2. Understanding sexual orientation identity development and its role in influencing career development. Excellent chapters have been written to aid in this understanding (see Broido, 1999; Fukuyama & Ferguson, 1999; Reynolds & Hanjorgiris, 1999). In addition, McCarn and Fassinger (1996) developed a model of lesbian development, and Fassinger and Miller (1996) developed a model of sexual minority identity formation.
3. Understanding and helping clients with issues of workplace discrimination and sexual identity management by using current models such as the workplace sexual identity management model (see Croteau et al., 1999; Lidderdale et al., 2006).
4. Understanding how societal messages about sexual orientation influence career interests, choices, and perceptions of the structure of opportunity for LGBT clients (Croteau et al., 1999).
5. Developing an awareness of one's own homophobic or heterosexist prejudices and taking active steps to overcome them and develop LGBT-affirmative attitudes. The work by Worthington et al. (2001) represents important new contributions in the area of LGBT affirmativeness.

The Career Counseling Process: Placing Gender Issues Within the Existing Counseling Process

Client Goal or Problem Identification, Clarification, and Specification

Identification—Opening and Forming the Working Alliance
The opening phase of career counseling has as its central goals (a) identifying the client's goals or problems and related internal thoughts and feelings, (b) forming a working alliance, and (c) defining and clarifying the client–counselor relationship and responsibilities. In planning this phase with the gendered context in mind, you as a counselor should keep in mind the following:

- You should help the client examine her goals through a gender and sexual orientation filter. Which goals are motivated out of socialization needs? Which presenting problems result from environmental pressures or a diminished sense of self? Are internal thoughts and feelings the result of socialized feelings of devaluation or lowered efficacy? Does the client appear to be setting authentic goals based on a full knowledge of relevant information? Are there references to discarded dreams?

- As you begin to develop the working alliance, you should be especially aware of the client's level of feminist identity development and what impact that might have on the relationship you are building. If a client is in the embeddedness–emancipation phase, for example, it may be particularly important for her to work with a gender-aware female counselor. A gender-aware man may also be acceptable, depending upon her current level of anger and separatism. Building the working alliance means building a bond of collaboration and hope. The client needs to see you as someone who understands her situation and relates to her concerns. Self-disclosure of relevant and appropriate information from your own life may help to build the bond. As you begin building the working alliance, this is also a time to reinforce client strengths and to stress the importance of valuing unique, traditionally female characteristics.
- As you work with lesbian and bisexual clients, be aware of their sexual orientation identity development and how this may impact their career development. This knowledge is also important in helping you gauge what interventions may be helpful. For example, if the client is at a very early stage in her sexual identity development, she may not be ready to discuss how her sexual identity influences her career development. Additionally, awareness on your part is important in communicating LGBT-affirmative attitudes and behaviors. Consideration of heterosexist assumptions, use of language (*partner* vs. *spouse*), and behaviors are essential to establishing a safe, trusting working alliance.
- When clarifying the client–counselor relationship and each individual's responsibilities, it is important to discuss your philosophy of counseling, particularly those aspects that relate to counseling women. If you prefer a feminist or gender-aware counseling relationship—a collaborative working relationship emphasizing equality—then this needs to be communicated. Because many clients come to counselors seeking an expert who will give them advice, this collaborative relationship may be foreign. The role of the environment in shaping the individual may also be an important philosophical issue to discuss. If you believe it is your responsibility to challenge gender-based and heterosexist assumptions, the client should know this. The client has a right to informed consent in the choice of a career counselor. The counselor's philosophical base is an important consideration for a client when making that choice.

Clarification—Gathering Client Information

The clarification and information-gathering subphase of the career counseling process has as its central goal learning more about the client.

Here, any or all of the assessment measures discussed earlier in this chapter can be used to supplement other standardized or nonstandardized assessment measures you consider appropriate to use. Using the Environmental Assessment of the Gendered Context Growing Up or the Environmental Assessment of the Gendered Context of Work would be appropriate ways of gathering information about the client's experiences that may have an impact on her career planning process.

If standardized tests are used, it will be important to discuss issues related to test bias and how women typically underestimate their ability on such measures.

Card sorts (see Chapter 12) are recommended as a way to understand more about how the client is processing her interests and skills related to each career field. Card sorts allow the counselor to challenge beliefs regarding the client's abilities in nontraditional career fields.

Specification—Understanding and Hypothesizing About Client Information and Behavior

The specification subphase of the career counseling process has as its central goal understanding the client more fully and hypothesizing about her unique dynamics and the psychological and environmental forces at work.

This phase probes deeper to understand more about how the client makes meaning out of herself and her occupational world. As we look through the gender filter, we try to understand the life choices from both an individual and an environmental perspective. We try to assess the authenticity of the client's earlier choices and those she has ahead of her.

In this phase, providing knowledge to the client to help her understand the impact of gender is appropriate. Depending on the situation, this may involve talking about the importance of continuing in the math and science fields, the ways in which self-efficacy beliefs about nontraditional fields can be altered, or what we know about the costs and benefits of traditional gender role beliefs.

This is an important phase in helping lesbian clients understand how various aspects of their sexual orientation may influence the career planning process. It is also important that the counselor understand the phenomenon of internalized homophobia and help the client recognize whether she has internalized heterosexist messages and beliefs. It is important for the counselor to recognize that sexual identity development represents an "emergent continuous life process" (Reynolds & Hanjorgiris, 1999, p. 36).

Techniques such as the genogram (see Chapter 11) may be used in this phase of counseling to understand better the client's gender-influenced life choices from a family systems perspective. This may also be the time to have the client construct a lifeline to help her understand issues such as how her self-efficacy beliefs have changed over time or what role compromise has played in her life choices.

Client Goal or Problem Resolution

This second phase of the career counseling process is one of taking action. Here we move from gathering and evaluating aspects of the gendered environment and their resultant gender-specific outcomes to actually taking steps to act on this information. Getting to this phase means that you have worked through all the major aspects of the client's situation and that she is in a position to make an authentic life decision based on as complete a set of information about herself and the work world as possible.

Taking Action

Whether the action is deciding to attend a vocational–technical school for auto body repair training, change from pre-med to a nursing program, join the Peace Corps to improve the lives of Third World women, or start one's own business importing ethnic textiles and baskets, a variety of gender-related issues should be explored. A few examples of these are the following:

- The client should practice interviewing skills so that she will not devalue herself in the job interview and will be able to recognize sex bias and homophobia in the interview and early signs of an unhealthy work environment.
- The client should learn the importance of networking with other women to gain support and should find female role models who have dealt with similar situations.
- A strong, self-enhancing résumé must adequately represent her skills and background. Women tend to underestimate their abilities on résumés, and, to make matters worse, evidence also shows that résumés are given less favorable ratings by employers when only the names are changed from male to female. Thus, it is critical that women have the strongest possible written presentation of their credentials.

Developing Career Goals and Plans of Action
In this subphase, the client benefits from a variety of interventions that help her develop an individual career plan. This happens when all the individual pieces gained from the earlier phases of counseling are brought together and integrated into a unique plan. This plan helps to make the step from the nurturing environment of the counseling setting to the outside world a little less frightening. When a plan is made and small, manageable steps are identified, the client can begin to feel a sense of confidence in her ability to make changes in her life. In addition to identifying the steps that the client will take, it is also important to identify potential stumbling blocks along the way and develop plans for overcoming them. This is a time for talking about the "what ifs": What if your boss refuses to discuss your request for additional training? What if you suffer harassment after you choose to come out about your sexual preference at work? What if you do not get into the vocational–technical program you desire? By having a plan of action, clients feel more confident in this phase of the process. In addition to identifying barriers, it is also important to identify the strengths that each woman brings to the situation and to find ways of reminding her about these strengths.

Evaluating Results and Closing the Relationship
The closure session is a time for evaluation of goal progress and process. When examining the closure session through a gender filter, consider the following:

- Reflect on the journey the career counseling process has taken—what the client brought in to the first session and how the goals of the sessions changed over time. This is an important time to reinforce what the woman brought to the session—her strengths, openness, and courage to explore the roots of some of her beliefs and choices—so that she owns her part in what made this counseling process successful.
- Discuss the relationship between the counselor and client over time. How did the working alliance develop? How were tears in the alliance mended? How do both parties feel about termination?
- Let the client know of your willingness for her to return if she wants more help or just wants to let you know how things are going. It may be especially important for female clients, given their greater relational focus, to know that the support system you have provided during counseling will remain available should they have difficulties after counseling.

Fortunately, a great deal has been written over the past decade about the career development of women. Although less has focused specifically on the career development of lesbian and bisexual women, there has been significant progress made in this field as well (Croteau et al., 1999).

Closing Thoughts

We have referred to numerous sources of both empirical and conceptual literature in this chapter. The purpose of this chapter was to highlight key aspects of the gendered context; to identify their resultant outcomes in female clients; to discuss strategies and assessments for integrating knowledge of the gendered environment into counseling sessions; and, specifically, to indicate key issues of relevance at each stage of the career planning process for lesbian, bisexual, and heterosexual women. In doing so, we hope to have prepared the counselor to feel more personal efficacy in empowering the choices of women through career counseling.

References

Arredondo, P., & Perez, P. (2003). Expanding multicultural competence through social justice leadership. *The Counseling Psychologist, 31,* 282–289.

Bailey, R. C., & Bailey, D. G. (1971). Perceived ability in relation to actual ability and academic achievement. *Journal of Clinical Psychology, 27,* 461–463.

Bandura, A. (1977). *Social learning theory.* Englewood Cliffs, NJ: Prentice Hall.

Bandura, A. (1982). Self-efficacy mechanism in human agency. *American Psychologist, 37,* 122–147.

Bandura, A. (1986). *Social foundations of thought and action: A social cognitive theory.* Englewood Cliffs, NJ: Prentice Hall.

Basow, S. A. (1992). *Gender: Stereotypes and roles* (3rd ed.). Pacific Grove, CA: Brooks/Cole.

Bell, L. A. (1997). Theoretical foundations for social justice education. In M. Adams, L. A. Bell, & P. Griffin (Eds.), *Teaching for diversity and social justice: A sourcebook* (pp. 3–15). New York, NY: Routledge.

Betz, N. E. (1989). The null environment and women's career development. *The Counseling Psychologist, 17,* 136–144.

Betz, N. E. (1994). Career counseling for women in the sciences and engineering. In W. B. Walsh & S. H. Osipow (Eds.), *Career counseling for women* (pp. 1–41). Hillsdale, NJ: Erlbaum.

Betz, N. E. (2006). Basic issues and concepts in the career development and counseling of women. In W. B. Walsh & M. J. Heppner (Eds.), *Handbook of career counseling for women* (2nd ed., pp. 45–74). Mahwah, NJ: Erlbaum.

Betz, N. E., & Fitzgerald, L. (1987). *The career psychology of women.* New York, NY: Academic Press.

Betz, N. E., & Hackett, G. (1983). The relationship of career-related self-efficacy expectations to perceived career options in college women and men. *Journal of Counseling Psychology, 28,* 399–410.

Bieschke, K. J., Perez, R. M., & DeBord, K. A. (Eds.). (2006). *Handbook of counseling and psychotherapy with lesbian, gay, bisexual, and transgender clients* (2nd ed.). Washington, DC: American Psychological Association.

Bieschke, K. J., & Toepfer-Hendey, E. (2006). Career counseling with lesbian women. In W. B. Walsh & M. J. Heppner (Eds.), *Handbook of career counseling for women* (2nd ed., pp. 351–386). Mahwah, NJ: Erlbaum.

Boaler, J., & Irving, T. S. (2007). Mathematics. In B. Bank (Ed.), *Gender and education: An encyclopedia* (pp. 287–293). Westport, CT: Praeger.

Bores-Rangel, E., Church, A. T., Szendre, D., & Reeves, C. (1990). Self-efficacy in relation to occupational consideration in minority high school equivalency students. *Journal of Counseling Psychology, 39,* 498–508.

Broido, E. M. (1999). Constructing identity: The nature and meaning of lesbian, gay, and bisexual identities. In R. M. Perez, K. A. DeBord, & K. J. Bieschke (Eds.), *Handbook of counseling and psychotherapy with lesbian, gay, and bisexual clients* (1st ed., pp. 13–34). Washington, DC: American Psychological Association.

Carayon, P. (1993). Effect of electronic performance monitoring on job design and worker stress: A review of the literature and conceptual model. *Human Factors, 35,* 3–11.

Chronister, K. M., McWhirter, E. H., & Forrest, L. (2006). A critical feminist approach to career counseling with women. In W. B. Walsh & M. J. Heppner (Eds.), *Handbook of career counseling for women* (2nd ed., pp. 167–192). Mahwah, NJ: Erlbaum.

Cook, E. P., Heppner, M. J., & O'Brien, K. M. (2005). An ecological model of women's career development. *Journal of Multicultural Counseling and Development, 33,* 165–179.

Correll, S. J. (2010). Gender and the career choice process: The role of biased self-assessments. *American Journal of Sociology, 106,* 1691–1730.

Croteau, J. M. (1996). Research on the work experiences of lesbian, gay, and bisexual people: An integrative review of methodology findings. *Journal of Vocational Behavior, 48,* 195–209.

Croteau, J. M., Anderson, M. Z., Distefano, T. M., & Kampa-Kokesch, S. (1999). Lesbian, gay, and bisexual vocational psychology: Reviewing foundations and planning construction. In R. M. Perez, K. A. DeBord, & K. J. Bieschke (Eds.), *Handbook of counseling and psychotherapy with lesbian, gay, and bisexual clients* (1st ed., pp. 383–408). Washington, DC: American Psychological Association.

Croteau, J. M., & Lark, J. S. (1995). On being lesbian, gay or bisexual in student affairs: A national survey of experience on the job. *NASPA Journal, 32,* 189–197.

Fassinger, R. E. (1995). From invisibility to integration: Lesbian identity in the workplace. *The Career Development Quarterly, 44,* 149–167.

Fassinger, R. E. (1996). Notes from the margins: Integrating lesbian experience into vocation psychology of women. *Journal of Vocational Behavior, 48,* 160–175.

Fassinger, R. E., & Asay, P. A. (2006). Career counseling for women in science, technology, engineering, and mathematics (STEM) fields. In W. B. Walsh & M. J. Heppner (Eds.), *Handbook of career counseling for women* (2nd ed., pp. 427–452). Mahwah, NJ: Erlbaum.

Fassinger, R. E., & Miller, B. A. (1996). Validation of an inclusive model of sexual minority identity formation on a sample of gay men. *Journal of Homosexuality, 32,* 53–78.

Fischer, A. R., & Good, G. E. (1994). Gender, self, and others: Perceptions of the campus environment. *Journal of Counseling Psychology, 41,* 343–355.

Forrest, L., & Mikolaitis, N. (1986). The relational component of identity: An expansion of career development theory. *The Career Development Quarterly, 35,* 76–88.

Freeman, J. (1979). How to discriminate against women without really trying. In J. Freeman (Ed.), *Women: A feminist perspective* (2nd ed., pp. 194–208). Palo Alto, CA: Mayfield.

Freire, P. (1970). *Pedagogy of the oppressed.* New York, NY: Continuum.

Frome, P. M., Alfeld, C. J., Eccles, J., & Barber, B. L. (2008). Is the desire for a family-flexible job keeping young women out of male dominated occupations? In H. M. G. Watt & J. S. Eccles (Eds.), *Gender and occupational outcomes: Longitudinal assessment of individuals, social and cultural influences* (pp. 195–214). Washington, DC: American Psychological Association.

Fukuyama, M. A., & Ferguson, A. D. (1999). Lesbian, gay, and bisexual people of color: Understanding cultural complexity and managing multiple oppressions. In R. M. Perez, K. A. DeBord, & K. J. Bieschke (Eds.), *Handbook of counseling and psychotherapy with lesbian, gay, and bisexual clients* (1st ed., pp. 81–106). Washington, DC: American Psychological Association.

Ghaill, M. M., Haywood, C., & Popoviciu, L. (2007). Heterosexism and homophobia in the hidden curriculum. In B. Bank (Ed.), *Gender and education: An encyclopedia* (pp. 549–554). Westport, CT: Praeger.

Good, T. L., & Brophy, J. E. (2003). *Looking into classrooms.* Boston, MA: Allyn & Bacon.

Gottfredson, L. S. (1981). Circumscription and compromise: A developmental theory of occupational aspirations. *Journal of Counseling Psychology, 28,* 545–579.

Gottfredson, L. S. (2005). Applying Gottfredson's theory to circumscription and compromise in career guidance and counseling. In S. Brown & R. W. Lent (Eds.), *Career development and counseling: Putting theory and research to work* (pp. 71–100). Hoboken, NJ: Wiley.

Grant, L., & Kimberly, K. (2007). Teacher–student interactions. In B. Bank (Ed.), *Gender and education: An encyclopedia* (pp. 571–576). Westport, CT: Praeger.

Griffin, P. (1992). From hiding out to coming out: Empowering lesbian and gay educators. In K. M. Harbeck (Ed.), *Coming out of the classroom closet* (pp. 167–196). Binghamton, NY: Harrington Park Press.

Hackett, G., & Betz, N. E. (1981). A self-efficacy approach to the career development of women. *Journal of Vocational Behavior, 18,* 326–339.

Hackett, G., & Kohlhart, J. D. (2012). Feminist vocational/career theory and practice. In C. Z. Enns & E. N. Williams (Eds.), *The Oxford handbook of feminist multicultural counseling psychology* (pp. 255–276). New York, NY: Oxford University Press.

Hausmann, R., Tyson, L. D., & Zahidi, S. (2010). *The global gender gap report.* Geneva, Switzerland: World Economic Forum.

Heppner, M. J. (2013). Women, men and work: The long road to gender equity. In S. D. Brown & R. W. Lent (Eds.), *Career development and counseling: Putting theory and research to work* (2nd ed., pp. 187–214). New York, NY: Wiley.

Heppner, M. J., & Jung, A. K. (2013). Gender and social class: Powerful predictors of a life journey. In W. B. Walsh, M. L. Savickas, & P. J. Hartung (Eds.), *Handbook of vocational psychology: Theory, research, and practice* (4th ed., pp. 81–102). New York, NY: Routledge.

Hershberger, S. L., & D'Augelli, A. R. (1999). Issues in counseling lesbian, gay, and bisexual adolescents. In R. M. Perez, K. A. DeBord, & K. J. Bieschke (Eds.), *Handbook of counseling and psychotherapy with lesbian, gay, and bisexual clients* (1st ed., pp. 225–248). Washington, DC: American Psychological Association.

Hotelling, K., & Forrest, L. (1985). Gilligan's theory of sex role development: A perspective for counseling. *Journal of Counseling & Development, 64,* 183–186.

Jacobs, J. E., Chhin, C. S., & Bleeker, M. M. (2006). Enduring links: Parents' expectations and their young adult children's gender-typed occupational choices. *Educational Research and Evaluation, 12,* 395–407.

Kerr, B., & Maresh, S. E. (1994). Career counseling for gifted girls. In W. B. Walsh & S. H. Osipow (Eds.), *Career counseling for women* (pp. 197–235). Hillsdale, NJ: Erlbaum.

Kerr, B. A., Vuyk, A., & Rea, C. (2012). Gendered practices in the education of gifted girls and boys. *Psychology in the Schools, 7,* 647–655.

Larose, S., Ratelle, C. F., Guay, F., Senecal, C., & Harvey, M. (2006). Trajectories of science self-efficacy beliefs during the college transition and academic vocational adjustment in science and technology programs. *Educational Research and Evaluation, 12,* 373–393.

Lent, R. W., Brown, S. D., & Hackett, G. (1994). Toward a unifying social cognitive theory of career and academic interest, choice, and performance. *Journal of Vocational Behavior, 45,* 79–122.

Lidderdale, M. A., Croteau, J. M., Anderson, M. Z., Tovar-Murray, D., & Davis, J. M. (2006). Building lesbian, gay, and bisexual vocational psychology: A theoretical model of workplace sexual identity management. In K. J. Bieschke, R. M. Perez, & K. A. DeBord (Eds.), *Handbook of counseling and psychotherapy with lesbian, gay, bisexual, and transgender clients* (2nd ed., pp. 245–270). Washington, DC: American Psychological Association.

Lips, H. M. (1992). Gender- and science-related attitudes as predictors of college students' academic choices. *Journal of Vocational Behavior, 40,* 62–81.

Mac Naughton, G. (2007). Early childhood education. In B. Bank (Ed.), *Gender and education: An encyclopedia* (pp. 263–267). Westport, CT: Praeger.

Mandel, L., & Vitelli, R. (2007). Heterosexism and homophobia in the peer group. In B. Bank (Ed.), *Gender and education: An encyclopedia* (pp. 597–603). Westport, CT: Praeger.

Martin-Baro, I. (1994). *Writings for liberation psychology.* Cambridge, MA: Harvard University Press.

Matlin, M. (2012). *The psychology of women.* Belmont, CA: Wadsworth.

McCarn, S. R., & Fassinger, R. E. (1996). Revisioning sexual minority identity formation: A new model of lesbian identity implications for counseling and research. *The Counseling Psychologist, 24,* 508–534.

McDaniels, C., & Gysbers, N. C. (1992). *Counseling for career development: Theories, resources, and practice.* San Francisco, CA: Jossey-Bass.

McWhirter, E. H. (1994). *Counseling for empowerment.* Alexandria, VA: American Counseling Association.

Morrow, S. L., Gore, P. A., & Campbell, B. W. (1996). The application of a sociocognitive framework to the career development of lesbian women and gay men. *Journal of Vocational Behavior, 48,* 136–148.

Multon, K. D., Brown, S. D., & Lent, R. W. (1991). Relation of self-efficacy beliefs to academic outcomes: A meta-analytic investigation. *Journal of Counseling Psychology, 38,* 30–38.

National Center for Education Statistics. (2012). *Digest of education statistics: 2012.* Washington, DC: Author.

National Science Foundation. (2002). *Science and engineering indicators: 2002.* Washington, DC: Author.

Nelson, M. L. (1996). Separation versus connection, the gender controversy: Implications for counseling women. *Journal of Counseling & Development, 74,* 339–344.

O'Brien, K. M., Friedman, S. M., Tipton, L. C., & Linn, S. G. (2000). Attachment, separation, and women's vocational development: A longitudinal analysis. *Journal of Counseling Psychology, 47,* 301–315.

Ormerod, A. J., Joseph, D. L., Weitzman, L. M., & Winterrowd, E. (2012). Career issues and challenges viewed through a feminist multicultural lens: Work-life interface and sexual harassment. In C. Z. Enns & E. N. Williams (Eds.), *The Oxford handbook of feminist multicultural counseling psychology* (pp. 277–303). New York, NY: Oxford University Press.

Ossana, S., Helms, J., & Leonard, M. M. (1992). Do "womanist" identity attitudes influence college women's self-esteem and perceptions of environmental bias? *Journal of Counseling & Development, 70,* 402–408.

Pajares, F., & Miller, M. D. (1995). Mathematics self-efficacy and mathematics performances: The need for specificity of assessment. *Journal of Counseling Psychology, 42,* 190–198.

Paludi, M. (2007). Sexual harassment policies and practices. In B. Bank (Ed.), *Gender and education: An encyclopedia* (pp. 793–800). Westport, CT: Praeger.

Perez, R. M., DeBord, K. A., & Bieschke, K. J. (Eds.). (1999). *Handbook of counseling and psychotherapy with lesbian, gay, and bisexual clients* (1st ed.). Washington, DC: American Psychological Association.

Prince, J. (2013). Career development of lesbian, gay, bisexual, and transgender individuals. In S. D. Brown & R. W. Lent (Eds.), *Career development and counseling: Putting theory and research to work* (2nd ed., pp. 275–298). Hoboken, NJ: Wiley.

Ratts, M. J., Toporek, L., & Lewis, A. (2010). *ACA advocacy competencies: A social justice framework for counselors.* Alexandria, VA: American Counseling Association.

Reynolds, A. L., & Hanjorgiris, W. F. (1999). Coming out: Lesbian, gay, and bisexual identity development. In R. M. Perez, K. A. DeBord, & K. J. Bieschke (Eds.), *Handbook of counseling and psychotherapy with lesbian, gay, and bisexual clients* (1st ed., pp. 35–56). Washington, DC: American Psychological Association.

Robertson, J., & Fitzgerald, L. F. (1990). The (mis)treatment of men: Effects of client gender roles and life-style on diagnosis and attribution of pathology. *Journal of Counseling Psychology, 37,* 3–9.

Russell, J. E. A. (2006). Career counseling for women in management. In W. B. Walsh & M. J. Heppner (Eds.), *Handbook of career counseling for women* (2nd ed., pp. 453–512). Mahwah, NJ: Erlbaum.

Sadker, M. P., & Sadker, D. M. (1994). *Failing at fairness: How our schools cheat girls.* New York, NY: Touchstone.

Sadri, G., & Robertson, I. T. (1993). Self-efficacy and work-related behavior: A review and meta-analysis. *Applied Psychology, 42,* 139–152.

Swanson, J. L., & Lease, S. H. (1990). Gender differences in self-ratings of abilities and skills. *The Career Development Quarterly, 38,* 346–359.

Szymanski, D. M., & Hilton, A. N. (2012). Feminist counseling psychology and lesbians, bisexual women, and transgender persons. In C. Z. Enns & E. N. Williams (Eds.), *The Oxford handbook of feminist multicultural counseling psychology* (pp. 131–154). New York, NY: Oxford University Press.

Unger, R., & Crawford, M. (1992). *Women and gender.* New York, NY: McGraw-Hill.

U.S. Department of Labor. (2007). *Facts on U.S. working women* (Fact Sheet 88-1). Washington, DC: Office of the Secretary, Women's Bureau.

Walsh, W. B., & Heppner, M. J. (Eds.). (2006). *Handbook of career counseling for women* (2nd ed.). Hillsdale, NJ: Erlbaum.

Watt, H. M. G. (2006). The role of motivation in gendered educational and occupational trajectories related to math. *Educational Research and Evaluation, 21,* 305–322.

Watt, H. M. G., & Eccles, J. S. (Eds.). (2008). *Gender and occupational outcomes: Longitudinal assessment of individual, social, and cultural influences.* Washington, DC: American Psychological Association.

Worthington, R. L., Savoy, H. B., & Vernaglia, E. R. (2001). *Beyond tolerance: An integrative model of LGB-affirmativeness.* Unpublished manuscript.

Chapter 5

Empowering Men's Life Choices: An Examination of Gender and Sexual Orientation

With P. Paul Heppner

In recent decades if you looked for information on the career development of men in our professional counseling literature, you likely came up empty handed. Because men were seen as privileged in the labor market and elsewhere, little attention was paid to any particular career issues they might have. There was a sparse literature on men at the margins, such as men with disabilities, gay men, and men with lower socioeconomic status, but even that literature was meager. It was thought that men were largely doing well with higher prestige jobs and greater incomes and holding all but a handful of the CEO positions in Fortune 500 companies. Thus, the conclusion seemed to be that we should focus on girls and women, who have been consistently disadvantaged in the labor force and elsewhere (Heppner & Heppner, 2014).

It is important to note that this dearth of information about men in our professional career literature is a relatively recent phenomenon. For example, close to 4 decades ago psychologist Leona Tyler (1977) wrote, "Much of what we know about the stages through which an individual passes as he prepares to find his place in the world of work might appropriately be labeled 'The Vocational Development of Middle Class Males'" (p. 40). In effect men's career development was largely seen as universal career development, with little attention paid to women or other groups who did not fit the norm. Our theories of career development, our assessment measures, even our normative work patterns were all developed from a male perspective. If women worked in the male world, they were implicitly instructed to try to be like men.

With Tyler's commonly held view as the backdrop, the question quickly becomes "Why include a chapter on empowering men's career choices when the whole field of career psychology was, until the past few decades, concerned almost exclusively with male career development?"

We answer this question in two ways: First, although the professional literature continues to be largely ignoring boys' and men's issues in education and employment, the lay literature has been prolific over the last decade. For example, *Boys Adrift* (Sax, 2007), *Save the Males* (Parker, 2008), *The Broken American Male: And How to Fix Him* (Boteach,

2008), *The Decline of Men* (Garcia, 2009), *Why Boys Fail* (Whitmire, 2010), and *The End of Men and the Rise of Women* (Rosin, 2012) have all been published in the last decade. Written by journalists, family practice physicians, educational administrators, and rabbis, these books paint a quite different picture of the role of men in today's society and one that calls on counselors and career planning professionals to take notice. These books highlight such data as boys are doing academically worse than girls at every educational level (Whitmire, 2010), women are now earning 60% of the bachelor's and master's degrees at universities (Rosin, 2012), 2009 was a tipping point year when there were more women than men in the labor force (Rosin, 2012), and 12 of the 15 fastest growing occupations are currently predominantly occupied by women (Bureau of Labor Statistics, 2013). Although the themes of these books differ, the message is consistent: Men are underperforming women in education and the labor force and need dramatic and quick interventions on the part of helping professionals (Heppner & Jung, 2013b).

Second, we argue that even when our literature focused on the male experience, it was examining a highly selective group of men—primarily White, able-bodied, heterosexual, economically and educationally privileged men who chose to work in traditionally male occupations outside the home. Little was written, and we argue that little is still being written, about the experiences of men who are outside of this select group, for example men of color, men with disabilities, gay or bisexual men, men in poverty, men who have not had educational privilege, men who choose nontraditional career paths, and men who are stay-at-home dads. It is particularly important both from a human resource perspective and from a social justice perspective that we understand more about the vocational lives of *all* men (Heppner, 2013; Heppner & Jung, 2013a).

Career counseling that homogenizes men or decontextualizes men's experiences does not provide the richness of information necessary for informed career planning. For example, one form of decontextualization that has occurred in the career literature over the years is the separation of love and work, especially for gay and bisexual men. As we mention in Chapter 4, it is important to note that although we have attempted to integrate career research on lesbian, gay, bisexual, and transgender (LGBT) individuals wherever possible, this body of literature remains quite small and incomplete. In addition, much of this research was conducted on one group, such as gay men, but not lesbian women (Chung, 2003). Whereas the literature on lesbian women and gay men is small, the literature on the career development of bisexual and transgender individuals is virtually nonexistent (Carroll, Gilroy, & Ryan, 2002; Chung, 2001, 2003; Prince, 2013). Thus, we caution the reader that our ability to discuss and offer assistance in working with LGBT clients is limited because of the limited research base. We do, however, believe that it is important for LGBT issues to be addressed in the mainstream career literature, and thus we have tried to include references to this scholarship whenever possible.

Likewise, it is critical that our profession recognize and embrace the construct of intersectionality. That is, we must recognize that being male is not an independent social identity but rather this maleness intersects with being rich or poor, minority or majority, able bodied or disabled (Heppner & Heppner, 2014). Each of these intersections alters the needs of the individual men we are seeing in career counseling and in effect forms "mutually constitutive relations among social identities" (Shields, 2008, p. 301).

Thus, the purpose of this chapter is to highlight key aspects of the gendered context and their resultant gender-specific outcomes. The first section is an overview of these complex and varied issues. The past decades have brought a number of excellent texts on issues related to men and gender role development (e.g., Brooks & Good, 2001; Englar-Carlson, Evans, & Duffey, 2014). The landmark book *Handbook of Counseling and Psychotherapy With*

Lesbian, Gay, and Bisexual Clients, edited by Perez, DeBord, and Bieschke (1999), is now in its second edition (Bieschke, Perez, & DeBord, 2006) and should be consulted for a more in-depth analysis of LGBT counseling and psychotherapy issues. In addition, Pope and his colleagues' (2004) article on culturally appropriate career counseling with gay and lesbian clients offers a host of potentially useful career interventions.

Although career development issues for transgender individuals are no doubt prominent in their lives (discrimination, experiencing transphobic employment cultures, navigating employment-related legal status as male or female, etc.), there is virtually no literature directly related to helping counsel transgender individuals on their career development (Chung, 2003). Transgender "is a range of behaviors, expressions, identifications that challenge the pervasive bipolar gender system in a given culture" (Carroll et al., 2002, p. 139). An article that provides much useful information on evolving definitions of transgender, as well as implications for counselors' attitudes and knowledge, was written by Carroll and her colleagues (2002) and provides excellent background for counselors in working with clients who challenge the binary gender system. Hopefully, in the years to come, there will be more research-based guidelines to assist career counselors in working with transgender individuals.

Particular constructs are discussed here in order to highlight key aspects of the gendered and heterosexist context in childhood, adolescence, and the adult workplace that most directly influence male clients who come for career counseling. The second part of this chapter suggests particular assessments, techniques, and areas of knowledge to share with clients to make career counseling more empowering for men. Finally, we provide an overview of the impact of gender and sexual orientation identity on the different phases of career counseling discussed in Chapter 1.

The Gendered Overlay: Sex Role Socialization in Childhood

The term *socialization*

> refers to how individuals learn about the roles and expectations that they play within a society and the way in which they develop a sense of self. . . . The term sex role socialization, also termed gender socialization, involves developing beliefs about gender roles, the expectations associated with each sex, and, also, gender identity, an understanding of what it means to be male or female. (Stockard, 2007, p. 79)

The gendered context begins when parents first learn their child is a boy. Whole interaction patterns begin to be established (Kite, Deaux, & Haines, 2008). Boys are given different toys than girls. Boys are much more likely to be played with in a rough and aggressive way. They are told not to cry or express sadness or hurt feelings. The male role models in their children's books and cartoons are aggressive, dominant, and always in control: They can fix any situation, rescue any damsel in distress. Because traditional fathers have been raised in environments that foster autonomy and independence, they may in turn perpetuate this pattern by emotionally distancing themselves from their sons (Gilligan, 1982). These early experiences with sex role socialization lay a firm groundwork for the gender-based characteristics these men portray throughout life. Up until recently, the issues girls faced as a result of this stereotyping were much more prominent in books and media outlets than were those of boys, leading Levant (2001) to conclude, "We have a cultural blindness to the problems of boys, in part because of our assumption that males should be self-sufficient, and in part because boys are required to keep their problems to themselves" (p. 355). There has also been growing awareness of the importance of verbal skills for success in both education and employment, an area where boys have traditionally fallen behind early and stayed behind. As Whitmire indicated in his book *Why Boys Fail* (2010), the world has become more verbal and boys have not.

Thus, this early socialization influences initial perceptions of occupational options. In their very early years, boys are already able to sex role stereotype occupational fields as women's work and men's work (Armstrong & Crombie, 2000; White & White, 2006), with these views becoming more and more rigid from kindergarten to fourth grade (Matlin, 2012). For boys, the need not to identify with anything feminine, including traditionally feminine occupations, is paramount. The worst fear is to be called a sissy, so boys repress the side of themselves that is vulnerable or scared and put on the facade of toughness (Heppner & Heppner, 2014; O'Neil, 2008; Rabinowitz & Cochran, 1994). This early gender socialization may be especially salient for LGBT individuals as they are receiving some of the first messages about what the narrow gender prescriptions may mean for their futures.

The Gendered Context of Adolescence

Adolescence is a time of trying to fit in and find a place in the world. It is a time when peer culture is highly influential. "Peer cultures consist of descriptive and evaluative meanings that peer groups assign to behaviors and relationships, and the interaction among peer group members consists of talk and behaviors that construct, maintain, consolidate, challenge or change these meanings" (Bank, 2007, p. 605). A critically important peer culture task is defining what it means to be a boy or a man. Many adolescent boys are trying to figure out who they are and how they can "be someone" in the world. This can mean joining groups that are interested in particular activities, such as sports, chess, or cars, or it can mean joining gangs (Sheldon, 2007). There is great pressure to conform to group norms and to prove manhood through these activities. Sports provide a major socializing experience for some boys and have a direct connection to attitudes and behaviors in the workforce. Boys play games that have clear winners and losers. They are taught to compete and win. They are socialized to the rules of the game, similar to the traditional rules of the adult, male-centered workplace: teamwork, competitiveness, a facade of invulnerability. In Skovholt's (1990) analysis of the socializing force of sports in men's lives, he suggested that emotional intimacy is as dysfunctional as extreme individualism is in most sports. Boys need to learn a certain level of cooperation but resist any real connectedness with other boys. Thus, adult men tend to say that they have many acquaintances and people whom they can cooperate with on projects but that they lack close intimate connections, especially with other men. The messages of the football field live on in the corporate office building, with socialized life scripts being perpetuated and reinforced through time. Consequently, through sports and other activities, adolescence continues to be a time of restricted emotionality for boys. They learn to be tough and not express their tender or vulnerable sides (Levant, 2001; O'Neil, 2008). They are, in effect, further severing the feeling sides of themselves.

Demonstrating masculinity through sexual conquest with girls is of utmost importance, making these years particularly hard for gay adolescents who feel they have to fit in to the heterosexual world or risk being ostracized or becoming victims of verbal and physical abuse (Hershberger & D'Augelli, 1999; Mandel & Vitelli, 2007; Rosin, 2012). For adolescents who are struggling with sexual identity issues, vocational identity may be delayed (Croteau, Anderson, Distefano, & Kampa-Kokesch, 1999; Tomlinson & Fassinger, 2003). Although much of the literature focuses on the negative, harmful aspects of traditional male socialization, it is important for the counselor to understand and reinforce traditional male strengths as well. As Levant (1996) argued, this same traditional adolescent socialization also plants the seeds for adult male strengths—the ability to persist in difficult situations until problems are resolved and the ability to strategize, think logically, solve problems, take risks, and stay calm in the face of danger. Both the positive aspects as well as the more detrimental aspects of the traditional male role are important for the counselor and the client to understand (Heppner & Heppner, 2014; O'Neil, 2008).

The Gendered Workplace Context

Often young men begin carving out their identities in the adult world in their first jobs (Heppner & Heppner, 2001, 2014). Keen (1991) spoke of the first job as a boy's rite of passage into manhood. It is a role he has been training for since birth. Achievement, competition, and goal orientation are all familiar concepts to him. Thus, work begins to form identity to the point where, for many men, the two become virtually inseparable. As Skovholt (1990) expressed, "Painting a picture of men's lives often results in a work-dominated landscape" (p. 39). Once in the work environment, men tend to strive for those elusive characteristics that define success. The definition usually includes predominantly materialistic components: owning a home, owning a car, providing for a family, taking nice vacations (Skovholt & Morgan, 1981). The dream for many men is a middle-class professional job with all its inherent rewards, as portrayed repeatedly on television. Men have many traditional role models for "the way you do a life" (Skovholt, 1990, p. 42). Fathers and grandfathers, male neighbors, and friends all provide information to young men about appropriate work behaviors. The message is clear: Men are supposed to work outside the home throughout their lives.

> Whether the job is loved, hated, intrinsically satisfying, or boring is much less relevant than the expectation that a man will work. For the thousands of young men growing up in poverty finding a job, any job is a must to provide for basic needs. For these men it is a luxury to think about the meaning a job has; rather their quest is one of survival. A long-term nonworking male adult violates this strong male principle and is usually shunned and rejected. (Skovholt, 1990, p. 42)

As this quote highlights, it is important to acknowledge the unspoken privilege of choosing a career. As Blustein (2006, 2011) has poignantly described, the vast majority of women and men in the world have limited volition or choice in what they do to support themselves and their families. This is especially important for career counselors to understand in times of recession, when large numbers of men who are still counted on as breadwinners in our society find themselves unable to find work and thus lose a large portion of their identity as men (Heppner & Heppner, 2014; O'Neil, 2008).

The modern workplace has also changed in ways that make it more difficult for traditional men. Previously characteristics such as being in control, having others listen to your commands, being competitive, and working in hierarchical ways were important for success in many organizations (Srivastava & Nair, 2011). These were roles that many nontraditional men were familiar and comfortable with. Today many organizations work in less hierarchical ways, using teams to accomplish tasks. Here cooperativeness, interpersonal skills, social intelligence, an ability to work with diverse individuals (including many more women), and written literacy skills have become more valued workplace traits. These tend to be traits that women have developed to a greater extent than many men. In essence, as Whitmire (2010) noted, the world has become more verbal and boys and men have not.

For many men, role models of how to be a man in the modern work environment are lacking. Gay men are particularly limited in terms of visible role models to increase their awareness of occupational possibilities and to demonstrate and discuss work-related issues specifically in relation to sexual orientation. Although all minority groups suffer from lack of role models, the invisibility of gays, in some cases even to one another, compounds the problem. Thus, "gay men may need to make career decisions without awareness of how other gay men employed in the occupations under consideration made their decisions and how their choices were implemented" (Hetherington, Hillerbrand, & Etringer, 1989, p. 453). In addition, discrimination against LGBT workers is very prevalent. From 25% to 66% of respondents across three studies reviewed by Croteau (1996) reported experiencing discrimination in the workplace because of sexual orientation. Thus, the gay or bisexual worker has this added pressure in his work life, which may be highly influential in his decision about whether to be "out" with regard to his sexual orientation at work (Chung, 2001, 2003).

Although there used to be choices and options for men with limited education and skills, largely in the industrial sector, most of those jobs have gone overseas or become much more automated, leaving limited options for these men. Prominent economists are calling this phenomenon of job loss for working-class men the most destructive social force of our era (Greenstone & Looney, 2010). In the recent recession three quarters of the jobs lost during the recession were lost by men (Kochhar, 2012). This is because in a recession jobs in construction and manufacturing are typically the first to go. This trend of male job loss does not seem particularly likely to change, as the Bureau of Labor Statistics (2013) indicated that of those occupations predicted to have the most growth in the next decade, 12 of the top 15 are currently dominated by women.

The impact of male unemployment is especially important for career counselors to understand in that it has been shown to be highly related to depression, anxiety, and a variety of physical problems (Paul & Moser, 2009). Once unemployed, it appears individuals do not return to their previous level of life satisfaction even when they have become employed once again (Lucas, Clark, Georgellis, & Diener, 2004). In addition, male unemployment has also been linked to divorce, being a more powerful predictor of divorce than unhappiness in their relationship (Sayer, England, Allison, & Kangas, 2011).

Men in Nontraditional Career Fields

Although the second wave of feminism brought the notion that men and women could be whatever they wanted to be, the reality then and now is a highly gender-segregated occupational structure in many fields. Yet as we indicate in Chapter 4, the literature on women going into nontraditional career fields, especially those in the science, engineering, technology, and mathematics areas, has expanded greatly over the past 2 decades (Fassinger & Asay, 2006). There have also been increased investigations, albeit at a much slower rate, of men in nontraditional fields (Heppner & Heppner, 2009). For career counselors to work most effectively with men going into nontraditional fields, it is important that they know the key results of this research. What do we know about men who go into nontraditional careers? For one thing, we know that these men tend to have more liberal social attitudes, higher degree aspirations, and higher socioeconomic statuses (Lease, 2003). In addition, we know that they tend to endorse fewer antifemininity and toughness norms, have less concern with restricting their emotion or expressing affection toward other men, and have less homophobia (Jome & Tokar, 1998). In a follow-up study, Tokar and Jome (1998) examined the mediating role of vocational interests. In this study they examined how the same masculinity-related variables may be mediated by interests to predict nontraditional career choice. They found partial support for men's endorsement of masculine gender roles predicting their vocational interests and those interests, in turn, predicting career choice traditionality. In addition, they found support for the mediational role of men's vocational interests in the relation between masculinity and career choice traditionality. Thus, it appears that the relationships between gender role constructs and traditional or nontraditional choices may be more complex than earlier thought and may influence interest formation, which in turn may predict choice.

The Nontraditional Career Choices of Men of Color

The studies discussed above were conducted on primarily White, heterosexual men. Given that the field of career development is just beginning to explore the career development patterns of people of color, it is perhaps not surprising that the specific research area of the nontraditional career choices of men of color is virtually nonexistent. An exception is a recent study by Flores, Navarro, Smith, and Ploszaj (2006), who examined the career choice goals of Mexican American adolescent boys by using an extended version of Lent, Brown, and Hackett's (1994) career choice model. Findings from this investigation indicated that Mexican American adolescent boys' nontraditional career self-efficacy was predicted by parental support and by the boys' acculturation level. They also found that nontraditional career self-efficacy predicted nontraditional career interests and fathers' career nontraditionality. It is critical to conduct this kind of theory-based research on the nontraditional choices of men of color if we are to be able to specify and generalize our findings to a broader array of men in our society.

The Nontraditional Career Path of the Stay-at-Home Dad

One of the most nontraditional of career paths still seems to be that of men who stay home and serve as primary caretakers of their children. Although researchers emphasize that stay-at-home dads are growing in number, the latest U.S. figures available indicate there were still only 161,000 men who stayed at home with their children for at least 1 year when their wives were working outside the home (U.S. Census Bureau, 2012). Thus, although the numbers may be growing, it appears psychological, social, and financial barriers are keeping the vast majority of fathers from choosing this particular life path. Some studies have been conducted that have examined the experiences of stay-at-home dads. The early studies in this area tended to have very small samples. For many participants, the stay-at-home status had not been voluntary but was due to unemployment or disability; often, even when the man was staying home and the woman was working outside the home, the woman still contributed more hours to homemaking responsibilities (see Robertson & Verschelden, 1993).

Two studies actively recruited men who were voluntarily staying home with children while their wives worked outside the home. These studies are particularly helpful in understanding the experiences of couples who make a choice to reverse traditional roles. Robertson and Verschelden (1993) conducted a mixed methods study with stay-at-home dads. Through both quantitative assessments and qualitative interviews, the researchers examined the experiences of these couples. What they found were men who were quite happy with their chosen roles. They concluded,

> We had expected, based upon previous research on homemaking, that male homemakers would view their experience somewhat negatively and that the role would have some negative impact on them. Although the men certainly recognized some drawbacks with the role reversal, their personal attributes and the quality of their reports were more positive than expected. (p. 398)

In terms of their measured satisfaction with life, both men and women in the study scored significantly higher than people in the general population. The researchers went on to highlight some other findings based on their data: (a) They found that the men were psychologically healthy, that the men had not entered the role because of some psychological deficit, and that psychological problems did not surface as a result of the role; and (b) they found little of the gender role identity incongruence evident in many of the studies related to men going into nontraditional careers outside the home. Although the men in this study did get perplexed and negative reactions, primarily from other men, the overall reactions they received were positive, and they felt reinforced in their role. The most consistent benefit of the arrangement was the men feeling grateful for having the opportunity to develop relationships with their children and being there to see them grow and develop.

By far the largest and most representative study in this area was conducted by Rochlen, McKelley, Suizzo, and Scaringi (2008), who found high levels of relationship and life satisfaction among a sample of 213 stay-at-home fathers. Using data collected through the Internet, Rochlen and his colleagues indicated that these dads appeared well adjusted and content with their lives. This study supported the importance of strong social support, high parenting self-efficacy, and low conformity to traditional male norms. Men who had lower adherence to restrictive male gender norms seemed to be able to be more content with their identity and able to face the negative views some may still hold regarding their choice. Specifically, parental self-efficacy was a significant predictor of psychological well-being and life satisfaction. In essence, men who were more confident in their parenting reported higher levels of life satisfaction and less psychological distress.

The Counselor Role With Male Clients

Given the importance of career in most men's lives, it seems likely that they would seek career counseling. Studies of gay men particularly have indicated that they have more uncertainty and confusion about their careers than either lesbian women or heterosexual men or women (Hetherington et al., 1989). Unfortunately, the constellation of traditional male characteristics, which includes emotional restrictedness and a strong need for control, may keep men from seeking mental health or vocational services. It has been demonstrated that men underuse all forms of social services, including career planning assistance, as compared to women. Although it is unfortunate, given male socialization, this is to be expected (Addis & Mahalik, 2003; Scher, 2001). There has been encouragement from some recent writers to rethink traditional counseling to make it more man-friendly (Kiselica, 2001). Although aimed primarily at school-age boys, many of Kiselica's (2001) suggestions seem fitting for men of all ages. These suggestions include (a) reexamining the 50-min hour, (b) reexamining the formal office setting, (c) using humor and self-disclosure, and (d) using rapport-building tactics that build on male strengths (Kiselica, 2001). These suggestions are attempts at closing the gap between the personality of many men and the "personality" of most counseling sessions. Being sensitive to what will make for a more natural and comfortable counseling environment for boys and men is an important issue for the counselor. The counselor's role in the perpetuation of the status quo has been studied extensively with women who choose nontraditional employment options.

A parallel examination of the impact of men's nontraditional choices on counseling process and outcome is sparse. In an interesting analog study, Robertson and Fitzgerald (1990) found that with regard to nontraditional male clients, counselors (a) considered them to have more severe pathology, (b) behaved differently toward them, (c) were more likely to attribute their depression to their nontraditional choices, and (d) were more likely to target their nontraditional behavior as a focus for counselor intervention. Robertson and Fitzgerald concluded, "It is still somewhat startling to find that a group of experienced mental health professionals is likely to diagnose severe pathology essentially on the basis that a client has chosen not to engage in the good provider role" (p. 8). Therefore, it seems that in initial exploratory studies, the same gender role bias identified in counseling with nontraditional women may also be true with nontraditional men. For men who are trying to break away from cultural norms to find new and more healthy paths for themselves, it is disturbing that sex role bias exists within the counseling profession.

In addition, it is important for counselors to practice LGBT-affirmative counseling. *LGBT affirmativeness* (Worthington, Savoy, & Vernaglia, 2001) is conceptualized as "the range of attitudes, beliefs, emotions and behaviors that express and assert the positive valuing of the sexual identity of, and an understanding of the realities faced by LGBT individuals within an oppressive society" (Worthington et al., 2001, p. 2). Affirmative individuals are not only knowledgeable about LGBT issues but understanding of and comfortable with their own sexual identity and diverse sexual orientations. Having contact and involvement with LGBT individuals is an important component of the process of becoming an LGBT-affirmative career counselor. This contact is presumed to occur not only in one's professional role but also in other contexts, including personal, social, and familial networks. The model describes five states: Passive Conformity, Revelation and Exploration, Tentative Commitment, Synthesis and Integration, and Active Commitment. Becoming LGBT affirmative is a developmental process of movement from an unexamined, unconscious heterosexist or homophobic construction of the world, through a phase of intellectualized understanding of what it means to be LGBT affirmative, and finally to a more fully integrated level of awareness and expression in which knowledge achieved in earlier phases is incorporated into one's personal, professional, and political spheres. LGBT-affirmative counselors use their self-awareness, knowledge, skills, and involvement with LGBT individuals to inform their practice with all clients, including lesbian, gay, bisexual, and heterosexual clients. The American Psychological Association's Public Interest Directorate has also come out with *Guidelines for Psychological Practice With Lesbian, Gay, and Bisexual Clients* (www.apa.org/pi/lgbc/publications/guidelines.aspx), which provides much useful information for providing affirmative career counseling.

Gender-Specific Outcomes

The previous sections provided an overview of some of the career-related aspects of the gendered environment that appear during early development, during adolescence, and in the adult workplace for gay, bisexual, and heterosexual men. Learning more about aspects of this environment is an important step in improving career counseling for all men. Only when we as counselors have adequate information about the extent of the gendered context can we be effective in our interventions with clients. This section discusses some of the most prevalent gender-specific outcomes that may result from these environments and that may dramatically influence the career counseling process.

The Relationship of Gender-Related Behaviors to Mortality and Morbidity

Probably one of the most tangible results of the gendered context on male lives is that, on average, women live 7 years longer than men (Courtenay, 2001). Although a variety of biological factors are involved in determining longevity, Harrison, Chin, and Ficarrotto (1989) studied mortality rates across the life span and concluded that biological factors alone cannot account for these dramatic and consistent differences in longevity. Other researchers have argued that as much as 75% of the difference in longevity between men and women can be attributed to the gender role behaviors of men (Waldron, 1976). A growing body of literature has linked traditional masculinity and men's beliefs about what it means to be a man to greater health risk (Courtenay, 2001).

The Relationship of Gender Role Ideologies to Stress and Coping

The relationship of gender role ideologies to stress and coping has been examined by Eisler and Blalock (1991). These researchers applied Lazarus and Folkman's (1984) work on the role of the cognitive appraisal of events in predicting stress and coping reactions to the issue of male gender role stress. Specifically, Eisler and Blalock predicted that strong adherence to traditional gender role ideology may result in a restriction of the type of coping strategies men feel are available in stressful situations. For example, when experiencing stressful events at work, such as a rumored downsizing of the company, men may need more social and emotional support but feel that it is inappropriate for them to ask for it. The kinds of thinking emphasized by Kiselica's (2001) man-friendly counseling and what Courtenay (2001) referred to as "humanizing help-seeking" seem like critical changes that could greatly enhance men's ability to seek needed support and services. To test these hypotheses about the relationship of adherence to the male role and the way men cope with stressful life events, Eisler and Skidmore (1987) developed the Masculine Gender Role Stress Scale (which is reviewed later in "Assessments for Empowering Men's Choices"). They proposed that excessive commitment to the male gender role tends to severely limit men's flexible responses to stressful events. Eisler and Blalock outlined four broad gender-related coping mechanisms that men use that tend to promote dysfunctional coping. These are discussed here under their general topic headings of (a) commitment to masculinity; (b) reliance on aggression, power, and control; (c) importance of performance, achievement, and success; and (d) emotional inexpressiveness. The interested reader is referred to the Eisler and Blalock article for a more specific description of these coping strategies. The current discussion applies each coping strategy to career- and work-related issues of relevance to the career counselor.

Commitment to Masculinity

Eisler and Blalock (1991) contended that one aspect of a rigid adherence to sex-typed masculine ideology is a fear of femininity and subsequently anything that is considered feminine. This aspect may be reflected in career counseling in a number of salient ways. It may be reflected initially in men's avoidance of help seeking and in their rational and logical presentation style. Appearing masculine and in charge while asking for assistance is a difficult balancing act. Because the expression of anger is much more acceptable for men than the expression of distress or vulnerability, the career counselor is likely to be presented with the expression of anger, if not toward the counselor then toward others in the man's environment. Eisler and Blalock found that anger is more frequently associated with masculine gender role stress and conjectured that it may lead to the prevalence of Type A behavior in the workplace. *Type A behavior* is described as consisting of "an aggressive, time-urgent, competitive orientation to task with a hostile, impatient interpersonal style" (Eisler & Blalock, 1991, p. 54). Eisler and Blalock proposed that the pervasive aura of hostility so characteristic of Type A behavior may be "due to the frustration of trying to live up to unrealistic definitions of masculine achievement and success" (p. 52). Type A behavior has been found to be much more prevalent in men, and the sex-linked nature of the Type A construct can be traced back to as early as kindergarten (Matthews & Angulu, 1980; Waldron, 1976). In the workplace, too, this commitment to masculinity may be reflected in the conflict and stress men feel when working with women as colleagues or bosses. Because men tend to control most managerial positions within organizations, this adherence influences the whole culture of the organization and has profound negative consequences on women and nontraditional men who work in these environments. Consequently, career counselors are more likely to see clients who are suffering the effects of working in environments run by men who have an excessive commitment to masculine ideology and thus create a rigid environment that reinforces male characteristics and punishes feminine qualities. These work environments can also be very difficult for gay and bisexual men, whether out in the work environment or not; the fear of formal and informal harassment is great. If the workplace is dominated by men who exhibit rigid adherence to sex-typed masculine ideologies, the environment can be even more stressful and difficult for gay and bisexual men.

Reliance on Aggression, Power, and Control

As a result of the sex role socialization process, aggression, power, and control are evident in all domains of a man's life, including the workplace. Men have learned that to be respected and valued they need to display these characteristics. Obviously, some measure of these characteristics is functional; however, the "unrelenting reliance on competitive and aggressive coping behaviors to solve problems consistent with rigid masculine schemata is likely to produce stress" (Eisler & Blalock, 1991, pp. 52–53). Career counselors may deal with this coping mechanism from both a process and a content perspective. The process of career counseling may be affected if men feel the need to use their power and control mechanisms to be comfortable in the counseling context. Demanding counselor credentials, having unrealistic expectations of the counselor, or attempting to control the course of counseling may all be process outcomes of this coping strategy. The content of the career counseling itself may also be shaped by men's use of aggression, power, and control. The workplace is currently in a state of transition from a strict hierarchy characterized by a dominant, aggressive leader and compliant workers to a more egalitarian work culture that emphasizes greater cooperation and group consensus. This change may create great stress and career conflicts for the traditional man who was comfortable with and felt competent in the old workplace structure.

Importance of Performance, Achievement, and Success

Because male self-identity is inextricably tied to the worker role, much importance is placed on performance and achievement in men's career lives. The importance given to the work role at the expense of other life roles can be conceptualized as an obsession (Eisler & Blalock, 1991). As a result, it is likely that the career counselor will see men when some aspect of this performance achievement success paradigm breaks down. Examining strictly environmental changes in the work setting, we see many opportunities for this breakdown to occur. As is discussed in Chapter 7 on the changing workplace, companies are downsizing to become "leaner and meaner," different kinds of skills are needed and valued, and lateral career moves are occurring more often than vertical ones. All of these changes affect a man's ability to feel successful and gain identity in the workplace.

Emotional Inexpressiveness

Eisler and Blalock (1991) contended that, for men, the construct of emotional inexpressiveness "results in their frequent appraisal of certain types of interpersonal situations as stressful, restricts the range of coping behaviors available to them, and impairs the success of their relationships" (p. 55). Although Eisler and Blalock focused almost entirely on the consequences of this construct for romantic relationships and friendships, one can clearly see the role of emotional inexpressiveness in the workplace and career counseling setting as well. By restricting emotional expression, men may appraise the variety of interpersonal interactions at work as being much more stressful than would their female counterparts, who may be more likely to express their emotional reactions at work to resolve differences. More than ever before in the workplace, a worker's abilities to cooperate, hear others' perspectives, and problem solve to reach consensus all require the ability and willingness to express his or her feelings. The theoretical and empirical work of Eisler and Blalock appears to have much relevance to understanding men's coping mechanisms in stressful situations. Applying these constructs to work-related issues helps career counselors understand and interpret behavior and provide more effective career counseling.

Search for Meaning

For an adult man who has spent a great share of his life striving to achieve in the work world, there often comes a time when his perspective changes from asking "Can I do it?" to "What meaning does this have for me?" Adult developmental theorists call this a change from a search for competence to a search for meaning. The man may come to the realization that he can do many things; he then asks himself whether what he is doing is important in the bigger picture of his life. He may also begin questioning the impact of his striving on his health, friendships, and family connectedness. Some men decide that their current jobs no longer provide what they need and are propelled into a career transition. Given the paramount role that work has in men's lives, being in this ambiguous transition time can be especially stressful. If they are also questioning gender role attributes, even more conflicting feelings can arise.

Themes in Men's Career Transition Experiences

O'Neil and Fishman (1986) identified four central gender-specific outcomes that emerge during times of occupational transition: (a) discrepancy and incongruity, (b) devaluation, (c) restriction, and (d) violation.

Discrepancy and Incongruity

Discrepancy and incongruity occur when men realize a difference between their real and ideal self-concepts. Especially during times of career transition, men may feel they are not living up to the idealized notion of what a man should be. Depending on the circumstances of the transition, men may feel inadequate, depressed, angry; they may also exhibit self-hatred. Although O'Neil and Fishman (1986) appeared to be describing primarily men who equated the traditional male role as the ideal, the discrepancy could also occur when men are awakened to a new, less traditional mode of living but feel they are not able to measure up to that ideal either.

Devaluation

Devaluation occurs as a result of self-blame and blame deriving from others, such as spouses, partners, or family members. Self-blame usually occurs when men do not feel they are measuring up to the masculine ideal. They may be in a career transition because of losing a job and may feel that they are not providing for their family by being the proper breadwinner. This self-blame can lead to fear and anger, a loss of confidence in themselves, and depression.

Restriction

Restriction occurs when traditional masculine roles limit the flexibility men have in their work or family roles. When restricted men exhibit rigid roles at home and work, this leaves little room for self-growth and much room for interpersonal conflict and stress.

Violation

Violation occurs when men's rights are taken away and the men are forced to conform to the rigid patterns of male achievement and success in the workplace. If men question or reject the masculine standards of success, they may become alienated or ostracized in the work environment.

Assessments for Empowering Men's Choices

Now we turn to an examination of various assessments and techniques for promoting men's awareness and understanding how gender has influenced men's career development. Fortunately, the past decade has seen the development of a variety of assessment measures that examine various aspects of the male gender role.

Thompson and Pleck (1995) provided a review of instruments that are available on men and masculinity-related constructs. It is imperative that counselors be aware of their own gender-related biases, the conflicts they may feel with their own gender role, and how these biases and conflicts may influence their work with clients. As we have seen, the few empirical studies that have been conducted to date have uncovered gender bias on the part of counselors in their treatment of nontraditional male clients. Thus, we discuss five instruments that we have found to be particularly useful in applying male gender role concepts to the career counseling process. These may be helpful for counselors to use to assess themselves and may also be helpful in assisting male clients to make more authentic life-planning decisions.

Gender Role Conflict Scale

The Gender Role Conflict Scale (O'Neil, Helms, Gable, David, & Wrightsman, 1986; see also O'Neil, 2008, for a review) measures the construct of *gender role conflict*, which is defined as "a psychological state arising from the inherently contradictory and unrealistic messages within and across the standards of masculinity. Gender role conflict exists when masculinity standards result in personal restriction and devaluation" (Thompson & Pleck, 1995, p. 150). This 37-item scale measures four constructs: (a) men's concerns with success, power, and competition (sample item: "Moving up the career ladder is important to me"), (b) restrictive emotionality (sample item: "I have difficulty expressing my emotional needs to my partner"), (c) restrictive affectionate behavior between men (sample item: "Expressing my emotions to other men is risky"), and (d) conflicts in work/family relations (sample item: "My need to work or study keeps me from my family or leisure more than I would like").

Conformity to Masculine Norms Inventory

The Conformity to Masculine Norms Inventory (Mahalik et al., 2003) was constructed to measure conformity to gender role norms. The 94-item scale consists of 11 factors: (a) Winning, (b) Emotional Control, (c) Risk-Taking, (d) Violence, (e) Power Over Women, (f) Dominance, (g) Playboy, (h) Self-Reliance, (i) Primacy of Work, (j) Disdain for Homosexuals, and (k) Pursuit of Status. This scale may be particularly useful in examining the role conformity to masculine norms has in career development patterns, including men's career choice and adjustment.

Masculine Gender Role Stress Scale

The Masculine Gender Role Stress Scale (Eisler & Skidmore, 1987) was constructed to measure stressful life situations that are more common in men's than women's lives, given gender role socialization. The instrument measures five areas of gender-linked stress: (a) situations that demonstrate physical inadequacy (sample item: "Losing in a sports competition"), (b) expressing tender emotions (sample item: "Telling someone that you feel hurt by something she/he said"), (c) placing men in subordination to women (sample item: "Letting a woman take control of the situation"), (d) threatening a man's intellectual control (sample item: "Working with people who are brighter than yourself"), and (e) revealing performance failures in work and sex (sample item: "Finding you lack the occupational skills to succeed").

Male Role Norms Scale

The original creation, development, and psychometric work on the Male Role Norms Scale (Brannon & Juni, 1984; Thompson & Pleck, 1986) was conducted by Brannon and Juni (1984) to measure men's approval of the norms and values associated with the male role. The original form is known as the Brannon Masculinity Scale. Thompson and Pleck (1986) conducted a factor analysis on the Brannon and developed a shorter (26-item) three-factor scale they called the Male Role Norms Scale. The three factors composing this scale are (a) Status Norms, (b) Toughness Norms, and (c) Antifemininity Norms.

Gender Role Journey Measure

This Gender Role Journey Measure (O'Neil, Egan, Owens, & McBride, 1993) was constructed to help both men and women explore the stage they are in with regard to their own gender role changes and transitions. The scale is based on the idea that individuals can grow and change in their gender role ideology, moving from stages of traditional and rigid gender-segregated social worlds to more flexible and less restrictive views. The five original theorized stages were collapsed into three factors that make up the current instrument. These three stages are (a) acceptance of traditional gender roles (sample item: "Men should be in charge at work"); (b) gender role ambivalence, anger, confusion, and fear (sample item: "I sometimes feel confused about gender roles"); and (c) personal–professional activism that promotes social change (sample item: "I have taken some action in my personal life to reduce sexism").

Strategies for Exploring Gender Role and Career Issues

As assessment tools, the five instruments described in the previous section provide a context and a language for discussing the complex issues of gender and career planning. By using them with male clients, the counselor can open up a dialogue with the client in which gender role constructs become a category of analysis within the career counseling process (Heppner & Heppner, 2001). In addition to using assessment measures in the career counseling process, using a number of other interventions may be helpful. We discuss three strategies that may be particularly helpful to male clients in their exploration of gender role and career: (a) expressiveness training, (b) the use of *Man Alive: A Primer of Men's Issues* (Rabinowitz & Cochran, 1994), and (c) the use of a gender-focused journal especially designed for men to use to examine career-related issues.

Expressiveness Training

Because restricted emotionality is one of the most pervasive outcomes of men growing up in the gendered context, interventions aimed at helping men become more expressive have been advocated (Dosser, 1982; Kahn & Greenberg, 1980; Zunker, 1994). Zunker described two goals of expressiveness training: The client needs to learn (a) situations when the expression of emotion in the workplace is appropriate and (b) the specifics of how to express a variety of emotions. A host of counseling techniques can be creatively applied to expressiveness training, including role play, in which group members play the roles of key figures in the work environment while men practice appropriate ways of expressing themselves with those individuals. The Gestalt technique of the Empty Chair may also be a powerful tool in expressiveness training (Kahn & Greenberg, 1980).

For example, one client identified a situation from the past when he wished he had been able to express appropriate emotion. His secretary had been emotionally distraught over the loss of her husband to cancer. He had managed to tell her to take as much time off as she needed but had been unable to express his empathy for her loss. Through using the Empty Chair technique, the client was able to practice ways of speaking to her and to switch roles to feel how she would have felt in response to both his nonexpressive and expressive modes. Skillful counselors can help men explore the full range of their emotions, thus giving them a much wider repertoire of responses from which to choose.

Man Alive: A Primer of Men's Issues

The *Man Alive: A Primer of Men's Issues* (Rabinowitz & Cochran, 1994) book can be used either as a self-help guide or as part of ongoing individual or group work to assist male clients in understanding and working through key aspects of the male role that might be destructive to their mental, physical, or spiritual health. It contains chapters on a range of topics, including early socialization messages; male health issues; and work, money, and male identity. Each chapter has a narrative that examines some aspect of the male role, followed by exercises designed to help men reflect on and explore these aspects of their lives. Some of these are consciousness-raising exercises; others are personal development ones. Additional readings are also provided for men to fully explore each topic. *Deepening Psychotherapy With Men* (Rabinowitz & Cochran, 2002) is a newer and very helpful resource that integrates theory, research, and practice in helping counselors deepen their relationships with male clients. Rabinowitz and Cochran (2002) also provide in-depth case studies that demonstrate ways of helping men understand important issues in their lives and more deeply connect with who they are and what they want from their lives.

Gender-Focused Journal

The use of journal writing in counseling and psychotherapy has been helpful to many clients (Progoff, 1975). Through reflection and writing, male clients may come to a new understanding of themselves and their work. Although the technique of journaling has been used most often with female clients (Kahn & Greenberg, 1980), it would seem appropriate for addressing the internal and introverted characteristics of many men. The autonomy and independence that journaling allows may be particularly appealing to men. Writing about one's thoughts and feelings may also be a good preparatory step to discussing them in the counseling session. It is recommended that the counselor give the client stimulus questions, quotes, or ideas to explore in the journal. For example, men could be asked to trace their heroes and role models through time, from their earliest memories to the present day, and to analyze characteristics consistent in their role models and those that have changed over time. Kahn and Greenberg (1980) suggested asking men to display graphically how they spend their time, or asking them to draw a lifeline to highlight the peaks and valleys of their life experiences. Planning and developing exercises to help male clients explore how their gender role has facilitated and hindered their career development can be a creative process for the counselor. The stimulus issues for the journal should be carefully planned to match the particular needs of the client.

The Structure of Career Counseling: Placing Gender Issues Within the Counseling Process

In Chapter 1 we outline the structure of career counseling, which consists of two major phases and a number of subphases. In this section we discuss ways of integrating the issues relevant to the gendered context for men into this structure and process. This section highlights those aspects of each phase that may have gender-related implications for gay, bisexual, and heterosexual clients.

Client Goal or Problem Identification, Clarification, and Specification

Identification—Opening and Forming the Working Alliance
The opening phase of career counseling has as its central goals (a) identifying the client's goals or problems and the internal thoughts and feelings that might be involved, (b) beginning to form a working alliance, and (c) defining and clarifying the client–counselor relationship and responsibilities. In planning this phase with the gendered context in mind, you as the counselor should consider the following issues.

You should help the client examine his goals through a gender filter. Which goals are motivated out of socialization? Which presenting problems result from environmental pressures and a need to prove some aspect of the traditional male role? Is the client able to express emotions honestly, even if they include feelings of vulnerability? Does the client appear to be setting authentic goals based on a full knowledge of relevant information?

As you begin to develop the working alliance, you should be especially aware of the client's level of gender role identity and sexual identity orientation and what impact these might have on the relationship you are building with him. It is critically important not to assume a heterosexist stance but rather to use inclusive terminology when building the working alliance and finding out about the man's situation. Small signs, such as whether there is a place to indicate "partnered" as opposed to "married" on an intake form or a Safe Space poster in one's office, communicate a message of affirmation important to building a strong alliance.

It is very difficult for most men to admit that they need help. Men's training fosters self-reliance. Thus, if a man actually comes to counseling, it may be important to recognize the likelihood that he is experiencing a fair amount of turmoil and pain. Building a strong working alliance is paramount. Little has been written about how best to establish a strong working alliance with a traditional man. An understanding of the typical male socialization process tells us that building a relationship of honesty and collaboration with a male client will often be difficult. If the counselor is male, often the male client is confused by the unfamiliar intimacy with another man and may have a homophobic reaction (Scher, 2001).

Building the working alliance involves building a bond of collaboration and hope. The client needs to see the counselor as someone who understands his situation and will relate to his life experiences. Appreciating the pride of the man and empathizing with his discomfort and inadequacy are critical for forming a working alliance. Self-disclosure of relevant and appropriate information from your own life may help model the appropriate expression of emotion and help to build the bond. As you build the working alliance, client strengths should be reinforced, because the client may feel that he has no strength of his own if he has reached the point of needing help. This is a time when emphasizing the strengths that are part of the traditional male role is especially important. Helping the client understand that his development has fostered such positive characteristics as integrity, steadfastness, loyalty, and the ability to persevere (Levant, 1996), for example, can help build self-esteem and increase the bond between counselor and client.

Recognize that the counseling setting may not be a comfortable place for men to be. Talking about feelings directly, sitting for 50 min, and being vulnerable are not behaviors that most men relate to. It may be important to alter the typical counseling session to better meet the needs of male clients. When clarifying the client–counselor relationship and responsibilities, it is important to discuss your philosophy of counseling and particularly those aspects that relate to counseling men. If you concur with the feminist or gender-aware counseling position discussed in Chapter 4—seeing the client–counselor relationship as one of equality, a collaborative working relationship—then that needs to be communicated. Because many clients come to counselors seeking an expert who will give advice about their lives, this characterization of a collaborative relationship may be foreign. Men often view the counselor as an answer dispenser. They expect to go in and "get fixed," not to work in a collaborative relationship that emphasizes self-awareness. Also, the role of the environment in shaping the individual may be an important philosophical issue to discuss. If you believe it is your responsibility to challenge gender-based assumptions, this should also be communicated. The client has a right to informed consent in the choice of a career counselor. Knowing where you stand and your philosophical base is important information in making that choice. As discussed in Chapter 4, it is also important for counselors to be aware of and knowledgeable about the sexual identity development of men and how this may impact men's vocational development. The reader is referred to Chapter 4 for more information and resources about sexual identity models that may be helpful.

Clarification—Gathering Client Information

The clarification and information-gathering subphase of the career counseling process has as its central goal learning more about the client.

Here, any or all of the assessments discussed earlier in this chapter can be used to supplement any other standardized or nonstandardized career-related assessment measures. Using the Gender Role Conflict Scale, Masculine Gender Role Stress Scale, Male Role Norms Scale, or Gender Role Journey Measure are all appropriate ways of gathering information about the client's experiences that may impact his career planning process. It is important to discuss your rationale for choosing a particular measure with the client. You might say something like this: "Career development for men is often intertwined with how they see themselves as men. This scale helps you assess your own gender role and how aspects of this role might affect your career planning."

These instruments have also been used effectively when clients have brought their test results home, reflected on them, and written about how these fit their perceptions of themselves. For example, the following is a portion of a client's writing after taking the Male Role Norms Scale:

> I hadn't really realized how driven toward status and material things I have become. As a product of the sixties, I always prided myself on living the simple life, but now I find myself working three jobs in order to be able to afford things I used to ridicule people for wanting.

The assessment of gender role constructs can also be very helpful when the results of such an assessment are integrated with more traditional career assessments, as this case example illustrates:

> Lester had a very low, flat profile on the Self-Directed Search, with strong scores only in the realistic area. His scores on the Gender Role Journey Measure indicated that he was at the second stage, characterized by gender role ambivalence, confusion, anger, and fear. By talking through the antecedents of his ambivalent feelings, it became clear that he wanted to be more open to broader roles but never felt his social skills were good enough to do other kinds of occupations. Thus, the path of counseling was shifted slightly toward examining ways of improving interpersonal skills in order to feel that he had greater career options.

Specification—Understanding and Hypothesizing About Client Information and Behavior

The specification subphase of the career counseling process has as its central goal understanding clients more fully and hypothesizing about their unique dynamics and the psychological and environmental reasons behind their actions.

In this phase, it is important to probe deeper to understand more about how the client makes meaning of himself and his occupational world. As we listen through the gender filter, we are trying to understand the life choices from both an individual and an environmental perspective. We are trying to help the client explore the gender-based career choices he has made and to evaluate how they are working for him at this point in his life.

As a counselor, you can also use your awareness of gender role constructs during this phase to assess their influence on men's lives in more informal ways. The instruments can provide you with language and constructs to use as filters when talking to male clients. They can help you build hypotheses about the client's behavior, such as the following:

> Mike is talking a lot about his anger toward his coworkers, how they aren't measuring up. I want to check out whether this is out of his own need to feel superior, or whether he feels angry at himself for being at the office every night, or whether there is another explanation for why he feels so upset by their behavior.

Another hypothesis might be that his anger at others is masking his feelings of inadequacy that result from his feeling inferior to his coworkers.

These hypotheses can then be tested in various ways so that the counselor and client can become more aware of the underlying gender-related dynamics that may be creating certain behaviors and attitudes.

In this phase it is appropriate to provide knowledge to the client to help him understand more about the impact of gender on people's lives. Depending on the client's situation, this may mean talking about such issues as the importance of learning to define success on one's own terms; expressing emotions rather than withholding them; how to replace the importance of achievement in defining one's identity with other, more balanced life options; and what we know about the costs and rewards of traditional gender role beliefs for psychological and physical well-being.

This may be an important phase for helping gay clients understand how various aspects of their sexual orientation may be influencing the career planning process. The counselor must also understand the phenomenon of internalized homophobia and help the client recognize if he has internalized heterosexist messages and beliefs. Some bisexual and gay men need to spend an enormous amount of energy "passing" for heterosexual at work. Understanding more about where the client is in terms of his coming-out process can be a vital aspect of helping to understand and negotiate various career-related issues and transitions.

Finally, this may also be the phase to use techniques such as the genogram (presented in Chapter 11) to understand more specifically about the client's gender-influenced life choices from a family systems perspective. At this time, the client might construct a lifeline to help him understand issues such as how his achievement orientation was manifested over time. He could take the Career Transitions Inventory (see Chapter 13) and then take the results home to use as inspiration for journal writing about the psychological resources and barriers he is bringing to his career transition. It might also be helpful for the client to reflect on the gender-related themes that men experience during times of transition discussed by O'Neil and Fishman (1986) to see how they fit the client's own experience.

Client Goal or Problem Resolution

The second major phase of the career counseling process involves taking action. Here we move from gathering and evaluating aspects of the gendered environment and their resultant gender-specific outcomes to actually taking steps to act on this information. Reaching this phase means that you have worked through all the major issues surrounding the client's situation, and he is now in a position to make an authentic life decision based on as complete a set of information about himself and the work world as possible.

Taking Action

Taking action is sometimes an easier phase of the counseling process for men than women, because taking action is ingrained in their gender role training more than talking about themselves is. For the male client, taking action may be the quickest way to quell anxiety. It is important, therefore, to be sure men have the necessary self-knowledge and occupational knowledge to make career decisions before charging ahead with the process. A poignant personal memory comes to mind that may help to highlight this point:

> Having come into the career center where I work, I saw a man in his late 50s sitting on the bench waiting for me. There was a young woman, maybe in her early 20s, with him. He was dressed like a college student and had carefully combed his little remaining hair over the large bald spot on top of his head. As he began the session with me, he explained that he had just lost his job, his wife had left him, and he wanted to get into another career field as quickly as possible. Even though he had built up a financial nest egg, his anxiety was clearly driving him to jump into another life as quickly as possible. The young woman with him was his new romantic partner, whom he had started dating 1 week after his wife had left him.

As this situation illustrates, it is important to try to help the client slow down and learn to live with the ambiguity of the career transition in order to increase the odds of making better choices.

Developing Career Goals and Plans of Action

Individualized career plans are particularly important for helping male clients incorporate parts of their gender role ideology into the career planning process. Carefully examining each step of the process with an eye to how the client is likely to handle particular action steps given his gender role upbringing can be invaluable to him. Different aspects will be important given the uniqueness of each man's situation. For example, when counseling a traditional man who is likely to appear arrogant when interviewing with women, building his awareness about the consequences of various interpersonal styles might be helpful. When helping a gay man apply for positions in a potentially discriminating employment setting, discussing each choice point he has in the job application and interview process would be vitally important. This also emphasizes the need for counselors to be aware of laws protecting and discriminating against gays in employment settings, as well as issues related to HIV testing in the workplace (Hedgepeth, 1979/1980).

Evaluating Results and Closing the Relationship

The closure session is a time for evaluating whether goals have been met and what the process was like for the counselor and the client. When one is examining the closure session through a gender filter, the following issues are important.

Reflect on the journey the career counseling process has taken. For many men, this might have been the first time that they identified the need for help and sought counseling. It is important to reflect on and reinforce the courage of that act. It may be helpful to the client to see the experience of asking for help as a sign of strength rather than a weakness.

Discuss the relationship between the counselor and client over time. How did the working alliance develop? How were tears in the alliance mended? How are both parties feeling about termination? Developing the types of intimate relationships that often result between a counselor and client is difficult for all clients, but especially for men. It is helpful to talk about how the counseling relationship developed, how communication became more honest, how trust developed, and how all of this felt from the client's perspective. You can point out that the strengths of the client that helped to foster this relationship are transferable to other relationships in the man's life.

Let the client know that you are here should he wish to return for more counseling or just to let you know how things are going. Male clients should know that the support system you have provided during counseling will remain should he have difficulties after counseling has closed, because this may be one of the few support systems he really has.

In each phase of the counseling process there are important gender-related issues to incorporate. If you plan each session knowing the individual man's life experience and its many gender-socialized aspects, the career counseling process is more likely to be an empowering and reinforcing one.

Closing Thoughts

The purpose of this chapter was to highlight key aspects of the gendered context; to identify their resultant outcomes in male clients; to discuss strategies and assessments for integrating knowledge of the gendered environment into counseling sessions; and, specifically, to point out key relevant issues at each stage of the career planning process. We have also tried to integrate the very limited literature on the unique career-related issues of gay and bisexual men. In doing so, we hope to have prepared the counselor to feel more personal efficacy in empowering the choices of all men through career counseling.

References

Addis, M. E., & Mahalik, J. R. (2003). Men, masculinity, and the context of help seeking. *American Psychologist, 58,* 5–14.

Armstrong, P. I., & Crombie, G. (2000). Compromises in adolescents' occupational aspirations and expectations from grades 8 to 10. *Journal of Vocational Behavior, 56,* 82–98.

Bank, B. (2007). Peer cultures and friendships in school. In B. Bank (Ed.), *Gender and education: An encyclopedia* (pp. 605–611). Westport, CT: Praeger.

Bieschke, K. J., Perez, R. M., & DeBord, K. A. (Eds.). (2006). *Handbook of counseling and psychotherapy with lesbian, gay, bisexual, and transgender clients* (2nd ed.). Washington, DC: American Psychological Association.

Blustein, D. L. (2006). *The psychology of working: A new perspective for career development, counseling, and public policy.* Mahwah, NJ: Erlbaum.

Blustein, D. L. (2011). A relational theory of working. *Journal of Vocational Behavior, 79,* 1–17.

Boteach, S. (2008). *The broken American male: And how to fix him.* New York, NY: St. Martin's Press.

Brannon, R., & Juni, S. (1984). A scale for measuring attitudes toward masculinity. *JSAS Catalog of Selected Documents in Psychology, 14,* 6 (Ms 2012).

Brooks, G. R., & Good, G. E. (Eds.). (2001). *The new handbook of psychotherapy and counseling with men.* San Francisco, CA: Jossey-Bass.

Bureau of Labor Statistics. (2013). *Databases, tables, & calculators by subject.* Retrieved from http://data.bls.gov/timeseries/LNS14000000

Carroll, L., Gilroy, P. J., & Ryan, J. (2002). Counseling transgendered, transsexual and gender-variant clients. *Journal of Counseling & Development, 80,* 131–139.

Chung, Y. B. (2001). Career counseling with lesbian, gay, bisexual and transgendered persons: The next decade. *The Career Development Quarterly, 50,* 33–44.

Chung, Y. B. (2003). Work discrimination and coping strategies: Conceptual frameworks for counseling lesbian, gay and bisexual clients. *The Career Development Quarterly, 52,* 78–86.

Courtenay, W. H. (2001). Counseling men in medical settings: The six-point health plan. In G. R. Brooks & G. E. Good (Eds.), *The new handbook of psychotherapy and counseling with men* (pp. 59–91). San Francisco, CA: Jossey-Bass.

Croteau, J. M. (1996). Research on the work experiences of lesbian, gay, and bisexual people: An integrative review of methodology and findings. *Journal of Vocational Behavior, 48,* 195–209.

Croteau, J. M., Anderson, M. Z., Distefano, T. M., & Kampa-Kokesch, S. (1999). Lesbian, gay, and bisexual vocational psychology: Reviewing foundations and planning construction. In R. M. Perez, K. A. DeBord, & K. J. Bieschke (Eds.), *Handbook of counseling and psychotherapy with lesbian, gay, and bisexual clients* (1st ed., pp. 383–408). Washington, DC: American Psychological Association.

Dosser, D. A. (1982). Male inexpressiveness: Behavioral interventions. In K. Solomon & N. B. Levy (Eds.), *Men in transition* (pp. 343–432). New York, NY: Plenum.

Eisler, R. M., & Blalock, J. A. (1991). Masculine gender role stress: Implications for the assessment of men. *Clinical Psychology Review, 11,* 45–60.

Eisler, R. M., & Skidmore, J. R. (1987). Masculine gender role stress: Scale development and component factors in the appraisal of stressful situations. *Behavior Modification, 11,* 123–136.

Englar-Carlson, M., Evans, M., & Duffey, T. (Eds.). (2014). *A counselor's guide to working with men.* Alexandria, VA: American Counseling Association.

Fassinger, R. E., & Asay, P. A. (2006). Career counseling for women in science, technology, engineering, and mathematics (STEM) fields. In W. B. Walsh & M. J. Heppner (Eds.), *Handbook of career counseling for women* (2nd ed., pp. 427–452). Mahwah, NJ: Erlbaum.

Flores, L. Y., Navarro, R. L., Smith, J., & Ploszaj, A. (2006). Testing a model of career choice with Mexican American adolescent boys. *Journal of Career Assessment, 14,* 214–234.

Garcia, G. (2009). *The decline of men.* New York, NY: Harper Perennial.

Gilligan, C. (1982). *In a different voice.* Cambridge, MA: Harvard University Press.

Greenstone, M., & Looney, A. (2010). *An economic strategy to renew the American community.* Washington, DC: The Hamilton Project, Brookings Institution.

Harrison, J., Chin, J., & Ficarrotto, T. (1989). Warning: Masculinity may be dangerous to your health. In M. S. Kimmel & M. A. Messner (Eds.), *Men's lives* (pp. 296–309). New York, NY: Macmillan.

Hedgepeth, J. M. (1979/1980). Employment discrimination law and the rights of gay persons. *Journal of Homosexuality, 5*(12), 67–78.

Heppner, M. J. (2013). Women, men and work: The long road to gender equity. In S. D. Brown & R. W. Lent (Eds.), *Career development and counseling: Putting theory and research to work* (2nd ed., pp. 187–214). Hoboken, NJ: Wiley.

Heppner, M. J., & Heppner, P. P. (2001). Addressing the implications of male socialization for career counseling. In G. R. Brooks & G. E. Good (Eds.), *The new handbook of psychotherapy and counseling with men* (pp. 369–386). San Francisco, CA: Jossey-Bass.

Heppner, M. J., & Heppner, P. P. (2009). On men and work: Taking the road less traveled. *Journal of Career Development, 36,* 49-67.

Heppner, M. J., & Heppner, P. P. (2014). The changing nature of work in men's lives: Implications for counseling. In M. Englar-Carlson, M. Evans, & T. Duffey (Eds.), *A counselor's guide to working with men* (pp. 71–86). Alexandria, VA: American Counseling Association.

Heppner, M. J., & Jung, A. K. (2013a). Gender and social class: Powerful predictors of a life journey. In W. B. Walsh, M. L. Savickas, & P. J. Hartung (Eds.), *Handbook of vocational psychology* (4th ed., pp. 81–102). New York, NY: Routledge.

Heppner, M. J., & Jung, A. K. (2013b). Women, men and change: The role of career interventions. In P. Hartung, M. Savickas, & B. Walsh (Eds.), *APA handbook of career interventions.* Washington, DC: American Psychological Association.

Hershberger, S. L., & D'Augelli, A. R. (1999). Issues in counseling lesbian, gay, and bisexual adolescents. In R. M. Perez, K. A. DeBord, & K. J. Bieschke (Eds.), *Handbook of counseling and psychotherapy with lesbian, gay, and bisexual clients* (1st ed., pp. 225–248). Washington, DC: American Psychological Association.

Hetherington, C., Hillerbrand, E., & Etringer, B. D. (1989). Career counseling with gay men: Issues and recommendations for research. *Journal of Counseling & Development, 67,* 452–454.

Jome, L. M., & Tokar, D. M. (1998). Dimensions of masculinity and major choice traditionality. *Journal of Vocational Behavior, 52,* 120–134.

Kahn, S. E., & Greenberg, L. S. (1980). Expanding sex role definitions by self-discovery. *Personnel and Guidance Journal, 49,* 220–225.

Keen, S. (1991). *Fire in the belly: On being a man.* New York, NY: Bantam Books.

Kiselica, M. S. (2001). A male-friendly therapeutic process with school age boys. In G. R. Brooks & G. E. Good (Eds.), *The new handbook of psychotherapy and counseling with men* (pp. 43–58). San Francisco, CA: Jossey-Bass.

Kite, M. E., Deaux, K., & Haines, E. L. (2008). Gender stereotypes. In F. Denmark & M. Paludi (Eds.), *Psychology of women: A handbook of issues and theories* (2nd ed., pp. 205–236). Westport, CT: Praeger.

Kochhar, R. (2012). *In two years of economic recovery women, women lost jobs, men found them.* Pew Research Center Publications. Retrieved from http://pewresearch .org/ pubs/2049/unemployment-jobs-gender-recession-economic-recovery

Lazarus, R. S., & Folkman, S. (1984). *Stress, appraisal and coping.* New York, NY: Springer.

Lease, S. H. (2003). Testing a model of men's nontraditional occupational choices. *The Career Development Quarterly, 51,* 244–258.

Lent, R. W., Brown, S. D., & Hackett, G. (1994). Toward a unifying social cognitive theory of career and academic interest, choice, and performance. *Journal of Vocational Behavior, 45,* 79–122.

Levant, R. F. (1996). Masculinity reconstructed. *The Independent Practitioner, 16,* 36–39.

Levant, R. F. (2001). The crisis of boyhood. In G. R. Brooks & G. E. Good (Eds.), *The new handbook of psychotherapy and counseling with men* (pp. 355–368). San Francisco, CA: Jossey-Bass.

Lucas, R., Clark, A., Georgellis, Y., & Diener, E. (2004). Unemployment alters the set point for life satisfaction. *Psychological Science, 15,* 8–15.

Mahalik, J. R., Locke, B. D., Ludlow, L. H., Gottfried, M., Scott, R. P. J., & Freitas, G. (2003). Development of the Conformity to Masculine Norms Inventory. *Psychology of Men and Masculinity, 4,* 3–25.

Mandel, L., & Vitelli, R. (2007). Heterosexism and homophobia in the peer group. In B. Bank (Ed.), *Gender and education: An encyclopedia* (pp. 597–603). Westport, CT: Praeger.

Matlin, M. (2012). *The psychology of women.* Belmont, CA: Wadsworth.

Matthews, K. A., & Angulu, J. (1980). Measurement of the Type A behavior pattern in children: Assessment of children's competitiveness, impatience, anger, and aggression. *Child Development, 51,* 466–475.

O'Neil, J. M. (2008). Summarizing twenty-five years of research on men's gender-role conflict using the Gender Role Conflict Scale: New research paradigms and clinical implications. *The Counseling Psychologist, 36,* 358–445.

O'Neil, J. M., Egan, J., Owens, S. V., & McBride, V. (1993). The Gender Role Journey Measure: Scale development and psychometric evaluation. *Sex Roles, 28,* 167–185.

O'Neil, J. M., & Fishman, D. M. (1986). Adult men's career transitions and gender-role themes. In Z. Leibowitz & D. Lea (Eds.), *Adult career development: Concepts, issues and practices* (pp. 132–162). Alexandria, VA: National Career Development Association.

O'Neil, J. M., Helms, B. J., Gable, R. K., David, L., & Wrightsman, L. S. (1986). Gender-Role Conflict Scale: College men's fears of femininity. *Sex Roles, 14,* 335–350.

Parker, K. (2008). *Save the males.* New York, NY: Random House.

Paul, K. I., & Moser, K. (2009). Unemployment impairs mental health: Meta-analysis. *Journal of Vocational Behavior, 74,* 264–282.

Perez, R. M., DeBord, K. A., & Bieschke, K. J. (Eds.). (1999). *Handbook of counseling and psychotherapy with lesbian, gay, and bisexual clients* (1st ed.). Washington, DC: American Psychological Association.

Pope, M., Barret, B., Szymanski, D. M., Chung, Y. B., Singaravelu, H., McLean, R., & Sanabria, S. (2004). Culturally appropriate career counseling with gay and lesbian clients. *The Career Development Quarterly, 53,* 158–177.

Prince, J. (2013). Career development of lesbian, gay, bisexual, and transgender individuals. In S. D. Brown & R. W. Lent (Eds.), *Career development and counseling: Putting theory and research to work* (2nd ed., pp. 275–299). Hoboken, NJ: Wiley.

Progoff, I. (1975). *At a journal workshop: The basic text and guide for using the intensive journal.* New York, NY: Dialogue House Library.

Rabinowitz, F. E., & Cochran, S. V. (1994). *Man alive: A primer of men's issues.* Pacific Grove, CA: Brooks/Cole.

Rabinowitz, F. E., & Cochran, S. V. (2002). *Deepening psychotherapy with men.* Washington, DC: American Psychological Association.

Robertson, J., & Fitzgerald, L. F. (1990). The (mis)treatment of men: Effects of client gender roles and life-style on diagnosis and attribution of pathology. *Journal of Counseling Psychology, 37,* 3–9.

Robertson, J. M., & Verschelden, C. (1993). Voluntary male homemakers and female providers: Reported experiences and perceived social reactions. *Journal of Men's Studies, 1*(4), 383–402.

Rochlen, A. B., McKelley, R. A., Suizzo, M.-A. P., & Scaringi, V. (2008). Predictors of relationship satisfaction, psychological well-being and life satisfaction among stay-at-home fathers. *Psychology of Men and Masculinity, 9,* 17–28.

Rosin, H. (2012). *The end of men and the rise of women.* New York, NY: Riverhead Books.

Sax, L. (2007). *Boys adrift.* New York, NY: Basic Books.

Sayer, L., England, P., Allison, P., & Kangas, N. (2011). She left, he left: How employment and satisfaction affect women's and men's decisions to leave marriages. *American Journal of Sociology, 116,* 1982–2018.

Scher, M. (2001). Male therapist, male client: Reflections on critical dynamics. In G. R. Brooks & G. E. Good (Eds.), *The new handbook of psychotherapy and counseling with men* (pp. 719–734). San Francisco, CA: Jossey-Bass.

Sheldon, R. G. (2007). Gangs and school. In B. Bank (Ed.), *Gender and education: An encyclopedia* (pp. 591–596). Westport, CT: Praeger.

Shields, S. A. (2008). Gender: An intersectionality perspective. *Sex Roles, 59,* 301–311.

Skovholt, T. M. (1990). Career themes in counseling and psychotherapy with men. In D. Moore & F. Leafgren (Eds.), *Men in conflict* (pp. 39–53). Alexandria, VA: American Association for Counseling and Development.

Skovholt, T. M., & Morgan, J. I. (1981). Career development: An outline of issues for men. *Personnel and Guidance Journal, 60,* 231–236.

Srivastava, N., & Nair, S. K. (2011). Androgyny and rational emotive behavior as antecedents of managerial effectiveness. *Vision: The Journal of Business Perspective, 4,* 303–314.

Stockard, J. (2007). Sex role socialization. In B. Bank (Ed.), *Gender and education: An encyclopedia* (pp. 79–85). Westport, CT: Praeger.

Thompson, E. H., & Pleck, J. H. (1986). The structure of male role norms. *American Behavioral Scientist, 29,* 531–543.

Thompson, E. H., & Pleck, J. H. (1995). Masculinity ideology: A review of research instrumentation on men and masculinity. In R. F. Levant & W. S. Pollack (Eds.), *A new psychology of men* (pp. 129–163). New York, NY: Basic Books.

Tokar, D. M., & Jome, L. M. (1998). Masculinity, vocational interests, and career choice traditionality: Evidence for a fully mediated model. *Journal of Counseling Psychology, 45,* 424–435.

Tomlinson, M. J., & Fassinger, R. E. (2003). Career development, lesbian identity development, and campus climate among lesbian college students. *Journal of College Student Development, 44,* 845–860.

Tyler, L. E. (1977). *Individuality.* San Francisco, CA: Jossey-Bass.

U.S. Census Bureau. (2012). *Facts for features: June 2006.* Washington, DC: U.S. Government Printing Office.

Waldron, I. (1976). Why do women live longer than men? *Journal of Human Stress, 2,* 1–13.

White, M. J., & White, G. B. (2006). Implicit and explicit occupational gender stereotypes. *Sex Roles, 55,* 259–266.

Whitmire, R. (2010). *Why boys fail: Saving our sons from an educational system that's leaving them behind.* New York, NY: AMACOM.

Worthington, R. L., Savoy, H. B., & Vernaglia, E. R. (2001). *Beyond tolerance: An integrative model of LGB affirmativeness.* Unpublished manuscript.

Zunker, V. G. (1994). *Career counseling: Applied concepts of life planning.* Pacific Grove, CA: Brooks/Cole.

Chapter 6

Facilitating the Career Development of Individuals With Disabilities Through Empowering Career Counseling

John F. Kosciulek

Because of significant and ongoing changes in economic circumstances, people with disabilities are facing significant career development and employment challenges. The world of work is changing at a rapid pace, and the changes are likely to accelerate during the 21st century. According to Krepcio and Martin (2012), some of these changes in the economy are characterized as (a) shifting job functions, (b) increasing demands for certifications and technical skills, (c) rapid changes in technology, and (d) frequent and longer periods of unemployment, particularly for persons with disabilities. Further, employment arrangements, such as temporary employment, short-term hires, contractual positions, leased workers, and on-call and part-time workers, have influenced and will continue to influence the career development of all workers (Institute on Rehabilitation Issues, 1999). These changes are having a substantial impact on the life roles of individuals with disabilities, the settings in which these persons live and work, and the events that occur in their lives (National Council on Disability, 2008). Thus, career counselors must respond to these changes by asking the question: In this new economy, where and how can I add true and targeted value to achieve the goal of meaningful careers and independence for individuals with disabilities?

The purpose of this chapter is to help you expand and extend your vision of career counseling and your counseling repertoire to include those skills and techniques necessary to effectively serve individuals with disabilities. It will enable you to assist individuals with disabilities in becoming empowered to achieve their career goals and resolve their career problems. To this end, the following topics are presented: (a) the current employment and career statuses of individuals with disabilities, (b) a career counseling empowerment framework, and (c) the career counseling structure as applied to individuals with disabilities.

Current Employment and Career Statuses of Individuals With Disabilities

Work is a complex activity that is deeply connected to an individual's psychological well-being. Furthermore, work is social, cultural, and economic in nature (Rothman,

1987). Given that work is a central force in people's lives, dramatically high rates of unemployment and underemployment can adversely affect not only the economic and social status of individuals with disabilities but also their self-image. Disability, therefore, is a risk factor and individual difference that counselors should carefully consider when providing career planning, preparation, and counseling services to individuals with disabilities (Szymanski & Hanley-Maxwell, 1996).

The ever-changing nature of work presents challenges for individuals with disabilities in finding and maintaining suitable employment as well as challenges for career counseling professionals who work with them. Major trends such as globalization of the American economy, technology, and population shifts are changing the nature of work and worker skill requirements (Friedman, 2005; Ryan, 1995). Currently, a majority of Americans with disabilities between the ages of 16 and 64 are not employed, despite the fact that many nonemployed individuals with disabilities in the working-age population want to work (Fogg, Harrington, & McMahon, 2010; National Council on Disability, 2008; National Organization on Disability, 2000; Taylor, 1994).

Specific Difficulties Faced by People With Disabilities

Providing career development services to people with disabilities presents a challenge to career counselors. In general, the vocational adjustment of individuals with disabilities has been characterized by limited marketable work skills, low income, underemployment, and unemployment (Curnow, 1989; Stapleton & Burkhauser, 2003). In addition, regarding postschool outcomes for youths with disabilities, researchers have found the following persistent issues and problems: (a) poor high school graduation rate, (b) low employment rates after high school, and (c) low postsecondary education participation (Brolin & Loyd, 2004; Harrington, 1997).

The discouraging reports on the vocational preparation and employment outcomes for individuals with disabilities (e.g., Roessler, 1987; Wolfe, 1997) highlight the need for improved career counseling services for this population. A distinct set of challenges encountered by many people with disabilities that can be used as a reference point for the practicing career counselor includes (a) limitations in early life experiences, (b) decision-making difficulties, and (c) a negative worker self-concept as a result of castification processes in service delivery systems.

Limitations in Early Life Experiences
Frequently, individuals with disabilities arrive at adulthood with few career options (Chubon, 1995). The limited number of early vocational and social experiences encountered by people with disabilities restricts the array of career options they perceive, impedes decision-making ability, and impairs future vocational development (Brolin & Loyd, 2004; Kosciulek & Perkins, 2005). The effect of limited early vocational experiences was described by Holland (1985) as a precursor to the development of career-related problems. Specific career development problems resulting from limited vocational experiences may include the failure to develop a consistent and differentiated personality pattern or a clear vocational identity and the establishment of a career in an incongruent occupation (Holland, 1985). Unfortunately, such developmental patterns are not unusual among people with disabilities.

Decision-Making Difficulties
Lack of opportunities to participate in decision making, to form a perception of oneself as a worker, and to test self-competencies can be the outcome of limited early experiences and can impede career development. The poorly defined self-concept, ambivalence about obtaining work, and limited occupational knowledge reported by people

with disabilities are indicative of distortions that could result in unrealistic vocational aspirations or decisions (Kosciulek, 2007). Harrington (1997) aptly described how many individuals with disabilities have had little opportunity for successful experience in decision making and, therefore, lack competence in making decisions.

Negative Worker Self-Concept Resulting From Castification Processes
Lack of experience and difficulty in decision making are not solely the result of disability but also an outcome of social attitudes and stereotypes. Social attitudes toward disability may be as important as the disability itself in that the negative attitudes of others play a part in shaping the life role of the individual with the disability (Kosciulek, 2007). The outcome of this long-term exposure to prejudicial attitudes may be a negative self-appraisal and a negative worker self-concept.

Society generally holds diminished expectations of people with disabilities (Schroeder, 1995). These attitudes are pervasive; they influence all of us to some degree. As a class, people with disabilities have suffered discrimination. Individuals with disabilities (Fine & Asch, 1988), similar to members of racial and ethnic minority groups (Trueba, 1993), face common social problems of stigma, marginality, and discrimination. Furthermore, given that disability rates among racial and ethnic minority group members are proportionally higher than rates in the overall population (Rehabilitation Services Administration, 1993), many individuals with disabilities face double jeopardy.

Szymanski and Trueba (1994) maintained that at least some of the difficulties faced by people with disabilities are not the result of functional impairments related to the disability but rather are the result of castification processes embedded in societal institutions for rehabilitation and education and are enforced by well-meaning professionals. Castification processes have their roots in a determinist view in which people who are different are viewed as somehow less "human" or less capable (Trueba, Cheng, & Ima, 1993). Problems of castification plague service delivery to people with disabilities because the same categories of impairment and functional limitation (constructed mostly by people without disabilities) are used to determine eligibility for services, to prescribe interventions, and, on occasion, to explain failure. The constructs and those who use them become agents of castification (Szymanski & Trueba, 1994).

The disempowering nature of these classification systems is often all too apparent to people with disabilities applying for rehabilitation services in an effort to enhance self-sufficiency and personal independence (Scotch, 2000; United Cerebral Palsy Association, 2007). Rather than being treated as adults with free or equal status, they may be confronted by able-bodied persons asserting a right to determine what kinds of services they need. Thus, it is critically important that career counselors reject paternalistic castification processes and actively work to foster empowerment among their clients with disabilities. To aid you in accomplishing this task, I present below an empowerment framework that is useful for providing career counseling services to people with disabilities.

Empowering Career Counseling

Current disability policy and rehabilitation service provision in the United States focus on the inclusion, independence, and empowerment of people with disabilities (Kosciulek, 2000; United Cerebral Palsy Association, 2007). Thus, career counseling with individuals with disabilities must be a dynamic, creative, and highly individualized process. Effective career counseling can be instrumental in empowering the life choices, inclusion, and independence of people with disabilities. In turn, empowerment, inclusion, and independence will lead to high-quality employment and fulfilling careers for individuals with disabilities (O'Day, 1999).

Although some people with disabilities may receive career services exclusively from the state–federal vocational rehabilitation system, it is important that *all* career counselors be aware of the philosophical tenets related to the disability empowerment movement and develop a framework for providing career counseling services from an empowerment perspective. The goal of empowering people with disabilities to live independently, enjoy self-determination, make choices, contribute to society, and pursue meaningful careers should be a common one for all professionals serving individuals with disabilities (National Council on Disability, 2008).

An Empowerment Philosophy

Empowerment of individuals with disabilities may be viewed as ensuring that they possess the same degree of control over their own lives and the conditions that affect life as is generally possessed by people without disabilities (Harp, 1994). It is the transfer of power and control of values, decisions, choices, and directions of human services such as career counseling from external entities to individuals themselves (Bolton & Brookings, 1996). Thus, as hypothesized and tested by Kosciulek and Merz (2001), the career counselor committed to an empowerment approach to service delivery should facilitate and maximize opportunities for individuals with disabilities to have control and authority over their own lives.

Emener (1991) described the philosophical tenets necessary for an empowerment approach to rehabilitation. Extended, these tenets provide a valuable philosophical framework for the provision of career counseling services to people with disabilities. The four tenets are paraphrased as follows:

1. Each individual is of great worth and dignity.
2. Every person should have equal opportunity to maximize his or her potential and is deserving of societal help in attempting to do so.
3. People by and large strive to grow and change in positive directions.
4. Individuals should be free to make their own decisions about the management of their lives.

From an empowerment perspective based on these philosophical tenets, career counseling is not something that can be done *to* or *for* a client. Rather, it is a process in which clients must become active, informed participants who learn and control a planning process that they use for short- and long-term career development (Szymanski, Hershenson, Enright, & Ettinger, 1996; Wehmeyer, 2004). In addition, the life-long, developmental nature of the process means "unless we plan to work with an increasingly dependent client again and again across the decades, our professional responsibility is to assure [*sic*] that each person learns the [career planning] process" (Mastie, 1994, p. 37).

Active client involvement is the key element of successful career counseling interventions (Ettinger, Conyers, Merz, & Koch, 1995). In an empowerment approach to career counseling, clients are actively involved in (a) gathering information, including self-assessment and learning about occupations and the labor market; (b) generating alternative courses of action and weighing those alternatives; and (c) formulating a plan of action. The final section of this chapter applies the structure of career counseling to people with disabilities. The information and structure provided allow you to develop the skills necessary to provide efficacious services to people with disabilities from an empowerment perspective.

Applying the Career Counseling Structure to People With Disabilities

Unfortunately, reports on the current employment and career statuses of people with disabilities are discouraging (Fogg et al., 2010; National Council on Disability, 2008; Stapleton & Burkhauser, 2003; United Cerebral Palsy Association, 2007). Many people with disabilities are either unemployed or underemployed. Career challenges encountered by individuals with disabilities often result from a combination of limitations in life experiences and decision-making difficulties. In addition, individuals with disabilities may feel disempowered as a result of long-term exposure to prejudicial attitudes from castification processes in service systems. The need for improved career counseling for individuals with disabilities cannot be overstated.

An empowerment approach to career counseling is necessary to assist individuals with disabilities to achieve their career goals and resolve their career problems. In this section, the career counseling structure is applied to people with disabilities to aid you in developing the skills necessary to effectively serve this population. By applying this structure to a disability context, you can be instrumental in empowering the life choices, inclusion, and independence of people with disabilities.

Client Goal or Problem Identification, Clarification, and Specification

Phase 1 of career counseling involves client goal or problem identification, clarification, and specification. In this phase, the counselor and client proceed mutually from forming the working alliance to gathering client information to understanding and hypothesizing about client information and behavior.

Identification—Opening and Forming the Working Alliance
It is important to note at this juncture that, at least theoretically, career counseling for people with disabilities should not differ from career counseling for any other client. In practice, however, this is less than totally true, primarily because the person with a disability presents unique issues that were not presented by the population of individuals without disabilities on whom career counseling approaches were developed (Hershenson, 1996). For example, in forming the working alliance with clients with disabilities, it is important to distinguish clients whose onset of disability was precareer (e.g., congenital or in early childhood) from those whose onset of disability was after they had entered into a career. As summarized by Brolin and Loyd (2004) and Goldberg (1992), past research has shown that people with acquired disabilities tend to choose occupations consistent with their predisability plans, whereas people with precareer disabilities tend to choose occupations consistent with their parents' aspirations and social class. It is critical from the onset that you have an awareness of the myriad ways disability may potentially influence a person's career development. Being aware of such disability-related factors is a critical ingredient in establishing an effective working alliance (Kosciulek, Chan, Lustig, Pichette, & Strauser, 2001).

In the opening stage of Phase 1 of career counseling, the counselor and client identify initial client goals or problems and the internal thoughts and feelings and underlying dynamics that may be involved. Multiple authors (e.g., Ettinger et al., 1995; Hershenson, 1996; Wolfe, 1997) have emphasized the importance of forming an effective working alliance when counseling individuals with disabilities by clearly identifying presenting problems and defining the client–counselor relationship and responsibilities. For an effective and useful career counseling process to occur, clients should be encouraged to be active participants in the counseling process (Kosciulek et al., 2001).

An empowerment approach to forming the working alliance in career counseling includes elements that both clients and counselors bring to the relationship. Primary client elements include the fact that clients (a) take responsibility for their own actions and for the consequences of their actions and (b) are responsible for their own decision making. Counselor elements in the working alliance demonstrate the following characteristics: (a) Counselors know and admit to their limitations (e.g., lack of knowledge of a specific disability), and (b) counselors display unconditional positive regard for the clients they serve (National Institute on Disability and Rehabilitation Research [NIDRR], 1994). Specific counseling techniques that contribute to client empowerment and the development of an effective working alliance also include treating all clients as adults regardless of the severity of the disability condition, using age-appropriate language and techniques, placing emphasis on client strengths, and respecting client values and beliefs.

Clarification—Gathering Client Information

Following the development of an effective working alliance and the establishment of an empowerment approach to career counseling, you should proceed to gather information about the client's specific situation. A series of questions may be helpful in the information-gathering process. It may be beneficial to inquire about the client's overall worldview. For example, asking clients how they view themselves, others, and the world may provide a valuable starting point for the career exploration process.

Another question that applies directly to working with people with disabilities relates to the personal and environmental barriers or constraints within which a client operates. The data generated from responses to this question may give the career counselor clues about the primary difficulties encountered by a client, including limitations in life experiences and feelings of disempowerment as a result of castification processes in previous educational and vocational pursuits. Another question important to address with clients with disabilities relates to their decision-making styles. Simply asking a client about his or her decision-making processes and the life matters on which he or she makes decisions may elicit valuable information about the client's comfort with decision making regarding career planning.

Specification—Understanding and Hypothesizing About Client Information and Behavior

The final stage of Phase 1 of career counseling involves understanding and hypothesizing about client information and behavior. Following the development of an empowering working alliance and the gathering of information about client worldviews, personal and environmental barriers, and decision-making patterns, the counselor and client are prepared to hypothesize how this information relates to the client's career development process. At this stage, it may be instructive for you to apply the language and constructs from career development, counseling, and personality theories, and the literature and research concerning individuals with disabilities, to understand and interpret client information and behavior. Identification of the specific disability-related variables (including interaction with the client's family, social, and labor market environments) that may be contributing to a career-related problem or inhibiting maximal career growth may be particularly useful for the client and counselor to focus potential actions and interventions.

Client Goal or Problem Resolution

Phase 2 of career counseling involves taking action, developing career goals, and evaluating and closing the relationship. In this phase, the counselor and client undertake actions that will begin to foster positive career progress, identify specific career goals, close the counseling relationship to the extent necessary, and plan appropriate services for monitoring progress and assessing goal attainment.

Taking Action

Career counseling with people with disabilities, as with all individuals, may best proceed into an action phase by using theory-based counseling and assessment procedures. Empowerment counseling assists clients with striving to achieve their goals or resolve their concerns in a positive atmosphere created by an effective working alliance. It is important to remember that empowerment career counseling with people with disabilities involves treating all clients as adults, using age-appropriate language and techniques, and respecting client values and beliefs.

For example, a 20-year-old client seeking job placement assistance may present with cognitive limitations due to intellectual disability. In this case, you should address the individual as you would any other 20-year-old, respecting his or her goals and making accommodations as necessary for individual needs. In addition, assessment processes must be comprehensive and individualized so that you can understand client needs, wants, skills, and weaknesses. It is also particularly important to remember that clients' strengths play a major role in their empowerment. Assessment procedures should focus on identifying and capitalizing on these strengths in the goal development process. Protocols should also be tailored to individual needs and preferences to avoid castification and disempowering service processes. For example, standardized assessment batteries that did not include individuals with disabilities in the development and norming processes may further accentuate disability limitations rather than identify individual strengths.

Finally, clients' disabilities affect their families, spouses, friends, and other individuals who can be assets to counseling and its outcomes. In the past, many professionals have underused these valuable resources. You may wish to include a family member or friend in some aspect of the career counseling process (e.g., intake, client homework) to facilitate integration of information and goal-directed behavior outside of counseling sessions. Involving significant others (with client consent) in counseling can be a critical element in creating empowering relationships (NIDRR, 1994) and facilitating client career development.

Developing Career Goals and Plans of Action

Career counseling is an active process that must be done in an empowering context. Successful goal development and interventions require active client involvement in all phases of the process. When developing career goals, clients with disabilities must be encouraged to take responsibility for (a) gathering and integrating information about themselves, occupations, and the labor market; (b) generating and evaluating alternatives; (c) making decisions and formulating plans of action; (d) implementing career plans; and (e) evaluating their results (Szymanski & Hershenson, 1997).

A wide range of career interventions is available to assist counselors and their clients with disabilities with effective goal planning. General interventions include career planning systems, assessment tools, career classes and workshops (including those specially designed for people with disabilities), and career portfolios. Career interventions that may accompany school-to-work transition, adult training, and direct job placement programs include apprenticeships, cooperative education, school-based enterprises/entrepreneurship, internships and practica, and community-based volunteerism. As discussed by Wolfe (1997), the use of a combination of both individual and group-based career counseling and job search interventions has a positive effect on the employment status of individuals with disabilities.

Two major rehabilitation approaches are also highly applicable to the career counseling goal identification and development of people with disabilities. One of these is *supported employment*, which provides ongoing, work-related supportive services that permit persons with severe disabilities to engage in competitive employment. A second approach is *job accommodation*, in which job tasks and job sites are modified to make them accessible to workers with disabilities (Hershenson, 1996). By allowing for exploration and attending to specific disability-related factors that may be adversely affecting career growth, supported employment and job accommodation processes may greatly assist clients and counselors with identifying realistic and satisfying career options. As people with disabilities are a heterogeneous population, no single counseling, assessment, or intervention approach will be applicable to all individuals. Therefore, as with all career counseling clients, the focus should be eclectic—that is, on identifying and meeting individual needs, removing specific barriers, expanding the person's range of options, and supporting the person through his or her transition to work (Szymanski & Hershenson, 1997).

Evaluating Results and Closing the Relationship

As previously stated, active client involvement is the key element of most successful career counseling interventions. A critical question at the close of a career counseling relationship with individuals with disabilities is whether the client was actively involved in (a) gathering information, (b) generating alternative courses of action and weighing those alternatives, and (c) formulating a plan of action. The quality of the working alliance, level of empowerment generated, usefulness of interventions, and appropriateness of career goals identified are likely to be closely related to the answer to this question.

A critical ingredient for successful career development for people with disabilities is effective follow-along and follow-up services. Thus, when closing the career counseling relationship, counselors and clients may want to establish a monitoring process to ensure achievement of established career plans (e.g., completion of an educational or vocational training program, or successful job maintenance). Follow-along services that are not intrusive but continue to support empowerment can be critical for achieving desired long-term outcomes. Counselors should recognize that clients might choose to discontinue ongoing supports at any time. Counselors should not foster dependency, because clients may see too much follow-up as lack of confidence. An empowered client will feel free to reinitiate counseling contacts if the need arises (NIDRR, 1994).

Once clients leave counseling, their success may depend on their ability to access community resources. Counselors can enhance self-reliance by teaching clients how to get information and tap into supportive workplace and community networks. Clients who discover and use community-based resources will be more independent and will transfer their personal empowerment beyond the counseling arena into all realms of life.

Closing Thoughts

Because of the ever-changing nature of the world of work and service system castification processes, assisting people with disabilities to achieve positive, challenging, and stimulating career development is an increasingly difficult task. Effective career counseling can thus be instrumental for empowering the life choices and career success of your clients with disabilities. The information provided in this chapter should help you expand your counseling repertoire to include those skills and techniques necessary to effectively serve individuals with disabilities. Applying the career counseling structure within an empowerment framework will enable your clients with disabilities to become active, informed participants who learn and control a planning process that they use for both short- and long-term career development. In this manner, you will promote opportunities for your clients with disabilities to have control and authority over their own lives.

References

Bolton, B., & Brookings, J. (1996). Development of a multifaceted definition of empowerment. *Rehabilitation Counseling Bulletin, 39*(4), 256–264.

Brolin, D. E., & Loyd, R. J. (2004). *Career development and transition services: A functional life skills approach.* Upper Saddle River, NJ: Pearson.

Chubon, R. A. (1995). Career-related needs of school children with severe physical disabilities. *Journal of Counseling & Development, 64,* 47–51.

Curnow, T. C. (1989). Vocational development of persons with disability. *The Career Development Quarterly, 37,* 269–278.

Emener, W. (1991). Empowerment in rehabilitation: An empowerment philosophy for rehabilitation in the 20th century. *Journal of Rehabilitation, 57*(4), 7–12.

Ettinger, J., Conyers, L., Merz, M. A., & Koch, L. (1995). *Strategies and tools for counselors, educators, and consumers* (Working Paper No. 3). Madison: University of Wisconsin–Madison, Rehabilitation Research and Training Center.

Fine, M., & Asch, A. (1988). Disability beyond stigma: Social interaction, discrimination, and activism. *Journal of Social Issues, 44,* 3–21.

Fogg, N. P., Harrington, P. E., & McMahon, B. T. (2010). The impact of the Great Recession upon the unemployment of Americans with disabilities. *Journal of Vocational Rehabilitation, 33,* 193–202.

Friedman, T. L. (2005). *The world is flat.* New York, NY: Farrar, Straus & Giroux.

Goldberg, R. T. (1992). Toward a model of vocational development of people with disabilities. *Rehabilitation Counseling Bulletin, 35,* 161–173.

Harp, H. T. (1994). Empowerment of mental health consumers in vocational rehabilitation. *Psychosocial Rehabilitation Journal, 17,* 83–90.

Harrington, T. F. (1997). *Handbook of career planning for students with special needs.* Austin, TX: PRO-ED.

Hershenson, D. B. (1996). Career counseling. In A. E. Dell Orto & R. P. Marinelli (Eds.), *Encyclopedia of disability and rehabilitation* (pp. 140–146). New York, NY: Simon & Schuster Macmillan.

Holland, J. L. (1985). *Making vocational choices: A theory of vocational personalities and work environments* (2nd ed.). Englewood Cliffs, NJ: Prentice Hall.

Institute on Rehabilitation Issues. (1999). *Meeting future workforce needs.* Menomonie: University of Wisconsin–Stout, Stout Vocational Rehabilitation Institute.

Kosciulek, J. F. (2000). Implications of consumer direction for disability policy development and rehabilitation service delivery. *Journal of Disability Policy Studies, 11*(2), 82–89.

Kosciulek, J. F. (2007). The social context of coping. In E. Martz & H. Livneh (Eds.), *Coping with chronic illness and disability* (pp. 73–88). New York, NY: Springer.

Kosciulek, J. F., Chan, F., Lustig, D., Pichette, E., & Strauser, D. (2001, October). *The working alliance: A critical element in the rehabilitation counseling process.* Paper presented at the Alliance for Rehabilitation Counseling Symposium, St. Louis, MO.

Kosciulek, J. F., & Merz, M. A. (2001). Structural analysis of the consumer-directed theory of empowerment. *Rehabilitation Counseling Bulletin, 44,* 209–216.

Kosciulek, J. F., & Perkins, A. (2005). Transition to work and adult life of youth with disabilities. In F. Chan, M. J. Leahy, & J. L. Saunders (Eds.), *Case management for rehabilitation health professionals* (pp. 293–308). Osage Beach, MO: Aspen Professional Services.

Krepcio, K., & Martin, M. M. (2012). *The state of the U.S. workforce system: A time for incremental realignment or serious reform?* (Research Report). New Brunswick: John J. Heldrich Center for Workforce Development, Rutgers, the State University of New Jersey.

Mastie, M. M. (1994). Using assessment instruments in career counseling: Career assessment as compass, credential, process and empowerment. In J. T. Kapes, M. M. Mastie, & E. A. Whitfield (Eds.), *A counselor's guide to career assessment instruments* (3rd ed., pp. 31–40). Alexandria, VA: National Career Development Association.

National Council on Disability. (2008). *National disability policy: A progress report.* Washington, DC: Author.

National Institute on Disability and Rehabilitation Research. (1994). Empowerment counseling: Consumer–counselor partnerships in the rehabilitation process. *Rehab Brief, 16*(6), 1–4.

National Organization on Disability. (2000). *Survey of the status of people with disabilities in the United States: Employment.* Washington, DC: Author.

O'Day, B. (1999). Policy barriers for people with disabilities who want to work. *American Rehabilitation, 25*(1), 8–15.

Rehabilitation Services Administration. (1993). *The Rehabilitation Act of 1973 as amended by the Rehabilitation Act Amendments of 1992.* Washington, DC: Author.

Roessler, R. T. (1987). Work, disability, and the future: Promoting employment for people with disabilities. *Journal of Counseling & Development, 66,* 188–190.

Rothman, R. A. (1987). *Working: Sociological perspectives.* Englewood Cliffs, NJ: Prentice Hall.

Ryan, C. P. (1995). Work isn't what it used to be: Implications, recommendations, and strategies for vocational rehabilitation. *Journal of Rehabilitation, 61*(1), 8–15.

Schroeder, F. K. (1995, November). *Philosophical underpinnings of effective rehabilitation.* Sixteenth Mary E. Switzer Lecture, Assumption College, Worcester, MA.

Scotch, R. K. (2000). Disability policy: An eclectic overview. *Journal of Disability Policy Studies, 11*(1), 6–11.

Stapleton, D. C., & Burkhauser, R. V. (Eds.). (2003). *The decline in employment of people with disabilities: A policy puzzle.* Kalamazoo, MI: Upjohn Institute.

Szymanski, E. M., & Hanley-Maxwell, C. (1996). Career development of people with developmental disabilities: An ecological model. *Journal of Rehabilitation, 62*(2), 48–55.

Szymanski, E. M., & Hershenson, D. B. (1997). Career development of people with disabilities: An ecological model. In R. M. Parker & E. M. Szymanski (Eds.), *Rehabilitation counseling: Basics and beyond* (3rd ed., pp. 273–304). Austin, TX: PRO-ED.

Szymanski, E. M., Hershenson, D. B., Enright, M. S., & Ettinger, J. M. (1996). Career development theories, constructs, and research: Implications for people with disabilities. In E. M. Szymanski & R. M. Parker (Eds.), *Work and disability: Issues and strategies in career development and job placement* (pp. 79–126). Austin, TX: PRO-ED.

Szymanski, E. M., & Trueba, H. T. (1994). Castification of people with disabilities: Potential disempowering aspects of classification in disability services. *Journal of Rehabilitation, 60*(3), 12–20.

Taylor, H. (1994, October 24). National Organization on Disability survey of Americans with disabilities [Special advertising section]. *Business Week.*

Trueba, H. T. (1993). Castification in multicultural America. In H. T. Trueba, C. Rodriguez, Y. Zou, & J. Contron (Eds.), *Healing multicultural America: Mexican immigrants rise to power in rural California* (pp. 29–51). Philadelphia, PA: Falmer Press.

Trueba, H., Cheng, L., & Ima, K. (1993). *Myth or reality: Adaptive strategies of Asian Americans in California.* London, England: Falmer Press.

United Cerebral Palsy Association. (2007). *The state of disability in America.* Washington, DC: Author.

Wehmeyer, M. L. (2004). Self-determination and the empowerment of people with disabilities. *American Rehabilitation, 28*(1), 22–29.

Wolfe, K. E. (1997). *Career counseling for people with disabilities.* Austin, TX: PRO-ED.

Chapter 7

Helping Clients Understand and Respond to Changes in the Workplace and Family Life

The worlds of work and family are changing at a rapid pace, and the changes are likely to accelerate in the 21st century.

> Globalization, declines in manufacturing and rising service sector employment, growth of nonstandard schedules, and technological developments (such as cell phones, wireless internet, and laptops) have made it easier for work to intrude on family and home life. . . . As such, work can become increasingly blurred with the non-work domains of family and personal life. (Ammons, 2013, p. 49)

Changing workplaces, increasing diversity in society and in the workplace, extended life expectancy, life-long learning, and changing family structures with the challenges, tensions, stress, and anxiety they bring about in individuals and society are not abstractions. They are real. They are challenging and changing the traditional rules that have governed life in the workplace and in the family. As a result, they impact substantially the life roles of individuals, the settings where they live and work, and the events that occur in their lives. Many of the problems clients bring to career counseling are manifested in their life roles, settings, and events and are caused directly or indirectly by one or more of these changes (Bianchi & Milkie, 2010). They are also manifested in clients trying to maintain balance between work and family in their lives. Hernandez and Mahoney (2012) made this statement about the work–family balance issue.

> The career–family balance represents a common area of struggle for many families, and is as much of an issue for men who are husbands and fathers as it is for women who are wives and mothers. (p. 152)

This chapter focuses on how to help your clients respond to the challenges and consequences of these changes through career counseling. First, we focus on changes that are occurring in the workplace and in family life, followed by a discussion of the problems your clients may be facing as a result of the challenges and consequences of these changes. Next, specific attention is given to helping your clients respond to workplace and family life problems through career counseling. Five major areas of required knowledge are presented that will prepare you to work with clients who are dealing with these problems. Finally, the chapter closes with a checklist of roles that are critical to the success of career counseling as we help our clients understand and respond to changes in the workplace and in family life.

Changes in the Workplace and in Family Life

Changes in the workplace and in family life have been under way for some time. Some commentators have used the term *revolutionary* to describe them, whereas others have used the term *evolutionary*. Whichever term you prefer, the changes taking place now in these two worlds will continue into the foreseeable future. What are some of these changes?

The Workplace

The workplace of today continues to undergo significant restructuring. It is being reinvented and reengineered so that it can compete successfully both nationally and internationally. Terms such as *globalization*, *downsizing (rightsizing)*, *upsizing*, *outsourcing*, *deregulation*, and *technology* describe various forces at work that are causing this ongoing restructuring (Shapiro, Ingols, & Blake-Beard, 2008). Lent (2013) stated that the ongoing restructuring of the workplace is increasing at a rapid pace.

> Wrought by sweeping change in such areas as technology, the global economic environment, and demographic and immigration patterns, the work world has become faster paced, more diverse, and less and less predictable for more and more workers. (p. 2)

In addition to these forces reshaping the workplace, another powerful force is at work. This force is the dramatic demographic changes occurring in our society that are producing an increasingly diverse labor force. So not only are forces at work changing the very nature and structure of the workplace, but the people who do the work are changing as well, mirroring the diverse demographics of our society. Here are some examples noted by Sommers and Franklin (2012, pp. 3–4):

- The labor force will grow slowly and become much older as the baby-boom generation moves entirely into the 55-years-and-older age group, whose labor force participation rates are significantly lower.
- The labor force will continue to become more diverse, with Hispanics making up 18.6% of the total by 2020.
- Consistent with slow labor force growth and assumptions concerning a full-employment economy in 2020, the gross domestic product is projected to grow by 3.0% annually. Productivity growth is projected at an annual rate of 2.0%, similar to its long-term trend.
- Nonfarm payroll employment is projected to increase by 1.4% annually, regaining the jobs lost during the 2007–2009 recession and expanding further, to reach 149.5 million by 2020. Total employment, including agriculture and self-employed and unpaid family workers, is projected to increase by 20.5 million over the decade.
- The health care and social assistance industry is expected to be the most rapidly growing sector in terms of employment, followed by the construction sector. Despite rapid growth, the construction sector is not projected to return to its prerecession peak employment level.
- Occupation groups related to health care, personal care services, social services, and construction are expected to be the most rapidly growing; however, office and administrative support occupations are projected to add the largest number of new jobs.

- Employment in the construction and extraction, production, and transportation and material moving occupation groups fell by 10% or more from 2006 to 2010. Although all three groups are expected to grow between 2010 and 2020, none is projected to regain its 2006 employment level.
- Occupations in which a master's degree is typically needed for entry are expected to grow by 21.7%, faster than the growth rate for any other education category. Among occupations in which a high school diploma or the equivalent is typically needed for entry, occupations that have apprenticeships as the typical kind of on-the-job training are projected to be the fastest growing and to have higher pay. These two results are based on the new education and training system introduced with the 2010–2020 projections.

Family Life

As changes continue to take place in the work world, so, too, do they continue to occur in family life. Work life and family life are intertwined, and families are becoming increasingly less stable and more diverse (Appelbaum, 2012).

> Families have become less stable (e.g., higher divorce and non-marital birth rates) and more diverse (e.g., more "nontraditional" family structures, dual-incomes). Many families have also come to experience decreased job security and less income after adjusting for inflation. In addition, couples are more diverse in their spirituality (e.g., more inter-faith marriages, less traditionally religious). (Hernandez & Mahoney, 2012, p. 135)

Whether one agrees or disagrees that there is increasing family diversity, most commentators on families in America do agree that family structures are changing. The traditional family structure of two parents and two or more children with only the father working is no longer the majority. It has been displaced by a wide variety of family combinations, including dual-career families, dual-income earners, and single-parent families:

> A defining trend of the 2000–2010 decade was the increased diversity of families and workplaces. Families increasingly diverged from the two-parent, two-child family with a male breadwinner and female homemaker, as other types of families (e.g., gay and lesbian families, divorced parents with joint custody) increased. Single-parent families and stepfamilies remained a large share of households with children in the decade, and many scholars examined their work–life conditions and consequences. (Bianchi & Milkie, 2010, p. 706)

Another trend in family life is the emergence of what a number of writers have called the *sandwich generation*. The sandwich generation is defined as families "providing care to both children and parents or in-laws" (Chassin, Macy, Seo, Presson, & Sherman, 2010, p. 38). This phrase describes families that must pay for the education of their children while needing to pay for the nursing home care of an aged parent.

Challenges and Consequences of Changing Workplace and Family Life

What are some of the challenges and consequences individuals face as a result of the changes that are occurring in the workplace and in family life? What impact do these changes have on their worker and family roles? This section focuses on some of these issues.

Worker Role Loss

A major consequence for some individuals as the workplace undergoes changes is job loss. When workers lose their jobs because of downsizing, for example, they lose a major anchor in their lives; they lose part of their identity. They feel devalued as individuals, and often the feelings that result affect every aspect of their lives and all of their life roles.

Job loss has economic meanings as well as social and psychological meanings. The loss of steady income; daily social contacts, friendships, and support; and identity and self-worth accompany job loss. Correspondingly, increased stress often creates strains in individuals (anger, frustration, anxiety) and in their family lives and family relationships.

> Little consideration has been given to the complex emotional dynamics of grief associated with job loss. Understanding grief in the context of job loss and lifestyle adjustment is particularly important when clients are confronting a major life change. Oftentimes, an overwhelming sense of loss distracts or impedes a person's readiness to conduct a job search or effectively move forward with a positive career-life change. (Simmelink, 2006, p. 1)

A number of writers (Bridges, 2004; Simmelink, 2006) have adapted Elizabeth Kubler-Ross's (1969) five stages of grieving to describe what happens to individuals who experience job loss. First there is denial: "They made a mistake," "They must mean somebody else." Then comes anger: "It was that free trade agreement," "It's Washington's fault." This is followed by bargaining: "Things don't have to be like this," "Let's all get together and maybe we can lick this situation." Then comes despair: "All hope is gone," "There is nothing out there for me." Finally, after these progressively deeper stages of grieving, individuals reach Kubler-Ross's final stage of acceptance: "I am ready to get on with it," "I miss what I did, but I can't sit around waiting." Not all workers who go through job loss go through these stages. But when they do, written descriptions of the stages cannot begin to touch their thoughts, emotions, and feelings.

Helping clients deal with job loss grief begins by listening, by asking clients to tell their story. It is important to listen for feelings, any work-related issues, and possible family-related concerns. Providing clients with the opportunity to tell their story about job loss is a key first step in the career counseling process (Simmelink, 2006).

Anger in the Workplace

Although all of the stages of grieving are connected and are important, the anger stage merits special attention because of the possible consequences of behavior that individuals may exhibit in the workplace or at home. The anger stage needs special attention because anger may be expressed in the workplace or at home as a result of incidents other than job loss. It also needs attention because "workplace aggression costs companies millions of dollars every year" (Novick, 2007).

Confrontation and dialogue usually form part of the normal working environment. Workers and managers are confronted on a daily basis with their personal and work-related problems. They have to face the anxieties and frustration of coworkers, organizational difficulties, personality clashes, aggressive intruders from the outside, and problematic relations with clients and the public. Despite this, dialogue usually prevails over confrontation, and people manage to organize efficient and productive activities within the workplace. There are cases, however, when dialogue fails to develop in a positive way—when relationships between workers, managers, clients, or the public deteriorate—and the objectives of working efficiently and achieving productive results are affected. When this happens, workplace violence may occur. Workplace violence "can take various forms, ranging from abusive language, threats, and bullying to physical assault and homicide" (Wassell, 2009, p. 1049).

Sometimes workers bring anger to work. At other times they become angry because of work and then take this anger home. Although job loss may be the precipitating event, there may be any number of other reasons, some rooted in an individual's past and others in the present.

What are the thoughts and feelings that may lead clients to become angry and act on that anger? Suppose you are working with clients who are expressing anger because they did not get promoted to their next job level. What sequence of thoughts and feelings might you anticipate? Allcorn (1994, pp. 29–30), citing the work of Hauck, suggested that you can anticipate the following: First, the clients might express feelings of frustration because they expected to be promoted but were not. This could be followed by thoughts that not being promoted is terrible and that they should have been treated more fairly. Now, as anger builds, they may begin to think that they should not be treated this way. Finally, they may think that the bosses who denied them their promotions should be punished severely, because people in management deserve severe punishment.

Given this example, how should you respond? Allcorn (1994, p. 56) recommended the following responses: Address anger directly by listening. Try to determine the source of the anger. Try to determine if the anger being expressed is covering up something, such as feelings of helplessness and powerlessness. As you listen, begin to focus on solutions. Help clients shift and sort, separating facts from fantasies.

Bullying in the Workplace

As noted by Wassell (2009), workplace violence can take the form of bullying. What is workplace bullying? It is "repeated, health-harming mistreatment of one or more persons (the targets) by one or more perpetrators that take one or more of the following forms: verbal abuse; offensive conduct/behaviors (including nonverbal) which are threatening, humiliating, or intimidating; and work interference—sabotage—which prevents work from getting done" (Workplace Bullying Institute, 2013).

According to Ramsay, Troth, and Brauch (2011), bullying has serious implications for the workplace. It can result in absenteeism, illness, lack of commitment, and a decrease in job satisfaction. They also pointed out that more than one person may be involved; it can involve groups.

While not often considered a workplace, schools are workplaces, and bullying in schools is serious. "This year alone, 13 million kids in the United States will be bullied. Three million will be absent from school at some point each month because they feel unsafe there" (Shallcross, 2013, p. 31). Bullying in schools takes various forms, including physical bullying, verbal bullying, cyberbullying, social aggression, and relational aggression. In cyberbullying the target may or may not know who is doing the bullying.

Work–Family Relationships

Given the changes in work life and family life described previously, how can the challenges and consequences individuals face in family life roles be understood? After an extensive review of the literature, Zedeck and Mosier (1990) described five approaches for understanding and explaining the complexities and dynamics of work–family relationships, focusing more on individuals in families than on families as units.

The first approach to explaining the complexities and dynamics of work–family relationships is called *spillover theory*. According to spillover theory, there are no boundaries between work and family; what happens at work spills over into the family sphere and vice versa. Modern technology that allows employees and family members to communicate freely and flexible work arrangements that allow employees to complete work at home have increased the likelihood of work–family spillover (Ilies et al., 2009).

The second approach is *compensation theory*, which hypothesizes that work and family roles are inversely related. Because individuals invest differently in their work roles and family roles, they may compensate in one for what is missing in the other. Zedeck and Mosier (1990), building on the work of Crosby, pointed out that "events at home provide 'shock absorbers' for disappointments at work, and vice versa" (p. 241).

The third approach is *segmentation theory*, which suggests that work and family roles can exist side by side without influencing one another. In other words, people can compartmentalize their lives. Zedeck and Mosier (1990) stated that "the family is seen as the realm of effectivity, intimacy, and significant ascribed relations, whereas the work world is viewed as impersonal, competitive, and instrumental rather than expressive" (p. 241).

The fourth approach is *instrumental theory*, wherein one role is used as a means of obtaining the necessities and luxuries that are deemed important for another role. Individuals work to obtain goods for family life. They also work to finance the purchase of goods and services for leisure activities, such as a boat, sports equipment, or a media center for the home.

Finally, Zedeck and Mosier (1990) described *conflict theory*. This theory postulates that achieving success in one role may mean making sacrifices in another role. Or, even more directly, responding to family obligations may require individuals to be absent from their job, to sometimes arrive late, or to not work efficiently on the job. Kossek, Pichler, Bodner, and Hammer (2011) defined work–family conflict as "a form of inter-role conflict that occurs when engaging in one role makes it more difficult to engage in another role" (p. 290). It is interesting to note that according to Williams and Bousbey (2010), work–family conflict is higher in the United States because Americans work longer hours than workers in most other developed countries. Apparently working longer hours creates the possibility of such conflicts occurring more frequently.

Another way of understanding and explaining the complexities and dynamics of work–family relationships was suggested by Voydanoff (2007). She pointed out that there are two types of relationships: time based and strain based. "Time-based family demands . . . include time spent addressing family responsibilities" (p. 55). In contrast, "Strain-based family demands . . . are associated with family structure and social organization and include psychological demands from spouses (e.g., marital conflict), children (e.g., children's problems), kin (e.g., caregiver strain), and household work (e.g., perceived unfairness)" (p. 55). Both types of relationships can have a substantial impact on work–family relationships.

Responding to Workplace and Family Life Issues Through Career Counseling

A Life Career Development Perspective

As we stated earlier, many of the issues clients bring to career counseling are caused directly or indirectly by one or more changes that occur in the workplace and in family life. They are often complex issues interwoven with personal, emotional, family, and work issues. Because they are often complex, having a holistic perspective of your clients is beneficial so that these issues can be seen collectively as well as individually. The holistic perspective we advocate is the concept of life career development as described in Chapter 1.

The concept of life career development provides you and your clients with the language of life roles, life settings, and life events. It becomes a shared language because you can use it with your clients to identify, analyze, and understand their work and family issues, and clients can do the same. Although you provide clients with these constructs, they are easily understood and personalized by clients because they can link them to their real-life work and family situations.

In responding to clients' work and family problems, use of the shared language of life roles, settings, and events provides ways to place and understand work and family problems in context. The use of shared language opens the door to joint (you and your clients together) learning about and understanding of clients' problems so that interventions can be chosen and used to help clients solve their problems. Thus, career counseling is a shared experience, with clients and counselors working together.

Major Areas of Required Knowledge

Helping clients respond to workplace and family life problems requires selecting and using appropriate interventions. Although the specific interventions you choose to use with your clients will depend upon your hypotheses about them and the issues with which they are dealing, major areas of knowledge are presented here to remind you of important problems that often require your attention when dealing with clients' workplace and family concerns. Hotchkiss and Borow (1996) listed several action areas, including learning about labor markets, combating gender stereotyping, and reducing racial and ethnic barriers. To their list we add combating barriers for people with disabilities and dealing with work–family problems.

Learning About Labor Markets

Because the work world is dynamic and ever changing, individuals often have a difficult time understanding it. To many clients who come for career counseling, the work world has few boundaries. It is difficult to grasp. It is overwhelming. This can be true for clients who are first-time job seekers as well as for clients who have been employed in the workplace but have lost their jobs. When we add to this other possible client problems in career counseling that are connected to work but are related to race, culture, religion, gender, age, and family, the complexity and interrelatedness of the issues involved in career counseling increase substantially.

Many client problems addressed in career counseling originate in the work world and then spill over into other arenas of life. For example, some clients have presenting problems of finding and getting jobs for the first time or finding and getting other jobs after industry downsizing. This problem is often directly related to their worker roles but then can spill over into other life roles, such as spouse, family, parent, and learner. Client gender, ethnic and racial identity, sexual orientation, age, religion, and social class may also be involved. If clients have experienced any form of discrimination previously in the workplace or in other situations, these experiences may affect their job search. Even if clients have not experienced direct discrimination, the anticipation that discrimination may occur based on clients' identity group history may also affect their job search.

Given all of these possible dynamics and connections in clients' presenting problems of finding and getting jobs, a starting point is needed. Because these problems are connected to the work world, starting there makes sense. Helping clients learn a way to negotiate the work world can be a first step. By providing clients with the concept of labor markets, you give them a way to describe, label, and negotiate the work world. They will have a starting point to connect themselves directly to the workplace, one that plants the seed of hope that there is a way to begin to solve their problems.

So what are labor markets? *Labor markets* are geographic areas in which workers compete for jobs and find paying work, and employers compete for workers and find willing workers. Labor markets may be local, state/regional, national, or international.

A local labor market encompasses a geographic area in which workers are willing to change jobs without changing their residences. It contains workers who compose the *labor force* of the local labor market, or the number of individuals aged 16 or older (not including active-duty military personnel or institutionalized people, such as prison inmates) who are either working or looking for work. The local labor market also contains an array of *occupations*, defined as sets of activities or tasks that employees are paid to perform. Employees who perform essentially the same tasks are in the same occupation. Finally, local labor markets contain *industries* (employers) that employ workers. Industries are broadly grouped into two categories: goods producing and service.

Some clients may not be looking for work in their local area. They may be interested in exploring job opportunities in a broader geographic area such as a state or a region (e.g., the southwest), or nationally or internationally. No matter the size of the geographic area, all labor markets consist of the same elements found in the local labor market: workers (labor force), occupations (the activities or tasks workers perform), and employers (industries).

The job opportunity structure available to clients depends in part upon where they live, how far they are willing or able to travel to work, and if they are willing to move to a new location. An exception to this is internal labor markets. Instead of being described in geographic terms, internal labor markets exist within employing firms. Internal labor markets are characterized by organizational rules that define how employees are hired and promoted and how jobs are structured. In internal labor markets, "workers are hired into entry level jobs and higher levels are filled from within" (Lazear & Oyer, 2004, p. 527).

Client knowledge about internal labor markets is important because of the rules that govern employment. New employees are hired for only certain lower level jobs. Once an employee is inside, movement is mostly vertical, and on-the-job training is featured. In organizations in which internal labor markets operate, clients need to be aware that even though they may have skills for higher level positions, they must begin at the entry point. Then the rules presented here apply.

Combating Gender Stereotypes

"Deeply rooted socialization processes perpetuate rigid sex role perceptions that limit career options" (Hotchkiss & Borow, 1996, p. 318). Because of such socialization, it is imperative that female and male clients so affected be helped to overcome gender stereotype limitations, including those concerning initial occupational selection, earnings, rank, and job responsibilities. Chapters 4 and 5 cover this topic in detail, so we only include a reminder here to highlight the importance of the topic.

Reducing Racial and Ethnic Barriers

Because of the increasingly diverse population of the United States and the reflection of this diversity in the labor force, paying attention to racial and ethnic barriers is critical. We must appreciate and respond to the variety of racial and ethnic backgrounds that clients bring to career counseling as well as to their experiences with discrimination. Understanding their personal and group histories, their worldviews, their identity statuses, and their levels of acculturation will lay the foundation for the working alliance and the effective selection of appropriate action intervention strategies. Chapter 3 provides extensive background and practical action intervention strategies; we simply want to remind you of its importance here.

Combating Barriers for People With Disabilities

Because of greater awareness of the needs of people with disabilities, as well as federal mandates, more and more individuals with disabilities are seeking employment. It is critical that counselors understand the unique issues facing people with disabilities and work toward the inclusion, independence, and empowerment of these people. Counselors can be critical links in helping foster greater skill development and exploration for clients with disabilities. Counselors can also serve as change agents with employers, helping to open more doors for employment in a wider variety of occupations. Chapter 6 provides specific information on the current employment status of people with disabilities, describes an empowerment framework, and discusses specific issues relevant to the career counseling process when working with this client group.

Dealing With Work–Family Problems

As individuals become adults, many must deal with work–family problems:

> What happens at work often affects other aspects of their life, just as other commitments often affect employment attitudes and behaviors. One of the common refrains is the desire to balance work and other commitments more successfully. The most familiar version of this challenge occurs with parents of young children. However, the challenges do not cease when parents move into the middle years. In fact, family involvement often becomes more complex, with marital, parental, grandparental, and filial roles competing with work for energy. (Sterns & Huyck, 2001, p. 469)

The life career development perspective presented in Chapter 1 and discussed earlier in this chapter, with its concepts of life roles, life settings, and life events all interacting over the life span, is a useful way of understanding and dealing with work–family problems. As suggested earlier, the concepts of life roles, settings, and events provide you and your clients with a shared language to break apart, identify, and label the issues and contexts surrounding work and family problems. As this is accomplished, concepts derived from the work of Zedeck and Mosier (1990) and Voydanoff (2007) can be applied to help explain the dynamics of work–family relationships and the possible consequences of family–work problems.

A beginning point in this process is to translate clients' work and family problems into life roles, life settings, and life events terminology. Worker roles, family roles (parent, spouse, partner), the workplace, home, work-related events, and family-related events become the vocabulary used to analyze, specify, and understand client work–family problems. Clients' presenting problems and possible underlying problems, originally global and fuzzy, now can take on specificity. A vocabulary is available to clarify issues and pinpoint concerns—the vocabulary of life roles, settings, and events.

This specifying and labeling process helps you and your clients to begin to sort out, explain, and understand the complexities and dynamics of work–family relationships. Listen to clients describe their presenting problems, and listen as underlying dynamics emerge in the gathering information phase of career counseling. Does what happens (event) at work (work setting, worker role) spill over into family life (family setting, parent role, spouse role)? Does what happens (event) at work (work setting, worker role) as a result of spillover cause conflict in family life (family setting, parent role, spouse role)? Does compartmentalization occur where clients try to separate these two worlds (Zedeck & Mosier, 1990)?

A Checklist of Counselor Roles

The opening phase of the career counseling process, with its beginning development of the working alliance, is crucial. Although you focus your attention on presenting goals or problems, there is awareness that these may expand into other goals or problems as the process of career counseling continues. Then, with the establishment of the boundaries of the career counseling process, the gathering information phase is under way. This involves learning more about your clients and their problems by using quantitative and qualitative procedures and instruments so that hypotheses can be generated. Using interventions based on your hypotheses to help your clients achieve their goals or resolve their problems follows. Then, when clients' goals are achieved or their problems are resolved, closure ends the career counseling process and relationship.

As these phases of the career counseling process are unfolding, the working alliance between you and your clients is being further developed and strengthened. The use of shared language facilitates statements of clear goals to be achieved and specifies the tasks to be carried out to achieve these goals. This, in turn, creates a joining together of you and your clients, creating the foundation for developing bonds of mutual trust and respect.

Given the phases of the career counseling process that you and your clients will go through together and the importance of the working alliance, what are some important roles for you to consider when helping your clients understand and respond to changes in the workplace and in family life? Here is a beginning list:

1. Help clients view themselves and their situations and problems holistically so that they can see connections and relationships in their lives, their families, and their work.
2. Help clients understand and deal with the intertwined issues of psychological health, work, and career development (Blustein, 2008).
3. Help clients appreciate diversity of all kinds, including that of race, ethnicity, gender, and sexual orientation in the workplace.
4. Help clients appreciate changing gender roles in the workplace.
5. Empower clients with disabilities.
6. Help clients understand and work through the stages of life transitions.
7. Help clients separate their successes and failures at work and at home from who they are as people.
8. Help clients develop support systems to buffer workplace and family stresses and strains (Kinnunen & Mauno, 2008).
9. Help clients recognize that grief and loss are natural reactions to change.
10. Help clients deal with resistance to change.
11. Help clients turn workplace and family frustration and anger energy toward positive solutions.

Closing Thoughts

Helping clients understand and respond to changes in the workplace and in family life through career counseling requires knowledge, understanding, and skill. This chapter was designed to provide you with an overview of workplace and family life changes and to highlight needed foundation knowledge required to understand and respond to client problems that occur as a consequence of these changes. To understand and respond appropriately, we recommend you view client problems from the holistic perspective of human development called *life career development*.

The life career development perspective, as well as our understanding of the career counseling process, is described in Chapter 1. Chapters 3, 4, 5, and 6 highlight foundation knowledge and application skills counselors need when dealing with gender, racial, ethnic, and disability issues. The rest of the book focuses on the career counseling process, demonstrating how all of these issues and concerns are interwoven from the opening phase through closure. Throughout the entire book you see the concept of the active, involved counselor at work. We firmly believe in the necessity of a counselor's active involvement in the career counseling process. "Counselors should . . . be encouraged to consider constructive intervention when barriers loom that clients cannot surmount unaided" (Hotchkiss & Borow, 1996, p. 318).

References

Allcorn, S. (1994). *Anger in the workplace.* Westport, CT: Quorum Books.

Ammons, S. K. (2013). Work–family boundary strategies: Stability and alignment between preferred and enacted boundaries. *Journal of Vocational Behavior, 82,* 49–58.

Appelbaum, L. D. (2012). Introduction. In L. D. Appelbaum (Ed.), *Reconnecting to work* (pp. 1–16). Kalamazoo, MI: W. E. Upjohn Institute for Employment Research.

Bianchi, S. M., & Milkie, M. A. (2010). Work and family research in the first decade of the 21st century. *Journal of Marriage and Family, 72,* 705–725.

Blustein, D. L. (2008). The role of work in psychological health and well-being. *American Psychologist, 63,* 228–240.

Bridges, W. (2004). *Transitions: Making sense of life's changes* (2nd ed.). Cambridge, MA: Da Capo Press.

Chassin, L., Macy, J. T., Seo, D. C., Presson, C. C., & Sherman, S. J. (2010). The association between membership in the sandwich generation and health behaviors: A longitudinal study. *Journal of Applied Developmental Psychology, 31,* 38–46.

Hernandez, K. M., & Mahoney, A. (2012). Balancing sacred callings in career and family life. In P. C. Hill & B. J. Dik (Eds.), *Psychology of religions and workplace spirituality* (pp. 135–155). Charlotte, NC: Information Age.

Hotchkiss, L., & Borow, H. (1996). Sociological perspective on work and career development. In D. Brown, L. Brooks, & Associates (Eds.), *Career choice and development* (3rd ed., pp. 262–367). San Francisco, CA: Jossey-Bass.

Ilies, R., Fulmer, I. S., Spitzmuller, M., Johnson, M. D. (2009). Personality and citizenship behavior: The mediating role of job satisfaction. *Journal of Applied Psychology, 94*(4), 945–959. doi: 10.1037/a0013329

Kinnunen, U., & Mauno, S. (2008). Work-family conflict in individuals' lives: Prevalence, antecedents, and outcomes. In K. Näswall, J. Hellgren, & M. Sverke (Eds.), *The individual in the changing working life* (pp. 126–146). Cambridge, England: Cambridge University Press.

Kossek, E. E., Pichler, S., Bodner, T., & Hammer, L. B. (2011). Workplace social support and work–family conflict: A meta-analysis clarifying the influence of general and work–family-specific supervisor and organizational support. *Personnel Psychology, 64,* 289–313.

Kubler-Ross, E. (1969). *On death and dying.* New York, NY: Macmillan.

Lazear, E. P., & Oyer, P. (2004). Internal and external labor markets: A personnel economics approach. *Labor Economics, 11,* 527–554.

Lent, R. W. (2013). Career-life preparedness: Revisiting career planning and adjustment in the new workplace. *The Career Development Quarterly, 61,* 2–14.

Novick, A. (2007). Workplace stress and anger—Resolving it could save millions. *AJ Novick Group's Anger Management Weblog.* Retrieved from http://angermanagementonline.wordpress.com/2007/11/29/workplace-stress-and-anger-resolving-it-could-save-millions/

Ramsay, S., Troth, A., & Brauch, S. (2011). Workplace bullying: A group processes framework. *Journal of Occupational and Organizational Psychology, 84,* 789–816.

Shallcross, L. (2013). Bully pulpit. *Counseling Today, 55,* 30–39.

Shapiro, M., Ingols, C., & Blake-Beard, S. (2008). Confronting double binds: Implications for women, organizations, and career practitioners. *Journal of Career Development, 34,* 309–333.

Simmelink, M. N. (2006, September 1). *Understanding grief in the context of job loss & lifestyle adjustment.* Retrieved from http://209.235.208.145/cgi-bin/WebSuite/tcsAssnWeb-Suite.pl?Action=DisplayNewsDetails&RecordID=856&Sections=&IncludeDropped=1&AssnID=NCDA&DBCode=130285

Sommers, D., & Franklin, J. C. (2012). Employment outlook: 2010–2020. *Monthly Labor Review, 135,* 3–20.

Sterns, H. L., & Huyck, M. H. (2001). The role of work in midlife. In M. E. Lachman (Ed.), *Handbook of midlife development* (pp. 447–486). New York: Wiley.

Voydanoff, P. (2007). *Work, family, and community: Exploring interconnections.* Mahwah, NJ: Erlbaum.

Wassell, J. T. (2009). Workplace violence intervention effectiveness: A systematic literature review. *Safety Science, 47,* 1049–1055.

Williams, J. C., & Bousbey, H. (2010). *The three faces of work-family conflict.* Washington, DC: Center for American Progress.

Workplace Bullying Institute. (2013). *The WBI definition of workplace bullying.* Retrieved from http://www.workplacebullying.org/individuals/problem/definition/

Zedeck, S., & Mosier, K. L. (1990). Work in the family and employing organization. *American Psychologist, 45,* 240–251.

PART TWO

Client Goal or Problem Identification, Clarification, and Specification

Chapter 8

Opening Phase of the Career Counseling Process: Forming the Working Alliance

There is much to consider as we begin the career counseling process, but nothing is more important than an emphasis on building strong working alliances with our clients. In this chapter, we define what is meant by a working alliance, clarify how important these alliances are to achieving successful outcomes in career counseling, and include ideas on how to build alliances. Statements from clients illustrate the importance of the alliance, as seen through their eyes.

The Working Alliance

Establishing a solid working alliance is presented in Chapter 1 as a necessary first step in making things happen in career counseling. Skovholt, Ronnestad, and Jennings (1997), summarizing the research on counseling, emphatically stated, "If we had to choose the single most important research-based counseling/psychotherapy domain, it would be the ability to establish a very positive working alliance with clients" (p. 362). The classic statement of a working alliance was offered by Edward Bordin (1979). He suggested that three parts in the relationship are essential and need our constant attention:

1. Agreement between the client and the counselor on the *goals* to be achieved in counseling.
2. Agreement on the *tasks* involved.
3. The *bond* necessary between client and counselor that establishes the importance of both (i.e., goals for treatment and tasks needed to achieve the goals).

More research evidence (Castonguay, Constantino, & Holtforth, 2006; Gelso & Carter, 1985) supports this way of conceptualizing the relationship and further emphasizes the importance of establishing it early in counseling. In fact, Wei and Heppner (2005) provided some evidence that Asian clients make earlier (first session) assessments of the working alliance, a finding that should further influence how we proceed with the opening counseling session. The outcomes of (career) counseling may be very dependent on not only establishing this alliance early but maintaining it throughout the duration of our time with our clients. Krupnick and colleagues were quoted in Skovholt et al. (1997) as having done an exhaustive review of research on the therapeutic alliance, finding that "mean alliance ratings had a very large effect on outcome" (p. 363). Other modalities looked at did not.

Also, although there is some research evidence emerging that we should consider the working alliance as two separate factors—with relationship (i.e., something like bond) being one factor and task and goal the other factor (Andrusyna, Tang, DeRubeis, & Luborsky, 2001)—this only implies that we may need to reconsider how we assess the alliance. Success in establishing the relationship, for example, may be somewhat independent of task and goal. Either way, we cannot overstate the importance of the working alliance.

However, were it entirely up to counselors to establish this alliance, they might move easily to ways to establish it, but it is clear that we describe a dynamic relationship that draws heavily on both what counselors say and do and what the client says and does. Meara and Patton (1994) described the alliance as that part of counseling that can be characterized as collaboration, mutuality, and cooperation of two working together. Gelso and Hayes (1998) identified two fundamental components of the alliance: collaboration and attachment, or bonding. It is this interdependence that makes it both complicated and fascinating. Like any good relationship, it demands work from both parties.

Establishing a Mutuality of Goals

First, then, we must establish a mutuality of goals for career counseling. We do not do this following any particular format or with a clear set of predetermined goals. Rather, we begin by being a good listener. We must be careful to first let our clients express what they believe they want from counseling. Listening well will provide an early basis for establishing a set of goals and will allow for the time and opportunity to learn whether the client comes with well-established goals. If so, we must determine whether the goals are reasonable ones that can properly be addressed in career counseling. We cannot have agreement on goals if a client is not clear about them at the outset, and often clients are not. We may have problems establishing these goals early, but a good alliance is dependent on both counselor and client, through an ongoing effort, working to establish and modify goals as appropriate. This is an important component of building a working alliance and should be repeatedly assessed as we proceed with the other two components of the working alliance: tasks and the bond. Let us look next at what we mean by *task*.

Finding Tasks in Support of the Working Alliance

Numerous tasks in counseling can contribute to successful outcomes. We encourage talk, reflection, openness, honesty, commitment to trying various creative stimulus activities (interest inventories, tests, card sorts, fantasy trips, genograms, journaling, networking, creating personal narratives, reading books or articles)—all types of activities that might move one along in thought or action toward agreed-upon goals. Although there may sometimes be good reasons for not engaging in these tasks, it is always important to work at reaching mutual agreement on what would be helpful and why. The tasks that lead to successful outcomes should be agreed upon up front so that there is a shared agenda for proceeding in career counseling. Just as we establish mutually agreed-upon goals, we are aided by agreeing upon a set of tasks through which to accomplish these goals. Our experience, aided by our understanding of our clients when they come to us, can go a long way toward ensuring that our counseling time together is truly productive.

Working at Bonding as Part of the Alliance

Finally, the working alliance depends on establishing a bond with our clients. Theorists give us a wealth of ways to conceptualize, understand, and even measure this bond (Barrett-Lennard, 1986; Gelso & Carter, 1985; Orlinsky & Howard, 1986; Rogers, 1961; Tichenor & Hill, 1989), but they diverge in their thinking about what is essential, necessary, or sufficient. They do seem to be in agreement that there must be some kind of a bond between counselor and client—an attachment that includes caring and trust—for without it there is evidence that efforts (tasks) directed toward accomplishing goals will be compromised. Disregarding small differences of opinion presented in the research, we can say that it is difficult to have a constructive relationship if trust and support are not offered and felt by both parties.

We know that counselors need to be skilled at establishing good working relationships. What is not as clear is how to do this. Are there essential conditions, as Carl Rogers (1961) suggested, or can bonding be achieved in other ways? Are there other equally effective relationships that promote desired change? Should we give more or less attention to the importance of goals and tasks? The most recent evidence is that all three need attention in order for counselors to establish what we term a good working alliance. We define a *good working alliance* as one that attends to the establishment of mutually well-defined goals in the relationship, finds mutually agreed-upon tasks to promote pursuit of these goals, and, equally important, creates an effective bond in the relationship to make the most constructive use of the therapeutic time together. When this is done early in career counseling, we can provide appropriate direction for our clients, and, ultimately, we can expect better outcomes from our efforts.

Building Successful Working Alliances

In an effort to build successful working alliances, we should listen to what clients say about their good experiences in counseling. We hear what they like to have happen in counseling. Sometimes they come with preconceived ideas about what they want or what should happen, but these preconceived ideas must be incorporated into the process as mutually agreed-upon goals. Listen as we offer some summary statements from clients. Listen carefully to what each has to say, and then we can determine whether these statements can help provide a basis for ideas about what constitutes a good working alliance.

> *Client:* I didn't know what to expect from career counseling. The counselor made it clear from the beginning that we were going to work together to clarify my concerns, and that seemed good to me. She also said we would work out a plan of action by the next session and while that seemed ambitious at first, I came to see the importance of it and actually began to see myself as up to the challenge of doing it. It wasn't what I expected, but I liked the idea. I could tell she knew a lot about careers from what she said in response to my questions, but more important, she seemed really interested in me as a person. I respected her and I thought here was someone who was going to listen to me and help me plan some next steps. I left excited and optimistic.

The client first tells us she did not know what to expect from career counseling; this is typical, given that many clients only know secondhand what to expect. That we would be working together on issues was not what she expected, but it was acceptable to her. When the counselor suggested a task of eventually having a plan of action by the next session, this was viewed as an unexpected task and, upon reflection, as a challenge. We can see the goals and tasks being negotiated and agreed upon in a satisfactory way. Finally, the client lets us know she respects the counselor's competence as an expert and a good listener, so she left the session excited and optimistic. This suggests that the client believes that a healthy bond is developing. All that she has said, we think, might be offered as descriptive of a good bond between the client and the counselor.

> *Client:* I was completely lost and came for career counseling. At the time, I would have done whatever was suggested. I just wanted to get on with my life—get out of my job and my marriage. I don't think I received much advice at first, but I did find I could tell her all that was going on in my life, and she listened until I seemed to be getting clearer about my own situation. I came back regularly for weeks because I liked her and we seemed to be making progress with some things I hadn't thought about when I first came for help. I found myself becoming more focused on what I needed to do with my life. We both seemed invested in my finding some alternatives, and I have some now. I'm just not ready to act on them yet.

Again, we hear loudest the importance of the relationship. The counselor did not take over or act on the expressed concern, as might have been the initial expectation of the client. The client moved toward a modified goal and then talked about the strength of her relationship with the counselor. She indicated that weeks later there was a shift in focus to her career concerns. Seemingly, the breakup of her marriage and thoughts of leaving her job were intertwined. She had to deal with this before attending to the more specific goal of finding a new job. Clearly, an agenda can be brought to the interview, modified, and strengthened in a mutually agreed-upon manner. However, for the client and counselor to move effectively toward mutually agreed-upon goals, there needs to be a strong bond, or neither will hear the other's input.

> *Client:* It was a fascinating session. I had taken numerous tests and read various books on careers, and I had some vague ideas about what I wanted to do, but I knew I didn't have enough information or anyone to talk to about what I was thinking. I was ecstatic to find someone who would listen and at the same time offer to help with my dreams. The counselor didn't suggest that finding answers would be easy, but she was encouraging and I felt she knew more than she was telling me. We decided during the interview that this would be a real opportunity for me to put things together. We agreed to work toward my choosing a new career within the next 6 months, and she made clear some of what I would have to do if I was to be successful at it. I liked the way she made me state my goal, and then she helped me define what I needed to do to make it happen.

Clearly, the client is describing what it is like to have a good working alliance with a counselor. They have attended to goals and tasks and seemingly have bonded in a relationship. You can hear that she is motivated to work, likes the counselor, is impressed with the agreed-upon tasks, and is likely headed toward some agreed-upon and well thought out changes in her life.

We do not intend to suggest that establishing the working alliance is easy in career counseling, only that it is important. Heppner and Hendricks (1995), in a qualitative study of career counseling, carefully documented this fact. Horvath and Greenberg (1994) compiled an extensive collection of articles further supporting its importance. Too many times, we as counselors find ourselves confused by reluctant clients or early terminations, and we seek explanations. We wonder if perhaps the client was not ready for counseling, was not properly motivated, found it difficult to commit the time, or some similar explanation. But first we should examine how well we were able to establish a good working alliance in that first interview. Kokotovic and Tracey (1990) would argue for attempting to measure the working alliance after the initial session, as it could help avoid premature termination. It might not be easy, but it clearly must be a goal for us if we are to deliver effective services. One further thought on the working alliance—this may only further confound our thinking, but some recent research (Mackrill, 2011) has suggested that we look at life goals as sometimes separate from our therapeutic goals. If so, then separate assessments of the effectiveness of the two may need to be considered. We'll not pursue that possibility now, but we do see it as a refinement to consider, especially when we may have difficulty understanding an alliance that is not maturing as we expect.

A Counselor's Checklist on Building the Working Alliance

So much of what the counselor does in the initial session to establish a working alliance depends on the individual, but we can offer a list of questions that the counselor should consider before and after the first session and subsequent sessions. These are not listed here in order of importance, and this is not an all-inclusive list, but these basic questions should spark your thinking about how attending to the various parts of the working alliance can make a difference:

- Have I given optimal time to the three parts of the relationship: goals, tasks, and bond?
- Have I clearly established a set of goals to work on?
- Do we have agreement on these goals?
- Am I sure the client sees these as reasonable goals?
- Have I established the tasks that will move us toward these goals?
- Am I comfortable that there is agreement on the tasks involved, and have we discussed how easy or difficult it will be to accomplish these tasks?
- Do I sense the beginning of a strong working relationship between us? Has this been discussed? Is it a sufficient bond to carry us through the previously described tasks?
- Have I established an egalitarian relationship with the client (Al-Darmaki & Kivlighan, 1993)?
- Is the nature of the time and commitment to the career counseling process clear?
- Am I sure there is a clear plan, with appropriate assignments for the next session and beyond?
- Can I speak with optimism about initial progress with the three parts of the alliance: goals, tasks, and bond?
- If I have reservations about any of the three parts, do I have a plan for discussing them at the next session?

Answers to the questions above should help you assess how you are doing with the working alliance. You might ask the client to complete a set of questions similar to those we provide in our Career Counseling Progress Report (see Figure 8-1), a form routinely used at the University of Missouri Career Center.

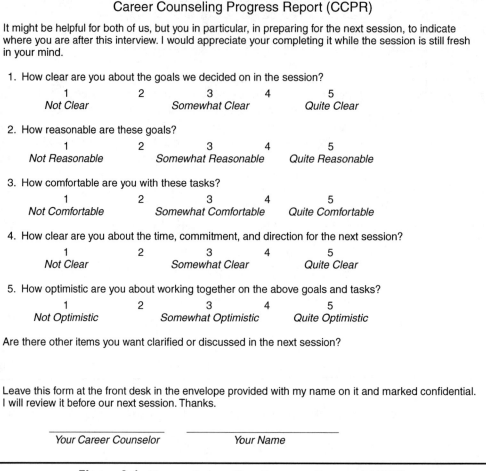

Figure 8-1. Career Counseling Progress Report (CCPR)

Or you could use a more formal and psychometrically sound approach, such as the Working Alliance Inventory–Form T (Horvath & Greenberg, 1989), or an equally valid and reliable short form of the instrument (Busseri & Tyler, 2003). There is also a form that you can ask the client to complete: the Working Alliance Inventory–Form C (Horvath & Greenberg, 1989). These inventories help us to focus on the developing relationship that is so important in career counseling. Use these instruments, but do not overlook the more obvious way of plotting or assessing the nature of the relationship: Regularly ask the client, "How are we doing?" Clients will often be forthright and helpful, if asked.

Closing Thoughts

There is room for discussion as to the best outcomes of career counseling, but there is little need for discussion as to the importance of the relationships needed in career counseling. We must start early and establish strong working alliances. These involve goals, tasks, and the development of a bond between counselor and client. We must begin attending to the working alliance in the initial interview and then regularly assess progress in attaining it. This chapter has offered some ways to measure the working alliance, and we suggest you use these measures early on as you hone your skills at developing the working alliance. Having effective alliances will clearly affect the outcomes of our counseling efforts.

References

Al-Darmaki, F., & Kivlighan, D. M., Jr. (1993). Congruence in client–counselor expectations for relationships and the working alliance. *Journal of Counseling Psychology, 40,* 379–384.

Andrusyna, B. A., Tang, T. Z., DeRubeis, R. J., & Luborsky, L. (2001). The factor structure of the Working Alliance Inventory in cognitive-behavioral therapy. *Journal of Psychotherapy Practice and Research, 10,* 173–178.

Barrett-Lennard, G. T. (1986). The relationship inventory now: Issues and advances in theory, method, and uses. In L. Greenberg & W. Pensoff (Eds.), *The psychotherapeutic process* (pp. 439–476). New York, NY: Guilford Press.

Bordin, E. S. (1979). The generalizability of the working alliance. *Psychotherapy: Theory, Research and Practice, 16,* 252–260.

Busseri, M. A., & Tyler, J. D. (2003). Interchangeability of the Working Alliance Inventory and Working Alliance Inventory, Short Form. *Psychological Assessment, 15*(2), 193–197.

Castonguay, L. G., Constantino, M. J., & Holtforth, M. G. (2006). The working alliance: Where are we and where should we go? *Psychotherapy: Theory, Research, Practice, Training, 43*(3), 271–279.

Gelso, C. J., & Carter, J. A. (1985). The relationship in counseling and psychotherapy: Components, consequences, and theoretical antecedents. *The Counseling Psychologist, 13,* 155–243.

Gelso, C. J., & Hayes, J. A. (1998). *The psychotherapy relationship: Theory, research, and practice.* New York, NY: Wiley.

Heppner, M. J., & Hendricks, F. (1995). A process and outcome study examining career indecision and indecisiveness. *Journal of Counseling & Development, 73,* 426–437.

Horvath, A. O., & Greenberg, L. (1989). The development of the Working Alliance Inventory. *Journal of Counseling Psychology, 36,* 223–233.

Horvath, A. O., & Greenberg, L. S. (1994). *The working alliance: Theory, research and practice.* New York, NY: Wiley.

Kokotovic, A. M., & Tracey, T. J. (1990). Working alliance in the early phase of counseling. *Journal of Counseling Psychology, 37,* 16–21.

Mackrill, T. (2011). Differentiating life goals and therapeutic goals: Expanding our understanding of the working alliance. *British Journal of Guidance and Counseling, 39*(1), 25–39.

Meara, N. M., & Patton, M. J. (1994). Contributions of the working alliance in the practice of career counseling. *The Career Development Quarterly, 43,* 161–177.

Orlinsky, D. E., & Howard, K. I. (1986). Process and outcome in psychotherapy. In S. L. Garfield & A. E. Bergin (Eds.), *Handbook of psychotherapy and behavior change* (3rd ed., pp. 311–381). New York, NY: Wiley.

Rogers, C. R. (1961). *On becoming a person.* Boston, MA: Houghton Mifflin.

Skovholt, T. M., Ronnestad, M. H., & Jennings, L. (1997). Searching for expertise in counseling, psychotherapy, and professional psychology. *Educational Psychology Review, 9*(4), 361–369.

Tichenor, V., & Hill, C. E. (1989). A comparison of six measures of working alliance. *Psychotherapy, 26,* 195–199.

Wei, M., & Heppner, P. P. (2005). Counselor and client predictors of the initial working alliance: A replication and extension to Taiwanese client–counselor dyads. *The Counseling Psychologist, 33,* 51–71.

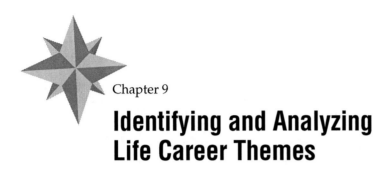

Chapter 9

Identifying and Analyzing
Life Career Themes

Counseling gives emphasis to identifying life themes because they indicate what
gives life purpose, meaning, direction, and coherence.

—Hartung, 2011, p. 111

Postmodern theories of career behavior and development place emphasis on the subjective, on individuals telling their stories in their own words. Assessments that are used
to facilitate clients telling their stories are "idiographic in nature, and the individual
serves as the reference point in both identifying pertinent experiences and interpreting
the meaning of those variables" (Whiston & Rahardja, 2005, p. 372). The goal is to help
clients narrate their lives and, as they are doing so, develop insights into their behavior
as the narration (story) unfolds (Gold, 2008).

Why is helping clients tell their stories important? It is important because we believe that what clients say about themselves, others, and the worlds in which they
live; what they say about their environmental barriers, racial identity statuses, and
levels of acculturation; and the language with which they choose to represent these
statements may be the crucial mediating processes in their lives. Understanding
these statements may provide you and your clients with insights into clients' internal thoughts and feelings concerning their presenting problems, hopes, dreams, and
other possible problems and issues that may emerge as career counseling unfolds. We
believe as Meier (2012) does that

> client stories are face valid, that is, they have intrinsic value, and narrative therapists
> assume that client stories reflect some meaningful aspect of that person. (p. 4)

Many years ago, Kelly (1955) described this phenomenon as individuals looking at
their worlds through self-created transparent patterns or templates in order to make
sense out of them. He used the term *personal constructs* to describe these patterns and
stated that personal constructs are ways in which individuals construe their worlds.
Later, Gerber (1983) suggested that the language people use represents the persons'

underlying conceptual schemata, and, in turn, their conceptual schemata determine their behavior.

One way to understand client information and behavior is to focus attention on these personal constructs, or *life career themes*, as we call them, that clients use to understand themselves, others, and their worlds. What language do they use? What is the nature and extent of their vocabulary? Is their vocabulary fully developed? Is it limited? Is it based on stereotypes? Does it contain distortions? What language do they use to describe possible environmental barriers, their racial identity statuses, and their levels of acculturation?

> The client's self-descriptions, recurring themes, incomplete life stories, distorted (from others' perspective) beliefs, polarities, and perceived contexts are all examples of important therapeutic content and client cognitions. (Meier, 2012, p. 6)

How important are life career themes in the lives of individuals? Savickas (2006) stated that themes matter because they give "meaning and purpose" to clients. Del Corso and Rehfuss (2011) suggested that they are very important because they form one's self or identity.

> Over the course of a lifetime, themes or patterns emerge that form the totality of one's self or identity. Therefore, when someone asks, "Who are you?" individuals share attributes they believe to be true about themselves. They may say they are smart, funny, or kind. When pressed further about how they know these attributes are true, people tell stories. They share experiences that validate their perception and worldview: "I know I am good at solving complex problems because I made all A's in math class, and I was usually the kid who other classmates went to for help." The focus, therefore, is not on objective truth, but rather on the way a person perceives him/herself. (p. 335)

To assist you in enhancing your skills to hear, see, interpret, and form hypotheses about client information and behavior in terms of life career themes, this chapter first describes the concept of life career themes. This is followed by brief discussions of the counseling techniques of interpretation and forming hypotheses that are used in life career theme identification and analysis. The rest of the chapter is devoted to sources of vocabulary that can be used to frame life career themes.

What Are Life Career Themes?

Life career themes are words that people use to express their ideas, values, attitudes, and beliefs about themselves ("I am" statements), about others ("Others are" statements), and about their worldviews ("Life is" statements). An understanding of life career themes is important because these themes provide us with ways to understand the thought processes of our clients (Savickas, 2013). They help us picture our clients' representational systems, and they help us gain insights into client information and behavior. Much like worldviews, life career themes

> suggest *directly* how an individual is solving a problem, moving towards self-completion, and striving for security, power, or love as they construct their careers; and *indirectly* points to an underlying pain or problem that an individual seeks to overcome as the protagonist in his/her life story. (Del Corso & Rehfuss, 2011, p. 338)

Steps Involved in Theme Identification and Analysis

The first step in life career theme identification and analysis begins in the first counseling session and continues into other sessions as you and your clients are gathering client self and environmental information. This can involve the use of qualitative procedures such as the Life Career Assessment, the career genogram, and an occupational card sort. It can also involve the use of quantitative instruments such as the Self-Directed Search (Holland, 1994), the INSIGHT Inventory (Handley, 2006), the Clifton StrengthsFinder (Roth, 2007), and the Career Transitions Inventory (Heppner, 1991). As the information these and similar sources provide is gathered, images are formed about what clients are like.

The next step involves translating the images you and your clients have formed into the language from one or more of the sources you may be using. In effect, you and your clients look at the images formed through the eyes of the source and interpret together what is seen in that source's language. For example, if you are using Holland's (1997) classification system as your source, you could use one or more of the personality types he describes as possible descriptors of the client images you and your clients have formed.

The last step in theme identification and analysis is developing an in-your-mind profile of the life career themes that you and your clients have derived from the client images you and your clients have formed. One way to do this is to visualize the client life career themes that have been identified as brief newspaper articles, complete with headlines. In your minds, you and your client write the article describing your client in terms of life career themes and then summarize the key themes as boldface news headlines. This is an excellent exercise to bring you and your client together, to correct any misperceptions, and to add details where needed. It is a way to bring life career themes into focus.

Some Points to Remember in Theme Identification and Analysis

Some career counseling approaches emphasize gathering all the data about clients before attempting to explain or hypothesize about client behavior. We believe that these approaches are not very effective or efficient because when you are working with clients, you will be dealing with their unique streams of behavior and their private logic (Nikelly, 1971). We recommend that instead of waiting to interpret client information and behavior into life career themes until all the information about the clients is gathered, you and your clients begin immediately in the first session to interpret client information and behavior into life career themes. As this unfolds, tentative hypotheses are formed by you and your clients about their unique combinations of themes and their resulting behavior. As the counseling process unfolds, you and your clients will accept or reject hypotheses in part or totally on a continuing basis. Rather than trying to impose psychological certainties after all the information is in, using interpretation and forming hypotheses invites you and your clients to continue with the task of understanding the life career themes they may be using, to test out your understanding of them with your clients, and to profit from mistaken or divergent views.

Sometimes in the career counseling process you will note life career theme inconsistencies in clients. These often are difficult to understand. A possible way to resolve inconsistent and contradictory themes is to use a technique called *two points of a line* (Dreikurs, 1966). This technique suggests that inconsistencies and contradictions in themes are simply a matter of our inability to grasp the logic that binds them into a coherent whole. If you are able to connect two divergent themes, it may be possible to understand your clients' behavior in a wide range of situations. As in geometry, the location of a line can be determined by two points. The key to resolving apparent inconsistencies and contradictions is to find the string that links the points together. Some clients who are aware of their weaknesses counter those weaknesses through compensation. Thus, you may observe their more primitive behavior at some times and their compensating behavior at other times. For example, a client may exhibit primitive behavior in a stressful situation. The fact that clients are using compensation is, in itself, a useful piece of information that will help you understand them better.

It is important to keep in mind that you need to avoid premature and absolute categorization of clients based on the life career themes you identify. Life career theme analysis is not a technique to help you gather perceptions about clients and then label them for all time on the basis of these perceptions. Instead, life career theme analysis is a technique that serves as a point of departure for you and your clients to explore, hypothesize, and plan together. As life career themes are identified, they serve as discussion points to aid both you and your clients in better understanding who they are, what their concerns are, and where they may be going.

Finally, as you are using life career theme identification and analysis as a part of the information-gathering phase of career counseling, keep in mind that you need to look at each bit of information about your clients in a number of ways. What does it mean as a sample? Is this a common or unusual occurrence? With what does the information correlate? Does it often follow or precede certain events? Is it a sign of an underlying condition? What does it symbolize?

Interpretation: A Needed Skill in Theme Analysis

The counseling technique of interpretation is a necessary skill to have if you are going to be effective in life career theme analysis. Although there are many definitions of *interpretation* in counseling, Clark (1995) observed that the common element in all of the definitions he reviewed was that "the client is introduced to a new frame of reference" (p. 483). It is important to note that this new frame of reference goes beyond where your clients are; something new is presented to them.

As information gathering in career counseling continues to unfold, the use of the technique of interpretation helps make explicit the life career themes present in your clients' responses even though these life career themes may still be meaningless to them. A major goal of career counseling "is to elicit inside information [from clients] so that it can be taught back to them or learned directly by them" (Field, 1966, p. 24). As career counseling progresses, such a framework makes it possible for you and your clients to make the connections between these life career themes on the one hand and client problem resolution or goal attainment on the other. Carlsen (1988) made this point in describing a type of therapy called *developmental meaning-making*:

> Clients who may never have explored themselves—and thus, never really known themselves—begin to understand the patterning and programs which have shaped their lives. Ordering and synthesizing this new information, they open their eyes to new possibilities and are often able to stand back with a new perspective on themselves. And, parallel to their cognitive understandings come new awareness and recognition of the influence and meaning of their affective experience—not one without the other, but intertwining and developing in a dialectical synergy of life development. (p. 4)

Kottler and Brown (1992) defined *interpretation* as an "attempt to impart meaning to the client by introducing new concepts and frames of reference" (p. 62). The selected models of human behavior organized around life roles that appear later in this chapter offer new concepts and frames of reference. They supply possible new language for expressing your clients' life career themes.

Interpretations usually start with your statements such as "Could it be that . . .," "You believe that . . .," and "It sounds like . . . ." How and when you interpret client information and behavior and what you focus on specifically will depend in part on your orientation to counseling. Your experiences may also play a part in interpreting client information (Clark, 1995). Remember, too, that this is a shared experience between you and your client.

Forming Tentative Hypotheses: Another Needed Skill in Theme Analysis

Another needed skill in life career theme analysis is the ability to form tentative hypotheses about the meaning of client information and behavior. What is a hypothesis? According to Walborn (1996), "In counseling and psychotherapy, a hypothesis is an educated hunch that is grounded in theory" (p. 224). What do hypotheses do in the counseling process? Walborn suggested that they keep sessions focused, they help "to keep the [counselor's] expectations in line with reality" (p. 227), they can challenge clients' interpretations of their problems, and they can foster the development of a collaborative relationship—the working alliance. Walborn put it this way: "The client's pain is exchanged for the [counselor's] understanding, as expressed in the hypothesis. Even an incorrect hypothesis is a gift" (p. 229).

As we pointed out earlier, gathering information about your clients begins with the presenting problem or issue during the first session. As gathering information using qualitative and quantitative procedures is under way, so are interpretation, theme analysis, and the forming of tentative hypotheses. One flows into the other. The dynamic and complex nature of these interacting processes requires you to be an active, involved counselor who is well grounded in various theoretical models of human behavior. The dynamic and complex nature of these interacting processes also requires that you be willing to take some risks in your interpretations and tentative hypotheses. You know that if your clients disagree with your hypotheses as the shared process of life career theme analysis continues to unfold, they will feel comfortable confiding their thoughts with you because of the strong working alliance you have formed together.

The major purposes of gathering information about your clients are to shed light on their presenting problems and issues, provide opportunities for them to go beyond their presenting problems if they wish, and begin to focus on problem solutions. This is accomplished through interpretation, providing your clients with vocabulary to describe problems and issues through forming tentative hypotheses about life career themes toward the goal of selecting interventions to assist them in reaching their goals and resolving their problems. How do we know if we are on the correct path in forming hypotheses? "The emphasis is not on the content of the hypothesis, but rather on the impact that the hypothesis has on the therapeutic relationship [working alliance] and, ultimately, on positive change" (Walborn, 1996, p. 242).

Selected Sources of Vocabulary for Life Career Themes

Life career theme identification and analysis require that clients have the necessary vocabulary to describe themselves ("I am" statements), others ("Others are" statements), and their worldviews ("Life is" statements). Unfortunately many clients lack such vocabulary. Meier (2012) stated that "many clients lack the emotional vocabulary necessary to express what they feel beyond a basic dimension of positive or negative affect" (p. 21). As a result, one of the tasks of career counseling, according to Savickas (2011), is to help "clients to enlarge their vocabulary of self" (p. 38) so that they are better able to understand and express themselves. To the vocabulary of self we add the vocabulary of others and worldviews.

There are many sources of self, others, and worldview vocabulary that can be used as life career themes in career counseling. Some sources are career theories (Anderson & Vandehey, 2012); others are word lists focusing on transferable skills (Bolles, 2012); and still others are quantitative assessments, such as the Self-Directed Search (Holland, 1994), the INSIGHT Inventory (Handley, 2006), the Clifton StrengthsFinder (Roth, 2007), and the Career Transitions Inventory (Heppner, 1991), that highlight individuals' traits and styles, and lists of strengths identified by Jones-Smith (2014).

In this section of the chapter we first present the concepts of data, ideas, things, and people used by American College Testing (ACT) in their world of work map to show how these concepts can be used as a source for life career themes. Then, we present Holland's (1997) theory of vocational personalities and work environments as a source of vocabulary for life career themes. Next, we use Bolles's (2012) concept of transferable skills as a source. Finally, we show you how these two last sources can be combined to offer ideas about vocabulary for life career themes.

Data, Ideas, Things, People

Prior to the creation of O*NET, the most widely used and influential occupational classification system was the *Dictionary of Occupational Titles* (U.S. Department of Labor, 1991) published by JIST Works, Inc., of Indianapolis, Indiana. Prediger (1976) extended the data, people, and worker function ratings described in the *Dictionary of Occupational Titles* to include ideas. Revisions of Prediger's original formulation appeared in several sources, including Prediger, Swaney, and Mau (1993), Prediger and Swaney (1995), and Swaney (1995). The most recent definitions of data, ideas, things, and people appeared in the *ACT Interest Inventory Technical Manual* (American College Testing, 2009, p. 5):

Data (facts, records, files, numbers, systematic procedures for facilitating goods/ services consumption by people)
> "Data activities" involve impersonal processes such as recording, verifying, transmitting, and organizing facts or data representing goods and services. Purchasing agents, accountants, and air traffic controllers work mainly with data.

Ideas (abstractions, theories, knowledge, insights, and new ways of expressing something—for example, with words, equations, or music)
> "Ideas activities" involve intrapersonal processes such as creating, discovering, interpreting, and synthesizing abstractions or implementing applications of abstractions. Scientists, musicians, and philosophers work mainly with ideas.

Things (machines, mechanisms, materials, tools, physical and biological processes)
> "Things activities" involve non-personal processes such as producing, transporting, servicing, and repairing. Bricklayers, farmers, and engineers work mainly with things.

People (no alternative terms)
> "People activities" involve interpersonal processes such as helping, informing, serving, persuading, entertaining, motivating, or directing—in general, producing a change in human behavior. Teachers, salespersons, and nurses work mainly with people.

Our purpose in presenting this source is to focus on its application to the process of life career theme analysis. Of particular interest is the language it can supply to help describe the images you form with your clients during the career counseling process. Some sample applications of theme analysis using the language of data, ideas, things, and people are shown in Table 9-1.

Vocational Personalities and Work Environments

Holland's (1997) theory of vocational personalities and work environments categorizes personalities and environments as described in Chapter 2. The language used by Holland to describe personality types and environments is very useful for deriving life career themes that can be used to assist clients in learning language to help them

Table 9-1. Sample Applications of Theme Analysis Using Data, Ideas, Things, and People

Typical Client Dialogue	Component Descriptors	Theme Statements
"I like to make copies of original artwork." "Monogramming clothing is fun."	*Data:* Creative—design reproduction, craft skills, composition, applied arts	Can duplicate originals Products show attention to detail Can be counted on to complete tasks
"It is important to have everything organized and in order." "They say I'm good with numbers."	*Data:* Abstract—numerical skills, symbols and ideas, information/data collection, data entry technology skills	Likes to manipulate financial data Intrigued by computer technology Prefers to organize information for budgets
"I love to write." "I lose track of time when I am putting ideas on paper."	*Ideas:* Artistic—entertainment interests, performing art (music, acting, etc.), literary creative design	Is a sensitive performer and artist Has the ability to express feelings in writing Has an original way of doing things
"I would like to devote my life to the study of the adrenal gland." "Each answer leads to another question."	*Ideas:* Investigative—social science, medical science, natural science, applied technology	Likes to construct theories to explain world conditions Constantly comparing and contrasting ideas Has the capacity to research and publish
"It feels good to be active and perspire." "Being outdoors makes me high."	*Things:* Physical—recreational skills, agriculture/outdoor stamina/strengths for jobs, performance oriented	Can show you how to do things Possesses physical skills for heavy work Contact with nature spurs activity
"People always seem to come to me for advice." "I like being around young people . . . they are so stimulating."	*People:* Instruct—persuade, help to perform, ability to communicate, serve others	Enjoys selling to others Wants to teach others Likes counseling and caring for others
"Being an office manager would be challenging." "I feel I have some expertise that would be of value to others."	*People:* Manage—supervise, consult, act as mentor, leadership	Aspires to be a consultant Wants others to follow one's lead Finds directing others to accomplish tasks rewarding

describe themselves, others, and their worlds. What follows are descriptions of Holland's six personality types and environments.[1]

Realistic Personality and Environment

Persons with a predominantly realistic personality tend to be more oriented to the present and to dealing with the concrete rather than the abstract. They are people who believe they have athletic or mechanical ability and prefer to work in the outdoors with their hands, tools, machines, plants, or animals rather than with people. They prefer the straightforward, measurable, and tried and true rather than the unknown and unpredictable. They often exhibit a straightforward stick-to-itiveness and a sense of maturity.

The environment is one that encourages and rewards success in the use of one's hands and in the manipulation of things. It is a world of the tangible and predictable that rewards with and values money, possessions, and power.

Investigative Personality and Environment

Persons with a predominantly investigative personality tend to be more oriented to the abstract and to problem solving. They like to solve problems that require thinking, especially those involving scientific, technical, and mathematical pursuits. They tend not to be particularly socially oriented and prefer academic and scientific areas. They value intellect and believe it is the tool with which to deal with the world.

The environment is one that encourages and rewards success in the use of intellect and in the manipulation of the abstract. It is a world of observing, investigating, and theorizing, and it values and rewards with status and recognition.

Artistic Personality and Environment

Persons with a predominantly artistic personality tend to be more oriented to the imaginative and creative, using feelings as a guide to whether something is right. They have, or believe they have, artistic, innovative, or intuitive abilities and prefer to avoid structured work settings and conformity. They value aesthetic and often prefer to relate to the world through the products of their work, such as paintings, plays, and music.

The environment is one that encourages and rewards displays of the aforementioned values. It is a world of the abstract, aesthetic, and original. It rewards with recognition, status, and increasing freedom to create in one's own way.

Social Personality and Environment

Persons with a predominantly social personality tend to be more oriented to the problems and growth of people and interpersonal relationships. They like to work with people directly and are good with words. They like to inform, teach, help, and train others. They often are academically oriented. However, they tend toward the impulsive and intuitive rather than the methodical and scientific.

The environment is one that encourages and rewards success in the aforementioned values and tends to promote social activities. It is a world of people and relationships that is often changing, and it values social skills and the ability to promote change in others. It tends to reward with recognition and approval from peers and those being taught and helped.

---

[1]*Note.* Reproduced by special permission of the publisher, Psychological Assessment Resources, Inc., 16204 North Florida Avenue, Lutz, FL 33549, from *Making Vocational Choices*, third edition, by J. L. Holland. Copyright 1973, 1985, 1992, 1997 by Psychological Assessment Resources, Inc. All rights reserved.

Enterprising Personality and Environment

Persons with a predominantly enterprising personality tend to be more oriented to the overcoming of political and economic challenges. They are, or believe they are, good at talking and using words to persuade, influence, and manage for organizational or economic goals. They tend to be more assertive and dominating than other types. They often value and seek out new challenges and tend to be self-confident as well as social, although this is often at a surface level.

The environment is one that encourages and rewards success in these endeavors. It is a world of new challenges to be continually overcome, valuing and rewarding with power, status, and money.

Conventional Personality and Environment

Persons with a predominantly conventional personality tend to be more conforming and conventional, preferring the structured and predictable. They like to work with data and have, or believe they have, clerical or numerical ability. They prefer to follow others' directions and carry out activities in detail. They tend to value the neat and orderly and prefer not to be responsible for the intangible and unpredictable.

The environment is one that encourages and rewards exacting management of data and details. It is a world of facts that is practical and organized, where dependability and attention to detail are rewarded. Rewards tend to be in the area of economic success and status involving material possessions and recognition of superiors and peers.

Transferable Skill Identification

In his book *What Color Is Your Parachute?* Bolles (2012) described transferable skills as "the most basic—the atoms—of whatever career you may choose" (p. 232). He pointed out that transferable skills can be grouped into three families: data/information, people, or things. In each of these families a number of specific skills are identified, and examples of where these skills may be used are provided. The language used to describe the skills and the examples provided can be used by you and your clients to help identify and describe skills (Coutinho, Dam, & Blustein, 2008). The language used provides the nucleus around which life career themes can be grouped.

Combining Two Sources of Vocabulary for Life Career Themes

Holland's (1997) theory vocabulary and the vocabulary from transferable skills can be used separately or in combination to derive life career themes. For the purposes of this chapter we have combined them to show how the two together can offer rich sources of vocabulary for identifying life career themes (see Boxes 9-1 to 9-6).

All of the examples use the same format. First a personality type is described. Then examples of transferable skills associated with that type are listed. Finally, possible life career themes are presented that may emerge from your interactions with clients during the gathering information phase of the career counseling process. Possible life career themes are presented in the form of tentative hypotheses, such as "As I have listened to you describe some of your experiences at work, it sounds as if you dislike routine and close supervision."

Practice in Identifying Life Career Themes

Because the concept of life career themes can be abstract, it is more difficult to explain than it is to demonstrate by example. Although some examples have been provided

---

Box 9-1. Realistic

The realistic personality uses physical skills to work on or make products. This interest can be satisfied in a variety of work ranging from routine to complex jobs. It may involve using physical skills to work on or make products. It also may involve dealing directly with things. Often tools, machines, or measuring devices are used to make or change a product or build, repair, alter, or restore products. Complex tasks are involved, such as adjusting and controlling things or using knowledge and reasoning skills to make judgments and decisions. Examples and prior experiences might include repairing a bicycle, mowing lawns, typing, doing highly skilled crafts, using a printing press.

Transferable Skills

Skills	Specific Operations
1. Using hands	1. Assembling, constructing, building; operating tools, machinery, or equipment; showing finger dexterity, precision handling, and repairing
2. Using body	2. Physical activity, muscular coordination, outdoor activities

Possible Life Career Themes

Likes detail; likes to complete tasks; systematic structured; efficient; confident; handles objects; works with tools; works with machines; conforming; precision work; practical; methodical; materialistic; frank; honest; humble; natural; persistent; modest; shy; stable; thrifty

---

throughout the chapter, more follow. As explained previously, life career themes are ideas, beliefs, attitudes, and values that people hold about themselves, others, and the world at large. These "I am," "Others are," and "Life is" statements have a lot to do with people's behavior. By looking at behavior—both words and actions—you can infer or directly observe life career themes. See Table 9-2 for examples.

To carry out theme identification and analysis, your task is to take the images formed about your clients from the samples of their information and behavior obtained during

---

Box 9-2. Investigative

The investigative personality has an interest in researching and collecting data about the natural world and applying them to problems in medical, life, or physical sciences. This interest may be satisfied by working with the knowledge and processes involved in the sciences. Conducting research and analyzing, evaluating, explaining, and recording scientific information as well as using scientific or technical methods, instruments, and equipment in work are involved. Planning, scheduling, processing, controlling, directing, and evaluating data and things also are involved. There may be contact with people, but dealing with people is not important to the work. Examples and prior experiences might include computer work, operating complex machines, assisting in a laboratory, finding the location of an unfamiliar street, tracing down a short in electrical wiring, finding the ingredients to a special recipe, doing comparative shopping, examining a cut or bruise.

Transferable Skills

Skills	Specific Operations
1. Using analytical thinking or logic	1. Researching, information gathering, analyzing; organizing, diagnosing, putting things in order, comparing, testing, evaluating
2. Using senses	2. Observing, inspecting, examining; diagnosing, showing attention to detail

Possible Life Career Themes

Analytical; efficient; cautious; likes to investigate; curious; methodical; seeks to understand; thinks to solve problems; precision work; independent; modest; seeks to organize; reserved

---

Box 9-3. Artistic

The artistic personality has an interest in creative expression of feelings or ideas. Complex mental skills are used to create new knowledge or new ways of applying what is already known. This includes solving different problems or designing projects and methods; using new ways to express ideas, feelings, and moods; and using imagination to create ideas and moods. Examples and prior experiences might include handicrafts, photography, art, painting, decorating, playing in a band, or singing in a choir.

Transferable Skills

Skills	Specific Operations
1. Using originality/creativity	1. Imagining, inventing, designing; improvising, adapting, experimenting
2. Using artistic ability	2. Composing, playing music, singing; shaping materials, creating shapes or faces, using colors; showing feelings and thoughts through body, face, or voice; using words expressively
3. Using intuition	3. Showing foresight, acting on gut reactions, quickly sizing up a situation

Possible Life Career Themes

Dislikes routine; dislikes supervision; expressive; intuitive; original; adventurous, likes novelty, change, variety; attention-getting; impulsive, independent, nonconforming; spontaneous; abstract thinking

---

the gathering information phase of career counseling and translate these images into the language of the sources of vocabulary just described. The language from these vocabulary sources then becomes the language used to express possible life career themes that may be present.

Remember, this process is a shared one in which you and your client need to think about life career themes together. It is a teaching–learning process in which you and your client are both teacher and learner. Your task as counselor is to supply vocabulary. Your client's task is to share experiences and information. Then, as you work together, the process of life career theme analysis unfolds, often tentatively at first, as ideas are exchanged and life career themes are identified and discussed. "Supported by career development theories that see patterns and purpose in life stories and recol-

---

Box 9-4. Social

The social personality has an interest in helping individuals with their mental, spiritual, social, physical, or occupational concerns. This interest can be satisfied through jobs in which maintaining or improving the physical, mental, emotional, or spiritual well-being of others is important. Speaking and listening well, communicating simple ideas, and having direct contact with the people being helped are also important. Examples and prior experiences might include being a disc jockey, doing public speaking, writing for the school paper, and organizing a basketball game.

Transferable Skills

Skills	Specific Operations
1. Using words	1. Reading, copying, editing, writing, teaching, training, memorizing
2. Using helpfulness	2. Drawing out people, motivating, counseling; appreciating, sharing credit, raising others' self-esteem

Possible Life Career Themes

Social contact; adaptable; interested; cooperative; kind; likes friends to approach; insightful; generous; sociable; guiding; understanding; popular; idealistic; convincing; friendly; expressive; committed

---

Box 9-5. Enterprising

The enterprising personality has an interest in influencing others and enjoys the challenge and responsibility of leadership. Activities involved may include setting up business contracts to buy, sell, talk, listen, promote, and bargain; gathering, exchanging, or presenting ideas and facts about products or services; leading, planning, controlling, or managing the work of others and as a result gaining prestige, recognition, or appreciation from others. Examples and prior experiences might include managing a paper route, selling candy or tickets, participating in Junior Achievement, being a candy striper, babysitting, or starting a money-making project.

Transferable Skills

Skills	Specific Operations
1. Using leadership	1. Starting new tasks, ideas, taking the first move; organizing, leading, making decisions; taking risks, performing, selling, promoting, persuading

Possible Life Career Themes

Dislikes routine; adaptable; adventurous; dislikes supervision; seeks reward and recognition; ambitious; energetic; independent; sociable; persuasive; manipulating; aggressive; competitive; impulsive; assertive; optimistic; self-confident

---

lections, students can identify themes that help define career possibilities" (Sacino, 2011, p. 136).

Closing Thoughts

This chapter has described the purpose of life career theme identification and analysis as well as the processes used to derive life career themes from selected vocabulary sources. Now that you have seen how the process works and you understand the importance of life career themes, you can practice this process in the next chapter. In Chapter 10, you can see how a qualitative assessment technique called the Life Career Assessment

---

Box 9-6. Conventional

The conventional personality is organized to get the most work done in the least amount of time. Setting up assignments and methods in advance and repeating the same task many times may be involved. These tasks can usually be done in a short time. Activities involved may be those requiring accuracy and attention to detail. Examples might include record keeping; billing, filing, or recording; keeping a checkbook; developing a budget; and working in savings.

Transferable Skills

Skills	Specific Operations
1. Using numbers	1. Taking inventory, counting, calculating; keeping financial records, managing money; number memory
2. Using follow-through	2. Following through on plans, instructions, attending to detail; classifying, recording, filing

Possible Life Career Themes

Likes details; likes to complete tasks; careful; persistent; systematic-structured; efficient; conforming; practical; conservative; orderly; inhibited; conscientious

---

Table 9-2. Sample Client Statements and Themes

Client Statement	Possible Theme/Identity
To have a job that provides many extra fringe benefits. To receive a large yearly pay increase or bonus. To have a job that provides personal comfort and good working conditions. To have ample work breaks or get time off. To be able to manage money or resources.	To receive direct benefits
To be my own boss. To be free to make my own decisions. To be directly responsible to no one at work. To work with little supervision. To be free to vary my working hours.	To be independent
To be able to question the customary way of doing things. To be able to explore various aspects of a job. To discuss which of a number of alternatives better explains a situation. To believe the work I do is important or significant to others. To be able to consider myself a creative person.	To achieve ideals
To know exactly how my supervisors expect a job to be done. To be able to see the results of my work at the end of each day. To be able to measure how much work I have done. To know the problem on which I am working has a correct solution. To know that when I have finished a task, it is done once and for all.	To be responsible
To size up a person or situation for decision making. To be responsible for making major decisions that affect the work of other people. To be responsible for hiring and firing people. To coordinate the work of others. To be able to verbally influence a group of people. To be responsible for making major decisions that affect the work of other people.	To provide leadership
To know a large number of the people with whom I work. To be around workers of the same age and interests. To be spoken well of by supervisors. To know and associate with fellow workers. To have other workers ask for my personal advice.	To have social contact
To make a deal with someone. To find ways to settle an argument. To act on gut reactions. To confer with people about solving problems. To listen and bring understanding to both sides of an argument.	To negotiate
To keep records, inventory, or charts and make appointments. To collect information; to gather materials or samples. To calculate, compute, or manipulate numbers. To classify information or organize it into categories.	To organize
To move something into place; to move or repair. To examine, inspect, and handle with precision. To groom, make up, or work with precision. To work, smooth out, grind, stress, press materials and products.	To handle
To do my best work the room must be free of distractions. To have an established daily routine. To have chores done on a regular schedule. To arrange my time so that each task is done at the same time every day. To allow me to work on one task at a time.	To establish routine
To be physically active. To participate in outdoor sports. To have hobbies and interests involving muscular coordination. To be involved in doing something active.	To be active

provides ample opportunity to see the process of life career theme identification and analysis in action. Remember, the goal is to provide clients with vocabulary to describe life career themes that can then be arranged into various behavior patterns useful in exploring educational and career options.

How important are behavior patterns? Law (2007) stated, "As a species we need frameworks to give our thinking shape—we seek patterns. Patterns are useful because they order data, direct our thinking, identify gaps and draw our attention to anything unusual" (pp. 4–5).

References

American College Testing. (2009). *ACT Interest Inventory technical manual.* Iowa City, IA: Author.

Anderson, P., & Vandehey, M. (2012). *Career counseling and development in a global economy* (2nd ed.). Belmont, CA: Brooks/Cole.

Bolles, R. N. (2012). *What color is your parachute?* Berkeley, CA: Ten Speed Press.

Carlsen, M. B. (1988). *Meaning-making: Therapeutic processes in adult development.* New York, NY: Norton.

Clark, A. J. (1995). An examination of the technique of interpretation in counseling. *Journal of Counseling & Development, 73,* 483–490.

Coutinho, M. T., Dam, V. C., & Blustein, D. L. (2008). The psychology of working and globalisation: A new perspective for a new era. *International Journal for Educational and Vocational Guidance, 8,* 5–18.

Del Corso, J., & Rehfuss, M. C. (2011). The role of narrative in career construction theory. *Journal of Vocational Behavior, 79,* 334–339.

Dreikurs, R. (1966). The holistic approach: Two points of a line. In *Education, guidance, psychodynamics. Proceedings of the Conference of the Individual Psychology Association of Chicago.* Chicago, IL: Alfred Adler Institute.

Field, F. L. (1966). *A taxonomy of educational processes, the nature of vocational guidance, and some implications for professional preparation.* Unpublished manuscript, National Vocational Guidance Association (now National Career Development Association), Alexandria, VA.

Gerber, A. (1983). Finding the car in career. *Journal of Career Education, 9,* 181–183.

Gold, J. M. (2008). Rethinking client resistance: A narrative approach to integrating resistance into the relationship-building stage of counseling. *Journal of Humanistic Counseling, Education and Development, 47,* 56–70.

Handley, P. (2006). *INSIGHT Inventory.* Kansas City, MO: Insight Institute.

Hartung, P. J. (2011). Career construction: Principles and practice. In K. Maree (Ed.), *Shaping the story* (pp. 103–120). Rotterdam, The Netherlands: Sense.

Heppner, M. (1991). *The Career Transitions Inventory.* Columbia: University of Missouri.

Holland, J. L. (1994). *Self-Directed Search, Form R* (4th ed.). Lutz, FL: Psychological Assessment Resources.

Holland, J. L. (1997). *Making vocational choices: A theory of vocational personalities and work environments* (3rd ed.). Odessa, FL: Psychological Assessment Resources.

Jones-Smith, E. (2014). *Strengths-based therapy: Connecting theory, practice, and skills.* Los Angeles, CA: Sage.

Kelly, G. A. (1955). *The psychology of personal constructs: Vol. 1. A theory of personality.* New York, NY: Norton.

Kottler, J. A., & Brown, R. W. (1992). *Introduction to therapeutic counseling* (2nd ed.). Monterey, CA: Brooks/Cole.

Law, B. (2007). *Career-learning narratives: Telling, showing and mapping.* Retrieved from the Career-Learning Café Web site: www.hihohiho.com

Meier, S. T. (2012). *Language and narratives in counseling and psychotherapy.* New York, NY: Springer.

Nikelly, A. G. (Ed.). (1971). *Techniques for behavior change.* Springfield, IL: Charles C Thomas.

Prediger, D. J. (1976). A world-of-work map for career exploration. *Vocational Guidance Quarterly, 24,* 198–208.

Prediger, D. J., & Swaney, K. B. (1995). Using UNIACT in a comprehensive approach to assessment for career planning. *Journal of Career Assessment, 3,* 429–451.

Prediger, D. J., Swaney, K. B., & Mau, W. (1993). Extending Holland's hexagon: Procedure, counseling applications, and research. *Journal of Counseling & Development, 71,* 422–428.

Roth, T. (2007). *StrengthsFinder 2.0.* New York, NY: Gallup Press.

Sacino, M. (2011). "Listen to my story": Identifying patterns and purpose in career counseling. In K. Maree (Ed.), *Shaping the story: A guide to facilitating narrative career counseling* (pp. 134–137). Rotterdam, The Netherlands: Sense.

Savickas, M. L. (2006). Career construction theory. In J. H. Greenhaus & G. A. Callanan (Eds.), *Encyclopedia of career development* (pp. 84–88). Thousand Oaks, CA: Sage.

Savickas, M. L. (2011). *Career counseling.* Washington, DC: American Psychological Association.

Savickas, M. L. (2013). Career construction theory and practice. In S. D. Brown & R. W. Lent (Eds.), *Career development and counseling* (pp. 147–183). Hoboken, NJ: Wiley.

Swaney, K. B. (1995). *Technical manual: Revised unisex edition of the ACT Interest Inventory (UNIACT).* Iowa City, IA: American College Testing.

U.S. Department of Labor. (1991). *Dictionary of occupational titles* (4th ed., rev. ed.). Indianapolis, IN: JIST Works.

Walborn, F. S. (1996). *Process variables: Four common elements of counseling and psychotherapy.* Pacific Grove, CA: Brooks/Cole.

Whiston, S. C., & Rahardja, D. (2005). Qualitative career assessment: An overview and analysis. *Journal of Career Assessment, 13,* 371–380.

Chapter 10

Life Career Assessment: An Interview Framework to Help Clients Tell Their Stories

> Narrative therapists help clients see that their worlds are constructed through language and cultural practice and that clients can subsequently deconstruct and reconstruct their assumptions and perceptions.
>
> —Meier, 2012, p. 2

Qualitative assessments such as the Life Career Assessment (LCA) are narrative interventions grounded in the postmodern approaches of constructivism and social constructionism. The goal of the LCA is to provide clients with a real-life framework that enables them to tell their stories using their own words. The emphasis is on clients' perceptions of themselves, others, and their worlds within their gendered, cultural, racial, socioeconomic, sexual orientation, spiritual, and disability contexts.

> The general aim of narrative career counseling [using the LCA] is to script a person's own life story. This focus makes the approach uniquely suited for an exploration of personal meanings and for helping resolve many kinds of problems involving meaning. In attempting to facilitate career development, a narrative approach attempts to effect personal agency, by viewing learners as active agents in their personal development and cultivating an increased emphasis on emotions and passions. (Maree & Molepo, 2007, p. 63)

The LCA is particularly useful when working with clients of all ages and differing cultural and ethnic backgrounds, when dealing with women's and men's issues, and when dealing with disability issues because clients' worldviews, environmental barriers, racial identity statuses, and levels of acculturation can be addressed directly and naturally. The LCA is very time flexible. The entire structured framework can be completed in 15 to 30 min, or, if desired, a more in-depth interview can be conducted over several sessions with clients. Also, sections of the LCA can be used separately.

The LCA is designed to focus on clients' levels of functioning in their life career development and the internal and external dynamics that may be involved. The LCA helps form working alliances with clients, because an atmosphere of concern and caring can be created through the nonjudgmental, nonthreatening, conversational tone of the LCA process. Printed forms, booklets, and paper-and-pencil instruments—which some clients may associate negatively with school, training, and evaluation—are not used. The LCA is a person-to-person process that allows clients to explore and talk about themselves by focusing on their own experiences in their own words.

The LCA helps to increase clients' career planning abilities. Clients' strengths, the environmental barriers they may face, and their levels of functioning in various life roles are discussed, followed by suggestion of goals and, finally, action to reach these goals. These discussions may uncover the need for other career assessment tools (such as those focusing on environmental barriers and disability issues) and may also uncover skills and abilities that may require further evaluation.

This chapter opens with a discussion of the theoretical foundations of the LCA, then the structure of the LCA is presented in detail. The chapter closes with some points about using the LCA, including how it can be adapted for use with a wide variety of people and issues. This is illustrated by a description of how the LCA can be adapted for work with younger clients.

Theoretical Foundation

The LCA is based in part on the individual psychology of Alfred Adler. He divided individuals' relations to the world into three areas of social living: work (or school), love (social relations), and friendship (Rule & Bishop, 2006). According to Adler, the three cannot be dealt with separately because they are intertwined; a change in one involves the others. Difficulty in one part of life implies comparable difficulties in the rest of a person's life. "Adlerian therapy affirms that humans cannot be understood apart from their social context and the relationships therein" (Watts, 2003, p. 139).

Individuals tend to solve problems and attempt to obtain satisfaction in a similar manner in all three arenas. We use the phrase *life career themes* to describe these consistent ways of negotiating with the world. In Chapter 9, we define life career themes as the ideas, beliefs, attitudes, and values people express about themselves, others, and the world—in general, their worldviews. The life career themes individuals use can be considered to constitute a lifestyle. Individuals are not always aware of their approaches toward life or the themes by which they operate, and they may not recognize the underlying consistencies that exist (Mosak, 1971). They may choose, rather, to dwell on specific, superficial feelings that serve to further obscure the ways in which they are developing.

In the following dialogue, a client is talking about her past job experiences. The client in this interview is a 25-year-old woman. Notice the possible themes that can be identified from this brief discussion.

Dialogue	Possible Theme
Counselor: Let's find out about your work experience. Could you tell me about your last job?	
Client: It was with a small insurance company. I was in the claims department. I sent out form letters and payment checks.	
Counselor: What did you like about the job?	
Client: The people were real nice, even though they were older. I liked	Likes social contact.

Dialogue (Continued)	Possible Theme
talking on the phone to all the different people. That's mainly why I got into claims, so that I could talk to people and wouldn't be all by myself. I liked working downtown where there's a lot of places to go, and I liked the insurance business. *Counselor:* Did you? *Client:* Yeah, I don't think I'd like car insurance, but I liked life and health insurance. It was pretty interesting. There were many different plans, and they were interesting to read.	Likes social variety.
Counselor: What are some of the things you didn't like about the job? *Client:* I just had a set thing that I did everyday. I'd check the mail, and I hated doing that and the form letters. I got to where that's all I could type were form letters. If I tried to type a letter that was handwritten, I just couldn't do it because I just wasn't used to it. It was just dull.	Dislikes routine.
Counselor: What about the job you had before that? *Client:* It was with a floral company. I liked it real well. Mom had gone to school with the owners. I really liked those people. They were a lot of fun. I loved to work with flowers. When I was on delivery I got to go out and run around and I liked that. That was a pretty fun job.	Contact with people is important.
Counselor: What about when you worked at the garment factory? *Client:* Oh, I hated that. That was terrible. I worked at night. I went to school all day long and worked until 1:00 in the morning. I just don't like to do all that routine stuff; that'll make a person go crazy. And I was on my feet all day long, and we got a 10-minute break and a half hour for lunch. It was just too much work.	Does not like to be closed in.

Recurring themes from this dialogue suggest that this client enjoys working with people to meet some of her social needs. She probably dislikes routine kinds of tasks but can adapt to them if she is receiving other satisfaction. As important as learning about what jobs she has held is learning about what kind of working environment is most reinforcing for her. A major purpose of the LCA in information gathering is to begin the process of helping clients identify and clarify their life career themes and the ways in which these themes guide their behavior.

Assessing clients' approaches to work (or school), love (social relations), and friendships provides a concrete way of analyzing and synthesizing clients' movement in their life career development. This assessment is a cooperative endeavor that not only helps you understand your clients but also helps your clients better understand their own life career themes, which reveal their unique sense of the meaning of life. By identifying such themes through the LCA, you and your clients can begin to understand their approaches to life and to do so in a comfortable and straightforward manner.

LCA Framework

The LCA framework is presented below in outline form. As you will see, there are four major sections: Career Assessment, Typical Day, Strengths and Obstacles, and Summary. Each section is covered in detail later in this chapter, but for now an important point to notice is that by following this format you can gather several types of information about your clients. One type is relatively objective and factual and regards your clients' work experiences and educational achievements. Another type is your clients' self-estimations of the skills and competencies they possess. Still another type is inferences made by you of your clients' skills and abilities. These inferences are based on life career themes and are derived from learning about the kinds of activities your clients are involved in at work, at home, in school or training, or at leisure. Another kind of information obtained concerns your clients' opinions of their value as persons and their awareness of self.

Although we suggest you follow the LCA format described here, there is no one prescribed way to use the format. You will need to discover your own personal style of using the LCA. In fact, it is preferable that you integrate the LCA structure into your own style as well as the style of your clients to keep the process from becoming mechanical and to make the gathering information subphase of career counseling as meaningful as possible.

Career Assessment
1. Work experience (part/full time, paid/unpaid)
   - Last job
   - Liked best about
   - Disliked most about
   - Same procedure with another job
2. Education or training progress and concerns
   - General appraisal
   - Liked best about
   - Disliked most about
   - Repeat for levels or types
3. Relationships/friendships
   - Leisure time activities
   - Social life (within leisure context)
   - Friends (within leisure context)

Typical Day
1. Dependent–independent
   - Relies on others
   - Insists on someone else making decisions
2. Systematic–spontaneous
   - Stable and routine
   - Persistent and attentive

Strengths and Obstacles
1. Three main strengths
   - Resources at own disposal
   - What do resources do for clients
2. Three main obstacles
   - Related to strengths
   - Related to themes

Summary
1. Agree on life themes
2. Use client's own words
3. Relate to goal setting or problem solving

Career Assessment

The Career Assessment section of the LCA is divided into three parts: work experience, education or training, and relationships/friendships. Descriptions of each part of the Career Assessment section follow.

Work Experience
To assess work experience, ask your clients to describe their last job or their current job. The jobs can be part time or full time, paid or unpaid. Ask your clients to describe the tasks performed and then relate what they liked best and least about the jobs. Listen for and discuss client worldviews, environmental barriers, and levels of acculturation, as these topics may emerge. As likes and dislikes are discussed, the life career themes that become apparent should be repeated, clarified, and reflected upon so that your clients are aware of the consistencies that run through them. Examining your clients' domestic responsibilities, such as mowing the lawn, caring for a younger sibling, or doing household chores, also can be revealing and is especially useful when clients have had little or no work experience. This process is illustrated by the following interview with a 30-year-old client in which his work experience is discussed:

Dialogue	*Possible Theme*
Counselor: The county hospital was the last job you had? You were working in the kitchen. You worked there quite a while?	
Client: Right, 2 years.	
Counselor: What was your job exactly?	
Client: I worked a tray line, a patient tray line. Afterwards, I'd clean up and then we'd have odds and ends to do, like	Takes care of details so that he can contact others.

(Continued)

Dialogue (Continued)	Possible Theme
go up on the floors and take the patients ice cream, milk, bread, or fruit. We weighed fruit for the next meal, just little odds and ends that you could get done once you knew what you were doing. They had a time schedule set, but me, once I got the hang of it, it didn't take me the time they had scheduled for me, so I just went from one thing to the next. I'd get done at 3:00 or 2:30; sometimes I'd get done at 2:00. Then I'd help the other people, and we'd all sit around 'til 4:30 'til the next meal.	
Counselor: You really like to keep busy. It seems that you like to have something to show for your work.	
Client: Yes, otherwise I get bored with it.	Completion of tasks is important.

The client's job priorities and life career themes begin to emerge in this short excerpt, although there is still much to learn. Note that his need for variety may interfere with his performance in a routine job. This is something to discuss with him later when you look at occupational options.

Education or Training

To begin this section of the interview, ask your clients for a general appraisal of their educational or training experiences. You can provide further structure by asking what your clients liked best and least about these experiences. Usually life career themes begin to appear as likes and dislikes. These themes should be repeated, clarified, and reflected so that your clients are aware of the consistencies or inconsistencies running through them.

After clients give you some general impressions about their educational background or their training experiences, you can begin to ask more specific questions about preferences for subjects, teachers, instructors, and learning conditions. This type of focusing will yield several types of information. One kind is factual, surface information, such as "I like science and math and dislike art and English" or "I like Mr. Jones and Mrs. Green but don't get along well with Mr. Smith." Another type of focusing is on the themes discussed earlier in the clients' work experience, some of which will appear again and again throughout the LCA. You also can obtain clues regarding your clients' learning styles from this section as well as the possible impact that gender, race, and ethnicity issues and disability status may have had on your clients' experiences in education and training.

The following is an excerpt from an interview in which a client's school experience is discussed:

Dialogue	Possible Theme
Counselor: Tell me about your school experience.	
Client: I liked it, until I got into eighth grade. Then I just lost interest. Right around eighth grade.	

Dialogue (Continued)	*Possible Theme*
Counselor: What happened then to make you lose interest?	
Client: I have no idea. I guess I just kinda thought I knew everything and started running around.	
Counselor: When you think back to elementary school, you said you liked it pretty well. What were some things that you remember liking? What was good?	
Client: Um, I can always remember third and fourth grade . . . spelling and capitalization and stuff like that. We always had special games to make it a lot more fun, you know. The spelling bee. If you completed so many words right we got a star on the board. Things like that. I remember how the teacher always pointed me out as being the one person who always got the stars. I guess the things that I got rewards for made it more interesting.	Seeks rewards and recognition. Approval from adults is important.
Counselor: You felt like you could see that you had done something good?	Seeks acceptance.
Client: She would have me help other people.	
Counselor: You must have felt very worthwhile. Now tell me what you did not like about school.	
Client: Well, my worst class was fifth grade.	
Counselor: What was so bad about it?	
Client: The teacher was mean. I'm not kidding! Can you imagine somebody reading, what was it . . . the story *Gone With the Wind*. I had to read that story in the fifth grade. That thing was about this thick, and then she had me write a report.	Large assignments can be overwhelming.
Counselor: She made you do that as a punishment?	
Client: We got off to a bad start, and when she did that to me it just made it worse. I went to the library and me and some girls were passing notes, so as a punishment she gave us all these real big books to read . . . real hard books to read. Then I stuck a tack underneath her chair and somebody told on me. So for a month she would send home	Attention from adults is important. Acts out for revenge. Needs involvement.

(Continued)

Dialogue (Continued)	Possible Theme
progress reports to my father, and he would make me sit and write "I am sorry" . . . 500 times each night. But sixth grade was a lot of fun. My teacher in sixth grade liked to get outdoors and she always took us on field trips to the parks, made a whole afternoon of it. On the weekends she had this nice place out of town and she would always ask us if we wanted to come out on Saturday or Sunday. We would always go out there, if we needed help.	
Counselor: Seemed like she really cared.	
Client: Yeah, she was real nice. I think she left the next year.	
Counselor: You said when you got to junior high you kind of lost interest.	
Client: Seemed like once I got to junior high school nobody really took interest in what you were doing. That might have been part of it. I was used to the one class and everything. I'm kinda old fashioned.	Lacks assertiveness skills. No adult attention brings loneliness.
Counselor: You felt you were left on your own with no one to go to for help.	
Client: That was a lot of it, because I need a lot of help with the short time you've got there and all the students. I would leave class and still have questions. I wouldn't know what to do the next day. So I just got further and further behind. I'll have something to say, but I never say it until it's too late. I remember I talked to my counselor.	Lacks confidence and is dependent.
Counselor: What did your counselor suggest you do?	
Client: Hang in there. And whenever I had a question walk up to them and say, "Hey, I need some help." And I did it for awhile when I got my nerve up, and I would say, "Hey, I need help over here." It was okay for awhile.	Asking for assistance is difficult.

As this client enters into new educational experiences, it will be important for someone to be available to discuss progress and focus on positive experiences. Assertiveness training or related counseling may be needed so that the client can begin to learn how to take more responsibility.

Relationships/Friendships

To explore relationships/friendships, begin by asking your clients about how they spend their leisure time. It is important to note whether themes in the relationships/

friendships section are consistent with the life career themes discussed in the work and education sections of the LCA or are in contrast with them. This also is a good time to explore friendship relations. Exploring clients' social lives within the context of how they spend their leisure time is a relatively nonthreatening way to explore this sometimes sensitive area. The goal is to discover how social relations themes may reflect themes identified in work and education settings. Does the client have many friends? Few? None? Does the client make decisions about leisure activities, or does the client follow the suggestions of others?

In the following dialogue, leisure and social activities are explored with a client:

Dialogue	*Possible Theme*
Counselor: Now that you're out of high school, what do you do with your leisure time?	
Client: Well, we have horses and most of the time I ride them. I have two horses and I ride each of them 2 hours a day. Really, I don't have much time to do anything else.	Intense interest and commitment.
Counselor: Four hours of horseback riding a day?	
Client: Uh-huh, I get up at 6:00 in the morning and ride until 8:00. Now I'll have to ride them both when I get home. I guess I'll have to cut down to an hour apiece. But I've got to ride them during the week, because they're not worth a darn if I don't ride them during the week for the shows on the weekend.	
Counselor: So you show them on the weekends.	
Client: We go all over and show them.	
Counselor: So that takes up most of your time?	
Client: Yeah, quite a bit of it, and I got a Doberman Pinscher that I'm trying to train, and he's about to drive me crazy. I spend most of my time with animals. We did raise Dobermans. Two years ago we had 13 of them, and we sold all of them. Now we only have one, this little baby.	
Counselor: So most of your time is spent with your horses and animals. What about friends?	
Client: Most of my friends live in town, and they usually come out and see me. So it's just whoever comes out, and somebody's usually out there all the time. I run around with my friends at night. Our horse shows last 'til about	Friends come to her.

(Continued)

Dialogue (Continued)	*Possible Theme*
7:30, then I come home and go to the dances or whatever parties are going on.	
Counselor: What about weekends?	
Client: Well, our shows are on Sunday, so I usually spend the whole day Saturday with Mom. I don't get to see her too much during the week. I see her every once in awhile at night, but on Saturdays we go shopping. We go to breakfast first and then we shop. Sometimes we go to lunch. My mom and I are real close.	Her mother is important to her.
Counselor: You feel responsible for her in a way.	
Client: Yeah, because she's done real well in spite of having to raise all us kids. I know my mom is just a lot of fun; I have more fun with her than I do most of my friends.	
Counselor: She's a mother and a friend?	
Client: Yeah, we're real close, but the problem is that I am thinking about moving to look for a job. If I move to California, my sister may want me to live with her. If I stay here, I'd probably move to someplace close so I could run back and forth to see Mom.	Mom is someone to go back to. Relationship with mother may interfere with moving to where the jobs are.
Counselor: One of the things holding you back is your mother.	
Client: I guess. She's married, and my stepdad works an awful lot, and I hate for her to be by herself all the time. I just enjoy seeing her. I'm kind of used to it, I guess.	Will she be able to leave home?

It is relatively simple to move from leisure activities to relationships and friendships. In the above example, the client's dependency on her animals and her mother for emotional support may interfere with career exploration. This conflict may have to be faced later in career counseling.

Typical Day

Many of the themes that emerge during the LCA have natural opposites, such as active–passive and outgoing–withdrawn. Each of these opposite pairs can be considered a personality dimension. At least two personality dimensions should be examined during the Typical Day portion of the LCA. These are dependent–independent and systematic–spontaneous.

Dependent–Independent
- Relies on others
- Insists on someone else making decisions

Systematic–Spontaneous
- Stable and routine
- Persistent and attentive

The purpose of the Typical Day exploration is to discover how clients organize and live their lives each day. You can do this assessment by asking clients to describe a typical day in a step-by-step fashion. You can explore the dependent–independent dimension by asking, "Do you get yourself up in the morning or rely on someone else to wake you?" or, "Do you do things alone or insist on having someone with you at all times?" Similarly, you need to determine whether your clients organize their lives systematically or respond to each day spontaneously. For example, systematic individuals tend to do the same thing day after day in a fairly stable routine (e.g., eating raisin bran cereal every morning), whereas spontaneous individuals may rarely do the same thing twice.

An understanding of the life career themes that emerge from the Typical Day assessment can be very helpful to clients, for these themes sometimes cause problems in school, in training, or on the job. For example, if a client confides that she just cannot get up in the morning, you may foresee problems with punctuality and attendance on the job; this should be explored later in the career counseling sessions. As life career themes are identified, they should be repeated, clarified, and reflected so that clients begin to gain a clearer understanding of how they affect their behavior.

In the following dialogue, a client's typical day is discussed. Notice that the client and counselor explore activities that are common to all people, such as eating and sleeping, as well as those that are more unique to this particular female client.

Dialogue	*Possible Theme*
Counselor: I'd like you to think for a minute about what a day is like for you. It's time to get up. Does an alarm get you up, does somebody wake you up, or do you just wake up?	
Client: I wake up myself, get up, and go downstairs. I've already taken my shower the night before, so I just wash my face, put on a little makeup, find something to put on, get dressed, fix myself something to eat, and drink lots of milk because my stomach is upset when I get up. I have an ulcer.	Responsible, systematic.
Counselor: You fix your own breakfast?	
Client: Yeah. Eggs or toast . . . then the phone usually rings and I talk.	
Counselor: Who's calling you?	
Client: One of my girlfriends.	
Counselor: Let's say you got up and you didn't have anything to do. You could do anything you wanted to do.	
Client: You want to know what I'd do? I'd grab a blanket, go downstairs, get something to eat, turn on the TV; I would just sit there and watch TV.	Passive, seeks pleasure in immediate environment.

(Continued)

Dialogue (Continued)	Possible Theme
Counselor: You like TV?	
Client: Uh-huh.	
Counselor: Daytime TV? Nighttime TV?	
Client: It depends. I like three soap operas. At night I really don't like TV that much unless it's really a good show or a movie. Other than that I don't watch too much, unless I really like it.	
Counselor: What do you like about soap operas?	
Client: Just the story itself, uh, the suspense of what's going to happen next, who's gonna find out what. And, um, who's getting married and whose daughter's pregnant [*laughter*].	Social interests.
Counselor: Can you ever put yourself in their place? Do you ever think that it's happening to you?	
Client: I get so mad that I stomp my feet, saying, "Stop! Stop!" or crying, I end up crying. And I get so mad. You see somebody behind a curtain with a gun and you're saying, "Don't go that way, don't go that way! Call the police." It's really exciting. Sometimes you get so mad and sometimes you get so happy you start crying.	Identifies with and relates to others easily.

The client indicates that she likes a systematic routine in her daily living. However, it also sounds as though she is dependent on others and could get caught up in social relationship problems. She seems passive, and TV could be a pacifier for her.

Strengths and Obstacles

The Strengths and Obstacles section of the LCA consists of asking clients what they believe are their three main strengths and three main obstacles.

Three Main Strengths
• Resources at own disposal
• What resources do for clients

Three Main Obstacles
• Related to strengths
• Related to themes

This part of the LCA gives direct information about the problems that your clients are facing, their possible environmental barriers, and the resources they may have at their own disposal to help them. You can gather information by asking clients to look at the roles they play (e.g., mother, father, learner, or worker) and the skills they use to carry out these roles. After clients name their three strengths, it is useful to probe deeper by asking them what these strengths do for them. For example, if a client lists persistence as a strength, further probing might disclose that it is a strength because it makes him keep trying.

The same kind of probing and clarification also should be done for obstacles. For some clients it is easier to come up with obstacles, perhaps because of past failure or low self-esteem. For such clients, you should look at their obstacles and strengths together. For example, how can strengths be used to offset obstacles? This may help clients start thinking in light of the abilities, competencies, and skills they already possess.

The following dialogue is from a portion of the LCA in which strengths and obstacles are pinpointed:

Dialogue	*Possible Theme*
Counselor: What would you say would be some of your main strengths?	
Client: Oh, I'm a pretty good typist, especially with a little practice. I can run office machines. I've never had any trouble with any kind of office machine. I'm good over the telephone. I can always keep things pretty well organized. I can get things set up, so that if somebody came into the job they'd know exactly what to do. I always make a list of the things I do every day.	Feels confident in her skills. Uses her social skills on the telephone. Well organized.
Counselor: That's a good list. Now describe some of the obstacles you may need to overcome to be more employable.	
Client: Well, I probably talk too much. If I get started on something, it's hard for me to get off the subject, and I probably do run my mouth too often. Another thing is that I don't pace my time right. Either I'm too fast or I'm not fast enough. I never can get everything to work out just right in the amount of time I'd like. I'd always have things done an hour early, or I won't have them done at all. If I could just get things in a better order.	Must control social needs. Concern about being better organized is really a strength.
Counselor: Then it's important for you to be organized?	
Client: Uh-huh, I like to be organized. And I don't think that there would be anything else that I would have any trouble with.	

During the Strengths and Obstacles section of the LCA, clients may not be able to respond to a request to list three strengths or three obstacles. In such cases, break down the task into smaller parts by asking them to list just one strength or obstacle. After one has been discussed, ask for another. This approach takes the pressure off clients to come up with a quick list of things and allows for time to come up with more details.

You also may encounter clients who give short answers or answers that contain little information in the Strengths and Obstacles section. For example, a client may give as a strength "I'm a good worker." This response does not reveal much information. To gain more information, you can ask, "What does being a good worker mean to you?" or "What do you believe are the best things about the way you work?" Vague answers may be encountered in other sections of the LCA as well. In describing a typical day, a client may state, "I get up, go to work, come home, eat, and go to bed." Again, little information can be gleaned from this statement. Instead, ask, "How do you wake up? Does an alarm clock wake you, or does someone else get you up? How do you get breakfast?" Continue examining the client's day in similar detail.

Something else to which you should be ready to respond is a client who cannot think of any strengths. One strategy is to simply move on to the obstacles section and then be especially sensitive to strengths that may be hidden. For example, a client who lists as an obstacle "I work too slow" may reveal on further probing, "I pay a lot of attention to detail and want to be sure everything is right." Another strategy is to recall and reflect on some of the themes expressed in other parts of the LCA. You might say to the client, "When you were talking about your typical day, you explained that your schedule was different each day depending on the schedule of other people in your family. Yet you seem to be able to get done what you need to each day. It seems to me that you are very flexible and adaptable." Such statements help clients discover strengths that they can bring to a job, that can result in greater self-esteem, and that may stimulate them to think of other strengths.

One final strategy that you should consider whenever a client seems unwilling to talk freely is to examine your career counseling style. Although even the most skillful helpers encounter clients who do not open up to them, all counselors need to check their use of human relationship skills when their interaction with clients seems to be unproductive. Are you using good attending and listening skills? Good perceiving skills? Are helpful response styles present?

Summary

The Summary section is the last portion of the LCA. There are two primary purposes for conducting a summary. The first purpose is to emphasize the information that has been gained during the interview. During the Summary, it is not necessary to review every bit of information obtained, but prominent life career themes, strengths, and obstacles should be repeated. It is helpful to first ask your clients to summarize what they have learned from the session. Having them take the lead in expressing what has been learned increases the impact of the information, thus increasing self-awareness. It also lets you know what your clients have gained and, in some cases, missed. When your clients have finished, you can add any points that may have been omitted. It is important that you and your clients reach agreement about their life career themes. This agreement is effective particularly when it can be reached through your clients' own words and meanings.

The second major purpose of the Summary is to relate the information gained to goals that you and your clients may work toward to resolve their problems. The life career themes that have been revealed may suggest possible internal dynamics that require further exploration and environmental obstacles that will need to be overcome. From the strengths and obstacles discovered, positive aspects of your clients may be revealed that can be developed further. Then, too, obstacles that need to be overcome may be apparent; if so, together you can decide to establish goals and form plans of action to reach these goals.

The following example is from a Summary of an LCA interview. Notice that the counselor attempts to highlight important life career themes, skills, competencies, and obstacles; allows the client to express what has been learned; attempts to reach agreement with the client on the client's life career themes and skills by using the client's own words; and relates the information gained to goals and possible courses of action.

Counselor: Pam, we've been talking for awhile about a number of issues, and I now need to bring this all together for you and look at what we have talked about. What do you see yourself learning from today? What is it that you have learned about yourself that you didn't know before?

Client: Well, I'm not real sure.

Counselor: Look back at when we talked about your daily routines, doing the same things, being organized. What do you think that tells you about your abilities?

Client: Well, I guess I'm organized. I guess I'm kind of responsible.

Counselor: Responsible in what way?

Client: I'm real concerned for Jill, my daughter. I do want to raise her well. My mom is always giving me a hard time about making sure to bring her up right. So I think I am responsible with her.

Counselor: When we talked about your strengths, we came up with things like you were very dependable. We talked about how you hadn't missed very many days at work, that you are really conscious about getting to work on time, not being absent, that kind of thing. From your typical day, it sounds like you are very organized and have things at hand as to what you're going to do, and I get the feeling that you are responsible, too. How do you see that working to your advantage in the training program you are enrolled in?

Client: Well, I think it will be useful for me especially in my work experience, at the law office, you know. I think that I am going to be able to handle some of the things that they give me to do there.

Counselor: It is a chance to apply some of the skills you have.

Client: I've really enjoyed the typing that they give me to do, but I'm still kind of scared about whether I'm going to be able to pass the GED [general equivalency diploma].

Counselor: I can understand your concern about that. It is a big step. It sounds like the certificate is important to you since you didn't get a chance to graduate.

Client: Yeah, it is. If I'm going to go on and become a legal secretary, I think that maybe I would need my GED.

Counselor: Well, I think we've got a good start here today. One concern that you have is passing your GED. We can work on that next time we meet.

Some Closing Points

Using Transitions

The LCA will be most effective if you use a conversational tone of voice. One way to help maintain a conversational atmosphere is to use transitional statements. These are signals to clients from you that the focus or topic of the LCA is going to change. By using transitional statements, you let clients know that the topic is being changed and what the new topic is.

One way you can accomplish smooth transitions from one section of the LCA to another is to pay attention to wording. Make the first part of your statement a brief response to something your client has said in the previous section. The second part of your statement is an introduction of the next topic: "Well, it seems that working has been enjoyable for you and you see it as valuable. Did you have these same feelings about being in school, or did you have a different outlook there?"

When you are introducing a new topic, another helpful strategy is to avoid long introductions that could break the conversational tone. In the following example, the counselor briefly describes the areas covered, signals to the client that a change in focus is coming, and lets the client know what the new topic is, all using a minimum of words: "Okay, we've talked about work and school and about how you spend your free time. I'd like to shift now and ask you to describe your typical day."

At what points in the LCA are transitions likely to be needed? Usually transition statements will be needed whenever you wish to move from one major section of the LCA (e.g., Typical Day) to another (e.g., Strengths and Obstacles). Transitions also will be helpful when you are moving from one area to another within a major section, such as between work experience, education or training, and relationships/friendships.

Adapting the LCA for Use With Younger Clients

As we mentioned earlier, the LCA is useful in working with clients of all ages and circumstances. It is particularly useful because its four sections are very broad, allowing you and your clients to structure the content and interactions by the choice of leads you use and the topics you and your clients choose to discuss. In the Career Assessment section, for example, opening leads or follow-up leads that explore possible workplace barriers resulting from clients' gender, race, ethnicity, culture, age, or disability flow directly and naturally as clients share their likes and dislikes concerning work and education. The Typical Day section provides additional opportunities for you and your clients to discuss possible gender, racial, cultural, ethnic, age, and disability issues that are present in their everyday lives. The Typical Day section is particularly suited for this purpose because it not only focuses on typical work days but also extends beyond work into home, family, and community life. The focus of the last two sections of the LCA can be adapted in a similar manner for use with clients with diverse needs.

To illustrate the adaptability of the LCA, we show how it can be used with younger clients. Goals for using the LCA with younger clients may differ from those for using the assessment with older, more mature clients. For example, older clients may possess a higher level of career maturity and may be in need of help adjusting to a specific work setting, remedying past inappropriate work habits, or expanding their career options. As younger clients' experiences are generally more limited, your goals may include introducing the world of work, introducing appropriate work habits, and beginning to explore a variety of occupations as a prerequisite to occupational choice. The LCA can be adapted easily for use with younger clients. These adaptations are listed here by LCA section.

Career Assessment
Work Experience. It is likely that younger clients have not had paid work experience. Many young people perform tasks at home, however, and these can be used in the same way that jobs are used with adults. Domestic responsibilities such as mowing the lawn, caring for a younger brother or sister, or doing the dishes are examples of these tasks.

Education or Training. This is an important area to cover with younger clients and should be done in essentially the same manner as with older clients. Special emphasis should be placed on teachers, counselors, and administrators whom younger clients liked or disliked and why. This provides information regarding the types of people they respect, emulate, or have difficulty cooperating with. Subject matter preferences also are important considerations that can help in exploring later job placement possibilities and possible occupational interests and determining future school subject choices related to eventual occupation choice.

Relationships/Friendships. The area of relationships/friendships can be examined in terms of family recreational activities. It may be of interest to look at what kind of family activities are undertaken to understand family ties. Another area to explore is hobbies. Do your younger clients enjoy activities such as stamp collecting or more adventurous endeavors, such as skateboarding or exploring? Ask them to describe a best friend or friends to help determine the kind of peer influence that exists.

Typical Day

The Typical Day section can be explored in much the same way as it is for older clients. Again, you are looking for dependent–independent, systematic–spontaneous tendencies. Who gets younger clients up in the morning? Do they have a set schedule? Do they have daily chores? If so, are responsibilities monitored? Are privileges contingent on fulfilling responsibilities? What is the home environment like?

Strengths and Obstacles

This section is also done much the same as it is for older clients. The focus is on recognizing strengths used to overcome obstacles. By having their strengths reinforced, clients may become more cognizant of the skills they possess.

Summary

You can conduct the Summary by asking younger clients what they learned from the session. It is important to instill an awareness of likes and dislikes and to organize strengths and obstacles to show how these form an overall method of operation or lifestyle. For example, do younger clients like teachers because they give encouragement? This may indicate a need for reinforcement in order to carry out tasks most efficiently. Such points are important revelations that can have implications for future occupational and personal success.

Closing Thoughts

The LCA is an interview framework designed to help you and your clients gather information in a systematic way in a relatively short period of time. Please note the words *interview framework.* As such, the LCA is a point of departure for the next steps in career counseling, because it helps to form positive working alliances with clients from which future career counseling activities can take place.

The structure of the LCA provides stimuli that in turn evoke client responses. You acknowledge and dignify those responses by helping your clients identify and describe their responses in life career theme form. Together, you apply that knowledge to possible next steps, such as testing, counseling, educational and occupational information gathering, and career planning and decision making.

You will find that using the LCA sets the stage for test taking and test interpretation, because the process used in the LCA teaches clients beginning skills in making observations, inferences, and hypotheses about themselves through life career theme identification. These beginning skills can have direct carryover because the language used to identify and describe client life career themes is the same language often used in test interpretation.

As you use the LCA you also will find that it sets the stage for the phases of career counseling that follow. It provides a comfortable, nonthreatening way to begin to bring a variety of issues to the surface, including women's and men's issues, racial issues, age issues, and disability issues. The LCA also will bring to the surface the ways in which clients gather and process information about themselves and the world in which they live. The styles clients use may have implications for the kind of career counseling interventions you use.

The LCA supports and reinforces a holistic approach to career counseling. It helps begin a discussion of the life role arenas of work, school, leisure, and family and their relationships. This is important in career counseling for reasons Berman and Munson (1981) pointed out many years ago, reasons we believe remain true today:

> Significant career involvements do not exist in isolation of, nor can they be understood apart from, other life ventures. People can be helped to identify areas of meaningful individual–environment dialogue and to examine their work life experiences in conjunction with family, community, school, and other important roles. (p. 96)

References

Berman, J. J., & Munson, H. L. (1981). Challenges in a dialectical conception of career evolution. *Personnel and Guidance Journal, 60,* 92–96.

Maree, J. G., & Molepo, J. M. (2007). Changing the approach to career counselling in a disadvantaged context: A case study. *Australian Journal of Career Development, 16*(1), 62–70.

Meier, S. T. (2012). *Language and narratives in counseling and psychotherapy.* New York, NY: Springer.

Mosak, H. H. (1971). Lifestyle. In A. G. Nikelly (Ed.), *Techniques for behavior change* (pp. 77–81). Springfield, IL: Charles C Thomas.

Rule, W. R., & Bishop, M. (2006). *Adlerian lifestyle counseling: Practice and research.* New York, NY: Routledge.

Watts, R. E. (2003). Adlerian therapy as a relational constructivist approach. *The Family Journal, 11,* 139–147.

Chapter 11

Career, Multicultural, Marital, and Military Family Genograms: Helping Clients Tell Their Stories About Their Career–Family Connections

The use of genograms often brings clients to greater insight, awareness, and understanding about their own interpersonal patterns, as well as the communication patterns between themselves and others. In addition, greater mental clarity about such familial influences provides clients with a basis from which to challenge and change the world, as well as how they behave.

—Duba, Graham, Britzman, & Minatrea, 2009, p. 17

Genograms are qualitative assessments that can facilitate the understanding of clients in family contexts (Erkan, Turan, Oguzhan, Rasit, & Ismail, 2012). DeMaria, Weeks, and Hof (1999) grouped genograms into two types. The first type is called the *basic genogram*. It is the full genogram that contains all aspects of family system work. The second type is called the *focused genogram*. It uses the framework of the basic genogram but emphasizes specific topics, such as

Attachment: bonding, temperament, and attachment
Emotions: sadness, loss, and grief; fear; and pleasure
Anger: anger, family violence, and corporal punishment
Gender and sexuality: gender, sexuality, and romantic love
Culture: race, ethnicity, and immigration; religious orientation;
   socioeconomic status. (DeMaria et al., 1999, p. 10)

Weiss, Coll, Gerbauer, Smiley, and Carillo (2010) pointed out that there are other types of focused genograms as well. They suggested ones that emphasized spirituality, academics, and trauma. They also described one that is focused on military family culture.

In this chapter, a focused genogram called the *career genogram* is featured first. It uses the framework of the basic genogram but emphasizes career. Later in the chapter, three other focused genograms are presented, namely a multicultural genogram, a marital genogram, and a military family genogram.

The Career Genogram

The career genogram is a qualitative assessment that is used to help clients tell their stories. It provides a format and process for drawing a picture of a client's family over three generations. A career genogram "allow[s] the counselor to explore the development of the client's career identity while it pictorially isolates some of the root sources and influences of the client's career decision path" (Chope, 2005, p. 406). As you will see, the process used to achieve a completed career genogram is as important as the final product.

The career genogram is an adaptation of the work of Bowen (1980) in family counseling. In family counseling, the word *career* is not used with the word *genogram*, because the emphasis is on specific family issues and concerns. When the word *career* is added, many other avenues of exploration are available for you and your clients as they tell their socialization stories (Brown, 2007; Chope, 2005). The career genogram is particularly useful because it provides a direct and relevant framework for use with clients to shed light on many topics, including their worldviews, possible environmental barriers, personal–work–family role conflicts, racial identity statuses and issues, and levels of acculturation. "By exploring family-of-origin events, clients may come to understand their present beliefs or values" (McMahon, Patton, & Watson, 2003, p. 195). It also has substantial face validity for clients because it provides them with an opportunity to tell their stories within the career counseling context. Clients have a chance to talk about themselves and their childhoods from a perspective they know well. The career genogram encourages trust and curiosity and helps to create the bond necessary in the working alliance.

In presenting the career genogram, we first provide a rationale for its use in career counseling. This is followed by the details of the administration of career genograms. Three steps are involved in the administration: presentation of the purpose, the actual construction of career genograms by the clients, and clients' response to questions upon completion of their career genograms. This section closes with a discussion of how you and your clients can analyze and use the information and insights gained through the career genogram process as well as adapt the genogram for a variety of uses.

Rationale

Dagley (1984) summed up the rationale for the career genogram by suggesting that clients often can be understood best in the context of their sociological, psychological, cultural, and economic heritage—their family. Kakiuchi and Weeks (2009) stated that career genograms allowed counselors to elicit information about clients' attitudes about work and career. The career genogram can provide you and your clients with a process to connect clients' understanding of the past to the present in order to better understand the dynamics of the present. The career genogram is particularly useful with clients who are struggling with work–family–socialization–identity issues, concerns, and stresses. Chope (2005) made this point by stating,

> Family patterns of all types can be pointed out, and the pressures of differential family standards can be discussed. A career genogram can assist a career counselor in developing a new clinical perspective on a client while the counselor has the freedom to ask questions more reflective of family dynamics. (p. 406)

Because the career genogram process unfolds naturally, it is a comfortable procedure for you and your clients to use. As you show interest in and respond to the life experiences and life histories of clients, the bond within the working alliance is strengthened. Not only do you gain knowledge and understanding about clients but also clients learn about themselves as well. Clients often, for the first time, gain insights into their internal thoughts and feelings about themselves, others, and their worlds. The career genogram provides clients with a structure for integrating information about themselves and their growing-up experiences in ways they had not thought of before.

Administration

There are three steps involved in using career genograms with clients. Step 1 involves sharing with clients the purpose of career genograms. Step 2 involves explaining the process of how clients construct their own unique career genograms. Step 3 focuses on how you and your clients can analyze and understand the meaning of clients' career genograms through a series of questions posed by you and the interaction and discussion that follow.

Step 1: Purpose
The first step in the administration of career genograms is to share with your clients their purpose. You can do this by explaining that the technique will provide clients with insights into the dynamics of their families of origin, including grandparents. You can explain that the career genogram will provide them with insights into such issues as the career, work, gender, and cultural socialization they experienced while growing up; environmental barriers, if any; and how they have integrated and dealt with various life roles. Many other issues of relevance to clients' situations (including clients' worldviews and racial identity statuses) also can be explored as the career genogram process unfolds, depending upon the concerns clients may have. How and why clients' current worldviews and racial identities were formed through the socialization process in their families and community can come into sharp focus through the construction and analysis of career genograms.

Step 2: Construction
The second step is to explain to your clients how to construct their own career genograms. The following directions can be modified to fit your clients and their situations:

Counselor: Career genograms can help us understand you and your family of origin, including grandparents. Please draw a picture of your family of origin beginning with your mother and father. Draw it on the sheet of newsprint that is on the table in front of you. [A chalkboard or other comparable writing surface also could be used.] Place the following symbols [McGoldrick & Gerson, 1985] for your mother and father about two thirds of the way down the sheet. Write their names under the symbols [see Figure 11-1].

Figure 11-1. Parents

Counselor: Then, just above these symbols place the birthdates of your mother and father. If either of your parents has died, put an X within their symbol and put the year of their death next to their birthdate. Next, add yourself and any brothers or sisters to the picture. Make sure you place their names under the appropriate symbols. Suppose for the purposes of this career genogram you have a brother and a sister. Your name is Justin, your sister's name is Melissa, and your brother's name is Samuel. Then, add birthdates for yourself and your brother and sister to the diagram. Now the diagram will look like this [see Figure 11-2].

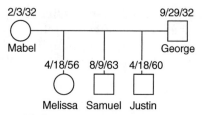

Figure 11-2. Parents, Brothers, and Sisters

Counselor: The next task is to add to the picture grandparents and any aunts or uncles from both sides of your family. Add names, birthdates, and dates of death if you know them for all of the people you add to your career genogram. Also add the titles of the occupations in which the members of your family of origin and extended family members are or were employed. Now your career genogram may look something like this [see Figure 11-3].

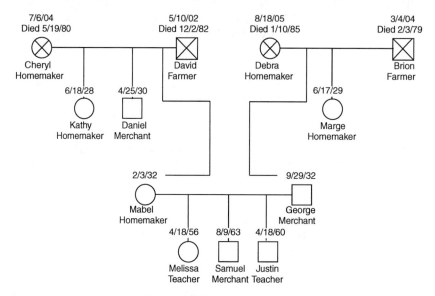

Figure 11-3. Extended Family

At this point in the construction of your clients' career genograms it is important to remember that there are many different kinds of family patterns today—single-parent families, blended families, stepfamilies, and two-parent families. Divorce, death, illness, remarriage, and no marriage have created these and other family pattern variations. As these and other variations occur, note these variations by writing in what the variations are. As shown in Figure 11-3, the client has already made notations by writing in dates of birth and death as well as the occupations of the individuals involved. Other notations could be added concerning divorce, illness, or other relevant conditions. In families with stepparents and stepchildren, circles and squares can be added and notations made concerning these circumstances.

Step 3: Analysis

Once your clients' career genograms have been constructed and information (birthdates, deaths, divorces, occupations, etc.) about family members (brothers and sisters, parents, and grandparents) has been recorded, the next step is to use the structures to explore with your clients what it was like growing up. The questions that are used in the exploration process depend in part on your clients' presenting problems and their internal thoughts and feelings. Rita and Adejanju (1993) suggested the following:

In the session, the counselor can facilitate the exploration of "what happened?" (identification of facts/events), "what was the impact upon your people and the family?" (analysis), and "what generalizations can be made?" (specific learnings), regarding the relationship of the "there and then" (one's living history), to the "here and now" issues which are the focus of the exploration.

The counselor endeavors to help the student [client] fill in gaps, make affective connections between significant events, perceive overt and covert patterns, and recall dormant positive images that have helped bond one person with others in the unique family. Verbal and nonverbal clues are carefully observed and, where deemed appropriate, explored to help make connections. The feelings, thoughts, and dreams experienced in the process completed are also examined. (p. 21)

Because the career genogram is not a standardized procedure, there is flexibility as to the questions you ask as you and your clients make decisions about what would be most helpful to explore and discuss. Here are some general questions that could be asked:

- How would you describe the family in which you grew up?
- If you grew up in a two-parent family, what is/was your father's occupation? What is/was your mother's occupation? (Also ask about your clients' parents, other work experiences, education or training, career satisfaction, and unfulfilled dreams.)
- What are/were your mother and father like? What adjectives would you use to describe them? What is/was the nature of their marital relationship (responsibilities)?
- What are the occupations of your brothers and sisters? What do your younger siblings aspire to be? Where do your brothers and sisters live? Describe the lifestyle of each. (Also ask whether the family lives close by, and explore cousin relationships such as competitiveness for grandparents' approval.)
- What is/was your grandmother's occupation? Grandfather's?
- What do your aunts and uncles do?
- What is/was your role in the family (now and when growing up)?
- What is/was your relationship with your mother? Father? (Ask about their career aspirations for the client.)
- Who are you most like in your family? (Ask about who took care of whom, coalitions.)
- What is your spouse's relationship with your family?

Dagley (1984) suggested another set of questions to be used in developing a career genogram:

- What are the dominant values in the family of origin?
- Vocationally, are certain "missions" valued?
- Are there any "ghosts or legends" that serve either as anchor points or "rightful roles" for the family?
- Are there myths or misconceptions that seem to transcend generations?
- Are there any psychological pressures or expectations emanating from "unfinished business" of the family?
- How does the individual's description of economic values and preferences fit in with the family's history?
- How has the family addressed the three boxes of life (learning, working, and playing)? Are there any imbalances?
- What family interaction rules and relationship boundaries have been passed along through generations?

- Are there any voids in the client's memory of family? Is there significance to those voids?
- Does the client have a sense of "owning" family traditions?
- How have the primary life tasks of love, work, and friendship been addressed by the family?
- What vocational patterns emerge, in terms of choices, as well as the choice and development process?

If you and your clients are focusing on educational/training issues, Rita and Adejanju (1993) have recommended the following line of questions:

1. What are the overt/covert messages in this family regarding education, academic success?
2. Who said/did what? Who was conspicuously silent/absent in the area of academic striving, academic success?
3. Who was the most encouraging/discouraging in terms of academic striving, and in what ways?
4. How was academic achievement encouraged? Discouraged? Controlled? Within a generation? Between generations?
5. What questions have you been reluctant to ask regarding academic success in your family tree? Who might have the answers? How would you discover those answers?
6. What were the "rules," "secrets," "myths" in your family regarding success (e.g., dangers, cut-off from family)?
7. What do the other "players on the stage" have to say regarding these questions? How did these issues, events, and experiences impact upon you? Within a generation? Between generations? With whom have you talked about this? With whom would you like to talk about this? How would you do it?
8. How would you change this genogram (including who and what) to meet your wishes regarding academic striving and success? (p. 22)

Career Genogram Commentary

As stated earlier, career genograms provide real-life frameworks onto which clients can visually organize and map perceptions of personal, work, and family concerns, tasks, and stresses into meaningful representations in the context of overall family life and family history. Career genograms are stimulus devices that provide clients with a natural, direct, and comfortable way for them to share their backgrounds and their life experiences. "Since individuals carry the history of past experiences with them continually, in understanding psychological aspects of development it may be more important to understand the individual's interpretations of his/her experiences rather than to have objective information about these experiences" (DeVries, Birren, & Deutchman, 1990, p. 4).

Although the analysis section follows the construction and discussion of clients' career genograms in this chapter, analysis actually begins as soon as clients undertake the construction of their career genograms. Tentative hypotheses about clients' presenting problems and the underlying dynamics that may be involved are formed fairly early with the understanding that they are to be modified or discarded and new ones added as new information and insights are gained from the career genogram interaction process. As this process unfolds, other issues or problems in addition to or in place of the presenting problem or issue may emerge. As Borgen (1995) suggested,

Assessment, ideally conducted in a counseling context, becomes a dynamic process. It stimulates dialogue between client and counselor, through which are merged the expert perspectives each brings. Together they construct a narrative, but often one that is in process, tentative, and incomplete. (p. 438)

As you interact with clients as they are telling their stories through the structure of their career genograms, it is important to listen to the words and phrases they use in addition to considering the emotional weight these words and phrases may carry. Some words and phrases may carry special meanings. For example, clients may talk in hushed voices about growing up in families with alcoholic parents. Other clients may describe experiences with mentors, and you can hear in the words they use and in their tone of voice how significant these mentors were to them. In addition, listen for any affective tones that may "reveal unconscious longings which, with the [counselor's] help can be used to establish new goals and directions" (Wachtel, 1982, p. 340).

We also recommend that you observe closely how your clients construct their career genograms. Pay particular attention to the amount of detail your clients put into their career genograms, the time it takes for them to complete the task, and the spacing between generations. How your clients record the details of their personal and family histories may provide clues as to their internal thoughts and feelings. These clues in turn can provide you with possible leads for further clarifying client concerns and issues.

It is important to remember at this point that a major goal of career genograms is to gather qualitative information about clients' growing up—their socialization and the impact that it had on how they view themselves, others, and their world. As career genograms are completed, more people of significance to clients are available for consideration so that "family scripts or legacies of an intergenerational nature" (Rita & Adejanju, 1993, p. 23) become visible and can be discussed. It is important to look for repetitive themes in the stories that clients tell (Peterson & Cortéz González, 2000).

Making family–socialization issues visible, putting them on the table out in the open, offers the opportunity for you and your clients to discuss them openly. Once information is gathered through the career genogram and added to client information collected in other ways, the counseling task is to use the tentative hypotheses that have been emerging to begin to consider interventions that may help clients achieve their goals or resolve their problems. Sometimes questions are raised about the use of career genograms with resistant clients. Will resistant, defensive clients respond to information-gathering devices such as career genograms? Wachtel (1982) suggested that genograms do work with such clients. In fact, according to Wachtel, genograms actually assist such clients in loosening up:

It is often quite helpful to use the genogram, particularly with rigidly defensive people who have trouble knowing and opening up about their feelings. Reassured by the structured questioning and by the illusion that they are merely telling the "facts," these guarded and controlled individuals gradually begin to loosen up. Impressions of interest and sympathy on the [counselor's] part as the "facts" are gathered help further emotional expressiveness. Since they are dealing with "past history" and supposedly "distant" relatives, they often do not feel the need to defend as much as when talking about what seems more obviously personally relevant. (p. 336)

Additional Uses of the Genogram

The genogram is a versatile technique that can be used to gather information on a variety of issues in addition to the ones described earlier. Three additional uses are presented here as examples. The first focuses on use of the genogram by clients who may wish to explore their racial/ethnic/cultural backgrounds (Sueyoshi, Rivera, & Ponterotto, 2001). The second focuses on use of the genogram by clients who may be experiencing marital difficulty with resulting impact on work and family life roles, while the third use focuses on military families.

Multicultural Genogram

DeMaria et al. (1999) suggested that the purpose of multicultural genograms "is to examine the impact of race, immigration, and ethnicity, religious orientation, and class upon individuals" (p. 177). The multicultural genogram can help individuals think about their racial/ethnic backgrounds and how these backgrounds may have influenced aspects of their lives. You and your clients can use multicultural genograms to note and reflect on clients' families' racial/ethnic heritages. The procedures for administering and constructing these genograms are the same as those presented earlier. The difference is in the analysis, in the questions you use to assist clients in analyzing their multicultural genograms (Rigazio-DiGilio, Ivey, Kunkler-Peck, & Grady, 2005).

The following questions can assist your clients in exploring their roots and the meanings these roots may have for their present and future lives:

1. What are your ethnic and racial roots?
2. What parts of this heritage do you most identify with today?
3. Have certain career behaviors or occupations been part of your ethnic or racial heritage?
4. What personal characteristics do you attribute to your racial or ethnic heritage?
5. What biases/prejudices/forms of racism have you experienced because of your racial/ethnic background?
6. What biases/prejudices/forms of racism did you see demonstrated by family members toward other groups?
7. What biases/prejudices/forms of racism do you find yourself carrying with you that were first learned in your family of origin?
8. How does your cultural background serve as both a strength and a hindrance in your work?

Marital Genogram

The genogram also can be modified to work with clients who may be experiencing marital difficulty that is possibly linked to work and family issues. Using the marital genogram, you and the client can explore the client's marriage from the courtship phase to the time a child was born. You would explain the purpose of the marital genogram and instruct your client on how to construct it. The process might unfold as follows as you say,

Counselor: On the large sheet of paper in front of you, please draw a circle and a square [as shown in Figure 11-4]. Then write your first name and your spouse's first name underneath the appropriate symbols.

Harriet   Robert

Figure 11-4. Wife and Husband

Counselor: As we go through this process I will be asking you some questions to help us gather information about the marital difficulties you are experiencing and any possible links to your work and family roles if these are of concern to you. Let's start with your courtship.

- What was the length of your courtship?
- What attracted you to each other?
- How much time did you spend together as a couple, and how was this decided? [Inquire about who may have pursued for more togetherness or time apart in the relationship.]
- When your relationship became exclusive, how did you handle your individual friendships?
- How did your parents view your relationship?
- Were either of you previously married? Are there children from these marriages?

Counselor: Let's now move to the time when you were married but before the birth of your child.

- What prompted you to get married when you did?
- How would you describe your relationship during this time?
- Describe the amount and nature of individual time and time with friends.
- As for your lifestyle, how much social, financial, and educational time is spent with in-laws?

Counselor: Now let's add your child to the marital genogram [see Figure 11-5]. Let's talk a bit more about your family now that your child has entered the picture.

- What entered into your decision to have a child when you did?
- How did your marital relationship change with the birth of the child?
- How did your individual roles change?
- Describe each child for me, from oldest to youngest.
- Which child takes care of whom, plays with whom, fights or argues the most, is the most different, is the most alike?

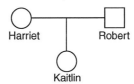

Figure 11-5. Wife, Husband, and Child

As you go through the marital genogram process to unfold the history of a marriage through the time a child was born, husband and wife behaviors and possible stress and strain points may be revealed. This may provide you and your client with possible hypotheses about the specific issues involved. At the very least, these issues can be discussed openly. Possible links to work world and family life behavior also can be seen, understood, and addressed.

Keep in mind that in this scenario you hear the story of these events from only one person. It would be useful to add the perceptions of the other spouse. In fact, the marital genogram could be used in couples counseling, in which case it could be constructed jointly.

Military Family Genogram

Weiss et al. (2010) pointed out that military families represent a culture different from civilian families. Military families live within military norms, beliefs, and traditions. Weiss et al. stated that "military culture brings a host of environmental, occupational, psychological, and family stressors. In response to these conditions and challenges the military genogram represents an effective tool to be used in clinical practice with military personnel and their families for therapeutic rapport building and providing culturally sensitive assessment and intervention services" (p. 405). Brelsford and Friedberg (2011) suggested that adding a spiritual discussion to the military family genogram "could support and open discussion of how . . . religious and spiritual beliefs, values, and affiliations affect their family, particularly during a stressful time like a military deployment" (p. 259). Finally, Papaj, Blumer, and Robinson (2011) suggested that a military family genogram could also be very useful when working with service women.

The following questions can assist military clientele in exploring family issues related to military service or deployment:

- What is the immediate family's attitude toward the military?
- What is the extended family's attitude toward the military?
- Have the service family members served during a time of war? If so, when? What war?
- Have the military family members ever experienced wartime trauma? If so, what? Has it affected their functioning? And if so, how?
- What was the service member's role prior to deployment? Has it changed post-deployment?
- What is the level of self-disclosure about the range of military experiences for the service member?
- What is the attitude toward mental health treatment or view of emotional illness? (Papaj et al., 2011)

If you are working with service women Papaj et al. (2011) suggested these questions:

- What does it mean to you to be a service woman? What does this mean to your spouse/partner? Your family? Your community?
- How have gender stereotypes, expectations, and assumptions affected you as the service member? Your partner? Your family?
- How have gender stereotypes, expectations, and assumptions affected you as the spouse of a service member? Your partner? Your family?
- Who has served as role models for you as a service woman in your family? Your community? How close are your relationships with these women? (p. 278)

Closing Thoughts

The focused genogram may not be an appropriate qualitative information-gathering technique for use with some clients. "The genogram construction or information may seem cumbersome, superfluous, or even distasteful to some counselors and clients" (Okiishi, 1987, p. 142). Some clients, because of their cultural, ethnic, racial, or religious backgrounds, may view the use of career, multicultural, marital, and military genograms as invasions of privacy. For them, family issues and family history are private matters that are not to be discussed in public. Some counselors may be concerned about the time it takes to gather information using a focused genogram and wonder whether the process is worth the work. Clients, too, may be concerned about the time, believing that devising action steps is more important than spending time gathering information toward something they think may not produce results.

We feel that the focused genogram is a useful qualitative information-gathering technique when used appropriately. It is your responsibility, with the advice of your clients as you share the purpose of genograms with them, to decide whether to use the technique. When the technique is explained clearly to clients, most will respond positively to the experience, and it will yield meaningful information that will be useful in the later phases of career counseling.

References

Borgen, F. H. (1995). Leading edges of vocational psychology: Diversity and vitality. In W. B. Walsh & S. H. Osipow (Eds.), *Handbook of vocational psychology* (2nd ed., pp. 427–441). Hillsdale, NJ: Erlbaum.

Bowen, M. (1980). *Key to the genogram.* Washington, DC: Georgetown University Hospital.

Brelsford, G. M., & Friedberg, R. D. (2011). Religious and spiritual issues: Family therapy approaches with military families coping with deployment. *Journal of Contemporary Psychotherapy, 41,* 255–262.

Brown, D. (2007). *Career information, career counseling, and career development* (9th ed.). Boston, MA: Pearson Education.

Chope, R. C. (2005). Qualitatively assessing family influence in career decision making. *Journal of Career Assessment, 13,* 395–414.

Dagley, J. (1984). *A vocational genogram* [Mimeograph]. Athens: University of Georgia.

DeMaria, R., Weeks, G., & Hof, L. (1999). *Focused genograms: Intergenerational assessment of individuals, couples, and families.* Philadelphia, PA: Taylor & Francis.

DeVries, B., Birren, J. E., & Deutchman, D. E. (1990). Adult development through guided autobiography: The family context. *Family Relations, 39,* 3–7.

Duba, J. D., Graham, M. A., Britzman, M., & Minatrea, N. (2009). Introducing the "basic needs genogram" in reality therapy-based marriage and family counseling. *International Journal of Reality Therapy, 28,* 15–19.

Erkan, I., Turan, A., Oguzhan, K., Rasit, A., & Ismail, C. (2012). Use of the genogram technique in counseling with Turkish families. *Journal of Family Psychotherapy, 23,* 131–137.

Kakiuchi, K. K. S., & Weeks, G. R. (2009). The occupational transmission genogram: Exploring family scripts affecting roles of work and career in couple and family dynamics. *Journal of Family Psychotherapy, 20,* 1–12.

McGoldrick, M., & Gerson, R. (1985). *Genograms in family assessment.* New York, NY: Norton.

McMahon, M., Patton, W., & Watson, M. (2003). Developing qualitative career assessment processes. *The Career Development Quarterly, 51,* 194–202.

Okiishi, R. W. (1987). The genogram as a tool in career counseling. *Journal of Counseling & Development, 66,* 139–143.

Papaj, A. K., Blumer, M. L. C., & Robinson, L. D. (2011). The clinical deployment of therapeutic frameworks and genogram questions to serve the service woman. *Journal of Feminist Family Therapy, 23,* 263–284.

Peterson, N., & Cortéz González, R. (Eds.). (2000). *Career counseling models for diverse populations.* Belmont, CA: Wadsworth/Thomson Learning.

Rigazio-DiGilio, S. A., Ivey, A. E., Kunkler-Peck, K. P., & Grady, L. T. (2005). *Community genograms: Using individual, family, and cultural narratives with clients.* New York, NY: Teachers College Press.

Rita, E. S., & Adejanju, M. G. (1993). The genogram: Plotting the roots of academic success. *Family Therapy, 30*(1), 17–28.

Sueyoshi, L. A., Rivera, L., & Ponterotto, J. G. (2001). The family genogram as a tool in multicultural career counseling. In J. G. Ponterotto, J. M. Casas, L. A. Suzuki, & C. M. Alexander (Eds.), *Handbook of multicultural counseling* (2nd ed., pp. 655–671). Thousand Oaks, CA: Sage.

Wachtel, E. F. (1982). The family psyche over three generations: The genogram revisited. *Journal of Marital and Family Therapy, 8*(3), 335–343.

Weiss, E. L., Coll, J. E., Gerbauer, J., Smiley, K., & Carillo, E. (2010). The military genogram: A solution-focused approach for resiliency building in service members and their families. *The Family Journal, 18,* 395–406.

Chapter 12

Gathering Client Information Using an Occupational Card Sort: Using Occupational Titles as Stimuli

As can be seen from the previous two chapters, there are a variety of ways to make use of career assessments. The Life Career Assessment and the career genogram can both help us gather information that can be helpful to us and to our clients. We cannot, however, rely on any one approach, as each client may require something different. Goldman (1983) made a convincing case for how the card sort can be a most effective approach with some clients. What should have become obvious as you read the previous chapters is how varied the approaches to gathering information are. Some approaches are quite objective and may provide information and norms that are truly unavailable from any other source. Other, somewhat more objective assessments (e.g., the genogram) are more dependent on the client producing information that is then interpreted with the help of the counselor. Still other assessments, such as card sorts, are more subjective in nature, and their effectiveness depends on the counselor's ability to help the client arrive at insights and ideas from the process.

This chapter introduces and then describes a process for using an occupational card sort in career counseling. We suggest how it might help clients who are inclined to resist, do not need, or already have explored more objective sources of information about themselves. We describe the benefits of the card sort and then take you through the use of one with a client. We conclude with an observation about how the card sort may help expand your understanding of your clients' ways of thinking about themselves.

Occupational Card Sorts

In general, card sorts are nonstandardized approaches to sorting almost any array of ideas. For career counseling purposes, let us begin with a card sort that involves the client sorting occupational titles from which all kinds of themes, ideas, issues, values, or feelings emerge. Unlike most standardized instruments, card sorts do not usually produce scores or have norms. The sort we describe consists of occupational titles listed on small cards. Clients are simply asked to sort the cards into three piles: those they like, those they are indifferent to, and those they dislike. A next step then might be to ask the clients to take one of the piles and sort it into smaller piles based on any common themes that might have influenced them placing the cards in the broader category. For example, a client may look at the cards in one pile and see that prestige or status or potential earnings seem to be common in some of the titles. Another theme might be that several occupations involve using math or numbers. The theme possibilities are limitless and often are best suggested by the client rather than the counselor. This is one reason this approach remains nonstandardized—each person has a unique way of organizing his or her thoughts.

Card sorts usually depend on clients' abilities to verbalize and eventually make sense of patterns they use to think about their worlds. This often depends more on your skill as a counselor than the clients' predispositions to verbalize. The card sort may help clients better understand life patterns as they talk about themselves and where they want to go with their careers.

Overview of Card Sorts

In the final analysis, individuals must act for themselves. We can offer information, advice, and assessments that substantiate their thinking, but, however we do it, eventually individuals must live with the consequences and own the ideas. Card sorts begin with the assumption that individuals have ideas about what they want to do but need to talk about them, and through the counseling process they come to some insight into or appreciation of how they can resolve issues for themselves.

A card sort is a semistructured way of sorting out or prioritizing the interests, skills, needs, values, or any predetermined array of ideas for a client. You can start from scratch and create some array of items, or you can simply use one of the many already published sorts. They exist for occupations (Holland, 1992; Jones, 1979; Krieshok, Hansen, Johnston, & Wong, 2002), skills (Knowdell, 1995a), college majors (Garson & Johnston, 2001), strengths (Clifton, Anderson, & Schreiner, 2005), and values (Knowdell, 1995b).

The number of cards may vary, as may the amount of information provided on the cards. But the cards are to be sorted by some predetermined procedure into piles that usually have clients describing their identification with, their possession of, their need for, or the importance of the items in their lives. So, for example, the cards might each have an occupational title with a brief description of what the title means, and the client may be asked to sort the cards into three piles depending on whether he or she likes, is neutral toward, or dislikes the occupation. That process of sorting reveals much about the client's facility with words, ideas, and concepts; his or her approach to tasks; his or her style and comfort with thinking about a complex task; his or her decision-making style; and a host of other things that may help you to understand and assess the status of the client at a later point. If done early, the card sort may help you predict the client's receptivity to more objective data provided later from standardized tests.

It is difficult to describe all of the nuances of a good card sort or a good card sort administration. No two are alike, nor do they need to be. Good use depends on the particular needs of the client and your own style or need in choosing to administer it. You may see it only as a tool for getting acquainted—an easy format or structure for talking about one's self and career concerns. Or you may see it as a way of helping one see relationships or priorities for items that may need to be considered in any career decision. It can be almost entirely open ended, or it can be very structured. It can be used as structure for conversation or for producing a fairly complete list of occupations, interests, values, or themes in much the same way a standardized test of the same material would.

We devote a complete chapter to occupational card sorts because they open up so many possibilities. With practice, the possibilities become endless, and the opportunities to help clients explore using their own existing resources become enormous.

General Benefits of Card Sorts

There are many types of card sorts, each of which has certain benefits that can be useful at particular times. Here we cover some of the common benefits of all card sorts, and then we follow this with a focus on one example of a card sort most applicable to career planning.

Provide Structure

Card sorts provide structure, and usually comfort, in dealing with a sometimes difficult or complex task. Almost everyone finds it easy, and often fun, to deal cards, perhaps because of earlier associations with card games. Having structure usually makes it easier to approach a difficult or unfamiliar task. Like with a puzzle, when you begin to see all the parts come together to form a picture, a complex task has become not only manageable but rewarding. To see patterns and closure with any difficult task, however, takes thought and sustained persistence. A card sort may provide this for a confused client who at that particular moment may need a step-by-step way of approaching a complex problem.

Promote Bonding

The card sorting process, as opposed to other tasks one might select early in career counseling, can be immediately engaging and can contribute directly to the bonding that is so important in establishing a solid working alliance on an interpersonal level. Alternatives, such as computerized career systems, paper-and-pencil inventories, or reading career materials, demand less interpersonal contact or may be initiated without contributing in any way to the bonding between you and the client. In Chapter 8 we emphasize the importance of establishing a bond with the client as early as possible. You will find that the card sort not only addresses your intention to work on developing a bond in the relationship, but it also enables you to engage yourself in a process that will help you become clearer about your client's needs, motivations, preferred ways of doing things, exploring style, and so forth. If clients are not engaged with the process, as may be the case when they take the initial steps with standardized tests, you will know it immediately, and you can correct or modify the intervention accordingly.

Authenticate Choices

In the process of sorting cards, and as you encourage clients to express their opinions or reasons for putting cards into particular piles, you also receive clues about the strength or logic of choices or discards. For example, clients may dismiss some occupations for weak or illogical reasons, but you will hear that part of their thinking. This is insight you would not necessarily obtain when immediately asking clients to complete a typical interest inventory. In short, it helps you begin a process of authenticating choices.

Promote Feedback

Feedback can be immediate and ongoing. You can continually incorporate new data as they are generated and constantly test them against data previously generated. If you have the time, administering a card sort will ensure that your later interpretation and use of objective data meshes with what the client is thinking—you will have already established what this is.

Promote Understanding in Communication

The card sorting process continually confirms what is being said and heard. A continual undercurrent in career counseling is knowing for sure that what you are saying is what the client is hearing. You build a model for what is happening in the client's head, but you continually want confirmation of it. In the proper administration of a card sort, there is continual verbalization and confirmation of what is being heard from what is being said. If this is done in a safe, nonthreatening atmosphere, it is likely to be an accurate reflection as well.

Minimize Dependency

A card sort minimizes the risk of a client depending too much on the counselor. By reinforcing what the client is saying, you are recognizing those perceptions as the ones that are most important. You can always add your perceptions, but you are building on what you have been told rather than the other way around.

Promote Inclusivity

Card sorts may be especially helpful with ethnic or nonethnic minority groups. In today's increasingly multicultural world, where the norming of standardized instruments lags somewhat, and where we are increasingly raising questions about a client's sense of identity with particular groups, card sorts offer another striking advantage. Interpretations are not dependent on norms, and, in fact, lacking norms we are more inclined to listen carefully to our client's perceptions of what something means. We cannot know what it is like to be raised in someone else's culture, to be unfamiliar with particular occupational titles or to have different impressions of some occupations, or to think as one who is disabled or who has restricted impressions of his or her roles. In all of these areas, we must continually learn about and appreciate someone else's perceptions or prior experiences in a decision-making process. The card sort has both counselor and client exploring and learning anew.

Are Easily Tailored to Clients' Needs

A final benefit of card sorts is that you can easily tailor the experience for the client. A reluctant or skeptical client can be coached to explore further, whereas a verbal client can be coached to be more focused. A client who wants a lot of structure can be asked to write or make lists of observations or career possibilities, whereas a client who would do better without structure can be left free to talk without much interruption.

Few will argue against using any card sort; those who do question using it may prefer a more standardized measure. We prefer to use it as another form of assessment—a particularly good one—through which, with practice, both clients and counselors can improve their ability to make more effective use of the information provided.

The Case of Tanya

At this point you may be asking when to choose to use a card sort. We can best answer that with a case study that shows the value of the card sort when you have already used a standardized test or when a client comes to you disappointed with the results of the usual standardized instruments.

> Tanya had come for career counseling before when she was a sophomore in college. She was the first in her family to go to college. Everyone had high expectations for her. She was a bright and articulate African American woman and could recall early on that her mother told her she should go to college, become a doctor, and return home and take care of the medical needs of the family. Her mother said the town needed a good doctor, and she was sure that would be her daughter. Tanya had gone along with this idea until her sophomore year in college. She enrolled in science courses, volunteered time at a local hospital, joined the pre-med club, and began talking with others who were in pre-medicine. She was bothered that they all seemed so different from her. They liked their science classes and she didn't, although she did quite well in them. She found them competitive as they talked about their classes, and she did not see herself that way. She felt they were too concerned about what their salaries

might be and not very concerned about the practice of medicine. She began to doubt her choice. She started thinking that maybe she had missed out on some experience that should have clarified her career directions earlier. Her roommate had taken a test at the career center that had confirmed she did not have interests like those of the other people with her major, so she was going to try something else. Tanya thought maybe a career test would help her as well. She took it with high expectations that she would find a new career for herself but was disappointed. In fact, the counselor said the test suggested she did not share interests with the people in any particular profession. Not only was she disappointed, but she left discouraged and did not return for a follow-up interview even though the counselor strongly urged her to do so. A year later she still did not know what to do. She was doing well in classes, but she knew deep inside that she was not happy. She opted to try career counseling again. Maybe another test would help this time.

This story is not atypical. Clearly Tanya was trying to fulfill the family dream. She had no other strong interests, so she simply went along with their wishes. She received continued reinforcement from family and friends and really did not give it all that much thought, as she was completely involved with school. Good in science and all her classes, Tanya was voted most likely to succeed in college. She listed pre-med as her expected major. It would have been hard not to think of going into medicine because she would have disappointed many others. She enjoyed the support and encouragement they offered, but when it came time to study, she did not find much support for herself. She knew somehow it just was not right.

It is not likely she would find another interest inventory of help. She indicated she would be willing to try one but was not enthusiastic about it. The initial conversation suggested the results would probably be somewhat similar to what they had been before. Would this not be a good time for a card sort? She was skeptical of the value of more tests, and she seemed eager to talk about her situation. We opted for an occupational card sort here, and, although we used a particular one (the Missouri Occupational Card Sort, 4th edition; Krieshok, Hansen, Johnston, Wong, & Shevde, 2008), you might use any of those listed in the references at the end of the chapter.

The Missouri Occupational Card Sort

This card sort is particularly helpful with traditional-age college students, but it can easily be adapted for use with a younger or older population (Heim & Johnston, 1991). A discussion of its development will make obvious what you might do to tailor a card sort for your particular clients.

The occupational card sort was developed for use at a large land-grant university that has many undeclared students and a great diversity of possible majors. The card sort also incorporates the Holland schema, which helps clients to learn about their personal identification with the six Holland personality types and their respective environments while they are sorting the cards. We listed most of the popular majors available at the university on cards and then sorted them into piles in accordance with how they match with the six environments. For example, *firefighter* was sorted into the Realistic pile, *anthropologist* into Investigative, *musician* into Artistic, *career counselor* into Social, *buyer/purchasing agent* into Enterprising, and *accountant* into Conventional. We then took approximately an equal number of these occupations for each of the six areas. In all, we chose a total of 90 occupations, about the number we thought could be easily sorted in 30 min. We also wanted titles to be the more popular or easily identifiable ones, so we worked in a somewhat arbitrary fashion to choose about 15 from each pile.

Because we also assumed clients would learn things about titles as they sorted, we put the titles on one side of each card and on the back of the card we provided a three-letter Holland code for the title, and the primary activities and responsibilities of the occupation. All the cards are described in the manual provided with the card sort (Krieshok et al., 2008). In addition to the three-letter code on the back of the card is the O*NET (Occupational Information Network) reference, the education typically required to pursue the occupation, other related careers, places where one might be employed, and the skills that might be needed in the career.

In a session with a client like Tanya, you might begin the interview using a format like this:

> *Counselor:* In front of you is a deck of cards. On each of the cards is the name of an occupation. These occupations will vary from unskilled to professional. Some of them you will have an interest in, and some you will not. Go through the cards and sort them into three piles: one pile for those you feel you would like to do (like pile), one for those you would dislike or not chose to do (dislike pile), and a third pile for those you are unsure about or could go either way with (undecided/neutral pile). If you can talk about why you are putting them in each pile as you go along, I'll take some notes that might serve as the basis for our discussion of these choices later on. This is not a timed activity, but your first impressions are probably the more important ones, so don't deliberate too long on any one of the cards.

If you want more structure or want to provide a written report of this activity for the client, you can follow or provide the client with the six-step handout that appears in the Appendix to this chapter.

For some clients, being watched over their shoulder may be too intimidating, so allow those people to get involved in the process on their own, and then check in on their progress a little later. This often provides the same outcome and allows you to do other things.

Most times, however, we recommend that you stay with your clients as they sort the cards. We suggest you make a mental note of the speed or decisiveness with which the cards are sorted. Sometimes you may need to prod a bit or suggest that clients deliberate a little less. Sometimes you can easily detect that a client is clear about what not to do, or that another is very focused on one occupation so that dismissing most occupations seems reasonable, although that problem might need discussion or clarification before the client gets too far into the process. You also can pick up on how much or how little the client knows about the various occupations by the number of times he or she resorts to turning over the cards or asking you questions about particular titles. With practice, you become more and more astute at observing significant influences in the pattern used by each client. You become more effective at probing for thoughts that may lie just below the level of consciousness or perhaps are at a conscious but not yet spoken level. Remember, probably no one has objectively spent this much time with the client on this topic before. You may be taking the conversation further than anyone before you because you are not encumbered by any previous agenda.

Once the sorting process is complete, you would ask Tanya to put the like and neutral piles aside and have her begin to categorize the dislike pile into several piles based on her reasons for not liking or choosing each occupation. Here is where themes begin to emerge. Tanya may say, "I couldn't do that kind of work, it's too physical" or, "It would mean I'd have to work with others on a team, and that's not for me." You might probe for what she means by that; she may not be able to articulate it. In particular, we look for what clients can offer as themes, although sometimes you may need to help them find the themes. Sometimes you may have to point out inconsistencies in what they are saying. It is a subtle process: You hope first to reinforce what emerges in their minds and then help them see how this relates to what they may have said earlier. It is not unlike a counseling interview in which you help clients to see patterns in what they are saying that may not be obvious to them. You would have Tanya sort all the titles in the dislike pile before trying to sum up with her what seem to be emerging themes for not entering these occupations. As Tanya reports the themes, you make notes for a later discussion. When the client is not clear about a particular occupation, you may try to help place it in an appropriate category. The less articulate client or a particularly confused client may need more help with this process. The challenge is to tailor the process to the particular needs of your client. Initially you may follow the six steps outlined in the Appendix, but with practice you can adapt your style to the particular needs of each client.

You then repeat the process with the like pile of occupations. You might argue for starting with this pile rather than the dislike pile, but usually it is best to end with the themes that will determine eventual choices, not with the ones being rejected. An initial inspection of the size of the three piles may also tell you where it is best to begin. Sometimes there will be too few in the like pile but a large neutral pile or dislike pile. That may favor starting with the neutral pile in an effort to tease some of those into the like pile. Although we outline the usual procedures here, we must emphasize again that there is no right way to proceed with a card sort. Experiment and decide what works best for you and a particular client. We suggest you vary the process so that you are able to choose the best process for each client.

A typical card sort interview might last an hour. If shorter, you may not be getting all you should from the process; if much longer, you may need to break it into parts. Here you would work only with the likes one time, the dislikes another time, and maybe even try to tie it all together in a third interview. You must be convinced that the process will yield some helpful data, and you must convey that impression to the client as well. Although one may be skeptical about undergoing another standardized assessment, typically one becomes convinced that is what one wants. Clients are apt to have doubts about these less standardized approaches. This is especially true considering that you are trying to convince them that they know best what they should do, and they come to you believing you know the answers.

You may or may not be able to convince the clients of the value of the process, but you should be convinced yourself. You should be comfortable knowing that you are trying to build on what the clients already know about themselves and that you are doing it through a process that should be helpful to them as they incorporate new information about occupations. There is evidence that this process of sorting out occupations may be the same process clients use for sorting ideas about other things, such as jobs, friends, mates, places to live, or goods to buy. All decisions may involve a similar decision-making process, and a client may become more skillful in one area as he or she learns more about the process in another area. You certainly minimize the client's dependence on you while optimizing the opportunity for him or her to use you as a resource. There is no waiting for scoring and no age, gender, ethnic, or cultural bias in the construction of the instrument. Contrary to what you might find with a standardized instrument, there is no need to conform to a set of rigid practices regarding administration.

Let us provide some hypotheses about why this process might better help Tanya at this particular point. She obviously felt she learned little from the earlier process with a standardized test. She had the most difficult of profiles to interpret—the flat profile. Her interests were not like the interests of any particular group, which is not very helpful to one looking for an alternative. You can say that further exploration will probably change the profile, but that is not too helpful to Tanya right now. You can say that having marked too many items as neutral or uncertain may have contributed to the flat profile, but again, that is not too helpful. You can say you are not sure how well the inventory represents the interests of minorities, but that, too, is not what Tanya needs to hear. None of these reservations applies to a card sort. It is likely that from the sorting process Tanya can begin to verbalize many themes that are likely to surround her sense of uneasiness about her career choice. She will find it helpful to express that she wants something different: perhaps something less competitive, something that rewards more individual initiative rather than team effort, something that promotes the theme of helping others but in a more people-oriented way, and something in which money is a less important goal. You expect that these and other ideas, given a supportive counseling relationship, are apt to emerge and be considered important variables in her ultimate career decision. These are not variables that emerge as easily from the usual format used in interpreting a standardized interest inventory. We expect that Tanya will at this point be better served by this process of talking through her concerns rather than again measuring her interests.

It is well known that students like Tanya know more about themselves than they think. Standardized interest inventories probably do little better at predicting career choices than simply asking clients what they want to do. Building on this evidence, there is good reason to believe that you can be quite helpful with card sorts in helping clients uncover what they already know but have not been able to put together for themselves. Combined with the more standardized instruments, use of the card sort helps you strengthen your ability to build good working alliances with your clients and makes other standardized test information more understandable and interpretable.

Common Themes and Subthemes

You may initially be concerned that finding themes with a client will be difficult, but we think you will be surprised. We offer the following list of some of the common themes and subthemes that have surfaced from various sessions.

1. *Achievement*
   Sense of accomplishment. Attain goals. Need to be successful. Fear of failure. See results. Make a contribution.
2. *Advancement Opportunities*
   Upward mobility. Dead-end jobs. Menial (no upward movement).
3. *Autonomy*
   Be my own boss. Use my own initiative. Choose and direct my own lifestyle. Self-sufficiency. Manage my own time. Do someone else's work.
4. *Benefits*
   Vacations. Unions. Retirement plans.
5. *Challenging/Boring*
   Physical (works body hard). Mentally stimulating. Meet others' needs or demands. Very hard to be successful. Need for competition. Boring.
6. *Creativity*
   Use my hands. Express myself. Use my imagination.
7. *Diversity/Repetition*
   Different tasks. Different people. Different places. Different things. Too much repetition.
8. *Early Influences*
   Fantasy. Parents. Others.
9. *Effort Required*
   Too much manual labor. Not enough manual labor. Occupation comes naturally.

10. *Excitement*
    Adventure.
11. *Genuineness/Dissonance*
    Feels false doing this. Makes me go against my values. Lets me be myself.
    Honesty in my work. Religious reasons.
12. *Geographic Bounds*
    Tied to hometown. Tied to one type of location (city, country, suburbs).
13. *Job Market*
    Occupation in demand. Occupation not in demand.
14. *Lifestyle*
    Family life. Night life. Farm. Settled. Familiarity.
15. *Meaningful/Meaningless*
    Practical. Superficial. Not needed.
16. *Monetary Reward*
    Pays well. Does not pay well.
17. *Pace of Work*
    Slow. Fast. Just right for me. Steady. Sporadic.
18. *Past Experience*
    Previous job. Previous education. People in occupation.
19. *Phobia/Repulsion*
    All animals. Snakes. Blood. Audiences. Sick people. Dirty hands. Pain. Flying.
    Physical contact. Guns. Doctors.
20. *Power*
    Control or direct others. Authoritarian role. Change society. Influence others.
21. *Preparation Required*
    Too long. Too demanding. Not enough payoff for investment. Realistic.
22. *Prestige*
    Do something important. Care about how others view me. Get attention from
    others. Dislike being a "peon." "Professional" stereotype. Menial occupation.
23. *Responsibility*
    Immediate. Delayed. Physical. Mental. Too much or too little responsibility.
24. *Safety or Health*
    Occupation would cause physical harm. Occupation would give me ulcers.
    Occupation would make me crazy. Occupation would keep me healthy.
25. *Security*
    Monetary. Job. Position.
26. *Self-Judgment*
    Ability. Talent. Personality (high, low, okay, questionable, patient, outgoing,
    introverted, aggressive, manipulative, perfectionist).
27. *Stereotype*
    Gender. Parental. Previous experience. Ability. Occupation as seen in general.
    Gay. Age role. Inconsiderate people in occupation.
28. *Stress*
    Makes me nervous. I'm too emotional.
29. *Structure*
    Structured. Flexible. Ambiguity. Orderly (hours, task, supervisor relations, goals,
    lifestyle).
30. *Travel*
    Excitement. Diversity. New culture. Away from home. Discovery. Fantasy. Relaxing.
31. *Understanding*
    Self. Others. World. Existential questions. How things work.
    Know how (get feedback, help others, their culture).

32. *Virtue*
    Altruism. Holier than thou. Do not like to force others. Lack of respect.
    Most in occupation do it for money. Help needy.
33. *Working Environment*
    Outdoors. Indoors. Alone. Social (too dirty, cannot take the elements, close to
    nature, office too confining).
34. *Working With Concepts*
    Researching, investigating. Using my head. Math or physics. Ambiguity.
    Foreign language. Science.

As you can see, the list is almost endless. More important, you will be surprised at
how easy it is for your client to come up with themes that are often ones you would
not think to include if you were attempting to standardize the process. It is precisely
for this reason that we urge you to let the themes flow from clients and then try to help
the clients make sense of them as presented. More attention is given to the process of
identifying themes in Chapters 13 and 15.

Closing Thoughts

Card sorts give you the opportunity to promote informal conversation with clients. The
process can be casual or structured, but it allows your clients the opportunity to provide
information about themselves in a nonthreatening manner. Consider using the card sort
along with other, more standardized assessments to better understand your clients.

References

Clifton, D. O., Anderson, E., & Schreiner, L. A. (2005). *StrengthsQuest: Discover and develop your strengths in academics, career, and beyond.* Washington, DC: Gallup Press.

Garson, R. A., & Johnston, J. A. (2001). *College major card sort.* Columbia: University of
Missouri–Columbia, Career Center.

Goldman, L. (1983). The vocational card sort technique: A different view. *Measurement
and Evaluation in Guidance, 16*(2), 107–109.

Heim, L. L., & Johnston, J. A. (1991). *Missouri Occupational Card Sort. Community/junior
college edition.* Columbia: University of Missouri–Columbia, Career Center.

Holland, J. L. (1992). *The vocational exploration and insight kit.* Palo Alto, CA: Consulting
Psychologists Press.

Jones, L. K. (1979). Occu-Sort: Development and evaluation of an occupational card sort
system. *Vocational Guidance Quarterly, 28,* 56–62.

Knowdell, R. L. (1995a). *Motivated skills card sort kit.* San Jose, CA: Career Research and
Testing.

Knowdell, R. L. (1995b). *Values card sort planning kit.* San Jose, CA: Career Research and
Testing.

Krieshok, T. S., Hansen, R. N., Johnston, J. A., & Wong, S. C. (2002). *Missouri Occupational
Card Sort.* Columbia: University of Missouri, Career Center.

Krieshok, T. S., Hansen, R. N., Johnston, J. A., Wong, S. C., & Shevde, E. (2008). *Missouri
Occupational Card Sort* (4th ed.). Columbia: University of Missouri, Career Center.

Appendix. Missouri Occupational Card Sort

Name _____   Date _____

Step 1

In front of you, you have a pack of cards. On each one of the cards is the name of an occupation. These occupations will vary from skilled to professional. Some of them you will have an interest in, and some you will not. Go through the cards and sort them into three piles.

On the right you should place the occupations that you might actually choose, that have some specific appeal to you, or that seem appropriate for a person like you—your "Like" pile.

On the left you should place the cards that have occupations that you are not interested in, that you would not choose, or that do not seem appropriate for a person like you—your "Dislike" pile.

The third pile should be placed in the middle. These should be occupations that you are indifferent to, you are uncertain about, there is some question about, or you do not know whether you would like—your "Undecided/Neutral" pile. (You will not use this middle group any further.)

Begin sorting into the three piles: *Dislike   Undecided/Neutral   Like*

Step 2

Now take the cards that have occupations you dislike and move the other two piles of cards out of the way. Spread the cards of occupations you dislike out in front of you, and group together occupations for which the reasons for not choosing them are the same or similar. You may have as many groups as necessary. One occupation can be considered a group.

Begin grouping your "Dislike" cards. After you have formed the groups, write the names of the occupations in the various groups below. It makes no difference which group is listed first. You do not have to have as many groups as are shown below. If you have more than five groups, then indicate the additional groups on the back of the page. Start by listing the occupations in Group 1 below:

Dislikes

Group 1: _____   _____
                _____   _____
                _____   _____

      What is similar about this group?
      Why are you not choosing this group?
      What do you not like about these occupations? Be as explicit as possible!

Themes: What generalities or themes do the above comments suggest?

_____
_____

Group 2: _____   _____
                _____   _____
                _____   _____

      What is similar about this group?
      Why are you not choosing this group?
      What do you not like about these occupations? Be as explicit as possible!

Themes: What generalities or themes do the above comments suggest?

_____
_____

Group 3: _____   _____
         _____   _____
         _____   _____

What is similar about this group?
Why are you not choosing this group?
What do you not like about these occupations? Be as explicit as possible!

Themes: What generalities or themes do the above comments suggest?

_____
_____

Group 4: _____   _____
         _____   _____
         _____   _____

What is similar about this group?
Why are you not choosing this group?
What do you not like about these occupations? Be as explicit as possible!

Themes: What generalities or themes do the above comments suggest?

_____
_____

Group 5: _____   _____
         _____   _____
         _____   _____

What is similar about this group?
Why are you not choosing this group?
What do you not like about these occupations? Be as explicit as possible!

Themes: What generalities or themes do the above comments suggest?

_____
_____

Now, do you want to make any changes in your "Dislike" group? Do you see any occupations that do not really belong in the same group? Indicate below any changes you would like to make and why.

Step 3

Now take the cards that have occupations you like and group them together so that the reasons for choosing them are the same or similar. It makes no difference which group is listed first. You do not have to have as many groups as are shown below. If you have more than five groups, then indicate the additional groups on the back of the page.

After you have found the groups, check them again and make any necessary changes. Now begin by writing the names of the occupations in Group 1 below:

Likes
Group 1: _____   _____
         _____   _____
         _____   _____

What is similar about this group?
Why are you choosing this group?
What do you like about these occupations? Be as explicit as possible!

Themes: What generalities or themes do the above comments suggest?

_____
_____

Group 2: _____   _____
         _____   _____
         _____   _____

What is similar about this group?
Why are you choosing this group?
What do you like about these occupations? Be as explicit as possible!

Themes: What generalities or themes do the above comments suggest?

_____
_____

Group 3: _____   _____
         _____   _____
         _____   _____

What is similar about this group?
Why are you choosing this group?
What do you like about these occupations? Be as explicit as possible!

Themes: What generalities or themes do the above comments suggest?

_____
_____

Group 4: _____   _____
         _____   _____
         _____   _____

What is similar about this group?
Why are you choosing this group?
What do you like about these occupations? Be as explicit as possible!

Themes: What generalities or themes do the above comments suggest?

_____
_____

Group 5: _____   _____
         _____   _____
         _____   _____

What is similar about this group?
Why are you choosing this group?
What do you like about these occupations? Be as explicit as possible!

Themes: What generalities or themes do the above comments suggest?

_____
_____

Now, do you want to make any changes in your "Like" groups? Do you see any occupations that do not really belong in the same group? Indicate below any changes you would make and why.

Step 4

Spread your "Like" occupation cards out in front of you and place them in rank order from 1 to 10 as to the occupations you most prefer. Take all relevant factors into account in the ranking of these occupations.

Your Top 10 Occupations

	Occupation	Values	Holland code
1.	_____	_____	_____
2.	_____	_____	_____
3.	_____	_____	_____
4.	_____	_____	_____
5.	_____	_____	_____
6.	_____	_____	_____
7.	_____	_____	_____
8.	_____	_____	_____
9.	_____	_____	_____
10.	_____	_____	_____

Indicate below any occupations that you would also like to include with the above list.

Step 5

Go back to your list of Top 10 Occupations and write a short phrase or word to the right of each occupation that best indicates why you value that specific occupation. For example:

Physician	makes lots of money, uses science, challenging
Lawyer	prestige, public speaking, utilizes detail
Nurse	helps people, uses science, good job market
Teacher	the working hours, works with youth, summers off
Artist	independent, being creative, works with hands

Step 6

Again, go back to your list of Top 10 Occupations and write down the three-letter Holland code for each occupation. These codes can be found on the back of each card.

Now summarize your Holland codes by counting how many times each letter appears on your list. Indicate the numbers below:

Most Frequent Code	Second Most Frequent Code	Third Most Frequent Code
(Highest Number Above)	*(2nd Highest Number)*	*(3rd Highest Number)*

What additional occupations do these Holland codes suggest? (To identify related occupations, you might use the *Holland Booklet*, *Occupational Finder*, or the *Dictionary of Holland Occupational Codes*.)

Chapter 13

Gathering Client Information Using Selected Standardized Tests and Inventories: An In-Depth Approach

The evidence for how tests improve the process by which clients understand themselves and their fit with particular environments is compelling (Holland, 1997). Not only do tests improve the process and the outcomes of career counseling, but also the use of such assessments promotes a more scientific orientation and gives us ways to support and confirm what might otherwise be little more than good speculation. Although many decisions are explained as leaps of faith, most clients want to make decisions with prior support from hard evidence. Clients expect us to use the best tools that are available to help them in their exploration. We want to do that as well, especially when we find that it not only enhances the outcome but also provides us with better data to help other clients resolve their problems and reach their goals.

Finding the Right Standardized Tests

It is estimated that hundreds of assessment instruments might be of help in career counseling. There are interest, aptitude, and ability tests; personality and values inventories; strengths inventories; environmental assessments; state and trait measures; survey forms; card sorts; computerized assessments; and the list goes on and on. Current reviews of most tests can be found in the *Mental Measurement Yearbook*, now in its 18th edition (Spies, Carlson, & Geisinger, 2010), or in *Tests in Print*, now in its 8th edition (Murphy, Geisinger, Carlson, & Spies, 2011). It is our belief, however, that counselors typically learn to use well only a select number of assessments in career counseling. These are ones that best support or affirm their points of view and, with practice and experience, ones they become more and more proficient at using. These are usually the tests they learned to use in their graduate training, and once on the job they simply continued with these rather than learned about new ones that might be better or more useful.

We applaud the use of a particular group of tests but caution against deciding on that number and not being open to learning about new instruments. Many good instruments are still being developed (or at least were developed after many counselors finished their graduate training). Furthermore, as we learn more about the appropriateness of tailoring tests to particular populations and developing norms specific to gender, ethnic origin, race, spirituality, sexual orientation, and social class, the profession is questioning the value of many of its earlier approaches to assessment. It is a burgeoning area, and one can expect it will continue to change fairly dramatically in the next few years.

We can, however, be relatively sure that it will continue to be appropriate to use a variety of assessments to help better understand where a typical client is in the career counseling and planning process. We need to confirm results from one assessment with results from another. We also need to recognize that many of our traditionally accepted measures may not be appropriate for use with many clients from nonmajority populations who are now becoming more frequent users of career services. This is one more reason for remaining open to new measures. We may continue to rely heavily and even become dependent upon a small number of instruments, but we should still remain vigilant about our own assessment of new or additional instruments that might better complement the career counseling process.

In this chapter, we first suggest criteria for selecting appropriate standardized tests and then identify and focus on a small battery of assessment tools that have proven particularly effective in our professional practices and settings. It is important to keep in mind your orientation and employment setting as you identify instruments that can be most useful. If your orientation is to be directive, for example, and you want to be able to tell clients what to do, you want to find instruments that best support that approach. If you are in a setting that encourages time-limited career counseling or one that expects clients to be fairly self-directed, then you will want to choose instruments that promote outcomes in a timely fashion or allow clients to work with assessments on their own. Because many of us will change orientation or setting over time, we should remain flexible and open to new instruments; we may suddenly have to find new instruments to better meet our needs and the needs of our clients.

It is not unusual for professionals to depend on a select group of assessments that work particularly well for them in their particular setting. These assessments complement a particular orientation and setting(s). Here we describe the criteria that we believe influence selections and that influenced our selections of the particular instruments described in this chapter. We expect that you will want to use a similar process in choosing ones that should be most helpful to you in your setting. We find it helpful first to be clear about the criteria; this both makes it easy to identify the appropriateness of what you choose and helps you evaluate the need for new instruments as you move to new settings. As we take you through this process, think about your own orientation and setting and whether the criteria suggest similar or different instruments for you.

Criteria for Choosing Assessments

Some of the criteria for choosing particular instruments include (a) validity, (b) reliability, (c) cost, (d) time required for administration, (e) client response to the instrument, (f) training needed for scoring, (g) scoring difficulty, (h) norms, (i) training needed for interpretation, and, perhaps most important, (j) usefulness of the instrument to the client. How important each of these is may depend on a careful observation of the staff, the setting, and the clients to be served. For example, in some settings paraprofessionals might provide the initial contacts for clients. If so, one might need or choose instruments they can competently use. There are many good ones with which paraprofessionals can become competent, such as card sorts, the Intake Scale (Hope Scale), computerized assessments (SIGI [System of Interactive Guidance and Information], DISCOVER, CHOICES, etc.), My Vocational Situation (MVS; Holland, Daiger, & Power, 1980), the Occupational

Dreams Inventory (Johnston, 1999), the Self-Directed Search (SDS; Holland, 1985), and other self-directed instruments. Paraprofessionals can describe well the availability of other assessments but not use them themselves. They can refer clients to others for individual assessments and career counseling. Those professionals will in turn use a different set of assessments with which they are most comfortable. Selecting which ones to use depends on the individual's background, training, place of employment, and personal preferences. It should also depend on some less obvious but equally important criteria, which assumes we must do some homework before making our decisions.

First Points to Consider: Validity and Reliability

Two test properties must be considered first in the selection of instruments regardless of who will be administering them: validity and reliability. We refer you to basic measurement books (Anastasi & Urbina, 1997; Hogan, 2007) to appreciate the importance of these concepts. We also remind you that both of these are relative terms: You never find completely valid or reliable instruments, only some that are more valid or more reliable than others. Nevertheless, both validity and reliability need our careful and professional judgment, especially because many clients come to us expecting more than we can honestly provide. We need to be sure we are working with the very best of what is available and that we are always open to finding something better. This is one of our professional obligations.

Validity

Perhaps the most important test property to consider is validity. How well does the test really measure what it says it measures? In the career area, this often means the following: If an instrument indicates a person has strong interests in certain occupations, how true is that? Counselors can gain validity information in a variety of ways, such as by looking at how well the test predicts the behavior and satisfaction of the test takers (predictive validity), how closely it is related to constructs that seem theoretically similar (construct validity), and how unrelated it is to measures that seem theoretically dissimilar.

It is also very important to examine the populations on which the instrument has been normed and the similarity of these populations to the clients to whom you will be administering the instrument. For example, if an instrument has been developed with college populations and you want to use it with adults, it would be very important to determine how valid the instrument is with your population.

This point is particularly true for instruments used with members of racial/ethnic minority groups, disabled individuals, and other underrepresented groups. Often the norming and psychometric development research indicates that the assessment measures have not been used with significant numbers of these persons. Thus, in many cases we have little information regarding the validity of instruments for these populations. Although we have no reason to think there would be any race-based biological difference in scores, we do know that we should recognize the different social and cultural histories and experiences of these underrepresented groups. For an excellent review of validity issues of career assessment instruments as they apply to the four major racial and ethnic minority groups in the United States, see Leong's (1995) *Career Development and Vocational Behavior of Racial and Ethnic Minorities*. For another excellent review of the current status of career assessments for women, see Walsh and Heppner's (2006) *Handbook of Career Counseling for Women*.

Reliability

Another critical property to examine is reliability. How stable is the instrument over time? If we give the instrument twice, spaced 3 weeks apart, and little has changed in our client's experience, will we get almost the same scores? This property is very important in career assessments. If a test has poor reliability, an individual may be told one week that she has interests similar to those of a psychologist and the next week interests similar to those of a tax collector; these data are not very useful to her. Even more harmful is the fact that clients usually do not retake tests; if they are given unreliable information one week, they may act on it, never knowing it is the product of an unreliable instrument.

The developer of an assessment instrument is always concerned with how valid and reliable the instrument really is and usually will be constantly refining it. New items can be added, or items that did not contribute much to the reliability can be deleted or replaced with better items. Depending on the construct being assessed, however, we need certain levels of assurances that what has been measured is valid and reliable. Yes, we can qualify our reporting in appropriate ways, but if we cannot speak with some certainty about the probability of success with the measurement of interests, aptitudes, skills, and other important traits, we lose credibility with our clients.

If the available measures in this field were as valid and reliable as they are in some of the hard sciences, we could move quickly beyond discussion of the nuances of validity and reliability. In the hard sciences, it may be possible to predict a happening with some certainty and be assured that it will always happen that way. That measure may be both perfectly valid and reliable. In dealing with people, and particularly when free choice is part of the equation, no measure is perfectly valid or reliable. The best instruments will always leave room for one to question the results. Even when the measure used is quite valid, the individual will take the information and process it with other information that is available. That is precisely why we need to spend time interpreting and integrating results from various standardized tests.

Several points should be made here. We must first attend to the validity and reliability of our measures in the interest of selecting good tests and because we later depend on that information to support our professional interpretations or judgments. Additionally, however, we must recognize that we will always be choosing instruments that are not as valid as we would like them to be. Standardized tests are available to help us make better judgments; they do not make judgments for us or for the client. Once we accept this, we can properly view these measures in the same way we do any other set of resources that are available to help us with the career counseling process. For further information regarding the validity and reliability of specific tests, see the references cited earlier in the chapter, particularly the various editions of the *Mental Measurement Yearbook* (Spies et al., 2010) and manuals that are available for each assessment you choose to use.

Other Points to Consider

Let us continue our discussion of criteria for choosing a standardized instrument. Are we looking for an instrument to administer to one client or to a large group? When one wants assessments to be available for large numbers, then the costs, time required for administration, ease of scoring and reporting results, extent to which one needs training to interpret the results, and usefulness of the results to the client all become issues. We sometimes choose a measure primarily because it is cost effective for large numbers, it can be scored immediately, or the results do not require professional interpretation.

Expanded criteria for consideration of which instruments to use in mass administrations would include not only the validity and reliability of the instrument but also the cost. Next would be how much time is involved in administration and the expected response of the client to taking the test. Also, if you give it to one or a hundred students, how easy is it to score? Or even more important, can it be self-scored in some situations? Can you receive immediate feedback on the results, or will it have to be sent away to be scored? Is training required to score the instrument? Are there good norms for the group you are testing? Is there an interpretive guide that might let the client understand the results without seeing a counselor? In our career center, all of these are important considerations in deciding on an instrument to administer to students. In Table 13-1, we list the criteria for choosing, for example, the MVS over other standardized tests. You can see that it measures up well to the criteria suggested.

You may want to start with several low-cost screening tools, like the MVS (Holland et al., 1980). A critical review of the usefulness of the MVS is provided in an article by Holland, Johnston, and Asama (1993). There are many good, short assessment instruments that are inexpensive, easily administered and scored, and useful for use in workshops or other situations where immediate scoring and feedback are important. Reviews of these appear in *A Counselor's Guide to Career Assessment Instruments* (Whitfield, Feller, & Wood, 2009) or any of the *Mental Measurement Yearbooks* (Spies et al., 2010), which is also where you will find extensive consideration of the issues of validity and reliability of most instruments. We also encourage you to read carefully the manuals for all instruments you choose. Authors are very concerned that you understand what is available to support their assessments. We should reinforce here, however, that typically one can and often must assess the usefulness of a measure as one part of an assessment battery. That is, usually it is only one of a number of measures or indexes that is available or that we have administered, and it becomes important to consider how well it works in concert with those other instruments.

A Basic Battery of Career Assessment

In a general way, we look for methods of assessing the state of people's vocational situations (e.g., MVS-type measures), their interests, their personalities, and perhaps their skills, strengths, aptitudes, values, and beliefs. We may need an assessment instrument that works well in each of these areas. When we are choosing a battery of instruments, we add to our criteria that the assessment instruments work well together or perhaps even complement one another. Sometimes you have to reassess the usefulness of an instrument when it is only one of many assessments you want to use. But let us look at a basic instrument for each of the areas we have identified and select one that might best meet the criteria we have suggested would be important. Although we apply the criteria to the use of the instruments in a career center, you should think about how well each instrument would apply where you work.

Table 13-1. Criteria Used for Selecting the My Vocational Situation

Criterion	Comment
Validity	See reference[a]
Reliability	See reference[a]
Cost	Minimal
Time for administration	Very short
Client response to taking instrument	Usually positive
Training needed for scoring	Minimal
Scoring	Self-scoring, easy
Availability of norms for particular population	Excellent
Training needed for interpretation	Minimal
Usefulness to client	Considerable

[a]Holland, J. L., Daiger, D. C., & Power, P. G. (1980). *My Vocational Situation*. Palo Alto, CA: Consulting Psychologists Press.

A Basic Interest Inventory: The SDS

The most widely used assessment of interests today is the SDS, written by John Holland (1985). It can be easily administered, self-scored, and self-interpreted, and it provides a vast array of information that a self-directed client can find particularly useful. It subtly helps teach a system or plan for further career exploration, and, with the aid of several guides, it can direct one to further explore possible jobs or careers that would be appropriate given a particular pattern of scores. It has good validity and reliability; is easily administered, scored, and interpreted; is reasonable in cost; is available in hard copy or online; can be given to almost any client (reading level is minimal, and Form E [Holland, Powell, & Fritzsche, 1994] is available for even lower reading levels); and fits well with other instruments routinely used in a career center.

What helped most in determining our choice of this instrument for use with students was our decision in 1985 to adopt Holland's six occupational themes (Realistic, Investigative, Artistic, Social, Enterprising, and Conventional) as an organizing feature of the University of Missouri Career Center. Information is stored in the pattern suggested by the scores received on the instrument. Individuals look for additional information in line with their scores on the instrument, and this is the way it is organized in our career center. It also permits broad consideration of a variety of factors relevant to career exploration—including occupational daydreams and interests and skills—and the client can easily ascertain how the scores were derived.

Other good interest inventories may be equally appropriate in other settings. These include the New Revised Strong Interest Inventory Assessment (Donnay, Morris, Schaubhut, & Thompson, 2005) and the Kuder Career Search (Zytowski, 2005). One can argue for having more than one assessment of interests for some clients, but the basic day-to-day practical value of the SDS for use in our career center is convincing. Paraprofessional staff members can be helpful with the administration and interpretation, and it reinforces what we teach and what we want students to learn about the career exploration process. We want students to explore on their own, and we want this exploration to organize and simplify a complex process. Moreover, the SDS allows for providing immediate feedback, which is also quite important.

A Basic Measure of Personality

Personality measures may assume more importance in some settings than others, but it is fair to say everyone needs at least one measure that can assess the basic dimensions of the personality. Which dimensions we measure may depend on who our typical client is and the typical concerns of the client. When making career assessments in a school or college setting, you are usually dealing with high-functioning individuals. You are looking for indexes of fit with particular majors, careers, or job environments, and you most often are sharing that information with the client. This makes some instruments more applicable than others. We opt for the short form of the NEO Personality Inventory by Costa and McCrae (McCrae, 1992) for some of the same reasons we provided for using the SDS. It has good psychometric properties (validity and reliability), can be self-directed and completed in a short period of time, has good interpretation guides or talk sheets to supplement an understanding of the results, and is inexpensive and unobtrusive for most clients. Not all measures of personality meet those criteria.

After many years of personality assessment, there appears to have emerged some consensus about the essential indexes to be considered. The NEO Personality Inventory is cited as measuring well all of "the Big Five" indexes: Neuroticism, Extroversion, Openness, Conscientiousness, and Agreeableness. All of these can be shown to be related to career decision making, and all are dimensions that can easily be used by clients in understanding their particular approaches to dealing with career issues and problems. The relationship of NEO Personality Inventory scores to SDS scores strongly supports the relatedness of personality and interests (Gottfredson, Jones, & Holland, 1993).

A Measure of Aptitudes and Skills

Career clients frequently ask for some test of their skills. They want to know what they really are good at, and yet, particularly with college students, they already know this based on their high school performance and often some work experience. What they are more likely asking is "What aptitudes or skills do I have that might better determine my choice of a major or eventually help me find employment?" Even when the evidence is already there, they seek confirmation of it or better ways to use the aptitude or skill they know they possess. One will hear something like "I'm good at math, but I don't know what to do with it" or "I'm good at drawing, but who would hire me?" Sometimes the inquiry begins when a student is having difficulty with a course that is required in the major, and that starts a reexamination of his or her strengths. It becomes a matter of believing that an alternative is needed. More times than not, students seek reassurance, and when you help them review their high school grades, their SAT or ACT scores, and the courses or life experiences they have enjoyed the most, they reconsider the need for any extensive reexamination of aptitudes or skills.

The SDS, for example, provides an inventory of skills and aptitudes as part of the assessment of an individual's identification with the six areas of interest. Most clients do not realize this and need to have it called to their attention. They complete the instrument with little hesitation, and, when confronted with the evidence of how well their estimates correlate with more objective measures of their aptitudes, they often elect not to take additional tests.

Laid-off workers or employees being asked to transfer to an entirely new job may be more insistent on taking and in need of aptitude or skill measures. When appropriate, a good aptitude or skill measure or measures can be quite helpful.

The Campbell Interest and Skill Survey (Campbell, 1995) is an assessment tool that meets many of the criteria we have established for practical use in our center. It has good validity and reliability, is easy to administer, can be taken online (www.pearsonassessments.com/tests/ciss.htm), and is relatively inexpensive. However, some compromise with our established criteria may be necessary to find a good measure. For example, choosing to measure aptitude in ways that will provide clients with evidence not already available to them may take some time. If clients have not accumulated enough evidence to be sure of their aptitudes and skills, they must expect to invest some time in finding more than reassurance.

At the high school level something else might make more sense. In many school districts, counselors are required to use particular aptitude measures; of course, you should first learn as much as you can about those measures and make use of them as opposed to introducing others.

A Measure of Internal Resources to Aid in the Career Transition

Although the field of career development has developed numerous psychometrically sound measures to assess career interests, values, and skills, until recently no measures had been designed to help clients assess and understand internal, dynamic psychological processes that may get in the way of the career transition process. Because having such instruments available to the career counselor is critical to effectively providing the holistic blend of the personal and career domains central to our model of life career development, we chose the Career Transitions Inventory (CTI) to help clients understand their unique psychological responses to aid in their transitions.

The CTI is provided here as an example of an instrument designed to assess critical dynamic factors operating for the client and to allow counselors to intervene in more targeted and specific ways. The CTI (Heppner, 1991) is a 40-item Likert-type instrument designed to assess an individual's internal process variables that may serve as strengths or barriers when he or she is making a career transition.

The responses for the items range from 1 (*strongly agree*) to 6 (*strongly disagree*). Factor analysis has revealed five factors: (a) Career Motivation (Readiness), (b) Self-Efficacy (Confidence), (c) Internal/External (Control), (d) Perceived Support (Support), and (e) Self Versus Relational Focus (Decision Independence–Interdependence).

High scores are positive and indicate that individuals perceive themselves to be doing well in that area; low scores indicate barriers. Thus, a high score on the Readiness factor indicates that one is highly prepared and motivated to make a career transition (e.g., "I am feeling challenged by this career transition process, and this knowledge keeps me motivated"). A high score on the Confidence factor means that one is highly confident in his or her ability to make a successful career transition (e.g., "I feel confident in my ability to do well in this career transition process"). A high score on the Control factor indicates that the person feels he or she has control over the career planning process (e.g., "The outcome of this career transition process is really up to those who control the system," reverse scored). Similarly, a high score on the Support factor indicates a greater amount of perceived social support associated with changing one's career situation (e.g., "Significant people in my life are actively supporting me in this career transition"). Finally, a high score on the Decision Independence factor indicates that the client feels he or she can make decisions regarding his or her career as an independent, autonomous individual (e.g., "Although family and relationship needs are important to me, when it comes to this career transition, I feel I must focus on my own needs").

Heppner, Multon, and Johnston (1994) calculated Cronbach's alpha coefficients for each of the factors and the total score for the CTI. These coefficients were as follows: .87 (Readiness), .83 (Confidence), .69 (Control), .66 (Support), and .83 (Decision Independence). The alpha for the total inventory was .90. The CTI has been found to correlate positively and significantly with age, marital status, length of time in the transition process, and five global ratings of coping (e.g., perceived level of stress in the career transition process). In addition, enduring personality traits such as those measured by the NEO Personality Inventory (Costa & McCrae, 1985) have been found to predict career resources as measured by the CTI. For example, openness to experience has been found to predict all five factors of the CTI, indicating that a willingness to try new things is an important personality variable predicting how one negotiates the career transition process. (The CTI has been translated into Mandarin Chinese, Arabic, Korean, Italian, and Japanese.)

Other Supplementary Measures

The Hope Scale is a good example of a brief measure that has proven particularly helpful to us in working with groups of clients facing layoffs. To establish in an easy fashion whether there are participants in these groups with minimal goals (low self-efficacy) or confusion as to how to achieve their goals (low on pathways), we routinely use the Hope Scale, a 16-item inventory initially devised by C. R. Snyder (Snyder et al., 1991) to be used with children. We found that adults who indicated little sense of goals or pathways were ones who needed individual attention in workshops. We changed the name of the inventory to The Intake Scale (with permission) and screened a number of people who then were given more individual attention in workshops. It also holds up well according to our criteria.

Numerous such inventories are available, and they often serve a useful role when other more time-consuming assessments might not be practical. The Hope Scale, like the MVS, can be used by the skilled practitioner with minimal training and can be scored in virtually no time at all. Using the Occupational Dreams Inventory, a stand-alone adaptation of the first part of the SDS, is an easy way to begin a conversation with a client about career plans. (You can create your own version of the Occupational Dreams Inventory or request a copy of it from Johnston, 1999; see also Figure 13-1.)

Other supplemental instruments of note are discussed in more detail in Chapters 10 through 12. Chapter 14 covers in some detail two related instruments: one on personal and work styles (INSIGHT Inventory) and one on personal strengths (Clifton Strengths-Finder). The latter, along with the Values in Action (VIA), are receiving considerable attention in the emerging field of positive psychology. Card sorts are considered somewhat standardized, but we chose to devote a separate chapter to this approach (see Chapter 12).

Bringing Test Data Together

We give tests to supplement other data we have on clients or data that clients have on themselves. In many cases, we gather assessment data to help establish a clearer picture of the client and then, in an individual session, convey that information to our client. Both tasks require gathering enough of the right information so it can then be presented in a coherent and credible fashion to help us understand the client and eventually to help the client better understand himself or herself. You can facilitate the process by putting all the test data on a single page or into a single report following a standard format. Figure 13-2 shows how we typically record standardized test data with the SDS as the

Name _____ Date _____

List five occupations you have considered in thinking about your future. List both ones you have dreamed about as well as those you have discussed with others.

Appeal   *Occupation*

_____ _____   _____

_____ _____   _____

_____ _____   _____

_____ _____   _____

_____ _____   _____

- Now arrange each in terms of its appeal to you today (i.e., place a "1" in front of the one that has the most appeal, a "2" in front of the one with the next most appeal, and so forth).
- Put a circle around the one(s) that others (e.g., parents, spouse, best friend, relative, teacher) think you should do.
- Put an "I" in front of any that seem impossible because of requirements (e.g., educational, financial, personal).
- Put an "F" in front of any that represent "fantasy" choices (i.e., fun but not realistic in your opinion).
- Put an "H" in front of any that might qualify more as what you would pursue as a hobby or avocation

Figure 13-1. Occupational Dreams Inventory

Client's Name __James_____ Date _____

Interpretive Guide for Understanding Client's *SDS* Scores™
(Copyright 1992 by Thom D. Rakes & Joseph A. Johnston. Revised 1/95. All rights reserved.)

1. Background Data: *(age, employment status, sex, race, education, family history, etc.)*
Caucasian, male, age 56, working toward GED, laid off shoe factory worker

• Current Occupation/Major: _____machine operator_____ Code: _RIE_

Work History	Code	Occupational Daydreams	Code
☐ Shoe cutter	RSE	☐ Patrol officer	SIE
☐ Inspector	RSE	☐ Accountant	CRS
☐ Factory	REC	☐ Tax Preparer	CES
☐ Machine Operator	RIE	☐ _____	___
☐ _____	___	☐ _____	___

Other Assessments: *(My Vocational Situation, Intake Scale, Career Transitions Inventory, Myers-Briggs Type Indicator, etc.)*
MVS = 04 Intake: Goal 13 Pathways 13 CTI—High on Readiness and Independence but low on Personal Control

Self-Directed Search™

Activities	5	8	1	7	5	8
	R	I	A	S	E	C
Competencies	4	1	2	8	5	3
	R	I	A	S	E	C
Occupations	3	6	0	10	4	10
	R	I	A	S	E	C
Self-Estimates	2	4	2	4	2	4
	R	I	A	S	E	C
	4	5	4	5	4	3
	R	I	A	S	E	C
Total Scores (Range 2–50)	18	24	9	34	20	28
	R	I	A	S	E	C

Summary Code

S	C	I/E
Highest	2nd	3rd

Counselor's Name _____

2. Codes to Explore— Full Exploration
(6–8 point rule)
SCI
SCE

3. Special Issues
(flat profile—low or high; opposing interests; summary code very different from career goals; summary code skewed by work experience, societal roles, etc.)
Age
Work experience
Uncommon SDS code

4. Hypotheses:
Would additional schooling be realistic?

Are daydreams realistic?

Figure 13-2. Interpretive Guide for Understanding Client's Self-Directed Search Scores™

main instrument. This process helps us see the relatedness of various scores. In putting all the scores on one page, we are forcing ourselves to be sure to use all the measures assessed in as integrated a way as possible. After all, we are looking at a single individual through multiple measures or lenses to support one composite picture.

The process just described—of being sure to properly use all the available data—is an appropriate approach for interpreting a single set of scores from any one assessment. We should remember that the test profiles are designed to be used primarily by professionals. The average client is not going to understand the results from a profile without our interpretation. As good as we are at interpreting data, clients do not always hear all we are trying to say or hear it as accurately as we hope. Our interpretations can be complemented with interpretive guides or "talk sheets" because these can help make the results more easily understood and provide a written record for later reference by the client.

These guides or talk sheets should be available for all standardized assessment measures. If one is not available, we encourage you to develop your own. You can request copies of ones used at the University of Missouri Career Center through its Web site (http://career.missouri.edu).

Integrating Test Data

We can best illustrate the integrated use of assessment data by showing our own use of a variety of measures with a single client. In this case, we present a client who was part of a 2-day workshop in which the assessments were administered and interpreted. This meant we needed to give careful consideration to several factors, including the time it would take to administer and score the measures, ease of scoring and interpretation, and, because follow-up would be difficult, how easy it would be for clients to understand the results later without our assistance. Because we typically work with each client as one member of a larger group and would need to do some of the interpretations in the group, we chose instruments that were easy to administer and complete; easy and quick to score and interpret; and unobtrusive, because clients would need to share results with others. Finally, as a battery of tests, the instruments should not take too much of clients' time to complete.

We settled on the Hope Scale, the MVS, the SDS, the NEO Personality Inventory, and the CTI. We had breadth of assessments that would not take too much of clients' time to complete, and we found that each assessment contributed in some meaningful way to how we approached the participants and what they wanted to know about themselves. With a broad brush, we used the Hope Scale and the MVS to quickly establish whether any participants felt they were without goals or pathways or without a reasonably clear sense of vocational identity to profit from the workshop format. If this were evident early, we could provide more individual time with these participants. We also used these two measures to help ourselves make appropriate sense of the other assessment scores.

We devised an "Interpretive Guide for Understanding Clients' SDS Scores" and completed it for each workshop participant (form available upon request). This form incorporates on a single page all the relevant observational and test data. First, we record the relevant background data, which usually includes age, employment status (previous and current), gender, race, education, family history, and other incidentals that might have a bearing on understanding and interpreting the test data. Some clues may come from an intake form, from introductions made in the workshop, or from information offered in a phone conversation as one enrolls for the workshop. Perhaps most important is identifying the expressed career choice(s) of the client. This is sometimes overlooked, and yet it clearly will be a significant part of a client's eventual career decision. Next we record the current occupation and work history of the client. (When we are working with a student, "occupation" often may be more appropriately recorded as "academic major.") Using the *Dictionary of Holland Occupational Codes* (Gottfredson & Holland, 1996), we give that occupation a three-letter code. Then we record the occupational daydreams as taken from a personal data sheet.

We then code each occupational daydream again using the *Dictionary of Holland Occupational Codes*. We later compare the codes of the dreams with measured interests as established from the interest inventory and from the occupational daydreams found on the first page of the Holland SDS interest inventory. The daydreams are recorded on the guide sheet because they, too, like the expressed career choice(s), are often not given their due weight in the eventual discussion of choices based on the more objective test data. It may appear as though we give too much attention to the daydreams, which are not as objective, but evidence shows that they predict eventual choice(s) about as well as any other measure one may use. In fact, if a client has already taken the SDS or some other interest inventory, we suggest you supplement this with the Occupational Dreams Inventory. Dreams should always be considered in any discussion of career plans.

Next we record other assessment data, such as the MVS, Hope Scale, or other intake scores. We include the relevant high and low scores from the CTI. A rough classification of scores as high, moderate, or low makes it easy to record and interpret these scores. You could devise a similar system for whatever inventories you use. We add any other measures that might influence the way we will interpret the eventual total array of test scores. For example, a low MVS score or Hope score would be important to note if we wanted to make appropriate use of one-on-one time with a client; that is, low scores suggesting individual time might be quite important or useful for the individual. All of these scores are important overlays to interpreting the SDS scores.

The SDS scores are recorded on the final page of the SDS in the form of actual raw scores from each of the five objective measures reported within the inventory: the activities scores, competencies scores, scores from the client's reactions to occupational titles, and the two self-estimates measures (one on abilities and the other on skills). Given that we have five measures and six scores on each measure, 30 scores in total are recorded. When total scores are compiled for each of the six areas, we have 36 scores from the interest inventory alone. All of these contribute to the summary code that is reported as the client's SDS code. One can by visual inspection see how each of the scores does or does not contribute to the final code. One also records self-estimates or self-efficacy ratings for the client and can flag any inconsistencies for later discussion.

Here we can make note of Holland's suggested rules for interpreting the SDS. We first remind ourselves to list all three-letter codes that should be explored with the client based on the actual pattern of summary scores. Often referred to as the "rule of eight," this implies that summary scores really are not different unless they total eight or more points (perhaps six or more points for older adults). Therefore, consider all possible patterns that should be explored. If the highest score, say R, and the second highest score, say E, are different by only five points, you should explore RE occupations and ER occupations, because both are equally appropriate based on what has been measured. The client may be inclined to take the ordering literally and not explore fully unless one makes a point of this as part of the interpretation. (See the manual [Holland et al., 1994] for a more complete discussion of the rule of full exploration.) You also need to make note of any special issues that need to be explained. For example, a low flat profile may need some explanation, as might measured interests that seem to be the opposite of what were expressed, a summary code that may seem to be overly influenced by previous work experience or a societal expectation, or a code that is rare and hence will not suggest many options when one looks for occupational alternatives. These are issues that may need to be pointed out and discussed with the client as you try to make the best use of the test data. Finally, record hypotheses that you believe are worth exploring based on what you have observed and measured. These can be written in such a way that they can be shared, refined, or refuted with the client. The SDS manual gives numerous examples of the proper use of scores. We urge you to consult the manual to improve your interpretive skills.

The Case of James

The use of the interpretive guide may be clearer if we apply the process to an actual case. In Figure 13-2 we present scores for James (a participant in a workshop), who was laid off as a factory worker in rural Missouri. James was 56, White, male, working on his general equivalency diploma, and planning to attend a community college now that he had time for it. The job he had was as a machine operator, which is coded RIE. Previously, he had held jobs as a shoe cutter (RSE), factory inspector (RSE), and general factory worker (REC), all in the same plant. His daydreams were to be a parole officer (SIE), an accountant (CRS), or a tax preparation assistant (CES). Other assessments included a very low score on the MVS (04); Hope Scale Scores of 13 on Goals and 13 on Pathways; and CTI scores high on Readiness and Decision Independence, moderate on Support and Confidence, and low on Control. SDS scores are reported in Figure 13-2 and were generally low, although most recordings of the eventual code supported the S code as highest and C next, except that James did not feel he had competencies in the C area (score = 3) or very high estimates of abilities or skills (4 and 3) in those areas. Codes to explore following the rule of full exploration include SCI and SCE. Special issues to be noted include his minimal years of education, his age, the relatively low profile of scores on the interest inventory, and the rather uncommon SDS code for an adult. At least two hypotheses present themselves: Is further schooling a realistic goal? And do the daydreams reflect appropriate next moves? Even before talking to him, we know at least two questions need answers.

The talk sheet helps one focus on all the available data on the client. With practice, it helps one develop hypotheses about the client, and it may help one see what is consistent and what still needs further exploration or explanation. The process is not unlike the one any professional—doctor, lawyer, or accountant—might use in compiling information before an interview with a client. You might in time do just as well without such forms, but initially the forms promote a discipline that can help make all of us better counselors.

Closing Thoughts

Throughout this chapter, we have illustrated both the types of standardized instruments that are useful and the logic of using a number of them in helping to construct a coherent picture of a client. We have emphasized how putting it all together in an interpretive guide helps with the process and how it takes effort and skill to do this for a client. This chapter adds standardized tests to other career assessment approaches already discussed, such as the structured interview and the career genogram. The next chapter introduces some less standardized approaches to career assessment. Although we probably will come to rely on a small group of assessments as we work with clients, we again stress that we always need to remain open to finding new measures and approaches to making information work for us and our clients. The two instruments discussed in the next chapter are examples of nuances that may prove both novel and useful to clients.

References

Anastasi, A., & Urbina, S. (1997). *Psychological testing* (7th ed.). Upper Saddle River, NJ: Prentice Hall.

Campbell, D. P. (1995). The Campbell Interest and Skill Survey (CISS): A product of ninety years of psychometric evolution. *Journal of Career Assessment, 3,* 391–410.

Costa, P. T., & McCrae, R. L. (1985). *The NEO Personality Inventory manual.* Odessa, FL: Psychological Assessment Resources.

Donnay, D. A. C., Morris, M. L., Schaubhut, N. A., & Thompson, R. C. (2005). *Strong Interest Inventory manual: Research, development and strategies for interpretation.* Mountain View, CA: Consulting Psychologists Press.

Gottfredson, G. D., & Holland, J. L. (1996). *Dictionary of Holland occupational codes* (3rd ed.). Odessa, FL: Psychological Assessment Resources.

Gottfredson, G. D., Jones, E. M., & Holland, J. L. (1993). Personality and vocational interests: The relation of Holland's six interest dimensions to the five robust dimensions of personality. *Journal of Counseling Psychology, 40,* 518–524.

Heppner, M. J. (1991). *Career Transitions Inventory.* (Available from Mary J. Heppner, PhD, University of Missouri, 201 Student Success Center, Columbia, MO 65211)

Heppner, M. J., Multon, R. D., & Johnston, J. A. (1994). Assessing psychological resources during career change: Development of the Career Transitions Inventory. *Journal of Vocational Behavior, 44,* 55–74.

Hogan, T. R. (2007). *Psychological testing* (2nd ed.). Hoboken, NJ: Wiley.

Holland, J. L. (1985). *Self-Directed Search.* Odessa, FL: Psychological Assessment Resources.

Holland, J. L. (1997). *Making vocational choices: A theory of vocational personalities and work environments* (3rd ed.). Odessa, FL: Psychological Assessment Resources.

Holland, J. L., Daiger, D. C., & Power, P. G. (1980). *My Vocational Situation.* Palo Alto, CA: Consulting Psychologists Press.

Holland, J. L., Johnston, J. A., & Asama, N. F. (1993). The Vocational Identity Scale: A diagnostic and treatment tool. *Journal of Career Assessment, 1,* 1–12.

Holland, J. L., Powell, A. B., & Fritzsche, B. A. (1994). *Professional user's guide.* Odessa, FL: Psychological Assessment Resources.

Johnston, J. A. (1999). *Occupational Dreams Inventory.* Columbia: University of Missouri.

Leong, F. T. L. (Ed.). (1995). *Career development and vocational behavior of racial and ethnic minorities.* Hillsdale, NJ: Erlbaum.

McCrae, R. R. (Ed.). (1992). The five factor model: Issues and applications [Special issue]. *Journal of Personality, 60*(2).

Murphy, L. L., Geisinger, K. F., Carlson, J. F., & Spies, R. A. (2011). *Tests in print VIII.* Lincoln: University of Nebraska Press.

Rakes, T. D., & Johnston, J. A. (1992/1995). *Interpretive guide for understanding clients.* Columbia: University of Missouri Columbia, Career Center.

Snyder, C. R., Harris, C., Anderson, J. R., Holleran, S. A., Irving, L. M., Sigmon, S. T., . . . Harney, P. (1991). The will and the ways: Development and validation of an individual-difference measure of hope. *Journal of Personality and Social Psychology, 60,* 570–585.

Spies, R. A., Carlson, J. F., & Geisinger, K. F. (Eds.). (2010). *The eighteenth mental measurement yearbook.* Lincoln: University of Nebraska Press.

Walsh, W. B., & Heppner, M. J. (Eds.). (2006). *Handbook of career counseling for women* (2nd ed.). Hillsdale, NJ: Erlbaum.

Whitfield, E. A., Feller, R. W., & Wood, C. (Eds.). (2009). *A counselor's guide to career assessment instruments* (5th ed.). Tulsa, OK: National Career Development Association.

Zytowski, D. G. (2005). *Kuder Career Search with Person Match: Technical manual version 1.1.* Adel, IA: National Career Assessment Services.

Chapter 14

Assessments That Focus on Strengths and Positive Psychology: The Clifton StrengthsFinder and the INSIGHT Inventory

With Patrick Handley

Several chapters in this book address qualitative and quantitative career assessments. This chapter highlights two quantitative assessments that can help you work with clients' personal strengths. This is not to suggest that we have not always focused on strengths and styles, but now more than ever this has become a major interest in psychology. Thus, it is appropriate for us to look at some of the promising assessments that focus on strengths and styles. Increasingly, evidence is emerging to support the fact that we can have the most impact by identifying what is right or positive with clients. This affects the nature of our career coaching relationships, it affects clients' motivations to continue to work with us, and it may be key to the success of our interventions. Although the profession has an admirable history of helping clients it is the discovery and enhancement of their personal strengths and styles that most excites them. Strengths exploration with clients may be the best investment of our professional time.

The Clifton StrengthsFinder and the INSIGHT Inventory help us keep the focus of career coaching on strengths, not weaknesses. Both are readily accessible either online or in paper format. They require little time to complete, self-score easily, and have good validity and reliability data. In short, they measure up to the criteria we establish in Chapter 13 for other assessment measures. Before we present these assessments, let us consider briefly where we have been in our profession and share our sense of where we are going.

The better part of the previous century saw phenomenal advances in psychological treatment approaches. Much of what career counselors claim as success comes from our learning to handle the deficits and shortcomings of clients. Such a focus, however, has kept us from attending to the positives or the strengths of our clients. True, we included some attention to client strengths, but usually we first had to focus on changing deficit behavior; that was why most clients came for help, or at least it was the basis for most referrals. It was our success at addressing the deficits that became the basis for how others judged our efforts. But what if we changed our thinking and asked, "What would happen if we studied what is right with people?" That was the question raised by Donald Clifton (Clifton & Nelson, 1996, p. 20). Recent research in positive psychology suggests that keeping the focus on the positive may be an equally effective approach to changing behaviors. In addition, there may be other reasons to take such an approach. Particularly telling is what Buckingham and Coffman (1999), two researchers at the Gallup Organization, reported after summarizing findings from tens of thousands of interviews: "People don't change that much. Don't waste time trying to put in what was left out (i.e., deficits). Try to draw out what was left in. That is hard enough" (p. 57). Do not focus on deficits, work with the positive! That is hard enough, but it is where we can make the best changes. Some might contend that this would not be a realistic approach in their work setting, but if it can be shown that focusing on strengths truly can affect how one comes to deal with deficits, then we need to be open to giving it a try. Perhaps we have been too enamored of stressing that one should try to improve in all areas rather than expanding the areas in which one is already performing well. It is with that in mind that we present these two instruments that help keep the focus on the client's strengths.

The Clifton StrengthsFinder

Once we decide clients should focus on their strengths, we need ways to promote their recognition of these strengths. This is not an easy task for the typical client. Clients may enjoy talking about themselves but be clueless as to what their strengths are. In Compton and Hoffman's text (2012) on positive psychology, there is a discussion of typical client characteristics to consider when helping clients recognize and own their particular strengths. Compton and Hoffman identified five characteristics. The first, they say, is a "yearning"—a pull to move toward certain interests, to use certain skills, to pursue a particular goal, or to engage with a particular project. Second, a particular strength may make one feel intrinsic satisfaction. The person does not feel pushed to do it, but doing it makes the person feel better about himself or herself. Third, it comes easily. It feels natural, like it is something one does without much effort. This leads to the fourth characteristic: The person does it extraordinarily well, although modesty may keep him or her from admitting it. And finally, when using identified strengths, all of the above may come into play, as does a feeling of a deeper sense of satisfaction.

General Description

With this in mind, let us discuss what the Clifton StrengthsFinder assessment is and how it helps clients identify their particular strengths. Through interviews with successful educators and business people, Clifton and associates at the Gallup Organization devised an instrument that provides a structured approach to identifying one's top 5 strengths from among a list of 34 possible ones (Clifton & Anderson, 2002). The assessment is a Web-based instrument constructed from the perspective of positive psychology. It takes less than 30 min to complete, and there are 177 items. Two items are paired with self-descriptors, and the person chooses the one that best describes him or her and the extent to which it does so. Once completed, the assessment gives a printout of the person's five strengths—"themes" of talent, often referred to as *Signature Themes*.

Supporting Materials

A person pays a fee to take the assessment (www.strengthsfinder.com), but the online supporting materials are extensive. In fact, although one can purchase books with an access code to the assessment (Clifton & Anderson, 2002; Liesveld & Miller, 2005), the online materials that accompany the results are such that little more is needed to help one make appropriate use of the instrument. It is important, however, to be creative in introducing clients to their strengths. For example, suggest that they focus on only one or two of the five strengths the assessment provides, or talk about the one they most often use. Once they see the application of one or two strengths, you can expand their consideration of the others. For many clients, it will be an entirely new way of thinking about themselves, and that implies a need for considerable exploration and reinforcement before they can accept and make use of the results.

Development and Theory

Donald Clifton spent his professional life studying successful people. He asked early in his career one simple question: "What would happen if we studied what is right with people?" One eventual outcome of his search resulted in what is known as the Clifton StrengthsFinder. The instrument has undergone extensive psychometric research, which was summarized in a 2005 technical report by Lopez, Hodges, and Harter (2005). Lopez et al. said, "Across samples, most scales (i.e., themes) have been found to be internally consistent . . . and stable over periods ranging from 3 weeks to 17 months" (p. 8). Also, "Specifically, coefficient alphas range from .55 to .81 and most test–retest calculations were above .70" (p. 8). What is also of interest is that once clients receive their results, they feel empowered and often are moved to share their findings with friends. This may be an important first step toward getting them to apply their strengths in their daily behavior.

The instrument is available in 17 languages and to those with reading levels at the 10th grade or higher. Gallup has another version of the instrument for children and youths (www.strengthsexplorer.com). It involves fewer themes, but it should be useful in helping younger students direct their energies more in line with their identified strengths.

The StrengthsFinder and the INSIGHT Inventory (reviewed later in this chapter) are two assessments clearly associated with the positive psychology movement. Both can be used in complementary ways to promote a fresh way of looking at personality and behavior. Using one in combination with or support of the other may help clients more easily apply what they discover about themselves.

One issue in using these instruments and adopting the associated orientation of positive psychology may involve finding ways to move clients beyond the positive "first impressions" of what they find about themselves. Although there is frequently a positive "Aha!" expression when clients first find their strengths, this impression can quickly fade. You need ways to help them apply the findings! You can find a host of online suggestions to help reinforce the use of strengths (Clifton, Anderson, & Schreiner, 2006). However, this is probably going to depend more on your infusing "strengths and styles" into your vocabulary and your behavior before clients will pick up on such thinking themselves.

Using the Results

Finding ways to reduce the number of strengths clients must remember is important. We know from experience that clients often cannot recall all five of their reported strengths. It may be an art to get them to focus on one or only a few of the five. We suggest having them look at a list of the 34 strengths before taking the instrument so they realize the difficulty (or ease) of narrowing this list down to 5. You might have them choose their expected strengths from a checklist of the 34 before taking the assessment (see Table 14-1). Or place the 34 strengths into three categories as in the book *First, Break All the Rules: What the World's Greatest Managers Do Differently:* ones that suggest "striving"

Table 14-1. Gallup Strengths Management Domains

Relating	Impacting	Thinking	Srtiving
Communication	Command	Analytical	Achiever
Empathy	Competition	Arranger	Activation
Harmony	Developer	Connectedness	Adaptability
Includer	Maximizer	Consistency	Belief
Individualization	Positivity	Context	Discipline
Relater	Woo	Deliberative	Focus
Responsibility		Futuristic	Restorative
		Ideation	Self-assurance
		Input	Significance
		Intellection	
		Learner	
		Strategic	

talents, ones that suggest "thinking" talents, and ones that suggest "relating" talents (Buckingham & Coffman, 1999, pp. 251–252). What you need are ways to reinforce a new vocabulary and perhaps a new way for clients to talk about themselves. You can also discuss how each of the 34 strengths belongs in one of four clusters as suggested by Winseman, Clifton, and Liesveld (2003): strengths that reflect either striving (personal motivation), relating (interpersonal skills), impacting (self-presentation), or thinking (learning style). Perhaps clients can focus on the one area in which they have the most interest or strength.

Buckingham and Coffman (1999) used a similar approach to bringing things down to size and suggested identifying "one critical talent" (p. 102) from each of three categories—striving, thinking, and relating. This may be still another approach to helping clients focus on their most important strength(s).

It is easy to assume that clients retain all we tell them, but too often that is clearly not the case. Finding ways to reinforce what they may be hearing or considering for the first time is important. That may involve restating their strengths, using documentation in logs or personal narratives that include writing about the strengths, or using other forms of communication. But we cannot simply assume clients are making the paradigm shift to thinking more about their strengths than their weaknesses.

We feel it best to use both the Clifton StrengthsFinder and the INSIGHT Inventory. If you have access to student orientation courses, career planning courses, leadership development offerings, learning communities, academic advising, peer mentoring, residential life programs, or any school or campus living arrangements—places where clients relate in ongoing fashion and can reflect on and try out their strengths and styles—those are where this strengths-based approach can best be implemented. If you can promote their use in encounters in these settings, you can make your efforts even more impactful. Introducing clients to their styles and strengths by themselves is not enough. You need to persist in helping your clients be comfortable with making changes in their behaviors.

An example may help clarify what we mean. Seeing clients come to understand their particular styles, and how these styles serve or disturb them or, more important, how they can flex to better meet clients' needs, is an outcome of a counseling session that is particularly rewarding. Clients appreciate learning how to use their strengths and flex their styles; it accentuates their uniqueness. We simply provide support for their learning how to do better what they do not realize they are probably already doing well. Giving attention to clients' strengths results in their feeling better about time spent in sessions. After all, they have some sense of what they do well; they appreciate reinforcement of it. Helping clients learn to better apply their strengths in different situations is helping them make the most of what they do best. We believe that working with strengths rather than focusing on weaknesses is a more effective approach to changing behaviors.

The INSIGHT Inventory

The INSIGHT Inventory and the Clifton StrengthsFinder provide a different yet complementary assessment of strengths. The StrengthsFinder reveals underlying talent themes, and the INSIGHT Inventory describes how the person with these themes looks and behaves. Whether used independently or together (a particularly powerful combination), they both help people discover positive dimensions within themselves and live these out in their careers and relationships.

The INSIGHT Inventory uses a strengths-based language for behaviorally describing four personality traits: (Influencing, Responding, Pacing, and Organizing). It also helps users identify the impact of certain environments (work and personal) on their behaviors. Finally, it clarifies which behaviors reflect users' natural strengths and which are caused by stress. Users rate their behavior in two global environments (Work Style and Personal Style) and receive two profiles describing the intensity of their preferences on four personality traits in each setting. The interpretive information uses positive, constructive language and helps users better identify their personality strengths and apply these to exploring career roles.

Support materials include an online Facilitator's Success Center that includes (a) a quick start guide, (b) a teaching/counseling manual, (c) presentation slides, (d) skill-building exercises and discussion activities, and (d) a technical manual.

Development and Theory

The INSIGHT Inventory was developed in 1984 by Patrick Handley, PhD, and has gone through several updates. Initially, when working in corporate and business settings, Handley began developing a personality assessment that yielded positive descriptions and helped users identify their strengths and apply these in career planning, team building, and leadership development. Later, the student version expanded this to include interpersonal communications, building self-esteem, and career-planning skills for students in high school and college.

Background research involved a factor analysis of an extensive list of behavioral descriptors. This process was similar to the one Cattell (1943, 1947) performed and that led to the Sixteen Personality Factor Questionnaire (16PF). The items chosen for the INSIGHT Inventory were limited to adjectives and short descriptors, paralleling the item selection methodology pioneered by Allport and Odbert in their classic work on identifying traits with commonly used terms (Allport, 1961, 1966; Allport & Odbert, 1936). The initial list of adjectives was reduced to a final list of 32 predictive terms that measured four personality traits. Each trait was identified and named through construct validity studies with the 16PF, Myers-Briggs Type Indicator, and Holland codes (Cattell, 1947; Cattell, Eber, & Tatsuoka, 1980; Holland, 1973; Myers & McCaulley, 1985). Once selected and named, they were carefully described in positive, strengths-based language. A unique characteristic of the INSIGHT Inventory is that it asks clients to rate themselves twice: first on how they see themselves at work, and a second time on how they see themselves at home in their personal worlds. This helps them identify how different environments (with inherent opportunities, pressures, and stresses) impact their behavior.

The two profiles clients receive reflect the underlying field theory base. Field theory, originally developed and popularized by Lewin (1935) in the 1930s, holds that behavior is a function of the interaction between one's personality within an environment. Lewin developed a mathematical formula for this: $B = f(P \times E)$, or *Behavior is a function of the Personality within an Environment*. Lewin (1954) believed that people have core personalities but that the behavior they display at any given time is influenced by the setting in which they find themselves. This is a particularly helpful concept in career planning, because people often find that certain environments bring out their strengths (and consequently feel like a fit), whereas other environments move them away from their strengths and feel like a poor or even stressful fit.

Lewin is known for having developed intricate formulas that factor in the supporting and restricting forces and pressures in a particular setting (environment) and applying mathematical weights to these. This was done in an effort to determine if one could predict how specific environments influence certain personalities (or personality traits). He labeled this process *force field analysis*, and it has become a widely used process for analyzing many situations, work problems, challenges, marketing approaches, and family and team dynamics. The INSIGHT Inventory applies this same theory to personality assessment and career counseling.

The INSIGHT Inventory asks users to describe themselves in two environments, work and personal (students use school and personal). The descriptive terms are primarily adjectives or short common phrases. No time limit is imposed on administering the INSIGHT Inventory; however, people complete the assessment in 10 to 15 min. Both self-scored paper and computer-scored online versions are available.

What the INSIGHT Inventory Assesses

The INSIGHT Inventory assesses four behavioral traits, each with two opposite extremes plotted on statistically normed continuums on each trait. The four traits are:

1. Scale A: Influencing—how people express their thoughts, present ideas, assert themselves, and influence others. The extremes are Indirect and Direct.
2. Scale B: Responding—how people approach and respond to others, particularly groups. The extremes are Reserved and Outgoing.
3. Scale C: Pacing—the speed and rhythm with which people take action and make decisions. The extremes are Urgent and Steady.
4. Scale D: Organizing—how people structure time, organize tasks, and handle details. The extremes are Unstructured and Precise.

These four traits are independent factors; therefore, numerous combinations of intensities can emerge. Many people also behave differently in different environments, and thus there are endless possibilities for profile shapes. Although there may be some wide variations between people's work and personal styles in certain environments, core underlying personality traits emerge that people tend to identify as their comfort zone. Most people demonstrate a small swing or range of movement on traits as they move between environments. However, some people are fairly fixed and behave basically the same regardless of the environment in which they find themselves. Either scenario is fine and leads to enlightening self-discovery and interesting application to career planning and communication patterns.

Reliability and Validity

The *INSIGHT Technical Manual* (Handley, 1999) provides all data derived from factor analysis techniques, normative studies, and reliability and validity statistics. Summary data are posted at www.insightinventory.com. Test–retest reliability ranges in the upper .70s (Nunnally, 1978) for the independent scales, and internal consistency reliability coefficients range between the .70s and .80s, consistent with Nunnally's recommendations for assessments of this nature. When INSIGHT Inventory traits were compared with similar scales on the Myers-Briggs Type Indicator, 16PF, and Holland codes, construct validity coefficients were consistently in the mid-.80s. Reviews of the INSIGHT Inventory can be found in the Buros Institute's *Mental Measurement Yearbook* series (Urgina, 1998).

The Interpretive Booklet

The interpretive booklet contained within the paper, self-scoreable version of the IN-SIGHT Inventory provides guidelines that help users understand and apply their results. The online version produces a personalized report with suggestions for improving personal effectiveness. Both versions help users identify their personality strengths, better understand their reactions to stress, and learn strategies for flexing their behavior to communicate better with others.

Online Versions

The online system presents the same assessment items in an easy-to-follow wizard and produces a *Self Report,* which describes the user's own strengths, reactions to stress, areas for flexing to better communicate, and self-development plan; and if selected, an *Observer Feedback Report,* which describes how observers view the user. Student/teen versions are also available and focus more on self-esteem, strengths, and career planning.

Understanding the Four INSIGHT Inventory Traits

Work Style and Personal Style Differences
Users' scores on the four independent traits on both their Work Style and Personal Style profiles are plotted on two horizontal charts. This helps users compare the differences that appear between the four traits in the two environments.

Trait A—INFLUENCING (Indirect and Direct)
Scale A provides an indication of how people express their thoughts, present their ideas, and assert themselves. The two opposite preferences are Indirect and Direct, and both can be effective when one is influencing others. People who favor the Indirect preference use strategy, tact, and diplomacy when attempting to get their ideas out and accepted. They tend to be modest, avoid conflict, and be cautious in their position. They are often good mediators and facilitators.

People who prefer the Direct preference use candor, assertiveness, and conviction when expressing their thoughts and opinions. They come across as forceful and self-confident. They are good at taking charge, especially in situations that need control and clear direction.

Trait B—RESPONDING (Reserved and Outgoing)
Scale B measures an individual's response to others, particularly groups of people. The two opposite preferences are Reserved and Outgoing. Reserved individuals are quiet, are retiring, and tend to minimize their engagement with large groups. They are introverted and prefer interacting with people one on one or in small groups. They keep their emotions rather private and self-contained, using few gestures and facial expressions. Reserved individuals are often good listeners and are comfortable working alone for extended periods.

The Outgoing preference describes people who are extroverted, animated, and very expressive. These individuals are "people people"; they enjoy others and are particularly comfortable in groups. They share emotions openly and freely, using lots of gestures and expressions when talking. Outgoing individuals shine when meeting and greeting others, putting people at ease, and staying connected.

Trait C—PACING (Urgent and Steady)

The third scale measures the pace, speed, or rhythm with which people make decisions and take action. The two opposite preferences are Urgent and Steady. Urgent individuals take action quickly and move ahead in a restless, fast-paced manner. They operate best with decisions made and action taken. When experienced at something, they are good at clarifying priorities, eliminating options, and moving ahead. If inexperienced, they may be impulsive and take premature action.

The Steady preference describes individuals who prefer to take their time when making decisions; they take action only after considering options carefully and deliberately. Because of their patience, they often perform well on long-term projects requiring consistency, persistence, and calculated responses.

Trait D—ORGANIZING (Unstructured and Precise)

Scale D provides an indication of a person's preference for structuring time, organizing tasks, and handling details. The two opposite preferences are Unstructured and Precise. People favoring the Unstructured preference tend to be very flexible and nonconforming. They can also be inattentive to the details of daily organization and resistant to systems and rules. They are often good at identifying innovative, atypical ways of completing projects or connecting people.

People who score as Precise are structured and ordered in how they manage time, organize tasks, and handle details. They are most often characterized as organized and efficient. They attend to the details of work and home life and place a high value on maintaining order and predictability. They are good at identifying ways to improve systems and procedures that help make work or personal projects flow more evenly and smoothly.

Work Style and Personal Style Similarities and Differences

When peoples' Work Style and Personal Style profiles are different, they are most likely adapting to certain responsibilities, pressures, or stressors in one or the other of these two settings. This causes their behavior to change on one or more of the traits. If their profiles stay the same, this indicates that they behave consistently, at least in these two environments. However, there may be other settings where their behavior does shift (e.g., when working around a certain person, driving in rush hour traffic, getting a performance appraisal).

Over time and across situations, most people develop a fairly predictable set of preferences. This is their core personality. The INSIGHT Inventory encourages people to explore how their behavior may change in different environments and helps people identify the settings in which they are comfortable. As users discuss their core personality traits with career counselors and facilitators, they get better at identifying the settings that bring out their strengths.

Impact of Stress

Situations that prevent people from using their preferred styles are often stressful. Most people will tend to "overuse" their strongest traits at those times. When this happens, their strengths can become weaknesses. For example, Direct people like being in control and taking charge. When they are tired or are in situations in which they have little authority or power to change things, they will feel stressed. They may react by becoming blunt, forceful, and domineering as a way of regaining control.

Flexing

When people have opposite styles, misunderstandings and conflicts may arise not over *what* is said but *how* it is said. As people learn to flex their style, they develop skill at reading others and communicating with people in the most appropriate manner. *Flexing* involves making temporary shifts in behavior and then moving back to one's own style strengths. This is also a core component of much of the work on emotional intelligence and high interpersonal intelligence (Gardner, 2006). Both of these models and theories emphasize the importance of self-awareness, talent in reading others, and skill at changing behavior when doing so enhances communications and relationships.

The INSIGHT Inventory provides a positive, strengths-based, and practical process for helping people develop emotional intelligence and link this to specific behavioral changes. Clients identify their behavior in different environments, learn how others see them, develop skill at reading others, and learn to flex their style to communicate better with a wide range of people. The INSIGHT Inventory labels this process style *flexing*, and it is one of the most important outcome goals.

Using the INSIGHT Inventory in Career Coaching or Counseling

The INSIGHT Inventory was designed as a strengths-based personality assessment that could be used in a constructive manner in career counseling, coaching, team development, leadership, and interpersonal communications. Its foundation rests in the field of positive psychology and in *field theory* (the premise that people can behave differently in different situations). Career counselors can use the INSIGHT Inventory to help people form positive and constructive images of their personality strengths and roles and the vocational paths that will bring out the best in them.

Goal: Helping Clients Identify Interests and Subgroup Personality Job Matches

Most career interest areas have multiple roles and subgroups toward which people can gravitate. For example, a person interested in becoming a medical nurse may first be drawn to science and helping but then has a full range of role selection. One nurse may be drawn to a career pathway that involves assertive leadership of others and quick decision making in emergency trauma rooms, whereas another nurse may gravitate toward laboratory research in a very technical area requiring patience and working alone.

Good planning and placement involves both identifying the best career interest area and matching personality preferences to specific roles in that interest area. Typically career counseling has emphasized the identification of interests and values. Personality and role fit has been left to the individual to sort out as he or she gets into a particular job. However, giving personality more attention early in the process and identifying specific strengths helps clients make even better career decisions.

Goal: Drawing Out Clients' Strengths

Some clients move out of their ideal personality/job fit because they trade their long-term satisfaction for short-term gains. These gains could take the form of tangible pay-offs such as increased salary, improved benefits, or more ideal job location. Or, these gains might be psychological payoffs such as prestige, status, or family approval. Neither trade-off leads to long-term satisfaction.

For example, Fred (Indirect, Reserved, Steady, Precise), a skilled technical person who enjoys detailed, structured work, decides to take a promotion for increased income. He soon finds himself stressed by having to manage others in a fast-growth, unpredictable leadership role that would be a better fit for a Direct, Outgoing, Urgent, Unstructured individual. Effective career guidance could have helped Fred better re-evaluate the trade-off (i.e., the loss of personality/job fit for increased income) before making his decision.

Students in high school and college may find themselves in similar positions. More typically young people are drawn away from their ideal personality/career fit by psychological payoffs. They may trade their "dream job or career track" for either parental or peer approval. For example, Teresa, an aspiring Outgoing, Unstructured young musician, might dream of a career in entertainment in which she can constantly be around people and live a flexible Unstructured lifestyle. However, she might abandon her study in piano because her parents (whose approval she highly values and needs for financial support) may believe she should get a degree in something more practical, such as business. So to retain their support, she switches majors. In this example, she trades off both her true career interest and personality/job match fit.

In a second scenario, Teresa might stay in the same interest area, music, but shift from becoming an artist in the entertainment industry to a private piano teacher. This may lead to just as much psychological job dissatisfaction down the road even though it appears to be a fit because the career is in music. However, career interest fit does not fully guarantee psychological fit. Her primary personality trait, Outgoing, gregarious, and demonstrative, might be shut down to such a level such that she experiences very little satisfaction in the private lesson teaching role.

Career counselors can help clients evaluate the trade-offs they are willing to make and clarify when clients are sacrificing personality job fit for external payoffs. The INSIGHT Inventory gives career counselors insights into personality traits and career fits and provides guidelines for facilitating these types of discussions with clients.

Goal: Helping Clients Combine Personality Preferences, Interests, and Competencies

Career and academic counselors need to be aware that some people have personality traits that naturally give them competence in certain job roles, but they may have little or no interest in careers that traditionally draw on those competencies. For example, most people scoring as Precise and structured on Scale D would probably enjoy jobs that give them the opportunity to organize details and plan carefully. But not always! There may be individuals who score as Precise and who have good organizing skills but who do not want to use those skills in traditional jobs.

The career counselor's challenge is to uncover a person's special interest areas and then take the step of identifying a good match between these interests and the person's personality traits. For example, Lauren scores as high Precise and is interested in work that involves attention to detail. Discussing careers in accounting or project management might be a first step. However, if this were combined with an interest area, say ancient history, where some jobs involve attention to detail (e.g., carefully recording museum artifacts), the conversation would become interesting and her eyes would light up. Career counselors must continually balance interest areas with personality strengths and help their clients identify those career paths that combine both.

Goal: Increasing Awareness of Family Preferences

As a counselor, you can help people at all life stages, but particularly students, learn to identify the subconscious and family patterns that relate to personality traits measured by the INSIGHT Inventory. For example, Family A might consist of two parents who are both very structured and Precise. They may give the message that it is "good" to be attentive to details, planned, organized, and predictable. However, a child of these parents may be Unstructured and feel out of place both in the home and in environments where these same traits are desirable. Career coaching can help clients discover the strengths of their own personality preferences and gain permission to follow these even if they do not match the messages they grew up receiving. This approach can apply to any of the traits and combinations of traits.

Goal: Helping Clients Deal With Job Stress

Sometimes people lose touch with what their underlying personality strength is because they have put themselves in positions where they overuse that trait and experience the negative side of this overuse. For example, Mary, a medical technician, scored as Direct and Urgent and was drawn to positions in which she could be in charge, take control of chaos, and make fast decisions. However, she ended up in a dysfunctional trauma rescue unit. And although her interest in medicine, her interest in helping others, and her personality preferences were ideal for the job, the particular team members she ended up working with were not working well together. There were constant power struggles and disrespect for one another's decisions. In response, Mary became more and more direct and forceful in presenting her ideas. This progressed to the point where she was becoming domineering, argumentative, and excessively controlling. Her work relationships were tense, and she became increasingly dissatisfied with her job and sought out career counseling, erroneously believing she needed to find a new career.

The goal for her career coach was not to help Mary find a new career but rather to help her identify how to avoid overusing her style and why she was doing so. If the situation were impossible, then perhaps Mary could look for a similar job with a different company and new team. More likely, Mary could benefit from some coaching on how to flex her style and not move to overuse, thus resulting in the accompanying stress.

Counselors and coaches can help people become aware of their reactions to stress and learn to moderate these before they resort to nonproductive style overuse and making knee-jerk career decisions.

Goal: Helping Clients Learn to Flex Their Traits

We can help clients identify the traits in which they can develop more flexibility and increase their satisfaction with a current career or clarify which positions might require less flexing and offer a more natural fit.

Some people have strong interpersonal skills and grasp immediately the concept of flexing their style to better communicate with others. However, there are people who struggle with these skills. A career counselor can help clients clarify which traits they are rigid in and identify specific behaviors they can learn to begin flexing better. This takes awareness, understanding, and action, all of which translates to discovery and guided practice. Both of these are outcomes that career counselors can offer and facilitate, particularly when the online Observer Feedback assessment is incorporated into the sessions.

Goal: Helping Clients Develop More Accurate Views of Their Personality Strengths

Counselors can use the online INSIGHT Inventory—Self Report and INSIGHT Observer Feedback assessment to help clients learn whether they see themselves the same as other people do. This is important, because in the work world clients soon discover that their interpersonal relationships are just as important as their job skills. Clients can find the job of their dreams—a perfect fit between their personality, interests, values, and the job requirements—but end up dissatisfied with the job because of strained working relationships with coworkers. Counselors can provide this feedback early in the career coaching process and help clients go into their selected careers with improved self-awareness and communication skills.

Using the INSIGHT Inventory With the Clifton StrengthsFinder

The INSIGHT Inventory and Clifton StrengthsFinder both focus on strengths and what is right with people, but they assess and define these characteristics differently. This makes it possible to use them together in complementary fashion. They build on each other's strengths!

The INSIGHT Inventory describes how people behave based on their personality traits and the environments they are in. The Clifton StrengthsFinder describes people's talent themes. Simply put, the StrengthsFinder describes which talents people prefer to engage in, and the INSIGHT Inventory describes how people behave when acting on their talents.

Following are two examples. The first describes Jack and Jennifer, who have the same StrengthsFinder talent theme but different INSIGHT Inventory Work Style profiles. In the second example, Ken and Barbara have different StrengthsFinder talent themes but the same INSIGHT Inventory Work Style profile. Note that the StrengthsFinder identifies people's top five talent themes, and the INSIGHT Inventory generates two profiles (Work Style and Personal Style). However, for the purpose of the following examples, only one talent theme and the Work Style profile are used.

Example 1: Jack and Jennifer: Two Achievers With Different INSIGHT Inventory Profiles

Both Jack and Jennifer have a constant need for achievement. According to the StrengthsFinder, the very nature of this theme suggests that no matter how much they achieve, shortly afterward the glory fades and they feel compelled to set another goal and begin anew working toward it. This gives them incredible energy and helps them accomplish a great deal, but they often have trouble just relaxing and enjoying some of the fruits of their success.

On the INSIGHT Inventory, Jennifer scores as very Direct, Outgoing, Urgent, and Precise. She pushes for results, drives herself and others hard, expresses her emotions readily, acts quickly, and makes sure all systems are perfectly organized. As an Achiever, she comes across as forceful, expressive, restless, and a perfectionist.

Jack, however, scores as very Indirect, Reserved, Steady, and Unstructured on the INSIGHT Inventory. He works quietly; negotiates his agendas diplomatically; avoids conflict; persists for hours; and thinks and acts in an unconventional, outside-the-box manner. As an Achiever, he comes across as tactful, reserved, patient, and creative.

Although both Jack and Jennifer are very driven as Achievers, they accomplish their goals with quite different sets of behaviors, and they come across quite differently to others. Career coaching would take quite different directions with Jack and Jennifer. The environments, job fits and issues that cause them stress, and job fit decisions would be quite different.

Example 2: Ken and Barbara: Two Direct, Reserved, Urgent, Unstructured Individuals With Different StrengthsFinder Talent Themes

Ken and Barbara both come across quite similarly to others. Based on their INSIGHT Inventory scores, they are candid, driven, forceful, rather quiet and reserved, quick decision makers who take action quickly and who are creative, nontraditional thinkers. However, they have quite different StrengthsFinder themes. One of Ken's top talents is Ideation, but Barbara's top theme is Arranger. Ken feels strongest when he is engrossed in the world of ideas and busy sorting out possibilities for combining creative thoughts into even bigger and greater concepts. He thrives on marketing and advertising positions in which he can focus daily on ideas for product launches. To his coworkers he comes across as rather brusque and intimidating at times (Direct), somewhat hard to read (Reserved), fast to take action and quite impatient with long meetings (Urgent), and always open to doing things differently (Unstructured).

Barbara comes across very similarly to Ken. Coworkers say she and Ken are mirror images of each other, and they often clear the room when Ken and Barbara bump heads on issues the two feel strongly about (two Directs just airing their opinions—forcefully). However, rather than dwell in the world of ideas where Ken thrives, Barbara draws on her Arranger talent theme to make things happen. She even says she has not had a new idea in years but can bring any good idea others provide to fast fruition. She immediately starts conducting the how-to-do-it, who-to-do-it, and when-to-do-it pieces required to bring the idea to measurable results. Plus, she can keep all the different parts spinning until the goal is met.

If they ever seek out career coaching, Ken and Barbara would benefit from quite different advice. They both would appear similar on the INSIGHT Inventory results, but their different StrengthsFinder themes mean they use their personality strengths in quite different talent areas. A career counselor or coach would need to focus on both personality and talent themes.

Organizational Talent Management and Career Development

Although employed predominantly in academic settings, career counselors are particularly well prepared and ideally suited for positions in corporate talent management and organizational career development. Their biggest challenge is identifying and using assessment instruments that fit the culture and language of business and draw upon career counselors' skill sets of coaching and training.

This could be the perfect match, because, pressed with the approaching retirement of the baby boom generation, organizations are giving increased attention to managing the careers of their key employees and retaining their top talent. These businesses can benefit from employment or consultant relationships with career counselors. We suggest a good start for a toolkit for career counselors or career coaches to use to provide services would be the INSIGHT Inventory and the Clifton StrengthsFinder. These two assessments can be used not only for developing and positioning talent but also for building a comprehensive strengths-based organizational culture.

Whether used in career development self-discovery or as pre-employment interviewing aids, the INSIGHT Inventory and Clifton StrengthsFinder better ensure that companies use a language of strengths, talents, and possibilities rather than one of weaknesses, shortcomings, and lack. There is no better way to ensure the hiring and retention of high-quality employees than to affirm the best in them, identify their highest potentials and dreams, and establish clear career paths for achieving these.

To order either of these assessments, and many of the others mentioned in this book, go to the University of Missouri Career Center Web site (http://career.missouri.edu), or order directly from the publishers: Clifton StrengthsFinder (http://www.gallup-strengthscenter.com/Purchase) or INSIGHT Inventory (www.insightinventory.com).

Closing Thoughts

In closing, we have shown how the use of two assessments, the Clifton Strengths-Finder and the INSIGHT Inventory, both with similar intended outcomes, can further increase the message about strengths. Strengths matter, and how we present them to clients, and how we help clients come to best use them, is something of an art and a science. We could add other assessments. For example, the Values-In-Action (VIA), which highlights one's individual values, is available online and free at http://www.viacharacter.org; adding the VIA as an intervention might have more impact on a particular client. No one approach is best or right for all clients. There are two things to keep in mind, however, as you put together which instruments you use. One, use only those instruments that you have taken yourself and with which you have become comfortable; and two, continue to look for and incorporate new instruments that you find are most useful to surfacing strengths for your particular clientele. No one assessment or combination of assessments necessarily will be useful for all of your clientele.

References

Allport, G. W. (1961). *Pattern and growth in personality.* New York, NY: Holt, Rinehart & Winston.

Allport, G. W. (1966). Traits revisited. *American Psychologist, 21,* 1–10.

Allport, G. W., & Odbert, H. S. (1936). *Trait-names: A psycho-lexical study.* Princeton, NJ: Psychological Review.

Buckingham, M., & Coffman, C. (1999). *First, break all the rules: What the world's greatest managers do differently.* New York, NY: Simon & Schuster, Gallup Organization.

Cattell, R. B. (1943). The description of personality: Basic traits resolved into clusters. *Journal of Abnormal and Social Psychology, 38,* 476–506.

Cattell, R. B. (1947). Confirmation and clarification of primary personality factors. *Psychometrika, 12,* 197–220.

Cattell, R. B., Eber, H. W., & Tatsuoka, M. (1980). *Handbook for the Sixteen Personality Factor Questionnaire (16PF).* Champaign, IL: Institute for Personality and Ability Testing.

Clifton, D. O., & Anderson, E. (2002). *StrengthsQuest—Discover and develop your strengths in academics, career, and beyond.* New York, NY: Gallup Press.

Clifton, D. O., Anderson, E., & Schreiner, L. A. (2006). *StrengthsQuest: Discover and develop your strengths in academics, career, and beyond* (2nd ed.). New York, NY: Gallup Press.

Clifton, D. O., & Nelson, P. (1996). *Soar with your strengths.* New York, NY: Delacorte Press.

Compton, W. C., & Hoffman, E. (2012). *Positive psychology: The science of happiness and flourishing.* Belmont, CA: Wadsworth.

Gardner, H. (2006). *Changing minds: The art and science of changing our own and other people's minds.* Boston, MA: Harvard Business School Press.

Handley, P. (1999). *INSIGHT technical manual.* Kansas City, MO: INSIGHT Institute.

Holland, J. L. (1973). *Making vocational choices: A theory of careers.* Englewood Cliffs, NJ: Prentice Hall.

Lewin, K. (1935). *A dynamic theory of personality.* New York, NY: McGraw-Hill.

Lewin, K. (1954). Behavior and development as a function of the total situation. In L. Carmichael (Ed.), *Manual of child psychology* (pp. 918–970). New York, NY: Wiley.

Liesveld, R., & Miller, J. A. (2005). *Teach with your strengths.* New York, NY: Gallup Press.

Lopez, S., Hodges, T., & Harter, J. (2005). *The Clifton StrengthsFinder technical report: Development and validation.* New York, NY: Gallup Organization.

Myers, I. B., & McCaulley, M. M. (1985). *Manual: A guide to the development and use of the Myers-Briggs Type Indicator.* Palo Alto, CA: Consulting Psychologists Press.

Nunnally, J. C. (1978). *Psychometric theory.* New York, NY: McGraw-Hill.

Urgina, S. (1998). Review of the INSIGHT Inventory. In J. C. Impara & B. S. Plake (Eds.), *The thirteenth mental measurement yearbook* (pp. 509–510). Lincoln, NE: Buros Institute of Mental Measurements.

Winseman, A. L., Clifton, D. O., & Liesveld, C. (2003). *Living your strengths: Discover your God-given talents, and inspire your congregation and community.* Washington, DC: Gallup Organization.

Chapter 15

Understanding and Working With Resistant Clients

Little has been written about client resistance in career counseling. Much more has been written about client resistance in the counseling and psychotherapy literature (Vogel, Wester, & Larson, 2007). Why is this so? One reason may be that some counselors have conceptualized and practiced career counseling as being devoid of process and relationship; career counseling for them focuses mainly on outcomes and methods within a relatively short period of time. The perspectives and structures they use to guide their work in career counseling do not provide for the concept of client resistance.

Blustein and Spengler (1995) pointed out, however, that client resistance, seen or unseen, can occur whenever counseling takes place, however the counseling is labeled. It does not matter whether counseling is labeled *psychotherapy* or *career counseling*:

> In psychotherapy, counselors give much attention to helping people make changes they can imagine but have not yet been able to invoke due to internal conflicts, anxiety, cognitive distortions, family restrictions, and the like. In actuality, career counseling may be no different. (p. 304)

Why do clients resist? In helping individuals make changes in their lives through counseling, whether labeled *career counseling* or *personal counseling*, we sometimes will evoke resistance in clients. In fact, Teyber and McClure (2011) defined *resistance* as the fear of change: "Often, as clients seek help and genuinely try to change, they simultaneously resist or work against the very change they are trying to change" (p. 95)

Amundson, Harris-Bowlsbey, and Niles (2009) suggested a number of reasons why some clients may be reluctant to participate in career counseling and hence resist. Clients may resist, at least initially, because they fear entering into a process with which they are unfamiliar. Clients may also resist because they fear taking responsibility for their actions. They may resist, too, because they are mandated to participate in career counseling. Vogel et al. (2007) suggested that social stigma, treatment fears, fear of emotion, fear of self-disclosure, and self-esteem are reasons why some clients may resist. Gold (2008) added that pain in their lives may also be a reason some clients may resist.

It is important to remember that for some clients, career counseling is straightforward. For them, change is minimal, so little or no client resistance is present. But for many clients, whether by conscious choice or unconscious action, resistance in some form at some level is part of career counseling because fear of change is involved (Pryor, 2010). Personality dynamics, irrational beliefs, motivational issues, environmental concerns, and distorted thinking may permeate clients' views of themselves, others, and their worlds and can often short-circuit the best use of tools and techniques in career counseling.

To be effective in working with clients who may be resistant, for whatever their reasons, it is important to acknowledge that resistance can and does occur in career counseling. If you do not acknowledge this, then you will not look for resistance in your work with clients. And if you do not look for resistance, you will not see it. As a result, you may misread and misunderstand some client behavior as career counseling unfolds.

What does client resistance look like? For the purposes of this chapter we present selected examples of different types of resistance that may be exhibited by clients in career counseling. These examples include fear of counseling, fear of taking responsibility, defense mechanisms, sabotaged communication, making excuses, irrational beliefs, faulty information processing, and overt physical behavior. Then we turn our attention to presenting selected specific techniques that can be used in responding to client resistance in career counseling. The techniques presented include forming a client–counselor working alliance, joining, using metaphors, using confrontation, and labeling and reframing. Although this chapter focuses on client resistance, it would not be complete without a brief examination of how and why counselors may resist too. Hence, the chapter closes with a brief discussion of counselor resistance.

Recognizing Resistance: Some Examples

Fear of Counseling

Client resistance due to fear of counseling is a type of resistance described by Meara and Patton (1994). It can take three forms: fear of the counselor, fear of the counseling process, or fear of discovery. Fear of the counselor focuses on clients' fears that counselors will not meet their expectations. Fear of the counseling process revolves around such concerns as a lack of faith on the part of clients in the counseling process, clients' feelings that they lack competence to be involved in the work of counseling, and clients' fear of working with authority figures. Finally, fear of discovery describes feelings of clients learning unwanted knowledge about themselves. Meier (2012) added that "clients may be very reluctant to share strong feelings because they do not expect to improve in psychotherapy, may be ashamed to reveal secrets or admit failure and thus expect to be critically judged, or fear losing control" (p. 9).

Fear of Taking Responsibility

Another type of client resistance can be labeled the *fear of taking responsibility* (King, 1992). Accepting responsibility for decisions is one of the most difficult things clients face in their lives. Counselors' awareness and appreciation of the potential burden and threat that taking responsibility represents to clients are prerequisites for dealing with resistance in a positive manner. In his treatment of clients, Low (1966) discovered that anything sounds more hopeful and more comforting than the bleak prospect of having to undergo training in self-discipline: "Even brain tumors, mental ailments and hereditary 'taints' are preferable to that dreadful indictment as being a weak character and needing training in self-control" (p. 279). Pryor (2010) underscored this point by stating that clients "struggle with transforming and transcending themselves because this involves self-discipline and suffering" (p. 34).

Some pain is only temporary; however, the fear of being unable to perform hits directly at clients' self-worth and the inability to adequately determine their existence. This presents the ominous prospect of continual, everlasting pain. Insulation and manipulation become necessary defense mechanisms for client survival.

Defense mechanisms and sabotaged communication serve as safeguards of self-esteem. This allows for an evasion of life tasks. It is always possible to collect more or less plausible reasons to justify escape from facing the challenges of life. Engle and Arkowitz (2008) supported this point by stating:

> Although the present pattern of behavior, thinking, or feeling may be undesirable and cause significant distress, it nonetheless persists because it serves important functions for the person. For example, drugs and alcohol temporarily help people escape from stress. People often feel that change means giving up a pattern that serves these functions to some degree for patterns that may not do so. (p. 399)

Clients often do not realize what they are doing. Some strategies are intended to ensure against failure, exposure, or other catastrophes. The strategy used may have the effect of making it impossible for clients to meet onerous responsibilities—or at least it may delay the "moment of truth." Clients may try to disqualify themselves from a race they do not wish to run. If the race must be run, can failure be justified?

Defense Mechanisms

Basic defense mechanisms are familiar. However, we are just beginning to appreciate the subtle and complex ways clients use various strategies in adjusting to threatening conditions. For example, a subtle strategy we all use is called *buying double insurance*. No matter what the outcome, one can afford to take a partial chance because one's safety is secured. Perhaps you can remember a report that you kept putting off and then, just before the deadline, you worked feverishly, completed it, and turned it in at the last minute. By doing so you ensured your self-worth. If your supervisor did not like the report, it was because you did not have enough time to do an adequate job. If your supervisor did like it, you proved your unusual superiority.

This strategy is even more complex in an academic environment that places value on superior performance. The problem presented is often described as an inability to concentrate on school studies. The real problem occurs with some students who may not dare to attempt a true test of their intellectual capacity. The strategy used is buying insurance against the failure of being of ordinary intellect. According to Shulman and Mosak (1967),

> Such students are overly ambitious and demand that they be on top. They cannot afford to take the chance that their best efforts may leave them in the average range of their class. At first they make resolutions to study and indeed fantasize that they will study exceedingly well and do much outside reading on the subject. But they rarely do the necessary work. In a few weeks they are behind, and the chances for doing well are diminishing. Now they feel disappointed in themselves and even less inclined to study. People who want to be on top have no interest in studying hard to achieve only an average passing grade. This is shown in their procrastination, inability to concentrate, and restlessness when they begin to study. Throughout this unproductive activity they maintain a feeling of intellectual superiority. Trouble with studying and poor grades are blamed on bad habits, nervousness, lack of discipline, dull teachers, or uninteresting courses. Such students console themselves with the thought that they are really bright but are just unproductive for the moment. If only they were able to study properly, they would be at the top of the class. If they should happen to get high grades in spite of not studying, that is all to the good. They may even boast, "I never opened a book." If a poor grade is received, it is not because they are stupid, but because they are lazy. In our society most people would prefer to be regarded as lazy rather than stupid. (p. 82)

As a last resort such students may recall their earlier IQ scores and tell themselves that they are bright. They tell themselves that they could make good grades if they really wanted to. A high IQ score allows them to maintain their superiority without having to take academic risks.

Sabotaged Communication

We are educated at an early age not to venture or risk statements that might eventually be proved wrong or described as foolish. We learn how to avoid "owning" statements. Very often during a discussion, statements of obvious belief are prefaced by "Don't you think . . . ?" We frequently use the words *you* and *it* to direct ownership away from ourselves in conversations. Owning is threatening.

There also is an advantage to mystifying situations so that there is always room for doubt and, therefore, justified inactivity. If the situation gets too threatening, one can always justify gracious withdrawal. Keeping communication incomplete allows for the freedom to do what one pleases.

Some communication tactics that allow the individual to maintain freedom from commitment and responsibility follow (Low, 1966).

Being Literal
Rejecting a statement made by another without opposing it openly is a device that can be used to block efforts, combat views, or reject suggestions by means of misinterpretation of the words the other person uses. The following is a situation that represents this sabotage approach:

> *Client:* I have been working on the behavior contract for several weeks, and I don't see any results.
> *Counselor:* You must not be discouraged.
> *Client:* I am not discouraged. But, of course, if no one sees progress . . .

Discrediting
Accepting the validity of another person's statement may imply one's own intellectual and moral inadequacy. Should the counselor's statement be fully accepted, the client's simplicity or stupidity is thereby implied. The tactic of discrediting ensures that the process of change does not proceed too fast or too far. A position of no obligation is maintained through a verbal pattern of "but-knocking." But-knockers acknowledge the premise and then proceed to attack or deny its applicability to their situation:

> *Counselor:* Here is an outline of a conflict resolution procedure that has been used successfully in a number of companies.
> *Client:* Very interesting. I can see how it would work with those large West Coast companies, but our company is quite different.

Disparaging the Competence or Method
The client must prove that the counselor is qualified and unqualified, expert and inept, proficient and unskilled, all at the same time. The dilemma is solved by a simple trick: The counselor's competence is asserted explicitly but solidly denied by implication. The client's conscience is saved. For example, a client who consults a counselor on improving his or her ability to handle stress may demonstrate trust by continuing visits but use phrases with disparaging implications, thus denying his or her ability to be helped:

Client: My uncle was telling me about a new stress reduction technique . . . it seems to work for him . . . there must be something . . .

Tactics of this kind permit the client to maintain the illusion of cooperation while at the same time disrupting or opposing the process. If the counseling process does not work, the method used or the counselor's incompetence was at fault, neither of which was the client's responsibility.

Challenging Accountability

A common rejection of pursuing further exploration is the recourse to heredity ("No one in our family does well in math"). No one on any account can be held responsible for a difficulty inherited from one's ancestors. Accountability also can be directed toward other sources, such as unique temperaments and moods, past traumatic experiences, and metaphysical or religious experiences. By presenting a "hopeless" situation, the client takes no responsibility. Labeling is one way to support this type of thinking. After all, what can be expected from a "dyslexic" child or a "mental" patient?

Making Excuses

Another way of understanding, interpreting, and working with resistance is to consider the concept of excuses. Snyder, Higgins, and Stucky (1983) defined *excuses* as "explanations or actions that lessen the negative implications of an actor's [client's] performance, thereby maintaining a positive image for oneself and others" (p. 4). Making excuses for their actions or inactions may be a way for clients to resist taking responsibility for their behavior, to not respond to the demands of the career counseling process and the tasks that may be involved.

What are some common excuses that clients may use? Snyder et al. (1983, pp. 4–7) described 11 different types of excuses. We paraphrase the descriptions of these 11 types as follows:

- Denial—I had nothing to do with it.
- Alibi—I didn't know about it.
- Blaming—Somebody else did it.
- It wasn't so bad—It was not as bad as it seemed.
- Minimization—It was only a small thing.
- Justification—There is a reason for my excuse.
- Derogation—The person had it coming.
- Yes-but—I did it, but . . .
- I couldn't help it—What can you expect from me?
- I didn't mean to—Something made me do it.
- It wasn't really me—It was my temper that made me do it.

Mistaken Beliefs

According to Bourne (2010), mistaken beliefs are basic assumptions we make about ourselves, others, and life in general. They are formed as we grow up and interact with parents, teachers, peers, and the community at large. Bourne suggested that we "take them for granted and assume that they reflect reality" (p. 216). We assume they are real and often act as if they are real, causing them to "become self-fulfilling prophecies" (p. 217). Examples of mistaken beliefs follow:

- I'm powerless. I'm a victim of outside circumstances.
- Life is a struggle. Something must be wrong if life seems too easy, pleasurable, or fun.

- If I take a risk, I'll fail. If I fail, others will reject me.
- I'm unimportant. My feelings and needs are unimportant.
- I always should look good and act nice, no matter how I feel.
- If I worry enough, this problem should get better or go away.
- I can't cope with difficult or scary situations.
- The outside world is dangerous. There is safety only in what is known and familiar. (Bourne, 2010, p. 218)

Faulty Information Processing

Another way to listen to and understand clients during career counseling is to focus on how they think and on how they process information. Dowd (1995, pp. 13–14) identified seven examples of what he called *faulty information processing*. We paraphrase descriptions of these seven examples as follows:

- Arbitrary Inference—drawing conclusions without evidence.
- Selective Abstraction—conceptualizing the whole from only a few facts.
- Overgeneralization—drawing conclusions about a situation that may be true and then generalizing these conclusions to situations where they may not be true.
- Magnification/Minimization—overestimating or underestimating the importance of an event.
- Personalization—assuming a relationship of external events to oneself.
- Dichotomous Thinking—all-or-nothing thinking.
- Catastrophizing—expecting the worst of a bad situation.

Overt Physical Behavior

Client resistance can be manifested not only in what clients say during career counseling but also in their overt physical behavior as career counseling unfolds (Meara & Patton, 1994). Some clients are silent and passive. Some clients show up late for career counseling sessions; some do not show up at all. Other clients terminate career counseling prematurely because they cannot (will not) deal with important issues or with change.

Such overt physical behavior on the part of clients creates a real challenge for counselors. How do we interpret such client behavior? Some counselors personalize this behavior and end up blaming themselves: "My client did not show up for our second interview; it must be my fault" or "My client is always late for our appointments; it must be something I am doing as a counselor that causes this."

Although issues of counselor competence may be involved in causing such client behavior, a more likely reason most of the time is client resistance. Being silent or passive, showing up late, or not showing up at all are ways clients can escape from the pain of change or from anxious situations. If the client is not there or is only there for a short time, then the pain of change can be postponed or at least lessened. Various defense mechanisms, including excuses, are used to explain why they did not show up or why they were late. Remember Low's (1966) admonition: "Even brain tumors, mental ailments and hereditary 'taints' are preferable to that dreadful indictment as being a weak character and needing training in self-control" (p. 279). Clients may go to extreme measures—being late, not showing up—to avoid dealing with changes that may require taking responsibility.

Dealing With Resistance

Clients may display resistant (defensive/evasive) behavior during any of the various phases of the career counseling process in order to protect themselves from change.

They may express fear of counseling. They may be afraid to take responsibility. They may make excuses. They may hold irrational beliefs or may use faulty information processing. Finally, as one more example of resistance, they may physically remove themselves from career counseling so that they are not in harm's way.

The question is why? Why do many clients put energy into resistance? As suggested previously, resistance protects clients from having to change, from having to face troublesome issues in their lives directly.

> When people come to the therapist's office, they are emotionally hurting. The last thing they want is to hurt more. It is no wonder that one of the client's major tasks is to not change, to avoid the risks of greater anxiety and emotional pain. (Walborn, 1996, p. 244)

Resistant clients have their own unique, idiosyncratic patterns for survival (Engle & Arkowitz, 2008). Understanding that resistance can and does take place in career counseling, recognizing the patterns resistant clients use, and knowing how to work with resistance within the career counseling process are crucial. Although no strategies are guaranteed to clear away resistance, the following counseling strategies (i.e., the client–counselor working alliance, joining, metaphors, confrontation, and labeling and reframing) may be helpful.

Working Alliance

Chapter 8 discusses the role of the working alliance in career counseling. However you come to understand and work with client resistance in career counseling, it is important to remember that a strong client–counselor working alliance is the foundation. As Walborn (1996) suggested, "Resistance melts with time and understanding, as the therapeutic relationship matures" (p. 244).

A strong client–counselor working alliance may also open the door to new insights about ways to interpret client behavior. Meara and Patton (1994) made this point when they suggested that where a strong working alliance exists, counselors

> can conceptualize behavior in career counseling the same way they do in personal counseling (e.g., resistance). A client who terminated early or seems reluctant to participate in building the working alliance might be labeled as resistant rather than uninterested or undecided. Client resistance can be worked with effectively if the counselor is able to recognize it and can then help the client overcome it. (pp. 174–175)

Joining

Joining is more than empathy, the reflection of feeling, or other relationship concepts associated with client-centered counseling. To join with clients, you must be able to appreciate their life struggles, not just the feelings of the moment. Miller (2006) suggested that we "view the clients' . . . resistance as a natural part of change, and join it by trying first to better understand the resistance, and then assist clients in recognizing it and understanding it themselves" (p. 1).

When you join with clients, you let them know that you are aware of their total life struggles. To do this you can draw on your own experiences and wisdom that relate to roles, stages, and events that structure the tasks of life. Clients are faced with different responsibilities as they move through life. Each brings a unique response to common life role and task responsibilities. You may need to relate clients' career change dilemmas to other aspects of their lives, such as parenting an adolescent, coping with an unexpected illness, or weathering a financial crisis. What is it like to be 8 years old, 26 years old, or 45 years old? Can you respect the power of such responses as depression, alcoholism, and delusions? This must be done in the context of daily living problems and career decision making.

Ultimately, you will need to identify clients' areas of pain, difficulty, or stress and acknowledge that, although these areas cannot be avoided, you will respond to them sensitively. Joining is letting your clients know that you understand them. It is letting them know that you are working with and for them. Only under this protection can clients have the security to explore alternatives, try the unusual, and change. You need to cross over the line to join with your clients to help them accept the responsibilities of their daily struggles. Your position is that of an active but neutral listener. You help your clients tell their stories.

As soon as possible, you should start working with your clients' strengths (Peterson, 2006). Focusing on weaknesses and negative barriers is not very fruitful. By confirming what is positive about your clients, you become a source of self-esteem. Look for and emphasize positive functioning while pursuing goals of change. It is important that you be nonjudgmental about previous attempts to cope. Even when an obviously negative situation is discussed, your clients should not feel that they are being criticized or being made to feel guilty. Stress that you are willing to work with them on the problem.

Focusing on what is positive about clients is important. Manthei (2007) found that clients appreciated being treated respectfully as intelligent individuals. He also found that

> clients also liked explanations or interpretations that provided them with new ways of looking at their situations and they especially liked being told they were competent, skillful, insightful people, in contrast to being regarded as fragile, a failure or unable to cope. (p. 271)

When clients feel they are being treated in these ways, joining has been accomplished.

Metaphors

> Metaphoric language has been an important therapeutic tool since the first counselor attempted to understand fully a client's experience of the world. Traditionally, counselors have developed metaphors to demonstrate empathy and to suggest alternative interpretations of presenting problems. This use of metaphor, created by the counselor, does not change a client's problems; rather, it changes perception of the problem and allows for solutions as yet unconsidered. In this manner, metaphor has provided both a linguistic tool to facilitate empathy and an intervention technique with a history of therapeutic value. (Wickman, Daniels, White, & Fesmire, 1999, p. 389)

Andersen and Vandehey (2012) stated that "metaphors are stories that offer a point of view that may be helpful in dealing with life. Usually metaphors imply an indirect meaning that softens a lesson or reframes issues for a client" (p. 177). Clients will take what is heard and relate it in terms of their own experience. As this is occurring, they may gain insight into their concerns. Experiences of the past become infused with their present models of the world. In addition, these new representations may provide counselors and clients with a mutually understandable way of discussing present problems. Metaphors "provide us with a useful method for integrating the emotional and symbolic aspects of our life experiences and career aspirations" (Barner, 2011, p. 100).

What follows are some sample metaphors. The first metaphor was used with a client who was afraid to leave home for a job offer in another community. The second metaphor was used with a client who was always excusing himself from taking responsibility because of a previous illness. The third metaphor was used with a client who often let play interfere with work.

Metaphor 1. Because you grow plants in your house, you will understand my concern. I had this cluster of plants in a large pot. They seemed to be getting along alright. I watered them and took care of them, but they didn't seem to have a healthy look. They were crowded together. So in spite of their apparently satisfactory survival, they didn't seem to be able to grow. I decided to separate them into several pots. I repotted them. At first they looked kind of lonely and puny. But after proper care, they began to grow. They did not have to share the water and nutrients in the common pot. Now they had their own pots. Even the plant I left in the original pot prospered. Everything grew better. Eventually, they were all equally strong and prospering. It may be difficult to imagine how a cluster of plants can be divided and then each one becomes a strong separate potting, but it happened to me.

Metaphor 2. There was this excellent baseball player. He was an outfielder, and his specialty was hitting and stealing bases. One day an unfortunate accident occurred. He was running from first base to third base and had to slide into third base. His cleats caught on the turf and he broke his leg. He went through a long rehabilitation process. During part of the process, he developed a limp, but gradually all traces of the broken leg disappeared. He seemed to be able to run almost as fast, but in the back of his head he wondered if he had lost speed. He went back to playing baseball. There were no apparent signs of the injury—except on those occasions when he would ground the ball to the infield and be thrown out at first base. He would limp after he crossed first base and returned to the dugout. Ironically, he did not limp when he got a hit and roared into second base with a double.

Metaphor 3. Life is a business. Granted, there ought to be time in everybody's routine to play, to amuse oneself with games, and to divert attention from the serious aspects of the business of living. Nevertheless, life is not a game; it is a business that must be toiled at and attended to. Its business is to create and maintain values (family, community, education, religion, sociability). To play with the business of life means to gamble.

If you start a game, you are not obligated to continue it. You may drop it because you don't like it or because it bores you or because luck is against you or because you have a headache. Conversely, if you engage in business (job, marriage, the rearing of children, helping a friend, civic activities) you are under obligation to continue it, to see it through, to finish what you have started. Headaches, boredom, dislike, and strain are no justification for shirking the duty you have assumed or the commission you have accepted. Games are personal inclinations; business is a group obligation. Games are pleasures; business is a task. A task may be pleasing, which means that pleasure and task can be combined. But if a game, no matter how pleasurable it is, interferes with the serious task of business, the thing to do is to stop the game and to continue the business. Tasks must have unquestioned priority over games. In life, even a plain conversation with a neighbor acquires the character of a task. It imposes the obligation to be courteous, to be friendly, to show humility, to create goodwill, and to avoid criticism and intellectual snobbishness.

Confrontation

Although you may experience a certain degree of discomfort in using confrontation, it can be a most useful approach in dealing with client resistance. To use it effectively, you may find it helpful to link it to other strategies. For example, the Adlerians often use the "stroke-and-spit" strategy. Cultivating a common social interest and tracking the focus of attention will build a joining-type process—positive stroking. In spitting, the counselor discloses the skillful maneuvers of clients by pointing to the specific behaviors they use to achieve their purposes. Here-and-now behavior is the usual focus, with the disclosure being unpleasant enough that the clients no longer desire to continue the behavior (Nikelly & O'Connell, 1971). If you "spit in someone's soup," they tend not to want to repeat the behavior. Humor and exaggeration can be used to soften a confronting focus. Such a disarming approach will reduce the likelihood of guarded or defensive behavior: "Let's see if we can make it worse" or "You are very clever; by pretending to be weak, you have become powerful."

If your clients are using irrational beliefs to guide their daily living at home, in school, or on the job, it is recommended that you help them become aware of this and deal with it in terms of a chain of events: A–B–C–D–E. To illustrate the use of this procedure, we present the following case, adapted by Weinrach (1980) from a case originally presented by Ellis (1977).

Jose: An Overview

Jose is trying to enter the labor force for the first time. He is an 18-year-old high school graduate with a background in automobile mechanics. His native language is Spanish. His oral English is adequate, but his written expression is poor. His other basic skills are also weak. He reported being depressed because he would never be able to get a job and told of having been rejected after his last job interview. This case is presented to demonstrate the applicability of Ellis's (1977, p. 44) Irrational Idea No. 1: I must do well and win the approval of others for my performance or else I will rate as a rotten person.

Activating Experience (A): Performed poorly during job interview and was subsequently not offered the job.

Beliefs (B)
- *Rational Beliefs* (rB) (wants and desires): I would have liked that job. I don't like getting rejected. Being rejected is a big inconvenience. It was unfortunate that I did so poorly in the interview. Getting a job may be harder than I expected.
- *Irrational Beliefs* (iB) (demands and commands): It is awful that I got rejected. I can't stand being rejected. Being rejected means that I am a rotten person. I'll never get a job that I want. I will always do poorly on job interviews.

Consequence (Emotional) of beliefs about activating experience (C): Depressed, worthless, rejected, helpless, hopeless.

Disputing or debating irrational beliefs (D) (stated in the form of questions): What is so awful about having not been offered a job? What evidence do I have that I can't stand having been rejected? How does having been rejected from one job interview make me a rotten person? How do I know that I will never get a job that I want? Why must I always do poorly on job interviews?

Effects of disputing or debating irrational beliefs (E)
- *Cognitive Effects* (cE): Nothing makes it awful to have been rejected, especially as a lot of people apply for the same job and it is impossible for everybody to get that job; I can stand rejection. This isn't the first time I was turned down, but I don't like the feeling. Being rejected only means that I wasn't offered this particular job and in no way does that make me a rotten person. It is too soon to tell whether or not I'll ever get a job that I like, but being 18 would suggest that I have time on my side. I'll just have to wait and try some more. I don't have to do poorly on job interviews for the rest of my life. Maybe a little practice will help. I do have some bad traits that seem to come out when I am under stress. But all humans have some bad characteristics. If they didn't, they'd be perfect and no human is perfect.

- *Emotional Effects* (eE): I am disappointed but not depressed.
- *Behavioral Effects* (bE): I will go for more job interviews; I will get some lessons from my counselor on how to act during interviews and then practice with my peers and parents. I will register with State Employment and local [Comprehensive Employment and Training Act] program for kids my age.

Summary: As a result of [rational-emotive therapy], Jose ceased making self-deprecatory statements. He also began to see that the situation was not, as he had previously defined it, hopeless. Nor was he helpless. There were things he could do to improve his chances for a job. Once he felt disappointed and not depressed, he regained the emotional energy to try to find a job again.

Note. From "A Rational-Emotive Approach to Occupational Mental Health," by S. G. Weinrach, 1980, *Vocational Guidance Quarterly, 28*(3), pp. 213–214. Copyright 1980 by the American Counseling Association. Adapted with permission. No further reproduction authorized without written permission of the American Counseling Association.

Labeling and Reframing

Labeling and reframing (Bandler & Grinder, 1979; Harman & O'Neill, 1981; King, 1992) clients' expressions provide a way to help them see themselves and their worlds differently. By providing new words and ways of organizing those words, you can help your clients by providing them with new patterns for organizing and viewing their worlds. Motivation and attitudinal changes often are associated with the labeling and reframing processes.

A change of frame is a primary event. A change of label is a secondary consequence. Reframing is changing the frame of reference we use to look at some particular behavior, such as a moral perspective versus a medical perspective or an individual/personal view versus a family systems view. Relabeling should be reserved for those instances in which there is a change in label with no change in frame of reference, for example, neurotic versus psychotic. Both labels are in the medical framework.

An excellent example of reframing occurred in Mark Twain's *Tom Sawyer*. Tom was able to reframe the painting of a white fence from something that was work and undesirable to something that was fun and desirable. His friends accepted his reframing of the task and proceeded to join in painting the fence enthusiastically. This does not mean that all reframing is controlling, but it does provide a different perception that suggests new behavioral responses to an old stimulus.

Labeling and relabeling skills are aimed at extracting your clients' experiences and bringing them to their attention with new verbal descriptions that punctuate their importance. Bolles (2012) did this when he helped people identify their functional job skills. He asked individuals to describe something that they do well. He then related these descriptions as functional job skills. For example, being a good mother and taking care of children is labeled as the functional skill of caring for people and helping others. The homemaker role is divided into various functional skills that can be relabeled as functional skills transferable to other jobs or roles. Labels provide a focus. When clients are considering career decisions, their experiences may need to be relabeled in terms of functional job skills. Academic skills often are relabeled, but social skills, leisure skills, and survival skills are sometimes overlooked.

Relabeling and reframing focus on the positive aspects of individuals. The emphasis is on what persons can do and the competencies they possess. For individuals who typically are described as having a low self-concept, relabeling and reframing techniques can be crucial and may need to be accented continually.

Reframing consists of a change of perception that implies a behavioral response that will be different or accented. This also may involve a change of values. For instance, a con artist and a salesperson have many of the same skills. Negatively described behavior often contains skills needed for survival. For example, reframing the ability to read nonverbal cues may allow the con artist to be successful. These skills also are valuable for a salesperson. Negatives can sometimes be reframed as positives.

Reframing also can be used to confront clients. A paradoxical situation can be created with resistant and unmotivated clients. Inappropriate classroom behavior may be reframed as a means of getting revenge and showing one's power so that the person will feel worthwhile. It is advantageous to reframe descriptions that are not behavioral into behavioral statements. This allows for specifying and interpreting.

Counselor Resistance

Counselor resistance—a strange topic of discussion for a chapter on client resistance? Not really, because resistance, wherever it originates, must be addressed in career counseling, and sometimes it originates in counselors.

Why would resistance originate in counselors? Cavanagh (1982) suggested that need gratification on the part of counselors may be involved. Counselors may have a need to punish, control, or convert clients. He also suggested that counselor dislike for some clients may be part of counselor resistance.

Cavanagh (1982) listed 10 possible signs of counselor resistance. He suggested that a counselor may do any of the following:

1. Cancel appointments or arrive late. (Counselors always have "good reasons" for being late; people in counseling seldom do.)
2. Talk at the person instead of listening *to* and talking *with* the person.
3. Daydream and doze off.
4. Talk about himself or herself instead of about the person in counseling.
5. Forget pertinent information about the person.
6. Set up impossible requirements.
7. Suddenly discover that the person has "a special problem" and try to refer the person to another counselor who specializes in the problem.
8. Refuse to consider as important the areas that the person perceives as important.
9. Be sarcastic or "buddy-buddy" with the person.
10. Introduce areas of discussion that are of interest to him or her but are not necessarily helpful to the person. (p. 261)

In addition to these signs, Meier (2012) suggested that some counselors may have difficulty in dealing with strong client affect and, as a result, may resist dealing with clients' emotional issues. Meier also pointed out that some counselors may resist focusing on client affect "through such acts as talking too much, giving advice, and premature problem solving" (p. 10).

Closing Thoughts

In this chapter we have identified and described ways in which clients or counselors may exhibit resistance during career counseling. Our purpose was to highlight the point that whenever clients are involved in change, client resistance is probably not far behind. In fact, client resistance is to be expected. The topic of change does not actually have to be discussed. Just the thought of possible change stimulated by the presence of a counselor may initiate client resistance. Another purpose was to provide you with a language system for identifying and describing client resistance so that when it is exhibited you will recognize it. Finally, we brought to your attention the fact that sometimes counselors themselves are the problem.

But being able to simply recognize client resistance is not enough, so we also presented sample counseling techniques that can be used to respond to client resistance. Our purpose was to underscore the active role you need to take in dealing with client resistance directly. If you know what the behavior (client resistance) is and you have hypotheses about why it is being exhibited, then you can respond to it directly and naturally within the context of the working alliance. Remember, client resistance impedes progress in career counseling and must be dealt with. At the same time, we have underscored the fact that resistance may not reside only in clients. As counselors, we must examine our motives and understand that although we believe we are part of the solution, at times we may actually be part of the problem.

References

Amundson, N. E., Harris-Bowlsbey, J., & Niles, S. G. (2009). *Essential elements of career counseling* (2nd ed.). Upper Saddle River, NJ: Pearson.

Andersen, P., & Vandehey, M. (2012). *Career counseling and development in a global economy*. Belmont, CA: Brooks/Cole.

Bandler, R., & Grinder, J. (1979). *Frogs into princes*. Moab, VT: Real People Press.

Barner, R. W. (2011). Applying visual metaphors to career transitions. *Journal of Career Development, 38*, 89–106.

Blustein, D. L., & Spengler, P. M. (1995). Personal adjustment: Career counseling and psychotherapy. In W. B. Walsh & S. H. Osipow (Eds.), *Handbook of vocational psychology: Theory, research, and practice* (pp. 295–329). Mahwah, NJ: Erlbaum.

Bolles, R. N. (2012). *What color is your parachute?* Berkeley, CA: Ten Speed Press.

Bourne, E. J. (2010). *The anxiety and phobia workbook* (5th ed.). Oakland, CA: New Harbinger Publications.

Cavanagh, M. E. (1982). *The counseling experience: A theoretical and practical approach*. Belmont, CA: Brooks/Cole.

Dowd, T. E. (1995). Cognitive career assessment: Concepts and applications. *Journal of Career Assessment, 3*, 1–20.

Ellis, A. (1977). *How to live with and without anger*. Pleasantville, NY: Readers Digest Press.

Engle, D., & Arkowitz, H. (2008). Viewing resistance as ambivalence: Integrative strategies for working with resistant ambivalence. *Journal of Humanistic Psychology, 48*, 389–411.

Gold, J. M. (2008). Rethinking client resistance: A narrative approach to integrating resistance into the relationship-building stage of counseling. *Journal of Humanistic Counseling, Education and Development, 47*, 56–70.

Harman, R. L., & O'Neill, C. (1981). Neuro-linguistic programming for counselors. *The Personnel and Guidance Journal, 59*, 449–453.

King, S. M. (1992). Therapeutic utilization of client resistance. *Individual Psychology, 48*(2), 165–174.

Low, A. (1966). *Mental health through will training* (14th ed.). Boston, MA: Christopher.

Manthei, R. J. (2007). Client–counselor agreement on what happens in counselling. *British Journal of Guidance & Counselling, 35*, 261–281.

Meara, N. M., & Patton, M. J. (1994). Contributions of the working alliance in the practice of career counseling. *The Career Development Quarterly, 43*, 161–177.

Meier, S. T. (2012). *Language and narratives in counseling and psychotherapy*. New York, NY: Springer.

Miller, G. (2006). *Using motivational interviewing in career counseling.* Retrieved from http://209.235.208.145/cgi-bin/WebSuite/tcsAssnWebSuite.pl?Action=DisplayNe wsDetails&RecordID=771&Sections=&IncludeDropped=1&AssnID=NCDA&DBCo de=130285

Nikelly, A. G., & O'Connell, W. E. (1971). Action-oriented methods. In A. G. Nikelly (Ed.), *Techniques for behavior change* (pp. 85–90). Springfield, IL: Charles C Thomas.

Peterson, C. (2006). *A primer in positive psychology.* New York, NY: Oxford University Press.

Pryor, R. G. L. (2010). A framework for chaos theory career counseling. *Australian Journal of Career Development, 19*, 32–39.

Shulman, B. H., & Mosak, H. H. (1967). Various purposes of symptoms. *Journal of Individual Psychology, 23*, 79–87.

Snyder, C. R., Higgins, R. L., & Stucky, R. J. (1983). *Excuses: Masquerades in search of grace.* New York, NY: Wiley.

Teyber, E., & McClure, F. H. (2011). *Interpersonal process in therapy: An integrative model* (6th ed.). Belmont, CA: Brooks/Cole, Cengage Learning.

Vogel, D. L., Wester, S. R., & Larson, L. M. (2007). Avoidance of counseling: Psychological factors that inhibit seeking help. *Journal of Counseling & Development, 85*, 410–422.

Walborn, F. S. (1996). *Process variables: Four common elements of counseling and psychotherapy.* Pacific Grove, CA: Brooks/Cole.

Weinrach, S. G. (1980). A rational-emotive approach to occupational mental health. *Vocational Guidance Quarterly, 28*(3), 208–218.

Wickman, S. A., Daniels, M. H., White, L. J., & Fesmire, S. A. (1999). A "primer" in conceptual metaphor for counselors. *Journal of Counseling & Development, 77*, 389–394.

PART THREE
Client Goal or
Problem Resolution

Chapter 16

Using Information, Taking Action, and Developing Plans of Action

We find ourselves in the midst of revolution, and the implications are far reaching. It is a revolution not of the sword but of the word. Career counselors, like most people, now have phenomenal access to the printed word and to information. This revolution brings power to everyone, particularly the educated. We may find ourselves with an additional responsibility to bring the benefits of the revolution to the less educated and to the many clients who, because of poverty or other forms of marginalization, do not have the same access to technology.

Not long ago this chapter would have focused primarily on how and where you could find career information and then would have stressed the importance of making it available to clients to use as they developed plans of action for themselves. We now are at a point where the information is often too readily available, and, in fact, sometimes there is too much of it to be useful. Whereas clients once might have been forced to make decisions with too little information, today they are more apt to be confronted with how to make decisions with too much information. Counselors need to be able to recognize symptoms or complaints of information overload—not necessarily good information, and too much of it. The key issue for career counselors today is identifying accurately the real needs clients have for career information. Once needs are established, other issues, such as why and when to provide career information, how to provide it, how much to provide, which sources are good, and how to help sort out the quality of the information, become important concerns.

In this chapter, then, we discuss how to identify clients' needs for information, clients' problems objectifying these needs, our own needs for gathering information, why and when we must provide information, assessments that help us with the process, and some good sources of information. This chapter demonstrates that the appropriate and effective use of career information is an important task, but not a simple one, and discusses how it comes into play as we help clients develop plans of action for themselves.

Identifying Client Needs for Information

We should not assume that all of our clients need career information. Although they may present themselves as needing information, this could mask other concerns. They may come to us believing they only need information, but in the first few minutes of the initial interview they may suggest that other issues are more pressing and that information may instead be useful later. Or you may see that responding to a simple request for information only further confuses rather than solves a problem. Information is powerful, but it can be confusing, overwhelming, or seemingly irrelevant if not offered at the right time (Schwartz, 2005). Knowing whether, when, and how to provide it is part of the essence of good career counseling. Information must be harnessed and offered in appropriate ways to be beneficial. Career counselors develop skills at doing this, which can make them particularly helpful at times when those without such skills may not be so helpful.

Review here some typical client requests that have been expressed in early career counseling sessions. Try to ascertain whether the need is for information and if (or when) providing it would be helpful.

A 55-year-old woman recently divorced:

> *Client:* I don't know what to do next. I never thought I would have to work outside the home, but now without a husband to support me, I need to find a career for myself.

An 18-year-old college freshman:

> *Client:* Everyone in the family is in medicine, and I always thought I would be, too. But now I'm not so sure. I'm good in science and I like it, but what else can I do with it? I'm not sure I want to be in school for 10 years, and besides, I don't see myself working with sick people or in a hospital.

A 50-year-old Navy officer about to retire:

> *Client:* I've enjoyed 20 years overseas doing maintenance and supply work, but where can I apply those skills in civilian life?

A seemingly disappointed college graduate:

> *Client:* I'm not doing the kind of work I thought I would, and I don't see any way out of the job I have. I don't know what else I can do with only a major in journalism.

These four clients represent quite different life situations, although not necessarily different needs. The recently divorced woman who never thought she would have to work outside the home may be much like the college freshman just discovering the need to think about something other than medicine. Neither felt much need to think about alternatives until recently. But how each will deal with this recent need for information may make our responses to their requests quite different. Both seem to need information, but we do not immediately know what other needs may be confounding their situations. For example, is the recently divorced woman still dealing with the end of a long-term marriage so that she cannot look objectively at alternatives? Is the college freshman looking for an alternative to medicine only because she is disappointed at not being in what she thought would be some exciting classes the first year in college? Clearly, we need more clarity about their situations before we can assess their needs for information.

The naval officer who spent 20 years overseas may seem like a classic example of someone in need of information, given that he wants to move into another career. But we must be careful not to assume he is not coming to us with a fairly clear agenda and much information, only asking us to confirm his choice. Again, we will need more clarity about his situation before deciding if and when more information would be appropriate. Finally, the disappointed college graduate working at an entry-level job that does not meet her needs may really be more concerned with remedying the present situation than with looking for an attractive alternative. We clearly do not yet have enough information to be helpful in any of the cases presented.

A common theme in all of these cases is that it is difficult to judge the need for career information before we have assessed a client's total situation. A request taken at face value in an opening session too often leads to the provision of career information either not needed or not valued at that time. Our diagnostic skills are important here: We are trying first to appropriately assess our clients' situations, and only then can we decide whether, when, how, and what kind of career information is needed.

A further nuance of making a decision to respond to the need for career information is the professional judgment you must make regarding how the client will make use of that information. You can build a case for a client who has a simple need for information, and you will provide it. You can observe that it is helpful and that it is being incorporated appropriately into the client's thought processes. Other times, however, you may provide information but observe that little use is being made of it or, worse yet, that it is being used inappropriately. A client is seemingly moving toward some new option but ignores the new information provided. These examples further argue for the need to adequately assess the need for information before providing it.

Career Information Needs From a Perceptual Point of View

In career counseling we are acutely aware of the importance of a perceptual frame of reference. So often the issue is not what reality is but what one perceives it to be. Our perceptions may tell us one thing, the client's perceptions another. When we engage in deciding on whether, when, and how to provide career information, we may err in favor of seeing this as an objective process. We may perceive a need for particular information and then try to find and provide it, considering ourselves experts at doing so. But let us look at why that approach, from a perceptual point of view, may not serve our clients' needs.

When a client comes to us with a perceived need for information, we accept this as an accurate perception. We provide the information, and then perceptions of career opportunities, for example, become more accurate. Encouraged by this, we provide more information but then begin to see that the additional information is not being used appropriately. For example, the client may ignore some of it or distort other bits of it. In our objectivity, we see the need to reinforce some ideas or correct others. The process becomes more complicated because the client filters what is said; only some parts are heard, and other parts heard are distorted. We begin to wonder if we are miscommunicating. The reality we see is not the reality the client sees. We can begin to understand that, like understanding the initial problem in counseling, we have a similar difficulty perceiving the need for the most appropriate time to provide career information and how it should or will be used.

It may appear that the simple process of the counselor providing career information is very complicated. We intend to present it that way. The process involves not simply drawing on resources from the library, computerized systems, or the Internet. It is a complicated process that demands the same care and attention we give all other parts of the counseling process. Because we need to be sensitive to the pervasive role of information at all phases of counseling, we must acquire an in-depth appreciation of not only what is available but also how, when, and in what form to provide it.

Looking at Our Own Needs for Information

Although we must examine carefully our clients' needs for information, we should also consider our own needs for acquiring and making use of these expanding sources of information. The information explosion and changing notions about work, leisure, employment, and life roles mean we must constantly search for new resources if we are to keep ourselves current. To be creative in helping clients prepare for an ever-changing world, we must become comfortable and conversant with materials from a variety of sources. It would appear as though one form of media may become particularly good at providing some kinds of information, whereas another form of media may become the key source for other kinds of information. Although we may prefer one source more than another, we eventually will have to draw on all sources. We must become masters of information and current technology to remain informed and effective. This means maintaining some subscriptions to printed materials, using resources on video, accessing company home pages and chat rooms, communicating via teleconferencing, and a whole lot more. In-service programs and continuing education in new media forms are essential for us, because professional expectations are changing for us as well as for our clients.

At the same time we are encouraged to learn more about information available through technology, we need to keep a perspective on the more traditional ways many of our clients will continue to access career information. We can, for example, speculate on the influence of computerized information in much the same way that we can look back on the influence of television. Although the potential was enormous, it took time before television became the pervasive influence it is today. Over time it became a dominant influence in most homes, but, more important, significant numbers of people still do not have access to television today. Similarly, large numbers of people still do not have access to computers or technology in general. Although career information may come to us in technologically sophisticated ways, there will continue to be significant numbers of people—many of them our clients—who will access information in other ways. In fact, for some, important resources for information will continue to be limited to more personal, informal sources that do not receive much coverage in this book. These important sources include family, relatives, community members, elders, ministers, peers, teachers, and other people with whom we as counselors may never interact. Nonetheless, these people may exert more influence on our clients through word-of-mouth communication than any information we may find electronically.

Whatever the sources, being able to know, retrieve, and access up-to-date information will become even more of a challenge. It is a task far beyond the reasonable efforts of any one individual. The journals of some of our professional organizations try to provide regular reviews of career-related materials, as do most publishers. Although initially these were almost exclusively reviews of print materials, you will increasingly find reviews of audio tapes, videos, films, CD-ROMs, and similar new sources of information.

Why We Provide Information

Beyond the fact that clients believe they have needs for information, providing information within the career counseling process serves numerous purposes. These purposes are either educational or motivational.

In the educational realm, we can hypothesize that information will inform thought, expand and extend it, or correct it. These are distinctly different purposes, and the ways in which we approach providing information in each of these categories are quite different. Informing the thought process is a far simpler task than correcting it.

To inform might be a straightforward process, whereas to correct may involve helping someone give up information that has served a seemingly useful purpose for some time. For example, a client may hold on to the distorted impression that she cannot go back to school because she did not complete high school or a college degree program years ago. By holding on to that information, she may not consider many attractive career alternatives, believing that she would not have access to them.

We may find it helpful to think of these differences as one would in advertising. Are we telling someone about the product, informing them of additional benefits of the product, or correcting their impressions of the product? If, for example, a person has a distorted impression of a product, we have a far different task than simply providing information.

In the motivational realm, we use information to stimulate, challenge, and confirm. Perhaps the biggest challenge in career counseling is learning to use information in a motivational way.

Some information by itself would not be motivating, but provided at the proper moment it may make all the difference in a career planning process. Some kinds of information can prove to be motivating before one makes a decision, and other kinds of information are more important after one makes a decision. Before making a decision clients may only hear the global or general information about a career possibility, but later, having made a decision to enter a particular field, they may be open to hearing more of the specifics about their choice.

When you consider the millions of dollars advertisers spend to motivate us to use their products, you have a perspective on our task. Counselors must stimulate or challenge clients with career information—a formidable task even for those with unlimited budgets. We must learn to do it with appreciation of what we refer to as *teachable moments*. These moments come when you have information to give your client that your client feels can be used at a particular time. This is another way we claim our professional identity: We are experts at knowing when to provide information.

When to Use Career Information in Counseling

Timing is everything. This adage is especially true in decisions about when to use career information. Given that making a career decision is an ongoing process, it is appropriate to find ways to provide information at all three phases of the process. In Phase 1 (Exploration), we may need to be assessing the clients' needs for information as they begin a process of exploring a variety of concerns. The process may have us hypothesizing about the clients' needs for information as well as their other needs. For example, a client might lack information and know it, or lack it and not know it; a client may have adequate information and be using it appropriately, or have adequate information and not be using it appropriately or be distorting it; or a client may have more than enough information and be coping with it, or he or she may be overwhelmed by it.

We can offer a 2 × 3 table as a way of conceptualizing where clients are initially: They come with too little information, about the right amount, or too much, and, on the other dimension, they either know it or do not know it (see Figure 16-1).

We could provide examples of clients who fit into each of these categories, and we could suggest hypotheses about when to provide information for each of them. The art and science of these hypotheses would not be that exact, but clearly clients with too little

	Information		
	Too little	About right	Too much
Client Status — Knows it			
Client Status — Does not know it			

Figure 16-1. Client Status Versus Available Career Information

information should initially be treated in a manner different from ones who have too much information. And clients who know what they need are different from those who lack insight into what they need. Our diagnostic skills, as always, are taxed and honed in identifying just where our clients are as they begin the career counseling process. What makes it even more complicated but fascinating is that the initial categorization can change quickly; we may find that one who begins with too little information and knows it suddenly becomes confused by too much information. Or, vice versa, a client with too much information may sort it out quickly and need more information.

Phase 1 (Exploration) in a career decision-making model leads to Phase 2 (Understanding). In Phase 2, we can confirm any hypotheses we made in Phase 1 about our clients' needs for information. If we thought they needed information and we provided it, we can observe in subsequent counseling sessions whether it has been incorporated and whether it has influenced their understanding. If not, we may need to try a different tactic. We know that sometimes clients do not understand the first time through, and this requires that we explore other ways. Because career counseling is an ongoing process, we can review and process again and again. We only hope to improve on our clients' understanding before they reach Phase 3 (Action), when they act on information. This three-phase model is portrayed graphically in Figure 16-2. It emphasizes the ongoing nature of the process, the way in which we constantly depend on feedback from our clients to refine the process, and the clear need to make ongoing assessments about the timing of the provision of information. It is a far more complex and interesting process than first meets the eye. It is one more place where we can practice and refine our skills as counselors.

Helping Assess the Need for Information

If clients find it difficult to assess their needs for career information, we might want to enhance their judgments or our own by looking for clues in some of the assessment tools frequently used in career counseling. The My Vocational Situation presented in Chapter 13, for example, provides a quick indication of what clients might need at the time they present themselves for counseling. It provides a vocational identity score (1–18), with a low score suggesting that clients have an unclear picture of their career situation. This

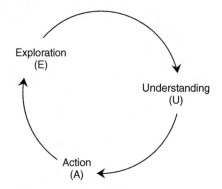

Figure 16-2. A Decision-Making Model Applied to Career Counseling

may be one indicator of a need for career information. In addition, Question 19 specifically asks clients about their needs for information in various areas. The Career Transitions Inventory, also discussed in Chapter 13, also helps both clients and counselors see particular needs. The Intake Scale or Hope Scale (Lopez, 2013) can suggest an apparent need to establish goals or find pathways for clients. In addition, clients with low or flat profiles on interest inventories may be ones who need more information. However, clients may be all too clear about their needs for information, or their initial presentation of a concern makes obvious their needs. We do not want to suggest that you not take their judgments seriously, but we do want to caution you to continually assess the need. It can be deceiving, because some clients believe the more information the better, and it can change quickly, leaving either the client or the counselor confused about the importance of providing information. Barry Schwartz's (2005) book *The Paradox of Choice: Why More Is Less* effectively makes the point that having more information does not make making decisions easier.

Establishing How Much Information Is Helpful

Nothing is more helpful in refining a process than feedback. We can ask clients for feedback, but sometimes it is not easy for them to provide it. We can suggest they look up something as homework, or we can ask that they try a computerized career information system like SIGI (System of Interactive Guidance and Information) or one of many such systems, or we can suggest they look at some information available on the Internet and then inquire in the next session as to how helpful it was. We can ask them to bring career information to the session for further discussion. If we make use of it within the counseling process, we can observe immediately how it is being used or incorporated into our clients' thinking. We then have one more clue as to the need and the effectiveness of the information being provided.

Feedback is important both during and after the counseling process. Too often we can be left wondering if the information provided was actually used and, if so, whether it was as useful as we thought. Without some kind of feedback from former clients, we miss the opportunity to improve our own use of career information. Encourage clients to stay in touch or drop a note after a reasonable time to let you know what was helpful. Some counselors or agencies routinely send form letters to clients several weeks after termination and request feedback. This practice encourages both reflection and evaluation that can be useful to both you and your clients.

Sources of Career Information

There are many good sources of career information. Some texts are particularly good at describing and defining the information available (D. Brown, 2012; Zunker, 2006). But there has been an explosion of new information and sources as well. More information is available on video, in computerized systems, and, most recently, on the World Wide Web. Clients are not apt to have equal access to all these sources, and yet, because "information is power," one of our roles is to help our clients grasp that power. To do so, we need to be comfortable with all of these sources ourselves.

We cannot overstate the impact of technology in making information available to people, including our clients. As we write this, we see many of our standard career informational references available on the World Wide Web. The *Occupational Outlook Handbook* (Bureau of Labor Statistics, 2013/2014), for example, is easily accessed complete with pictures on the Web. This is one of many resources promoted through the National Association of Colleges and Employers. Employment Opportunities and Job

Resources on the Internet, commonly known as the Riley Guide, provides users with immediate access to resources previously available only to a select few. The U.S. Department of Labor collects information on all major jobs and provides it in a database called the Occupational Information Network, or O*NET (http://onetonline.org). It also now includes a career interest inventory and a career values inventory. See the Appendix that appears at the end of this chapter for ways to access these resources online. Most companies maintain sites on the Web where users can access extensive, up-to-date information that may be of help in job searches. Home pages allow users to send information about themselves to prospective employers. Résumés can be constructed and sent via the Internet. CD-ROM technology and Web technology have merged to make available unlimited information with links to Web sites that can provide constant updates. Peterson's guides to both undergraduate and graduate schools are available on the Web. Virtual career centers are on the Web, as are career assessments. In short, whatever was available in print is now available electronically at competitive prices. We are probably at a point when various media—print, computer, video, and other sources—will merge in creative ways. In the meantime, we can expect a continued explosion of ever-changing career information.

Using the Internet to complement your sources of career information and other career planning resources is essential. However, it is not yet a science but more of an art. New sites appear almost daily. Sites you start to rely on one day are gone the next. It may, however, be useful to bookmark particularly good sites for your personal use. Find ones in those areas where you most need information on a routine basis. The Appendix to this chapter presents a representative (not exhaustive) sampling of current sites on the Web that may be helpful to both career counselors and clients. We list ones our staff members in a college career center have found to be particularly useful. As these invariably change, log on to the University of Missouri Career Center home page (http://career.missouri.edu/) for updates. Even though some links will have changed by the time you read this, by accessing them you will learn of links to other career-related sites. Bookmark those you find to be most useful in working with clients. Whether information is on the Web or in print form, on CD-ROM or on audio tape, our basic skills as counselors are further challenged by helping clients find this career information and use it to their advantage.

Some Less Obvious Sources of Career Information

Increasingly, we are counseling clients who either do not have access to the many sources of career information just described or, equally important, do have access and yet continue to rely on other sources. For many clients of different ethnic, religious, or cultural backgrounds the family, elders in the church or tribe, or a prophet, sage, or some other authority may be the ultimate source of information. We do not shape or influence these sources in the same way that we shape and describe the use of computerized systems, but we must learn to appreciate and understand the importance of these influences. This is another important reason why we need to listen for feedback from our clients. We cannot assume they will find our sources as useful as the ones they are already using. We need to listen for subtle clues about what the really meaningful sources of information are for our clients. Too often these are not brought into the conversation, significantly diminishing the impact of our time together with clients. The importance of understanding another's background in an increasingly global world is a fascinating and essential perspective for career counselors. We must try to weave together a variety of sources and recognize that the ultimate decisions made in career counseling are not ones we necessarily need to explain in any objective fashion. This may be one way to view the process, but clearly it is not the preferred way for many of our clients. The more you work with clients from different backgrounds, the more you learn that your way is only one of many ways.

Methods of gathering, sorting, evaluating, and deciding whether to use information and whether to act on it may be dependent on ethnicity, race, gender, sexual orientation, cultural or socioeconomic background, and a host of other variables. We can only learn so much about these differences from our textbooks. Much will always depend on listening well to our clients. In preparation for that, when assigned a client from a different racial or ethnic background, you might want first to inventory your own experience with such differences. Ward and Bingham (1993) created the Multicultural Career Counseling Checklist for Counselors (see Table 16-1), which is "designed to help you think more thoroughly about the racially or ethnically different client to whom you are . . . providing career counseling" (p. 250). You simply read and check the statements that apply. By doing so, you learn what you know and what you need to find out from your client.

Ward and Tate (1990) created the Career Counseling Checklist for Clients (see Table 16-2), later modified by Ward and Bingham (1993), which serves as a checklist for the client to tell you what he or she knows about the world of work and the influences of age, gender, disability, and socioeconomic background. It also includes questions regarding the role of the family in career decision making. When administered early or before counseling, it not only provides you with useful information from your client on important issues but also communicates that you are interested in making these issues part of career counseling. You may find you want to establish still other ways of ensuring that you remain open to learning about these differences.

Making effective use of career information, now available in a wide variety of forms, is a daunting challenge for career counselors. We now have all the information out there that we need; the challenge is to help our clients sort out what is needed, when it is needed, how and when it can best be used, and what the important sources are. Helping clients to put it all together for themselves can be a complicated but fascinating process that draws on many of our professional skills.

Developing Plans of Action

Seeing our clients take proactive steps with their career plans is one of the truly rewarding parts of the career counseling process. Helping them turn a dream into reality is validating and affirming for both the counselor and the client. How this happens is sometimes the result of a well-developed set of goals and a plan of action, and other times it happens in seemingly unsystematic and unexplainable ways. Career goals and a plan of action are best understood or explained when they follow a rational set of steps. We know other times the process seems quite intuitive, and, particularly for members of racial and ethnic minority groups and for women, the process of getting to where one wants to be can be nonlinear and perhaps even circular, with the process recycling through various layers of the decision. Either way, helping clients become clear about their career goals and establishing plans of action is another important step that deserves our attention as part of the career counseling process.

In this section, we begin by looking at the outcomes we can expect to emerge from career counseling. This leads us naturally to a closer examination of the process by which such outcomes or goals or plans come to be formulated. Finally, we conclude with a section on some techniques that will increase the chances that clients leave career counseling with the career plans and goals they envision for themselves.

Table 16-1. Multicultural Career Counseling Checklist for Counselors

If you have a client of a different ethnicity/race than yours, you may wish to use this checklist as you begin to do the career assessment with your client.

The following statements are designed to help you think more thoroughly about the racially or ethnically different client to whom you are about to provide career counseling. Check all the statements that apply.

My racial/ethnic identity _____
My client's racial/ethnic identity _____

I. Counselor Preparation
❑   1. I am familiar with minimum cross-cultural counseling competencies.
❑   2. I am aware of my client's cultural identification.
❑   3. I understand and respect my client's culture.
❑   4. I am aware of my own world view and how it was shaped.
❑   5. I am aware of how my socioeconomic status (SES) influences my ability to empathize with this client.
❑   6. I am aware of how my political views influence my counseling with a client from this ethnic group.
❑   7. I have had counseling or other life experiences with different racial/ethnic groups.
❑   8. I have information about this client's ethnic group's history, local sociopolitical issues, and her attitudes toward seeking help.
❑   9. I know many of the strengths of this client's ethnic group.
❑ 10. I know where I am in my racial identity development.
❑ 11. I know the general stereotypes held about my client's ethnic group.
❑ 12. I am comfortable confronting ethnic minority clients.
❑ 13. I am aware of the importance that the interaction of gender and race/ethnicity has in my client's life.

II. Exploration and Assessment
❑   1. I understand this client's career questions.
❑   2. I understand how the client's career questions may be complicated with issues of finance, family, and academics.
❑   3. The client is presenting racial and/or cultural information with the career questions.
❑   4. I am aware of the career limitations or obstacles the client associates with her race or culture.
❑   5. I understand what the client's perceived limitations are.
❑   6. I know the client's perception of her family's ethnocultural identification.
❑   7. I am aware of the client's perception of her family's support for her career.
❑   8. I know which career the client believes her family wants her to pursue.
❑   9. I know whether the client's family's support is important to her.
❑ 10. I believe that familial obligations are dictating the client's career choices.
❑ 11. I know the extent of exposure to career information and role models the client had in high school and beyond.
❑ 12. I understand the impact that high school experiences (positive or negative) have had on the client's confidence.
❑ 13. I am aware of the client's perception of her competence, ability, and self-efficacy.
❑ 14. I believe the client avoids certain work environments because of fears of sexism or racism.
❑ 15. I know the client's stage of racial identity development.

III. Negotiation and Working Consensus
❑   1. I understand the type of career counseling help the client is seeking (career choice, supplement of family income, professional career, etc.).
❑   2. The client and I have agreed on the goals for career counseling.
❑   3. I know how this client's role as a woman in family influences her career choices.
❑   4. I am aware of the client's perception of the woman's work role in her family and in her culture.
❑   5. I am aware of the client's understanding of the role of children in her career plans.
❑   6. I am aware of the extent of exposure to a variety of career role models the client has had.
❑   7. I understand the culturally based career conflicts that are generated by exposure to more careers and role models.
❑   8. I know the client's career aspirations.
❑   9. I am aware of the level of confidence the client has in her ability to obtain her aspirations.
❑ 10. I know the client understands the relationship between type of work and educational level.
❑ 11. I am aware of the negative and/or self-defeating thoughts that are obstacles to the client's aspirations and expectations.
❑ 12. I know if the client and I need to renegotiate her goals as appropriate after exploring cultural and family issues.
❑ 13. I know the client understands the career exploration process.

(Continued on next page)

Table 16-1. Multicultural Career Counseling Checklist for Counselors *(Continued)*

III. Negotiation and Working Consensus (Continued)

❑ 14. I am aware of the client's expectations about the career counseling process.
❑ 15. I know when it is appropriate to use a traditional career assessment instrument with a client from this ethnic group.
❑ 16. I know which instrument to use with this client.
❑ 17. I am aware of the research support for using the selected instrument with clients of this ethnicity.
❑ 18. I am aware of nontraditional instruments that might be more appropriate for use with clients from this ethnic group.
❑ 19. I am aware of nontraditional approaches to using traditional instruments with clients from this ethnic group.
❑ 20. I am aware of the career strengths the client associates with her race or culture.

Note. From "Career Assessment of Ethnic Minority Women" by C. M. Ward and R. P. Bingham, 1993, *Journal of Career Assessment, 1*, pp. 246–257. Copyright 1993 by Sage Publications, Inc. Reprinted with permission. All rights reserved. Further reproduction is prohibited without permission from Sage Publications, Inc.

What Clients Take From Career Counseling

When one looks carefully at the research evidence on outcomes from career counseling, it is easy to conclude that it is a valued and helpful process (Heppner & Hendricks, 1995; Phillips, 1992). In fact, the effects reported in a summative manner from a variety of studies of career interventions (S. D. Brown & Ryan Krane, 2000; Spokane, 1991; Spokane & Oliver, 1983) suggest that the outcomes may be even more impressive than what are reported as outcomes for psychotherapy. This should make us inquire as to what clients say happens for them in career counseling. What is it that they report as being so helpful?

For one thing, we often hear clients express a new or renewed sense of hope or determination about doing something they said they wanted to do. In terms we introduced earlier in the book, they may have a better sense of agency or hope (Lopez, 2013) and talk in clearer terms about the pathways to follow in pursuit of their goals. Their "goals" are not to be confused with our "goal" of creating a strong working alliance. In the working alliance, we reference goals to be achieved in the counseling relationship—goals important to our working together as counselor and client—whereas here we reference goals as some specifics to be worked on in creating a plan of action for the client.

Clients will attribute much to counseling and to the support, understanding, and encouragement they feel from their counselor and from the relationship they experienced (Fuller & Hill, 1985; Heppner & Hendricks, 1995). We should not overlook the importance of this relationship, and perhaps the process of career counseling will eventually prove to be far more important than has been reported. It may, however, be more difficult to collect evidence of its importance than of the more objective changes one can observe.

We will often hear about new discoveries or insights from career counseling; these can be clients' learnings or insights about themselves or about opportunities for themselves. Reports of changes in the way clients see themselves or their opportunities are common in the research on outcomes of career counseling (Holland, Magoon, & Spokane, 1981).

We should be encouraged by the evidence of all that can be attributed to career counseling, but we do not want to overlook what happens within the process. Clients come to new understandings and insights and see new opportunities for themselves, but how does this happen? How do they put things together for themselves? How do their goals and a career plan of action emerge, and what do we do to encourage such planning?

In a comprehensive review of 62 recent studies of career counseling (S. D. Brown & Ryan Krane, 2000), there emerged considerable support for the idea that positive outcomes are related to the inclusion of five critical ingredients. Although any one of them

Table 16-2. Career Counseling Checklist for Clients

The following statements are designed to help you think more thoroughly about your career concerns and to help your assessment counselor understand you better. Please try to answer them as honestly as possible. Check all of the items that are true for you.

❑ 1. I feel obligated to do what others want me to do, and these expectations conflict with my own desires.
❑ 2. I have lots of interests, but I do not know how to narrow them down.
❑ 3. I am afraid of making a serious mistake with my career choice.
❑ 4. I do not feel confident that I know in which areas my true interests lie.
❑ 5. I feel uneasy with the responsibility for making a good career choice.
❑ 6. I lack information about my skills, interests, needs, and values with regard to my career choice.
❑ 7. My physical ability may greatly influence my career choice.
❑ 8. I lack knowledge about the world of work and what it has to offer me.
❑ 9. I know what I want my career to be, but it doesn't feel like a realistic goal.
❑ 10. I feel I am the only one who does not have a career plan.
❑ 11. I lack knowledge about myself and what I have to offer the world of work.
❑ 12. I do not really know what is required from a career for me to feel satisfied.
❑ 13. I feel that problems in my personal life are hindering me from making a good career decision.
❑ 14. My ethnicity may influence my career choice.
❑ 15. No matter how much information I have about a career, I keep going back and forth and cannot make up my mind.
❑ 16. I tend to be a person who gives up easily.
❑ 17. I believe that I am largely to blame for the lack of success I feel in making a career decision.
❑ 18. I have great difficulty making most decisions about my life.
❑ 19. My age may influence my career choice.
❑ 20. I expect my career decision to take care of most of the boredom and emptiness that I feel.
❑ 21. I have difficulty making commitments.
❑ 22. I don't have any idea of what I want in life, who I am, or what's important to me.
❑ 23. I have difficulty completing things.
❑ 24. I am afraid of making mistakes.
❑ 25. Religious values may greatly influence my career choice.
❑ 26. At this point, I am thinking more about finding a job than about choosing a career.
❑ 27. Family responsibilities will probably limit my career ambitions.
❑ 28. My orientation to career is very different from that of the members of my family.
❑ 29. I have worked on a job that taught me some things about what I want or do not want in a career, but I still feel lost.
❑ 30. Some classes in school are much easier for me than others, but I don't know how to use this information.
❑ 31. My race may greatly influence my career choice.
❑ 32. My long-term goals are more firm than my short-term goals.
❑ 33. I have some career-related daydreams that I do not share with many people.
❑ 34. I have been unable to see a connection between my college work and a possible career.
❑ 35. I have made a career choice with which I am comfortable, but I need specific assistance in finding a job.
❑ 36. My gender may influence my career choice.
❑ 37. I have undergone a change in my life, which necessitates a change in my career plans.
❑ 38. My fantasy is that there is one perfect job for me, if I can find it.
❑ 39. I have been out of the world of work for a period of time and I need to redefine my career choice.
❑ 40. Making a great deal of money is an important career goal for me, but I am unsure as to how I might reach it.
❑ 41. My immigration status may influence my career choice.

Note. From "Career Assessment of Ethnic Minority Women" by C. M. Ward and R. P. Bingham, 1993, *Journal of Career Assessment, 1*, pp. 246–257. Copyright 1993 by Sage Publications, Inc. Reprinted with permission. All rights reserved. Further reproduction is prohibited without permission from Sage Publications, Inc.

is important, the combination of the five seems the most powerful. The five, in no particular order, are written exercises, individualized interpretations and feedback, information on the world of work, vicarious learning experiences such as exposure to models who have attained success in the career exploration process, and attention to building support for one's career choices. We suggest a few ways of incorporating each of these into career counseling and encourage you to think of other creative ways of doing so. If each is important, and a combination of all is more important, we need to attend to creatively incorporating all of them into our interventions. We also refer you to the chapter by S. D. Brown and Ryan Krane (2000) for a more thorough description of their important findings.

The first ingredient is the incorporation of written exercises. We might include a simple intake form that requires the clients to write briefly about themselves. We might ask them to complete a series of incomplete sentences about their career plans. Completing the Occupational Dreams Inventory, for example, may make clients focus on past, present, and future career plans.

The second ingredient to include in counseling is individualized interpretations and feedback. These may be comments on written papers or exercises, comments made about career plans in counseling sessions, or interpretations of tests or inventories. The usefulness of such feedback depends on providing it in the context of a strong working alliance. Only in that context will it be seen as important and meaningful to the client.

Third, we provide information on the world of work. We may assume our clients know and can use information and do not need help finding it. However, we devoted the larger part of this chapter to stressing not being too quick to assume what our clients' needs and understandings are regarding career information.

S. D. Brown and Ryan Krane (2001) added an interesting observation of their own a year later, after reviewing their earlier findings: "Studies that have asked clients to rate how helpful different aspects of the interventions were to them consistently [report] the most helpful activities [were] those designed to help clients search for and use occupational information" (p. 6). Specifically, the use of career information within counseling sessions was highlighted as opposed to the more common practice of giving a client homework to locate and examine career information.

Fourth, we provide vicarious learning experiences. We can expose our clients to role models who have attained success in their chosen fields of study. On the college campus, that may mean finding peers, faculty and staff members, community members, and alumni who are open to being interviewed about their work.

Fifth, we build support for clients' career choices. This may mean emotional or social support. It may mean helping clients make connections with people in our network or other ways of helping them expand on their own networks of professional contacts. We may promote rehearsals and immediate reinforcement of career plans that are brought up in counseling sessions.

Earlier in this chapter, we presented career decision making as a three-part process. The first phase was Exploration, the second Understanding, and the third Action. It is a continuous process, with one phase leading to the next and so forth. As you learn more about yourself, you may see a need for more information about the work world before taking action. This may be a good representation of the process as followed by some clients, and we believe it is probably close to the way a systematic person would proceed. It is a crude representation at best, but it does accurately represent three phases that are continually changing in an equation. It may be more difficult to represent the way other, less systematic clients proceed. We know, for example, that an intuitive and nonlinear process may be equally effective for some clients (Gelatt & Gelatt, 2003). We explore in Chapter 2 how a theory of planned happenstance and a personal career theory (Holland, 1997) might be equally effective processes. In short, we must be careful not to impose one process when another would better serve a client. By using one model or a combination of models, however, we try to help clients move toward some plan of action.

Whichever model proves most helpful to your thinking about the process, know that you should place an emphasis on eventually taking some action. It may be short-term or long-term action, within the time frame of counseling or well after it, but career counseling should provide a framework for good planning. And although clients may talk about other outcomes of counseling, some of those do not require you to do anything in particular. A good goal or plan of action usually requires discussion, refinement, rehearsal, modifications, and a whole lot more before being successfully implemented. Clients need help with these steps, and there are a variety of things we can do to improve the chances that they will eventually act on them.

Defining Career Goals and Plans of Action

To be logical, we want to have a plan before we take action. This may not always be true, but that is the order we give it—plan, then act. We often speak of our goals, for example, and then, with help from others, set about trying to devise a plan of action for achieving them. This plan can be simple or complex, short or long term, individual or group, specific or general, but it always involves some goal(s) that should be understandable and achievable. In career counseling, we help the client put together an understandable scheme for achieving particular goals that becomes the plan of action. It is true that most of us do not set goals or make plans on a regular basis, but we admire the few who do. Career plans usually emerge from a process of setting goals. Once goals are identified, we look for ways to achieve them.

The Basics of Planning

Like career counseling, a career plan needs to be seen as an ever-evolving process. Although we can characterize the planning part or action phase as the last part of the three-part process, the whole is more accurately a continuous process or loop in which one may be working simultaneously on all three parts—exploring and understanding about self, exploring and understanding about one's environment, and, equally important, exploring and understanding how to act on these insights or learnings.

Out of career counseling, then, should come plans of action, concrete objective steps for doing something differently from the way one did it before. What do we know about making plans that would be helpful to clients who may have had little experience with the process? There are a number of things to impart to clients during the process of counseling. Most important, recognize that counselors can set the stage for developing goals and making plans as early as the first session. In fact, it should be communicated early on that goals and plans of action are expected outcomes of career counseling. Clients may need to be instructed on this early and often. We can easily become comfortable with simply talking about a plan and never actually making one. That is why sometimes you hear clients with high praise for counseling and no mention of actions taken as a result of such efforts. It may be necessary to illustrate in concrete terms what you mean by an action plan. For example, early on in counseling a counselor might make a statement like this:

> *Counselor:* You may learn a lot about yourself and some new career options you hadn't thought of before, but, equally important, I hope you'll be able to be clear as to a course of action that you could follow. Could you see yourself, for example, with a goal of taking a new job in another field by the end of this year? I'd like you to be thinking about that and what specific plan of action that might require. I'd like to think I could be of some help to you as you develop that or a similar plan of action for yourself.

This statement emphasizes both the need for a plan and the need for a timeline. These are two concrete ideas to suggest early in the process. They may need to be reemphasized throughout career counseling, as clients often resist efforts to move toward action. In fact, often that is what brought them to career counseling—not being able to set a goal or establish a plan of action for themselves.

Keep in mind that a client's early attempt at stating a plan of action may only be a statement of an immediate need. It may come before he or she has engaged in any Exploration. What ensues may eventually change the Action that seems appropriate. It may not represent a long-term plan of action. Some clients come to counseling not knowing they need more information about themselves or their options before being able to state a plan of action. They come to counseling only expressing their immediate needs. Let us look at some examples of statements made in opening interviews that should illustrate our point:

Client: I must choose a major by tomorrow so I can preregister for next semester.
Client: I want to quit my job and go into something where there are fewer hassles.
Client: I've been fired again, and I need help finding a new job.

These statements may be good clues as to why a client came for counseling, but they do not provide all the information necessary for establishing an eventual plan of action. Choosing a major may be a long-term goal, but chances are that a client will need more time and probably some specific information about himself or herself or careers before setting it as the immediate goal of counseling. Quitting a job because one wants something with fewer hassles may or may not make sense, but clearly we need more information before agreeing to work with that as a goal or endorsing it as a plan of action. Likewise, in the third example, we see that helping a client find another job is an appropriate long-term plan of action, but we want the client to give serious consideration to what has gone wrong in previous jobs before seeking another job.

Two points can be made from these examples. First, it is important to make a distinction between what is offered as an immediate goal or plan and the eventual goal or plan. Second, we need to view the creation of goals and action plans as an ongoing process. This last point should not negate the initial statement of a goal and a plan of action, because it is that statement that brought the client to career counseling. It may well be a good indication of what may need to be clarified and refined in counseling. It is usually an accurate indication of where we must begin as we help clients establish a goal and develop a plan of action.

We need to be sure that clients give equal time to both short- and long-range plans of action. Some clients see only immediate goals; others see only the long-term ones and need help focusing on the necessary short-term goals. Whatever the case, we can help clients make plans according to criteria that better ensure them of success in meeting their goals.

Criteria for Career Goals and Action Plans

Goals and eventual plans of action should be formulated to meet objective criteria. This takes practice, but it makes it easier to later observe progress toward meeting the goals or recognizing the steps still to be taken. Krumboltz and others (Blocher, Heppner, & Johnston, 2001; Gysbers & Moore, 1987; Krumboltz, 1966) have presented particularly helpful criteria to use in establishing a goal and eventually a plan of action. In brief, goals should be specific, observable, time specific, and achievable. To help our clients with plans that meet these criteria, we need to provide some help. It is not simply doing what comes naturally.

Goals Should Be Specific
Attention to specificity is necessary to keep a client from simply making vague statements like "What I need is a new job . . . more money . . . a new major" when it will be more

helpful to have the client state the kind of job, the amount of money, or the specific major to pursue. Again, clients initially tend to be vague about goals, but with practice they can become quite specific. That is one of our roles: to see how goals or plans can be made more specific. It is hard to lay out a plan of action without first being specific about goals.

Goals Should Be Observable

A second criterion argues for goals to be observable. It helps when a client can see the goal: "I will enter graduate school," "I will take a new job," or "I will earn my diploma." These are all specific and observable goals. You can see that the client either did or did not do what he or she intended to do. Both the client and the counselor can observe this. Again, a client may not be inclined to state goals in such a manner. The counselor may need to help frame goals this way.

Goals Should Be Time Specific

Mentioning the time needed to meet a goal is also important. Those observable goals just mentioned might better be stated with some mention of a reasonable timeline: "I will enter graduate school by September of this year," "I will take a new job before the end of the year," or "I will earn my diploma by June of next year." These would all be specific, observable, and time-specific goals.

Goals Should Be Achievable

Finally, goals should be achievable. In the optimism of new learnings or the discovery of new possibilities, one can be overly optimistic or ambitious about goals. "I will enter graduate school by September and have my master's degree in a year" is unrealistic when serious inquiry reveals that the program is a 2-year program. Again, the counselor's role is to help the client set reasonable and attainable goals without dampening his or her enthusiasm for undertaking something new.

The goal-setting stage may be an important place to help minority clients or men and women who are taking nontraditional life paths plan and strategize for the probable environmental barriers that may stand in the way of reaching their desired goals. Racism, sexism, homophobia, and ageism all may influence societal and institutional willingness to support the goals of your clients. This may also be a time when counselor advocacy is important in helping clients actively overcome barriers that are standing in the way of their attaining their dreams.

Goals May Need to Be in Writing

It sometimes helps to have goals in writing. Some people relate positively to written reminders of what they intend to do; others find it unnecessary to put what they see as obvious in writing. Here we believe a counselor needs to attend to whatever is reinforcing for a particular client. After all, the intent is primarily to help clients find reinforcement for doing what they say they want to do. The career counselor should do whatever is helpful in documenting changes in counseling.

Goals Should Be Articulated

Another point to emphasize is the importance of articulating the plan. Although we may think a plan of action should be obvious, the client may not see it that way. We should encourage the client to work at verbalizing a plan throughout counseling. This promotes planning as an ongoing process and allows you to contribute to the refinement of the plan. It also gives you feedback on what is being heard in counseling. Often a client will verbalize a global or overly ambitious plan, much to your surprise. Because a good plan may take input from both of you, you need to hear it as it is being put together. Only a well thought out and articulated plan will ever be put into action.

Techniques That May Help to Establish Career Plans

There is no one way to establish a goal or goals for oneself. A plan of action may also be quite individualistic, but we should work to establish a repertoire of techniques and interventions that aid the process. Some of these are listed below, but be vigilant in adding to the list as you learn from your own experience.

1. Establish early and often the expectation and need for goals and a plan of action. Let clients know what they can realistically expect as outcomes.
2. Make goals and plans of action reasonable. Clients may need help seeing what is reasonable. Too often their prior experience has not helped them with either goal setting or organizing a plan of action, or they are seeking counseling because they have not been able to establish goals or make plans. Teach the process, if necessary. Provide time in counseling for clients to learn and practice the process, review goals and plans, critique them, rehearse them, and help refine them. Provide support and nurturing for these new skills.
3. See that goals and plans are built and can be evaluated according to meaningful and objective criteria. The client, as well as the counselor, should be able to observe and document progress.
4. Reinforce in as many ways as possible the means to effective goals and plans of action. It is far easier to create a goal or a plan than to act on it. Provide opportunities for clients to talk through their goals and plans, to write them out, to rehearse them, and to visualize themselves achieving them. Push clients to openly share these ideas with significant others. Consider establishing a routine during career counseling for formulating and reviewing progress toward setting goals and developing plans of action. Help clients adjust their goals and plans as appropriate, and help them recognize and celebrate any progress toward achieving their goals or implementing any part of the plan of action. These reinforcements are essential to clients' ultimate success. And because reinforcement is often hard to provide to clients who are unclear about goals or plans, this may be another reason clients value so much their time in career counseling.
5. Individualize the process according to the needs and preferred style of each client. What seems helpful for one client may be counterproductive for another. Structure, for example, may enhance one's ability to act, or it may be a hindrance. Teaching a client to focus may be helpful, or it may be unnecessary. Visualizing a plan, writing out a plan, and rehearsing the plan may be a help for one and only a meaningless exercise for another.
6. Do not be hard on a client or yourself when things do not go according to plan. There are a myriad of very good reasons why goals are not achieved and plans are not followed. Expect successful approximations from some; failure from others; and delay tactics, excuses, and unexplained inactivity from others. Complex and often demanding actions are being considered. Sometimes we may only know a fraction of the reasons why a client does or does not act. We often find that we can learn from one client how to better help another client.

Closing Thoughts

Making goals and plans work is the final and perhaps most difficult of the steps involved in career counseling. We need an equally varied repertoire of skills to make it a productive part of the entire process. To become good at it requires practice, follow-up, and feedback from our clients. With that kind of help, we become better at meeting the real needs of our clients.

References

Blocher, D. H., Heppner, M. J., & Johnston, J. A. (2001). *Career planning for the 21st century*. Denver, CO: Love.

Brown, D. (2012). *Career information, career counseling, and career development* (10th ed.). Upper Saddle River, NJ: Pearson Education.

Brown, S. D., & Ryan Krane, N. E. (2000). Four (or five) sessions and a cloud of dust: Old assumptions and new observations about career counseling. In S. D. Brown & R. W. Lent (Eds.), *Handbook of counseling psychology* (3rd ed., pp. 740–766). New York, NY: Wiley.

Brown, S. D., & Ryan Krane, N. E. (2001, August). *Critical ingredients in career counseling: Some new data.* Paper presented at the 109th Annual Convention of the American Psychological Association, San Francisco, CA.

Bureau of Labor Statistics. (2013/2014). *Occupational outlook handbook.* Retrieved from http://www.bls.gov.ooh/

Fuller, R., & Hill, C. E. (1985). Career development status as a predictor of career intervention outcomes. *Journal of Counseling Psychology, 29,* 388–393.

Gelatt, H. B., & Gelatt, C. (2003). *Creative decision making: Using positive uncertainty.* Los Altos, CA: Crisp.

Gysbers, N. C., & Moore, E. J. (1987). *Career counseling: Skills and techniques for practitioners.* Upper Saddle River, NJ: Prentice Hall.

Heppner, M. J., & Hendricks, F. (1995). A process and outcome study examining career indecision and indecisiveness. *Journal of Counseling & Development, 73,* 426–437.

Holland, J. L. (1997). *Making vocational choices: A theory of vocational personalities and work environments* (3rd ed.). Odessa, FL: Psychological Assessment Resources.

Holland, J. L., Magoon, T. M., & Spokane, A. R. (1981). Counseling psychology: Career interventions, research, and theory. *Annual Review of Psychology, 32,* 279–305.

Krumboltz, J. D. (1966). Behavioral goals for counseling. *Journal of Counseling Psychology, 13,* 153–159.

Lopez, S. J. (2013). *Making hope happen: Creating the future you want for yourself and others.* New York, NY: Atria Books.

Phillips, S. D. (1992). Career counseling: Choice and implementation. In S. D. Brown & R. W. Lent (Eds.), *Handbook of counseling psychology* (2nd ed., pp. 513–547). New York, NY: Wiley.

Schwartz, B. (2005). *The paradox of choice: Why more is less.* New York, NY: HarperCollins.

Spokane, A. R. (1991). *Career intervention.* Boston, MA: Allyn & Bacon.

Spokane, A. R., & Oliver, L. (1983). The outcomes of vocational intervention. In W. B. Walsh & S. H. Osipow (Eds.), *Handbook of vocational psychology* (pp. 99–136). Hillsdale, NJ: Erlbaum.

Ward, C. M., & Bingham, R. P. (1993). Career assessment of ethnic minority women. *Journal of Career Assessment, 1,* 246–257.

Ward, C. M., & Tate, G. (1990). *Career Counseling Checklist.* Atlanta: Georgia State University, Counseling Center.

Zunker, V. G. (2006). *Career counseling: A holistic approach* (7th ed.). Pacific Grove, CA: Thompson Brooks/Cole.

Appendix. Additional Resources

General Career Guidance and Information
    http://www.bls.gov/ooh/
    www.rileyguide.com (Riley Guide, general guide for job seekers)
    http://career.missouri.edu (University of Missouri Career Center)
    www.chronicleguidance.com (*Chronicle of Occupational Briefs*)
Résumés, Cover Letters, and Interviewing
    http://career.missouri.edu/resumes-interviews (University of Missouri Career Center)
Networking
    www.rileyguide.com/nettips.html (Riley Guide)
Online Career Assessments
    www.self-directed-search.com (Self-Directed Search Interest Inventory)
    www.keirsey.com (Keirsey Temperament Sorter)
    www.rileyguide.com (Riley Guide)
Internships
    http://college.monster.com/
    www.internshipprograms.com (InternshipPrograms.com)
    www.internsearch.com (InternSearch.com)
Job Searches
    www.cool2serve.org (national service)
    http://ww42.nationalservice.org/
    http://www.idealist.org/info/nonprofits
    www.escapeartist.com (international jobs)
Company Profiles
    www.vault.com (Vault Reports)
    www.wetfeet.com (independent directory for jobs and company profiles)
    http://company.monster.com (Monster.com)
    http://imdiversity.com (diversity perspective on jobs)
    www.businessweek.com (*BusinessWeek*)
    www.thestreet.com (TheStreet.com)
Graduate Schools
    www.gradschools.com (general information)
    www.princetonreview.com (Princeton Review)
    www.petersons.com (Peterson's Guide to Graduate Programs)
    www.kaplan.com/

Chapter 17

Using Social Media in Career Counseling

Amanda Nell

What Is Social Media?

Davis, Deil-Amen, Rios-Aguilar, and González Canché (2012) defined social media as "web-based and mobile applications that allow individuals and organizations to create, engage, and share new user-generated or existing content, in digital environments through multi-way communication" (p. 1). This includes blogs, social networking sites (Facebook, LinkedIn, Ning), microblogging (Twitter), sharing sites for photos and videos (YouTube, Instagram, Flickr), mobile technology, discussion forums (WindowsLive Messenger), live forums (Skype), geolocation services (Foursquare), social bookmarking (Pinterest), and publishing tools/wikis.

This chapter begins by exploring the importance and value of social media in career counseling as well as the key considerations necessary for social media to be an effective communication and counseling tool. Most examples reference social networking sites and video/picture sharing sites because those are most popular with the public and receive the most scrutiny from employers. The discussion then centers on defining and developing the social media literacy of clients to aid their career exploration and employment efforts. Numerous examples of social media best practices are shared, and the chapter closes with a recommendation of professional development action items for all career counselors.

Why Is Social Media Important?

There are several key factors driving the convergence of social media and career counseling. The rapid expansion of social networking sites is simply astounding. The numbers speak for themselves: There are 1.11 billion monthly active Facebook users (Facebook Statistics, 2013). Twitter accounts have topped 500 million, with users averaging 400 million tweets each day (Holt, 2013). And perhaps the most rapidly growing social networking site, LinkedIn, boasts the addition of two new members per second. Of the 225 million members worldwide, there are over 30 million students and recent college graduates on LinkedIn. They are LinkedIn's fastest growing demographic (LinkedIn Statistics, 2013).

Delivery of Services

With a vast majority of clients and the public accessing social media on a daily basis, career counselors must evaluate how they are delivering career counseling. The Pew Research Center's Internet & American Life Project found that young adults ages 18–29 are the most likely of any demographic cohort (83%) to use a social networking site (Duggan & Brenner, 2012). If we are to meet clients where they are (often with a laptop or hand-held device), we will be drawn into cyberspace. In fact, some research shows that online interactions can spur greater client engagement (Higher Education Research Institute, 2007) and therefore lead to more meaningful interactions. Online exchanges that are timely and responsive not only meet client expectations but also build trust and rapport.

Access to Services

With the growing career counseling needs of clients of all ages, social media provides e-learners and "remote" clients the opportunity to further engage with career counselors. As a free service, social media brings equity and access to all clients, removing potential barriers for distance learners, clients with disabilities, nontraditional clients, and other underserved populations.

External Expectations

There are also external expectations demanding greater career counselor time toward Internet and technology use. Understanding social media is critical to effectively counseling clients about the job market because it is consistently used in the world of recruitment. For example, college recruiters and employers are steadily increasing their use of social media to both recruit and screen candidates. A 2012 Kaplan survey of undergraduate admissions representatives showed that 26% included Google and Facebook in applicant evaluations and that 35% reported finding something online about an applicant that negatively impacted their application (Kaplan Test Prep, 2012). Likewise, employers spend time performing online searches of candidates. Nearly two in five companies (39%) use social networking sites to research job candidates, and 43% of those recruiters found information that caused them not to hire a candidate (CareerBuilder.com, 2013). In addition, employers are trying to discover background information about applicants, but research suggests social media activity can also be a predictor of future job performance (Kluemper, Rosen, & Mossholder, 2012). Kluemper and colleagues' (2012) study concluded that a Facebook profile could reveal insights about the personality traits that are often used to predict success within a work environment. So clients who write overly emotional posts, share inappropriate content, or highlight immature behavior are likely going to demonstrate those same characteristics in the workplace.

On the positive side, surveys have found that admissions professionals and employers are more likely to use Facebook and other social networking sites to actively recruit candidates and source potential applicants. A CareerBuilder.com (2013) survey determined that 87% of human resource recruiters were sourcing potential applicants for job vacancies, and a Kaplan Test Prep (2012) survey found that the vast majority of college admissions recruiters (78.6%) logged onto Twitter, Facebook, and/or YouTube to identify prospective students. So a positive and professional online presence can potentially yield great results for clients.

For these reasons, this chapter presumes that technology and social media are tools "to help young people and adults make informed and careful occupational, educational, training and employment decisions" (Vuorinen, Sampson, & Kettunen, 2011, p. 41). In a profession focused on interpersonal interactions, technological competence is often not a strength or priority of most career counselors. Research studies have demonstrated that career practitioners' personal conceptions about social media, as well as their practical knowledge, directly impact the extent to which they embrace and use technology. Career counselors with a holistic approach to their practice, rather than a directive approach, are far more likely to use social media (Kettuen, Vuorinen, & Sampson, 2013).

Social Media Considerations

If you are planning to launch or simply reevaluate the social media you use in your work setting, here are some points to consider from a national survey of career services professionals (Kubu, 2012b). The results revealed that the following points are key to social media success:

- Guidelines/standards of practice
- Goals and strategies
- Content management
- Staffing and training
- Assessment

Guidelines/Standards of Practice

The majority of career centers responding to the survey (52%) did not have departmental or institutional policies for social media practitioners. Offices should first consult with legal, Web communications, or information technology professionals who likely have adopted guidelines. Stated policies should address implementation, content (tone and voice), standards for responding to negative comments, and the handling of crisis communications (Kubu, 2012b).

Princeton University (Kubu, 2013) drafted a model of comprehensive guidelines that clearly state expectations of social media administrators and the appropriate engagement of employers, alumni, and students to maintain fairness and ethical standards for those unique audiences. It includes a brief rationale for all policies and recommendations for the personal use of social media by individual career services staff members.

Goals and Strategies

The hallmark of a successful social media strategy is to align it with institutional and/or agency goals and seek buy-in from leadership. The focus should be not only on the platforms you use but also on the story you are telling and the brand you are crafting. Most social media experts point to the importance of having a communications strategy and an editorial calendar that is based on goal attainment. Numeric goals are one benchmark, but don't forget about the engagement of users. You want your clients to fill out polls, make comments, click on links, and retweet posts. Two-way communication is the ideal model of social media so that your client audience is actively keeping up with and sharing your content (and vice versa).

Also, think broadly about all your intended client audiences across all platforms. Certain sites may speak better to certain end users. For example, if you want to target communication efforts to employers, you may want to focus on Twitter because companies actively use this medium. Many clients, on the other hand, are far more active on Facebook, so this is where you may focus career information and related posts. A LinkedIn group or page could serve as a communication device for the staff at your university or agency. Think critically about your intended goals: Is social media simply a way to promote your existing services, or are you using social media as a value-added service? There is no right or wrong answer. The key is developing a deliberate, rather than haphazard, approach.

In some cases, career centers that use social media conduct a needs assessment to determine how an online presence can help them deliver career services and reach key constituents. Identifying audience needs and behaviors helps drive good decision making about technology rather than giving way to social media trends (Timm, 2006).

Content Management

Your communications strategy should drive your content development, but there are other considerations to managing the substance of your social media platforms. Career counseling professionals should take ample time to identify source material, determine the frequency of those updates, and carefully avoid common but costly mistakes.

What to Post

The content of what you post needs to be creative and appealing. To engage clients, vary your approach by posting informative, creative, and entertaining content. For example, you can link to an amusing video clip, upload photos from a career event, link to an article or survey about job trends, conduct employer Q&A shorts, and so on. Multimedia posts (videos, animations, pictures) often get more attention than other posts, as do current events and campus or agency happenings. But don't feel responsible for drafting all original content. There are a number of bloggers and career sites (Wetfeet, Career-Builder, Brazen Careerist, and CareerThoughts, to name a few) that do an excellent job of creating frequent, topical content. Simply bookmark your favorite sites or sign up for e-newsletters and repost the content on your social media accounts with the click of a "share" button.

The more you integrate social media with other marketing tools, the better the results. For example, include social media icons on your email signature, include share buttons on your career Web site, or add QR codes on fliers that link to Facebook pages or career videos. This marketing integration will help your social media sites gain visibility and can save you some time by reusing existing content, such as career fair photos or newsletter articles.

When to Post

The information and media you share must be accurate, relevant, and consistently posted. Creating a calendar will help guide your updates, which will help you carry on a discussion with clients. Too many posts can end up hiding key page updates or annoy clients, who will leave. Too few posts and you'll be forgotten or viewed as irrelevant. Make sure your schedule includes variety, like a status update, a link, and a photo or video update. A calendar also allows you to schedule periods of time (days) for comments, if you feel this is helpful. Many career counselors are cautious about enabling comments, fearing inappropriate or negative client posts. But careful monitoring and short posting windows will foster a desired outcome: client interaction. Typically, most activity occurs within 24 hours of an update before it drops out of news feeds. Also, strategically plan for the time of day to post. In some cases, morning posts can be effective as a first piece of information a client receives for the day. Other career counselors prefer evening activity because they know clients are more likely to be on a device or perhaps procrastinating from studies. Social management sites, such as Hootsuite.com (a free resource), allow career counselors to schedule posts in advance on any given day or time for all of their social media sites. Scheduled activity also provides the advantage of assessing the effectiveness of your communication strategy. By planning and recording activity on a schedule, you can review your page insights and other analytics to determine what content got the most traction with your clients at particular times.

Things to Avoid

While online communication can reach the masses, it does have limitations. It is a truncated conversation, and statements often focus on character length rather than tone or substance. Studies show that despite the confidence of the sender and receiver, people have difficulty identifying tone and even project their own stereotypes because of the ambiguity of the method (Epley & Kruger, 2004; Kruger, Epley, Parker, & Ng, 2005). It is critical to be mindful of tone and to avoid nuanced or complex messages when using social media. Additionally, simple mistakes can reflect badly on your agency or institution. Poor judgment, such as an ill-advised joke, or misinformation and frequent errors, such as typos and broken links, can quickly tarnish an online reputation. Proofing and fact checking on your social media sites are critical to ensure that you are regarded as a good source of reliable information.

Staffing and Training

Who will manage and post social media content is a critical decision. Communications can belong to a dedicated communications/marketing staff, while other full-time staff are tasked with social media and other major job duties. In many cases, for example, career services rely on student staff to contribute to or administer social media sites. In some cases, all staff members are encouraged to make daily or weekly contributions to social media. According to the 2012 National Association of Colleges and Employers (NACE) social media survey, most respondents spent between 1 and 5 hours a week on social media implementation. The more advanced a career center's strategy was, the more hours they reported spending on social media management (Kubu, 2012a).

Whoever is charged with coordinating social media, their training and ongoing education is crucial as technology consistently evolves. Ideally, social media coordinators should consider professional development seminars provided by their institution or agency, participate in groups for social media users, join online discussion groups, attend webinars/seminars of professional associations, and/or benchmark with peer institutions or agencies. Implicit to the discussion of staff and training is budget, which often dictates the level of staff involvement and training. Even with limited resources, there are many free resources and social media communities that can support a small office or single career counselor juggling social media responsibilities.

Sites like Mashable, Technocrati, and SocialMediaToday are leading sources for news and information documenting industry trends and innovations. They organize information by social media platform and provide helpful articles and advice to effectively manage networking sites and maximize the potential of your social media. The "how-to" information provided can also be repurposed on your social media sites to advise your clients. Professional organizations at the national and regional levels also advise you on how to stay current with emerging issues, such as content management, social media promotion, laws, and ethics. The NACE, the National Career Development Association (NCDA), and the American Counseling Association have numerous print and online articles as well as sponsored events addressing social media usage. The NCDA Web site and *Career Convergence* online magazine often address social media issues and online training tools. In addition to surveys and research, NACE sponsors semiannual "Social Media Mash-Ups," which are intensive workshops designed for both the seasoned social media coordinator and the novice.

Assessment

There are a variety of online tools to manage and monitor social networks; however, there is no standard set of metrics to evaluate social media effectiveness and return on investment. However, you can evaluate your use of social media by taking some or all of the following steps:

- Use free analytics such as Google Analytics to evaluate Web site traffic and referrals. This can tell you everything from the individual number of page views to the types of browsers used to access the site and whether they got there from a social media platform.
- Review Facebook Insights, which include metrics for any Facebook fan page. An administrator can measure fan growth, "likes," and page interactions as well as demographic data of users to see if you are reaching your target audience. The data also show peak activity during the day and week.
- Check Twitter data to see how many followers, mentions, messages, and retweets your career center or agency has.
- Register with sites like HootSuite or Tweetdeck, which use a dashboard to manage and streamline your social media accounts. They also offer strong data and reports on traffic (retweets, mentions, etc.).
- Take advantage of URL shortener insights such as Owly or Bitly. This is another way to see how many people are actually clicking on links within your messages or posts on social media platforms. Social dashboard sites typically offer this option as well, which is key for embedding a link on a 140-character tweet.
- Survey your clients and employer audiences to see what information they are seeking and how they are accessing information about your services, resources, and events.
- Measure your "social influence" (Kubu, 2012b, p. 39) on sites that compare data from multiple social networks to determine the reach of your social media. Klout, Social Mention, and Topsy are just a few examples.
- Lastly, consult industry standards like Mashable.com and SocialMediaToday.com for ideas on how to best maximize your social media platforms and to monitor your progress. While analytics are helpful, the numbers can be overwhelming; without context, they are meaningless. Your reports and statistics need to tie back to your overall goals and communication strategy.

The State of Social Media in University Career Counseling Centers

In a 2012 survey of university career centers, Osburn and LoFrisco found that centers managed an average of 2.7 social networking sites: Facebook (93%), LinkedIn (77%), and Twitter (70%). According to this survey group, the purpose of social networking sites was to provide career information, including job search tips, career-related articles, employment announcements, employer connections, and promotion of career services. About one third of respondents had 500 or more followers, and 86% of career centers reported being satisfied or mostly satisfied with their social networking site usage (Osburn & LoFrisco, 2012).

As for the benefits of social media, most offices identified student engagement, increased visibility, event attendance, more frequent communication, and greater connection with alumni and employers. Drawbacks included staffing, absence of metrics, lack of student professionalism, and difficulty targeting communications (Osburn & LoFrisco, 2012).

Social Media Literacy of Clients

In this digital age, career counselors have a responsibility to educate clients on the basics of social media so that they can use all aspects of technology in their career exploration and post-graduation pursuits. Clients who fail to use social networking sites are at a distinct disadvantage from their peers who use these tools for occupational and company research, networking, and job search leads. Just as we have learned in past decades to embrace online tools, innovations in technology are compelling us to help clients develop social media literacy.

Basic Client Competencies

Here are suggestions for the basic knowledge all clients should master as it relates to the three most popular sites—Facebook, Twitter, and LinkedIn—which are almost universally used by clients and/or employers:

1. *Create an online presence.* Clients likely have a Facebook page but should be encouraged to create a LinkedIn profile. Those accounts should also be active, and career counselors should advise clients to manage their accounts on a regular (weekly) basis. It doesn't take a lot of effort to repost a story on Facebook or retweet a comment. At the same time, it is important to consider when a client should be involved in social media and on what platforms. LinkedIn is a great resource for seeking internships, full-time jobs, and networking contacts, but it may not be practical for undecided clients. Your approach with clients should vary according to each individual. Most important is sharing with them the purpose and value of social media sites so that they may develop their own strategic approach.

2. *Clean up digital dirt.* If clients already have social media accounts, they likely need to review those sites and purge them of inappropriate pictures, content, and links. Career counselors might ask clients if they are willing to review their profile together, or they can simply pose the question, "Is this something you would want a family member or significant other to see?" Clients need to carefully review their privacy and account settings. Facebook, in particular, gives users the ability to control who can view and post items on your timeline, approve any tags or outside content, and block users. You can also recommend resources like BrandYourself.com to highlight particular profiles and links in search engine results.

3. *Create employer-friendly sites.* After purging social media of negative content, clients should then focus on accentuating the positive. There are several ways to do this:
   - Use the highlight tool to identify career-related posts and key accomplishments on Facebook timelines.
   - (Re)tweet positive stories or topics related to a particular field of study or chosen profession.
   - Place career goals and interests in the headline of a LinkedIn account.
   - Upload a professional headshot or Twitter avatar.
   - Make sure that all social media sites have a link to a résumé and/or portfolio and include links to other social networking sites.

Personal Branding Tool

Career counselors can spend lots of time telling clients to clean up digital dirt, but the conversation is most productive when we talk about how to harness the power of social media by creating a positive, professional online presence. Whether you consider your-self Web savvy, Web-phobic, or somewhere in between, as a career counselor you can easily prompt your clients with basic questions about the types of social media they actively use and the nature of the content they post. The message career counselors can share is that clients should use online tools not just for social purposes but also to explore and pursue their personal and career interests. To do that, clients must create a thoughtful, intentional Web presence that reflects those values. Many clients have given little consideration to the image their online presence is portraying, so encourage them to think of their social media as a branding tool that can help them develop a positive and professional narrative. Ask clients to process their goals, interests, skills, and abili-ties and then review their social media to see if those values and traits are reflected on their sites. A blog post, tweet, Pinterest pin, or Facebook post can highlight an academic achievement, a passionate cause, or a career aspiration. Challenge them to join groups, post articles, and participate in discussions that address the issues and current events they care most about. Our role is to help educate clients about the power of social media and how to leverage online platforms to achieve their short- and long-term career goals.

Job Search and Networking Tool

According to a recent survey, 54.5% of college graduates failed to use social media what-soever in their job search (NACE, 2012). This is a tremendous waste of opportunity, especially when students have great proficiency with tools like Facebook and Twitter. More than 80% of recruiters have actively used social media to promote vacancies and search for applicants, and a whopping 98% of recruiters reported that they log in to LinkedIn to find and contact top candidates (Payscale.com, 2012).

As career counselors we must be versed in the ways that recruiters are seeking candi-dates and help clients realize the potential of social networking sites in their job search. Our advice to clients must take into consideration the varied options that different so-cial media sites provide. Recommendations from LinkedIn and Twitter are given here.

LinkedIn Recommendations

As a professional networking site, LinkedIn offers some unique features that can help clients network and find job leads. Here are some actions to recommend:

- Highlight your education, coursework, honors, and other academic achieve-ments. Develop a summary statement that describes your experience, talents, and career goals.
- Update your status on a regular (weekly) basis so you stay on the new feed of others.
- Join groups, display the group badge, and actively contribute to discussions.
- Seek recommendations from a variety of sources (faculty, work supervisor, etc.).
- Claim a unique LinkedIn URL that is your full name (or variation of).
- Link URLs to sample projects and other social media sites.
- Place your LinkedIn URL on your résumé.
- Search for people/organizations and review suggestions of possible connections to add to your network.
- Personalize all messages to help you make that first critical point of contact.

Twitter Recommendations

Not only is Twitter a great way to follow and network with individuals, but it also pro-vides a wealth of vacancies to job seekers. Here are some actions to recommend to clients:

- Follow Twitter accounts dedicated to job openings within companies (@mtvnet-worksjobs), industries (@medical_jobs), regions (@ChicagoTechJobs), and job types (@findinternships).
- Follow human resource recruiters, industry alumni, and "big names" to stay abreast of current events and hiring information.
- Use hashtags to gain greater visibility and relevance.
- Retweet posts that are related to your major or career goals to demonstrate your interest and commitment to your field.

Career Center Best Practices

The best ideas for social media come from sharing best practices among career professionals. For example, below are descriptions of innovative programs and uses highlighted in Evangeline Kubu's (2012b) national study of career centers' implementation of social media.

Student Mentoring and Networking

LinkedIn is often used as a way to foster mentorship relationships with students and alumni or young alumni with older alumni. LinkedIn is a great resource because it provides students with an electronic "rolodex" of contacts that needs no updating on the part of the student. Networking is streamlined, as students can easily research their connections to companies and individuals and send an automated request to connect with a particular contact. Although those requests should be personalized to each contact, the click of the button saves valuable time. Students can also identify common ties and shared interests based on work and educational history and group memberships. LinkedIn helps students identify professionals with similar career paths and interests they share. Rather than making a "cold call," this medium allows students to quickly build and maintain a broad network of professionals. The University of Pennsylvania career services created @PennCareerDay to feature alumni who tweet throughout their workday to give students and followers an idea of what it is like to work in a particular field. The daily transcripts are archived on the career Web site, and alumni bios are posted in the career center's blog.

Alumni Outreach

Alumni can easily connect with one another through LinkedIn groups and Facebook pages and follow job leads and career topics through Twitter hashtags. A motivated, active group often needs little administrative oversight except for occasional monitoring and the verification of new group members. Since alumni are often scattered all over the United States and the world, online tools are extremely effective in meeting their needs in real time.

Event Promotion

Career services can release content to coincide with career events. For example, some schools create weeklong countdowns on Facebook and Twitter to promote an upcoming career fair, including daily video tips on how to prepare. Social media is also a great way to send a last-minute reminder the day of or just an hour before an event, which can be ideal for workshops, speakers, or job/interview deadlines.

Employer Relations

Social media can quickly broadcast job and internship opportunities for students, in particular using Twitter to tweet job announcements. Other schools engage employers as LinkedIn discussion group experts or as workshop panelists using Skype. Some programs have asked employers to add content to social media by serving as guest bloggers or videotaping responses to brief questions for a video post.

Peer Advising

Student blogs and video shorts written and produced by paraprofessionals or student interns are effective ways of engaging undergraduates. Some also use Facebook as a discussion forum for students. For example, Facebook events can be organized for "send off" parties, connecting student interns and/or recent college graduates hired through the same company or relocating to a particular region.

Theme Days or Weeks

Using weekly or daily themes and topics is another example of ways that career centers organize their social media efforts, including theme days such as "Myth-Busting Monday" or "Retweet Tuesday." Another example is the University of Missouri's "MIZ-JOB" week where students who retweet career posts and share career success stories are entered into a drawing for a $100 bookstore gift card. The winner is prominently featured on social media the following day. In 2013, the event nearly doubled their followers.

Professionalism

Some schools are using the online pinboard Pinterest to educate students about professionalism. Career centers such as the University of Pennsylvania share images and resources about proper interview attire, career info-graphics, recommended book and resource titles, student success stories, as well as workplace tips for young graduates.

Multimedia

Videos and animations are great ways in which to attract today's student. Michigan State University created a YouTube channel that has four overarching themes: myCampus, myCareer, myBusiness, and myCommunity. The purpose of the channel is to provide students with a brief glimpse of career information and insight into job searches. They produce their own content and subscribe to other career- and university-related channels.

Contests

For brands that want fan pages to have added value (to increase engagement and visibility), career centers can offer contests and coupons specifically to social media users to entice students to join. The University of Delaware held a video contest with cash prizes, asking students to express why they valued career services. The "contestants" were generating buzz and content for the career center while providing valuable testimonials.

Advisory Boards

For quick feedback about an issue, a LinkedIn group, Ning site, or Skype call can easily put you into contact with key constituents like alumni, employers, or other career professionals. Many schools convene formal advisory boards in person, but when many of those members are geographically dispersed, social media can bring them closer to advise you on the pressing issues of the day.

Career Courses

Career courses can use online tools to reach new distance learners as well as connect with campus-based students. Coursework can be shared and enhanced through videos, assignments, slides, and other content. This can also be an effective tool for creating a community of learning, which can be effective for students who may be perhaps intimidated to participate in larger in-class discussions. In addition to delivering class content, social media can aid students in researching and completing assignments such as informational interviews and career narratives.

Community and Relationship Building

The Golden Rule applies to social media: If you follow and post the content of others, they will do so in return. Besides cross-marketing student services, social media activity can lead to greater collaborations among departments and student groups across campus. Social networking sites can also foster a sense of community and belonging, which is critical to the satisfaction and retention of students, particularly at larger institutions.

Professional Development

Whether or not you directly manage social media, career counselors should be skilled at using these platforms. This requires familiarity with and regular use of social media sites to stay current with emerging features and technology trends. Please take the following actions for your own professional development:

- Bookmark and reference the LinkedIn Career Services Resource Center: http://university.linkedin.com/career-services.
- Create a comprehensive LinkedIn profile and use it as your personal rolodex.
- Join discussion groups such as Career Counselor Technology Forum or NACE Social Media to actively follow and join the dialogue.
- Share your expertise and post your PowerPoint slides through the SlideShare LinkedIn feature.
- Find or create YouTube videos to share with career professionals and clients.
- Make connections with others through announcements and one-on-one messages.
- Arrange a Skype meeting with an alumnus or distance learner. (Just practice first!)
- Share career and social media news with career services professionals and other colleagues.

Closing Thoughts

Take small but measured steps to implement these strategies in order to more fully integrate social media into your professional interactions and career counseling. Social media is a vital tool to help us perform our career counseling roles more effectively and to reach the broadest possible audience. It seems fitting that as we advise clients to be life-long learners and build long-term career development skills, we should model that very behavior by braving the exciting and uncertain world of social media.

References

CareerBuilder.com. (2013). Retrieved from http://www.careerbuilder.com/share/aboutus/pressreleasesdetail.aspx?sd=6%2f26%2f2013&siteid=cbpr&sc_cmp1=cb_pr766_&id=pr766&ed=12%2f31%2f2013

Davis, C. H. F., III, Deil-Amen, R., Rios-Aguilar, C., & González Canché, M. S. (2012). *Social media and higher education: A literature review and research directions* (Research Report). Tucson: University of Arizona, and Claremont, CA: Claremont Graduate University.

Duggan, M., & Brenner, J. (2012, February). *The demographics of social media users.* Retrieved from Pew Internet & American Life Project Web site: http://pewinternet.org/Reports/2013/Social-media-users.aspx

Epley, N., & Kruger, J. (2004). When what you type isn't what they read: The perseverance of stereotypes and expectancies over email. *Journal of Experimental Social Psychology, 41*, 414–422.

Facebook Statistics. (2013). Retrieved from http://newsroom.fb.com/Key-Facts

Higher Education Research Institute. (2007). *College freshmen and online social networking sites.* Retrieved from http://heri.ucla.edu/PDFs/pubs/briefs/brief-091107-social-networking.pdf

Holt, R. (2013, May 21). Twitter in numbers. *The Daily Telegraph.* Retrieved from http://www.telegraph.co.uk

Kaplan Test Prep. (2012). Retrieved from http://press.kaptest.com/research-and-surveys/kaplan-test-preps-2012-survey-of-college-admissions-officers

Kettuen, J., Vuorinen, R., & Sampson, J. (2013). Career practitioners' conceptions of social media in career services. *British Journal of Guidance & Counselling, 41*(3), 302–317.

Kluemper, D. H., Rosen, P. A., & Mossholder, K. N. (2012). Social networking websites, personality ratings, and the organizational context: More than meets the eye? *Journal of Applied Social Psychology, 42*(5), 1143–1172.

Kruger, J., Epley, N., Parker, J., & Ng, Z. W. (2005). Egocentrism over email: Can we communicate as well as we think? *Journal of Personality and Social Psychology, 89*, 925–936.

Kubu, E. (2012a). *Assessing social media implementation in career centers.* Retrieved from the National Association of Colleges and Employers Spotlight for Career Professionals Web site: http://naceweb.org

Kubu, E. (2012b). Career center social media implementation and best practices: Findings of a nationwide survey. *National Association of Colleges and Employers Journal, 72*, 32–39.

Kubu, E. (2013). *Princeton University Office of Career Services social media and guidelines strategy.* Retrieved from http://www.princeton.edu/career/pdfs/Princeton-University-Office-of-Career-Services-Social-Media-Guidelines-Strategy 2013-2014.pdf

LinkedIn Statistics. (2013). Retrieved from http://press.linkedin.com/about

National Association of Colleges and Employers. (2012). *Class of 2012 student survey report.* Retrieved from http://www.naceweb.org/Research/Student/Student_Survey.aspx?referal=research&menuID=70

Osburn, D. S., & LoFrisco, B. M. (2012). How do career centers use social networking sites? *The Career Development Quarterly, 60*, 263–272.

Payscale.com. (2012). Retrieved from http://www.payscale.com/career-news/2012/04/social-media-recruiting-infographic?goback=.gde_135722_member_134640695

Timm, C. (2006). Technology decision-making in career services. *National Association of Colleges and Employers Journal, 66*, 33–39.

Vuorinen, R., Sampson, J., & Kettunen, J. (2011). The perceived role of technology in career guidance among practitioners who are experienced Internet users. *Australian Journal of Career Development, 20*(3), 39–46.

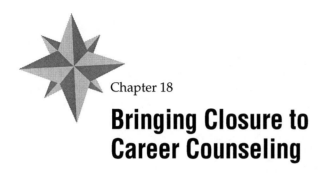

Chapter 18

Bringing Closure to Career Counseling

What we call the beginning is often the end and to make an end is to make a beginning.
The end is where we start from . . .

—T. S. Eliot, 1942, p. 12

Bringing meaningful closure to a counseling relationship is often a most difficult task for counselors, and recent research has indicated that counselors and clients tend to perceive aspects of the termination process quite differently (Corey, 2013; Manthei, 2007). In essence, it is important for counselors to think about why termination might be difficult for both the counselor and the client and to develop effective skills for closing the counseling relationship (Meier & Davis, 2011).

There are a number of reasons for this difficulty; perhaps foremost is people's general uneasiness with endings of all kinds (Young, 2013). Examples of this discomfort are visible in everyday endings, such as our leave-taking behaviors after a visit with friends or relatives. These endings are many times prolonged and include numerous references to when the parties will get together again. These behaviors seem to serve the purpose of denying the fact that the visit is in fact ending. Some of the most important, most honest communication we have with others is spurted out in the last few moments of a long visit. Endings make us uncomfortable. Thus, in counseling, both counselors and clients may resist closure. They may continue in the counseling relationship after it has ceased to be useful in order to avoid the feelings associated with the end of the relationship.

An important training issue for counselors is to examine their own attitudes toward endings. If endings are of particular difficulty for counselors, they may profit from reading books or articles related to dealing with loss. Time should be set aside during supervision to discuss counselor concerns with closing relationships. In some cases, the counselors may need to seek counseling themselves if their personal issue with closure is limiting their effectiveness as counselors. Sometimes counselors fear that their inadequacy as a counselor will become even more evident when they have a termination session with a client (Meier & Davis, 2011). For most counselors, however, the discomfort that accompanies endings can be alleviated through information about what elements contribute to effective closure in career counseling.

Very little has been written about the importance of closure in career counseling, but termination is as important as the initial phase of counseling (Corey, 2013). This lack of focus on closure may be due in part to the perception that career counseling is short term and structured, with few of the emotional loose ends common in socioemotional counseling sessions. As this book has pointed out, this description does not fit a large majority of career counseling cases. The role of work in people's lives cannot be neatly compartmentalized from their socioemotional lives. Thus, effective career counseling includes a broad approach to the person and one that encompasses all aspects of the person's context and emotion. Research has indicated that, contrary to popular belief, clients value and recognize the importance of the working alliance in career counseling (Bikos, O'Brien, & Heppner, 1995; Heppner & Hendricks, 1995). With this more holistic view of career counseling comes the need to attend to all aspects of the relationship, including the integral issue of bringing closure to the relationship, saying goodbye. It is important to plan for this "closing ceremony" (Amundson, 1998, p. 203) from the very beginning days of the counseling relationship.

This chapter addresses four related topics. First, we discuss the context of closure, including the various reasons for closure. Next, we cover a special kind of closure, the premature termination that occurs when the client ends counseling before the counselor believes that he or she is ready to do so. Following this, we discuss the feelings associated with closure, and finally, we provide information on what constitutes effective closure.

The Context of Closure

Closure happens at a number of different times for varied reasons. The context of closure is an important element in determining the form it will take. There are three primary reasons for closure.

Initial Goals Have Been Met

The client and counselor feel that the initial goals for counseling have been met and there is no longer a need to meet. In the best of scenarios, closure occurs when the needs that originally brought the client to counseling are satisfied. This may mean, for example, that the client has become clear about his or her major or career choice or has worked through difficulties felt on the job. Examining the progress that the client has made toward meeting his or her goals is a critical part of the termination process (Amundson, Bowlsbey, & Niles, 2005; Corey, 2013, Young, 2013). Although the client may need reassurance about the counselor's availability should additional needs arise, these closure sessions are usually the clearest and most rewarding for both the counselor and the client.

No Action at This Time

Clients know what needs to happen next in the career planning process but have decided not to take action at this time. In this situation, the clients have "gone to the edge of the lake" but are not quite ready to jump in. This describes clients who have clarified their interests, skills, and values and know exactly what path they need to take but, for a number of reasons, are unable or unwilling to take that path at the current time. One way to assess specific reasons for this inability to take action is through the use of the Career Transitions Inventory, which is described in Chapter 13. Clients may lack motivation, confidence, support, independence, or feelings of control. By helping clients understand the reasons for their inaction, you can help them understand that they can choose if they want to work on these psychological barriers and try to overcome them. Many times situational variables prevent forward movement: small children needing care, lack of financial resources to support the training necessary to change careers, or too little emotional energy following a divorce. It is important that clients do not feel blamed for their lack of activity. The counselor can normalize the situation and reassure clients that when they are ready to take the next steps, the counselor will be there to provide assistance.

Lack of Depth or Meaning

The counseling session itself lacks depth or meaning. The pain that originally brought clients to counseling has lessened, and the motivation to work in counseling has eroded as well. A certain amount of discomfort, confusion, or pain is usually necessary to give clients the motivation to initiate counseling. This pain can be caused by the stress of job loss, difficult relationships with coworkers, or the anxiety caused by indecision in choosing a major or career field. It may also result from the pain and uncertainty many adults feel when approaching particularly important trigger points in their lives, such as turning 40 or coming to the age that a same-sex parent was when he or she died. Sometimes this pain is eased by the cathartic effects of talking to a counselor for a few sessions. Even though the problem is not resolved, the clients no longer feel the powerful affective reaction that initially motivated them to work on these issues in counseling. Thus they choose to end the counseling relationship.

How the counselor chooses to handle this type of closure depends to a great extent on the consequences of closure for the individual client. For many clients, this type of closure is normal and will result in few dire consequences. They have received some immediate help to get them through the current issues, and they will opt to use services again should they have recurring problems. In the current health care arena, which places a value on time-effective counseling, this type of short-term problem resolution is becoming the norm.

In some situations, however, the counselor may need to encourage the client to continue even though the initial pain has subsided (e.g., in situations in which there is physical or psychological danger to the client should he or she choose to stay in an unhealthy work situation). In this case, the counselor's role may be to help the client recognize the following inevitable consequences: (a) The counselor feels he or she cannot work with the client, and these reasons have been discussed with the client, or, conversely, (b) the client feels he or she cannot work with the counselor, and these reasons have been discussed with the counselor.

Sometimes in the course of counseling a mismatch occurs between the counselor and client for a variety of reasons. For example, the client may be at a stage of identity development that makes it difficult to work with a particular counselor. As we discuss in Chapters 3, 4, and 5 on gender and diversity issues in counseling, if a client is at a stage of identity development characterized by a dichotomization of the sexes or races, it may be difficult for this client to constructively work with a counselor of the opposite sex or a different race. Another potential reason for a mismatch is when the counselor feels ill equipped to handle particular client issues because of lack of appropriate training or biases that the counselor holds about specific groups of people. In any case, it is vital that the counselor and client work through their differences before the counselor makes a referral to a more appropriate counselor. Thus, these different contexts of the closure session in many ways prescribe the form the closure session will take. For example, if a client is being referred because of an inability to work with a particular counselor, the closure session will focus on different issues than if the relationship were ending because of goal accomplishment (Hackney & Cormier, 2013).

The Special Case of Premature Closure

Perhaps one of the most difficult contexts of closure is that which has been referred to in the literature as *premature termination* (Ward, 1984; Young, 2013) or *premature closure*. This occurs when the client decides to end counseling before the counselor believes the client is ready to do so. Premature closures often occur when the client simply does not show up for the next scheduled appointment. Brown and Brooks (1991) mentioned four possible reasons for premature closure: (a) the client's belief that he or she has achieved his or her goal, (b) the client's fear of what may be uncovered in the counseling process, (c) failure of counseling to meet the client's expectations, and (d) lack of client commitment to counseling in the first place. Although premature closures occur in most settings, it is imperative that the counselor examine the reasons behind the termination. Sometimes this examination results in information concerning aspects of the career counseling setting or procedures that actually promote premature closure. In a study examining critical negative and positive incidents in career counseling (Heppner, O'Brien, Hinkelman, & Flores, 1996), the following comments were made that illuminate some possible reasons for premature termination:

> I got the feeling the counselor had little interest in me as a person. She had her little routine of giving me these tests and telling me what I should be. I felt she treated every client exactly alike—with the same mechanized roteness. Why would I go back for more of that?

This quote exemplifies the importance of building a working alliance, viewing career counseling as a process rather than a procedure, and valuing the uniqueness each client brings to the process.

> As a Black person, I just didn't feel like my counselor understood me or the issues I was addressing. She looked like she had always been one of the privileged. The counseling agency had a White feel to it—I didn't feel comfortable there.

Although premature closures occur with all client populations, there is strong evidence that they are especially prevalent with clients from underrepresented groups (Sue & Sue, 2007). This client's quote emphasizes the need to examine ways in which the counseling setting is discouraging to members of underrepresented groups.

> We worked together for a couple of sessions, then he referred me to the career resource library to "collect information." He said I should call him when I was done looking. I felt dumped—like he had no interest in helping me any further.

The art of integrating information into the career counseling process is critical. As discussed in Chapter 16, clients and counselors need to develop a specific plan for identifying and interpreting career information. Turning clients loose to explore on their own may be one of the quickest routes to premature closure. Clients need to feel assured that their counselor will work with them throughout the process and not abandon them in a sea of unfamiliar occupational information.

> Having never been to career counseling before I guess I just didn't know what to expect, but clearly I wasn't ready to pursue counseling right now.

As we highlight in Chapter 8, talking about client and counselor expectations is of critical importance in the opening sessions of career counseling. Being sure that the client understands what career counseling is and, perhaps more important, is not can avoid premature closures that are precipitated by unclear expectations.

Handling Premature Closure

A point of decision occurs for the counselor when a client does not show up for an appointment. How much responsibility the counselor should take in encouraging the client's return is a matter of professional judgment. Generally, calling the client has the following advantages:

- It allows for the expression of caring and concern for the client.
- It gives the counselor a chance to collect information about the reasons for the client's premature closure and to learn whether there were ways the counselor or counseling agency may have unknowingly contributed to the client's decision not to return.
- It allows for referral to another counselor or agency when appropriate.
- It gives the counselor the opportunity to leave the door open to future visits when the client feels ready to begin again.

Feelings Associated With Closure

Understanding the range and complexity of emotions related to closure will help the counselor normalize diverse feelings and facilitate the client's processing of his or her own emotions. A wide diversity of feelings is associated with endings in counseling.

"I'd Rather Talk the Talk Than Walk the Walk"

Although most effective career counseling is a blend of talk and action, clients may feel that ending counseling puts more pressure on them to take major steps on their own behalf. Clients may have become quite comfortable with the talk of the career planning process; the action may elicit much greater fear and discomfort.

"I Feel Nurtured in This Nest—Don't Kick Me Out"

For some clients, the nurturing and intimacy that are part of counseling are a unique experience. The relationships in their own lives do not provide the kind of support and caring they feel in counseling. This nurturing feels good, and they do not want to give it up. These feelings provide a rich environment for encouraging clients to develop more meaningful and nurturing relationships. You might emphasize that they have clearly been able to develop this relationship with you as the counselor and that these same skills may be used to foster other nurturing relationships.

"I Don't Have to Say Goodbye if I Don't Come Back"

Sometimes clients will simply avoid the whole process of closure by repeatedly canceling or not showing up for appointments. Through this form of avoidance they do not have to go through the discomfort of endings, but they also miss out on the satisfaction that comes with closure.

"It Wasn't All That Good Anyway, so Why Process It?"

Many times people are less uncomfortable with anger than with sadness or loss. Thus, when they feel an ending approaching they may distance themselves from it through a process of disenchantment (Bridges, 2004). This disenchantment may take the form of discounting the counselor and the counseling process. Clients may start believing that the counselor is withholding information or not being as helpful as originally thought. This disenchantment serves the purpose of making the ending easier because the relationship was "not that important anyway."

"Thank Goodness I've Accomplished My Goals and
Have My Thursday Evenings Free Again"

Being in counseling is work. It is not uncommon for a client to feel relief at not having to come to counseling any more. The counseling may have been very helpful in accomplishing needed goals, but the client may nonetheless feel freedom when it is over. Being able to talk about this relief in an authentic manner is an important goal of the closure session.

What Constitutes Effective Closure?

Closure sessions vary greatly depending on the level of working alliance that has developed and how effectively the goals or tasks of counseling have been achieved. But even within this individual variation there are at least seven commonalties in what makes for effective closure.

1. Typically there will be a review of the content of what has transpired during counseling. Effective closure sessions are a time for reflection on the journey of career counseling: where the client was when first coming to counseling and the path that brought him or her to this ending. This reflection may focus on the initial confusion and uncertainty the client felt and how, through the process of counseling, the client gained new clarity about the self and the world. Especially important in this review of content is emphasizing the role the client had in shaping the journey and the transferability of skills learned in the process to new situations. This discussion provides an opportunity for the counselor to describe the dynamic and reoccurring nature of career choice and change and to emphasize that the client may very well be using the skills learned in these sessions for future career planning. Reviewing the content helps the client understand more about how the individual parts of the process came to make up the whole. As Amundson (1998) described, "I have found it important to highlight 'Moments of Movement' . . . points in the process where there seem to be clear indicators of a change in perspective" (p. 191). This processing of context might sound like this:

   Counselor: We have been on quite a journey together for the past 6 weeks.
   Client: Yes, I feel pretty different from when I stumbled in here, not knowing what you do, or what I could even ask for.
   Counselor: Yes, you were pretty confused then. Your divorce had only been final for a little over a week and you didn't know what direction your life should take.
   Client: Yes, and I hadn't realized how dependent I'd become on Mike and how I had lost a great amount of self-esteem in the ending of my marriage.
   Counselor: You really demonstrated strength and resiliency in reaching out for help and coming to this place you knew nothing about.

2. Equally important to a review of the content of the sessions (what happened) is an examination of the process of the sessions (how it happened). Examining the process includes talking directly about the working alliance that developed between the counselor and client and how that relationship unfolded over time. Focusing on the process is especially important if there was conflict in the counseling relationship. A careful examination of how both the counselor and client dealt with the conflict can be a powerful learning experience. This review of the process of the session might go like this:

Counselor: I remember when you first came to counseling I felt your anger and despair at being overlooked for so many positions.

Client: I felt really bad and when I saw you, I wondered if a White person would really understand what I'd been going through.

Counselor: I really wanted to help, but I wasn't sure you would let me.

Client: Well, not until you passed my tests.

Counselor: Tests?

Client: I was checking you out. Were you racist? Did you really mean what you said? Would you follow through, or were you just saying what you thought I wanted to hear?

3. Closure sessions are also a time to reemphasize the strengths of the client in dealing with these important life issues. It is often difficult for a client to own his or her part in what was effective in counseling, so it is important to reflect on those strengths at this time of closure. Here is an example of restating the strengths of the client:

Client: You have really helped me understand how much I've let being a woman stop me.

Counselor: You have shown a lot of sophisticated understanding about the role of all kinds of environmental factors in limiting your perceived options.

Client: Yes, thanks to you I feel like I can explore many more areas now and that I might actually have some skills to succeed in them.

Counselor: I appreciate your reinforcement of my role in your new enlightenment about options. I also want to hear you own the part you had to play in reclaiming your dreams.

Client: Yes, I have gone after it with vigor.

Counselor: Indeed!

4. The closure session is also a time for evaluation (Corey, 2013). What went well? What went poorly? What was the most helpful event in counseling? What was the most hindering event? Reflecting on these questions together can provide extremely helpful information to both the client and counselor. It is often difficult for the client to express negative feelings to the counselor. The client may need help in doing so. We can normalize the fact that all counseling has highs and lows. Understanding more about individual clients' experiences helps the counselor and the client understand the change process in counseling. This is an example of how the evaluation might sound:

Counselor: In every counseling relationship there are peaks and there are valleys; there are interventions that go well and others that fall flat. I wonder if you feel you can share with me the most helpful and least helpful parts of this process for you.

Client: Sure. The most helpful part was you believing in me and affirming my choice to get out of law and pursue my dream of becoming a potter.

Counselor: And on the flip side, what was least helpful or what perhaps even hindered your progress?

Client: Well, I know you wanted to check me out, but those interest inventories were kind of a waste of time. I didn't need them, and I could have spent the time in more productive ways.

5. Often in interactions, things go unexpressed. Sometimes it feels like it is not the right time to say something, or we wonder how the comment might be received. Sometimes we are driving home from a session or reviewing a tape and we think, "I wish I had told my client. . . ." Providing a time and place for "things unsaid"

(Wheeler & Kivlighan, 1995) can be another important aspect of the closure session. The following is an example of a way to raise the issue of things unsaid:

Counselor: Sometimes in relationships, things are left unsaid. You (or I) may think or feel something but not express it. Then later, we might have wished we had been more assertive. Take a moment and reflect on anything unsaid or unfinished between us.

6. The closure session provides a place for discussing the varied emotions related to a relationship ending. Here it is important to normalize a range of feelings and reinforce honesty and candidness of expression. It may be important to discuss how some clients feel fear and abandonment, whereas others feel relief. Understanding more about the client's own feelings provides helpful closure to the relationship. As counselors we also need to be in touch with and authentically communicate our own feelings during this time. Introducing the topic of feelings related to termination might sound like this:

Counselor: As we talked about for the past couple of weeks, this is our last session. People have a range of feelings about endings like this—some feel relief, others feel fear or lack of self-confidence, others want to avoid any discussion of endings. I wonder how you are feeling about this being our last session together.

7. The closure session is also a time of next steps. This discussion may take several forms depending on the individual context. The counselor and client may review next steps in the career planning process. Sometimes these next steps are taken individually, sometimes through the help of a referral source, and sometimes there is a need to return to the counselor for additional assistance. The important point here is that the client should have a clear picture of next steps and feel confident in performing them. The client should also feel welcome and encouraged to return to the counselor as the need arises. What we know from psychotherapy research is that there is often a rebound effect after counseling has ended, such that the client may feel lost and in need of further assistance from the counselor. Developing an atmosphere that makes it as easy as possible for the client to reconnect with the counselor is important. Some counselors use the terms *booster shot* or *tune up* to describe these sessions. Because clients are familiar with these terms, the normalcy of getting a tune up makes it easier for them to call. Leaving the door open might sound like this:

Counselor: Even though this is our last formally scheduled time, I always tell my clients I'm available in case they feel the need for a tune up.
Client: A tune up?
Counselor: Yes. Sometimes clients feel like they come to a point where they are stuck, or struggling, or just need to check in and talk about how things are going for them. Sometimes they feel like they need a little reaffirmation of their choices, or reinforcement of their efforts. Whatever the reason, I want you to know my door is open for you.

Questions to Ponder Before the Closure Session

Closure sessions take time and planning to be effective. Thinking about our own feelings about the client and the termination prior to the session is critical. Preparing clients for the last session so that they feel comfortable and confident is also critical. One technique for this preparation is asking clients to think about the following five questions prior to coming to the last session. This serves to prepare clients and deepen their level of sharing.

1. What feelings are you aware you are having related to this termination?
2. Please take some time to reflect about what aspects of counseling were the most and least helpful to you.
3. What are the most important things you learned about yourself?
4. Are there things left unsaid between us that you could share with me now?
5. What are your next steps? What does the next part of the journey look like for you?

In addition, it may be helpful for counselors to look over this 7-point checklist and determine if their closure session was complete and thorough:

Closure Session Checklist. Did I:
Review the content of what happened in counseling?
Review the process of what happened in counseling?
Reemphasize the client's strengths that were evident in counseling?
Evaluate what went well and what went poorly?
Explore things unsaid in counseling?
Discuss feelings related to the ending of the counseling relationship?
Provide clear and direct structure for the client's next steps?

Closing Thoughts

In many ways the closure session is one of the most difficult, but also the most important, sessions of counseling. It is a time when the counselor and client each summarize the journey of counseling—both what happened and how it happened. The effectiveness of the process can be assessed, things left unsaid can be said, strengths of the client and counselor can be reinforced, and the client can be left with a clear plan for the future. When these issues are avoided, rushed, poorly timed, or delivered in a less-than-thoughtful manner, the whole impact of counseling is lessened. When the closure session is well thought out and planned, it can be one of the most satisfying and meaningful sessions for both the counselor and the client. We urge career counselors to take the time to plan for closure so that as clients go on to new beginnings, they will have this important time to reflect on the process they have just experienced.

References

Amundson, N. E. (1998). *Active engagement: Enhancing the career counselling process.* Richmond, British Columbia, Canada: Ergon Communications.

Amundson, N. E., Bowlsbey, J. H., & Niles, S. (2005). *Essential elements of career counseling.* Upper Saddle River, NJ: Pearson.

Bikos, L., O'Brien, K. M., & Heppner, M. J. (1995). *Therapeutic alliance as a component of career counseling: A comparison and outcome study.* Unpublished manuscript, University of Kansas–Lawrence.

Bridges, W. (2004). *Transitions: Making sense out of life's changes.* Reading, MA: Addison-Wesley.

Brown, D., & Brooks, L. (1991). *Career choice and development.* San Francisco, CA: Jossey-Bass.

Corey, G. (2013). *Theory and practice of counseling and psychotherapy.* Belmont, CA: Brooks/Cole.

Eliot, T. S. (1942). *Little Gidding*. San Diego, CA: Harcourt Press.

Hackney, H. L., & Cormier, S. (2013). *The professional counselor: A process guide to helping*. Boston, MA: Pearson.

Heppner, M. J., & Hendricks, F. (1995). A process and outcome study examining career indecision and indecisiveness. *Journal of Counseling & Development, 73,* 426–437.

Heppner, M. J., O'Brien, K. M., Hinkelman, J. M., & Flores, L. Y. (1996). Training counseling psychologists in career development: Are we our own worst enemies? *The Counseling Psychologist, 24,* 105–125.

Manthei, R. J. (2007). Client–counselor agreement on what happens in counselling. *British Journal of Guidance and Counselling, 35,* 261–281.

Meier, S. T., & Davis, S. R. (2011). *The elements of counseling*. Belmont, CA: Brooks/Cole.

Sue, D. W., & Sue, D. (2007). *Counseling the culturally different: Theory and practice* (3rd ed.). New York, NY: Wiley.

Ward, D. E. (1984). Termination of individual counseling: Concepts and strategies. *Journal of Counseling & Development, 63,* 21–25.

Wheeler, J. L., & Kivlighan, D. M., Jr. (1995). Things unsaid in group counseling: An empirical taxonomy. *Journal of Counseling & Development, 73,* 586–591.

Young, M. E. (2013). *Learning the art of helping: Building blocks and techniques*. Boston, MA: Pearson.

Index

Boxes, figures, and tables are indicated by "b," "f," and "t" following the page number.

A

Accommodation for individuals with disabilities, 136
Accountability, challenges to, 257
Acculturation, 62–64
Achievement, importance to men, 115
"Acting as if" technique, 13
ACT Interest Inventory Technical Manual (American College Testing), 168
Action phase of career counseling. *See also* Information gathering
    action plan development, 279–285
        benefits of, 277
        career counseling outcomes and, 279–282
        goals, criteria for defining, 282, 283–284
        process of, 282–283
        techniques for establishing, 285
    culturally diverse clients and, 68–69
    individuals with disabilities and, 134–136
    men and, 122–123
    women and, 97–98
Adejanju, M. G., 200–201, 202
Adlerian techniques, 13, 25, 180, 261–262
Adolescence, gendered context of, 81–83, 108–109
Adult career development transition model, 34–37
Advisory boards, 298
Affirmative action, 56
Affirmative counseling practices, 87, 89, 95, 113
Affluence, 55
African Americans. *See also* Race and class
    demographics, 52, 57, 58, 59
    nigrescence theory and, 64
    nontraditional jobs for men of color, 111
    prevalence in social occupations, 67–68
    racial identity development of, 64, 65
Aggression in men, 115
Aging clients, life career development approach for, 13
Alfeld, C. J., 86
ALGBTIC (Association for Lesbian, Gay, Bisexual, and Transgender Issues in Counseling), 95

Alibis, 257
Allcorn, S., 145
Allport, G. W., 241
Alumni outreach through social media, 297
American Counseling Association, on social media usage, 293
American Dream, 56
American Psychological Association, 26, 95, 113
Amundson, N. E., 4, 5, 8, 9, 253, 306
Ancis, J. R., 40, 41
Andersen, P., 260
Anderson, H. D., 25
Anderson, M. L., 21, 34, 35–36
Anderson, M. Z., 81
Anger in workplace, 114, 144–145
Anticipated transitions, 34
Aptitudes and skills measurements, 229
Arbitrary inference, 258
Arkowitz, H., 255
Army Alpha and Beta tests, 23
Army General Classification Test, 24
Artistic personality, 170, 173b
Asama, N. F., 227
Asay, P. A., 84–85
Asian Americans. *See also* Race and class
    collectivist values of, 55
    demographics, 57, 59
    perception of returning to counseling, 69
    racial identity of, 65
    working alliance and, 155
Assertiveness training, 186
Assessment. *See also specific assessment tools*
    of client's self, 35–36, 54, 163–164
    of coping strategies, 36
    of counseling philosophy, 87–89
    cultural bias in, 60, 96
    culture-specific variables and, 66–67
    environmental. *See* Environmental assessment
    history of, 23
    integration of different types, 121

(Continued)